PENGUIN

DAILY LIFE IN A

Jérôme Carcopino was born at Verneuil-sur-Avre (Eure) in 1881. He was educated at the École Normale Supérieure, where he specialized in history. From 1904 to 1907 he was a member of the French School at Rome, returning as *proffesseur* of history to the *lycée* in Le Havre. In 1912 he became a lecturer at the University of Algiers and inspector of antiquities for Algeria until 1920, but his career there was interrupted by the First World War, in which he served in the Dardanelles and the East. He was a professor at the Sorbonne from 1920 to 1937 when he became director of the French school at Rome. Having retired from there, he continued his membership of the Académie des Inscriptions and was elected in 1955 to the Académie Française. He died in 1970.

# DAILY LIFE
# IN ANCIENT ROME

## THE PEOPLE AND THE CITY
## AT THE HEIGHT OF
## THE EMPIRE

BY

JÉRÔME CARCOPINO

*Director of the École Française de Rome*
*Member of the Institute of France*

EDITED WITH BIBLIOGRAPHY AND NOTES BY

HENRY T. ROWELL

*Professor of Latin in the Johns Hopkins University*

TRANSLATED FROM THE FRENCH BY

E. O. LORIMER

PENGUIN BOOKS

PENGUIN BOOKS

Published by the Penguin Group
Penguin Books Ltd, 27 Wrights Lane, London W8 5TZ, England
Penguin Books Use Inc., 375 Hudson Street, New York, New York 10014, USA
Penguin Books Australia Ltd, Ringwood, Victoria, Australia
Penguin Books Canada Ltd, 2801 John Street, Markham, Ontario, Canada L3R 1B4
Penguin Books (NZ) Ltd, 182–190 Wairau Road, Auckland 10, New Zealand

Penguin Books Ltd, Registered Offices: Harmondsworth, Middlesex, England

First published 1941
Published in Pelican Books 1956
Reprinted in Peregrine Books 1962
Reprinted in Penguin Books 1991
1 3 5 7 9 10 8 6 4 2

Printed in England by Clays Ltd, St Ives plc
Set in Monotype Bembo

### TRANSLATOR'S NOTE

*In rendering quotations from Martial and Juvenal, Tacitus, Petronius, and Pliny the Younger, I have gratefully adopted – less often adapted – the phrasing of the Loeb Classics, edited by T. E. Page and Dr W. H. D. Rouse (Heinemann, London).*

E. O. L.

# CONTENTS

PREFACE                **9**

## PART ONE
## THE PHYSICAL AND MORAL BACKGROUND OF ROMAN LIFE

### I. THE EXTENT AND POPULATION OF THE CITY
1. *The Splendour of the Urbs*     13
2. *The Precincts of Rome and the City's True Extent*     20
3. *The Growth of the City's Population*     26

### II. HOUSES AND STREETS
1. *Modern Aspects of the Roman House*     34
2. *Archaic Aspects of the Roman House*     42
3. *Streets and Traffic*     57

### III. SOCIETY AND SOCIAL CLASSES
1. *Romans and Foreigners*     65
2. *Slavery and Manumission*     69
3. *The Confusion of Social Values*     74
4. *Living Standards and the Plutocracy*     78

### IV. MARRIAGE, WOMAN, AND THE FAMILY
1. *The Weakening of Paternal Authority*     89
2. *Betrothal and Marriage*     93
3. *The Roman Matron*     98
4. *Feminism and Demoralization*     104
5. *Divorce and the Instability of the Family*     109

### V. EDUCATION AND RELIGION
1. *Symptoms of Decomposition*     116
2. *Primary Education*     118
3. *The Routine Teaching of the Grammarian*     122
4. *Impractical Rhetoric*     129
5. *The Decay of Traditional Religion*     137

# CONTENTS

6. *The Progress of Oriental Mysticism*     144
7. *The Advent of Christianity*     152

## PART TWO
## THE DAY'S ROUTINE

### VI. THE MORNING
1. *The Days and Hours of the Roman Calendar*     161
2. *The Roman Begins the Day*     169
3. *The Barber*     175
4. *The Matron Dresses*     183

### VII. OCCUPATIONS
1. *The Duties of a 'Client'*     191
2. *Businessmen and Manual Labourers*     193
3. *Justice and Politics*     205
4. *Public Readings*     214

### VIII. SHOWS AND SPECTACLES
1. *'Panem et Circenses'*     223
2. *The Employment of Leisure*     227
3. *The Races*     234
4. *The Theatre*     243
5. *The Amphitheatre*     254
6. *Late Opposition*     267

### IX. AFTERNOON AND EVENING
1. *Strolling, Gaming, and Pleasure*     271
2. *The Baths*     277
3. *Dinner*     287

LIST OF ABBREVIATIONS     301

SOURCES OF INFORMATION     303

NOTES     315

INDEX     341

# PREFACE

IF 'Roman life' is not to become lost in anachronisms or petrified in abstraction, we must study it within a strictly defined period. Nothing changes more rapidly than human customs. Apart from the recent scientific discoveries which have turned the world of today upside down – steam, electricity, railways, motor-cars, and aeroplanes – it is clear that even in times of greater stability and less highly developed technique the elementary forms of everyday life were subject to unceasing change. Coffee, tobacco, and champagne were not introduced into Europe until the seventeenth century; potatoes were first eaten toward the end of the eighteenth; the banana became a feature of our dessert at the beginning of the twentieth. The law of change was not less operative in antiquity. It was a commonplace of Roman rhetoric to contrast the rude simplicity of the republic with the luxury and refinement of imperial times and to recall that Curius Dentatus 'gathered his scanty vegetables and himself cooked them on his little stove'.[1] There is no common measure, whether of food or house or furniture, between ages so different. Since a choice of period must necessarily be made, I shall deliberately confine myself to studying the generation which was born about the middle of the first century A.D., toward the end of the reign of Claudius or the beginning of the reign of Nero, and lived on into the reigns of Trajan (98–117) and of Hadrian (117–138). This generation saw Roman power and prosperity at their height. It was witness of the last conquests of the Caesars: the conquest of Dacia (106) which poured into the empire the wealth of the Transylvanian mines; the conquest of Arabia (109) which, supplemented by the success of the Parthian campaign (115), brought flooding into Rome the riches of India and the Far East, guarded by the legionaries of Syria and their desert allies.

In the material domain, this generation attained the highest plane of ancient civilization. By a fortunate coincidence – all the more fortunate in that Latin literature was soon to run so nearly dry – this generation is the one whose records combine to offer us the most complete picture of Roman life that we possess. The Forum of Trajan in Rome itself, the ruins of Herculaneum and Pompeii, the two prosperous resorts buried alive by the eruption of 79, supply an immense fund of archaeological evidence. Recent excavations have also restored to us the ruins of Ostia which date in the main from the time when the emperor Hadrian created this great commercial city as the realization of his town planning. Literature adds her testimony. We possess a profusion of vivid and picturesque descriptions,

precise and colourful, in the satirical romance of Petronius, the *Silvae* of
Statius, the *Epigrams* of Martial, the *Satires* of Juvenal, and the *Letters* of
Pliny the Younger. Fortune has indeed favoured the historian in this case,
supplying him with both the obverse and the reverse of the medal.

It is not enough to focus our study of the Roman's life on a fixed point
in time. It would lack foundation and consistency if we did not also focus
it in space – in the country or in the town. Even today, when the facilities
for communication, the diffusion of newspapers, the possession of radios
bring something of the pleasure, the thought, and the noise of the metropolis
into the humblest country cottage, there remains a vast discrepancy between
the monotony of peasant existence and the excitement of city life. A still
greater gulf divided the peasant from the townsman of antiquity. So
glaring was the inequality between them that, if we are to believe the learned
historian Rostovtzeff, it pitted the one against the other in a fierce and silent
struggle which pierced the dyke that protected the privileged classes from
the barbarian flood. The peasant pariah abetted the invading barbarian.

The townsman, in fact, enjoyed all the goods and resources of the
earth; the peasant knew nothing but unending labour without profit, and
lacked for ever the joys which warmed the heart of even the most wretched
in the cities: the liveliness of the *palaestra*, the warmth of the baths, the
gaiety of public banquets, the rich man's doles, the magnificence of public
spectacles.

We must renounce the attempt to blend two such dissimilar pictures
into one, and must make a choice between them. The period which I
propose to describe day by day is that of the Roman subject of the first
Antonines – days spent exclusively in the town, or rather in *The City*,
Rome, the *Urbs*, the hub and centre of the universe, proud and wealthy
queen of a world which she seemed at the time to have pacified for ever.

We cannot, however, hope to paint the daily life of our Roman in
its reality if we do not first try to form a summary but adequate picture of
the setting in which it was passed and by which it was coloured, and free
ourselves from false preconceptions concerning it. We must seek to reconstruct the physical milieu of the great city in which this life was lived;
the social milieu of the various classes of the hierarchy by which it was
governed; the moral milieu of thought and sentiment which explains both
its merits and its weaknesses. We can satisfactorily study the method in
which the Roman of Rome employed his time only after we have plotted
out the main lines of the framework within which he lived and outside
which the routine of his daily life would be more or less unintelligible.

*La Ferté-sur-Aube*                                                                              J. C.

# PART ONE

\*

## THE PHYSICAL
## AND MORAL BACKGROUND
## OF ROMAN LIFE

The material characteristics of Imperial Rome are full of contradictions. On the one hand the size of her population, the architectural grandeur and the marble beauty of her buildings proclaim her kinship with the great modern capitals of the West. On the other, the overcrowding to which her multitudes were condemned – piled on top of each other on her irregular hills within an area restricted alike by nature and by man – the narrowness of her tangled lanes, the scantiness of her sanitary services, and the dangerous congestion of her traffic reveal a closer relationship to those medieval towns of which the chroniclers tell, whose appealing yet sordid picturesqueness, unexpected ugliness, and swarming chaos survive in certain Moslem cities of today.

Our first task is to throw a light on this essential contrast.

# I

## THE EXTENT AND POPULATION OF THE CITY

\*

### 1. The Splendour of the Urbs

THERE is little need to dwell on the splendour of the city of Rome at the beginning of the second century of our era. The ruins which reflect it are incomparable; it would be superfluous to enumerate them, still more superfluous to describe them one by one. It is enough to dwell for a moment on the group which is linked with the name of Trajan and in which the genius of his time reaches its zenith.[1] In the warm light which bathes them, these ruins everywhere preserve the strength and harmony of those vanished monuments of which for the most part they are but the naked skeleton. Nowhere do they inspire us with a nobler or more satisfying idea of the civilization whose riches they display, of the society whose discipline they evoke, of the men – our ancestors and equals – to whose intellectual stature and artistic mastery they bear witness, than in the Forum of Trajan, which in the very centre of the Urbs prolongs the forum of Augustus to the north. In this spot, between the years 109 and 113, Trajan brought to completion a work which calls forth not only our admiration but our love. Thanks to the recent excavations of Corrado Ricci, we are able to reconstruct it in its earliest perfection. The spaciousness of the conception as a whole, the supple complexity and generous elaboration of every part, the sumptuousness of the materials, the daring sweep of the lines, the ordered movement of the decorations enable this creation of Trajan's easily to challenge comparison with the most ambitious work of modern architects. Even in its decay it has never ceased to supply them with lessons and with models. Brilliant and faithful expression of its own time, it seems under our very eyes to forge a link between its day and ours.

Defying the difficulties which the irregularity of the ground and the inconvenient proximity of earlier monuments opposed to its development, this group of buildings united in a coherent and harmonious whole a public square or forum, a judicial basilica, two libraries, the famous column which rose between them, and an immense covered market. We do not know the date at which the market was completed, but it must have been built before the Column, whose height, as we shall see, was governed by the proportions of the market. The Forum and the Basilica were inaugurated by Trajan on 1 January 112; the Column on 13 May 113.[2] The whole formed a sequence of daring magnificence.

To the south rose the Forum proper in majestic simplicity – a vast esplanade, 116 metres by 95, surrounded on three sides by a portico. On the south side, through which the public entered, this portico was supported by a single row of columns, and on east and west by a double colonnade. To east and west its back wall, built of peperino faced with marble, curved out into a semicircle 45 metres in radius. In the centre of the forum rose the equestrian statue of the emperor in gilded bronze, attended by more modest statues ranged between the surrounding columns, commemorating men who had served the empire well by the sword or by the spoken word. Three steps of yellow marble led up to the entrance of the Basilica Ulpia which derived its title from the family name of Trajan. The Basilica, which measured 159 metres from east to west and 55 from north to south, was raised one metre above the level of the Forum and excelled the Forum itself in opulence. It was an immense hypostyle hall, designed in oriental style and entered from the south on one of its longer sides. The interior was divided into five naves 130 metres long, the central one reaching a width of 25 metres; there were 96 pillars in all; the entire floor was paved with Luna marble, while the roof was adorned with tiles of gilded bronze. The hall was encircled by a portico with sculptures in the spaces, and the attic was ornamented with bas-reliefs distinguished for their animation and the delicacy of their modelling. Finally, the upper entablature repeated several times on each face the brief and haughty inscription '*E Manubiis*', proclaiming that the building had been erected from the spoils of war (the plunder taken from the Dacians of Decebalus). Beyond and parallel to the Basilica, and rising as high above it as it rose above the Forum, stretched the two rectangles of the twin libraries, the Bibliothecae Ulpiae, bearing, like the Basilica, the Gentile name of their common founder. One of these libraries was consecrated to Greek manuscripts, the other to Latin manuscripts and the imperial archives; in each of them the space above the *plutei*, or cupboards which housed the manuscripts, was decorated with a series of busts representing the writers who had attained greatest fame in the two languages of the empire.

A narrow quadrilateral 24 metres by 16 separated the two libraries, and in the centre of it there rose, and still rises almost intact, the marvel of marvels: the Column of Trajan.[2] The base is an almost perfect cube of stone 5·5 metres high, pierced by a bronze gate above which was the dedicatory inscription. The other three sides of the pedestal were decorated with arms and trophies and all four sides with bosses interlaced with laurel. The Column is composed entirely of marble, has a diameter of 3·70 metres and a height of 29·77, and contains a spiral staircase of white marble starting from the base of the pedestal and boasting 185 steps. The monumental Doric capital which crowns the column was originally surmounted by a bronze eagle with outspread wings. After the death of Trajan the eagle was replaced by a bronze statue of the dead emperor which was probably torn down and melted in the chaos of the invasions. That was replaced in 1588 by the statue of Saint Peter which we see today. The total height of the monument is approximately 38 metres, which corresponds to the 128½ Roman feet of which the ancient documents tell.

Grandiose as are the mere proportions of the Column of Trajan in themselves, the effect is heightened by the external arrangement of the marble blocks of which it is composed. Seventeen colossal drums of marble bear twenty-three spiral panels which, if ranged in a straight line, would measure nearly 200 metres. From base to capital these panels represent in relief the major episodes of the two Dacian campaigns in their historic sequence, from the beginning of the first campaign to the end of the second. They have been executed with so much skill that they conceal from view the forty-three windows which serve to light the interior of the column. Twenty-five hundred separate figures have been counted in these reliefs. Wind and weather have reduced them all alike to the warm but uniform colour of the Parian marble in which they were carved, but formerly they shone in brilliant colours which proclaimed the supremacy of the Roman sculptors in this type of historic relief.

Trajan's unexpected death occurred in the early days of August 117, when he had already set out on his return journey to Rome after handing over to Hadrian the command of the army he had raised against the Parthians. His ashes were brought back from Asia to Rome and placed in the chamber in the pedestal of his great Column. The burial of his ashes within the *pomerium* transgressed the laws which forbade the burial of ordinary mortals within the sacred space.[4] Though his successor Hadrian and the Senate unanimously declared that the deceased emperor was above the common law, they nevertheless took in this matter an initiative which Trajan himself had neither desired nor foreseen. He had not designed his Column as his tomb. His commemorative purpose in erecting it had been twofold: the reliefs it bore were to immortalize the victories he had won over the external enemy, and its unique proportions were to symbolize the superhuman effort he had made to conquer Nature for the adornment and prosperity of Rome. The two last lines of his inscription made his intention clear. Today a few letters of the inscription can no longer be read, but in the seventh century the unknown visitor whom we call the Anonymous Traveller from Einsiedeln was able to copy it entire. The meaning of Trajan's formula – '*ad declarandum quantae altitudinis mons et locus tantis operibus sit egestus*'[5] – has become clear since scholars realized that the verb *egerere* expressed the two contradictory meanings, 'to empty' and 'to erect', both of which are needed to interpret literally this noble phrase. The Column was intended to indicate how much the spur (*mons*) which the Quirinal Hill thrust out to meet the Capitoline had been levelled, and how great an area (*locus*) had been cleared for the giant monuments which to the east completed the emperor's work and which were rescued from the ruins in 1932 by the scientific faith of Corrado Ricci.

The majestic hemicycle of bricks which encircles the Forum proper on the side of the Quirinal and the Subura easily sustained the five storeys which housed the 150 booths or *tabernae* of the market.⁶ Shallow rooms on the level of the Forum formed the ground floor, and here fruit and flowers were probably set out for sale. The front of the first floor was a loggia of vast arcades, whose long vaulted halls served as storehouses for oil and wine. Rarer products, especially pepper and spices (*pipera*) from the distant East, could be bought on the second and third floors. The Middle Ages preserved the memories of the spice market in the name of a steep and winding street which served the spice merchants of antiquity before it came to serve the subjects of the popes – the Via Biberatica. Along the fourth storey ran the formal hall where *congiaria** were distributed and where, from the second century on, the offices of public assistance (*stationes arcariorum Caesarianorum*) were permanently installed.⁷ On the fifth and last storey were ranged the market fishponds, one set of them linked by channels to the aqueduct which supplied them with fresh water, and another designed to receive sea water brought from Ostia.

From the fifth storey spectators can still survey the immensity of Trajan's achievement, and note that they are standing exactly on a level with the halo of Saint Peter who now crowns the Column of Trajan. From this point of vantage they can feel the full significance of the inscription and appreciate the matchless grandeur of the works carried out by Apollodorus of Damascus to the order of the greatest of the Caesars. His massive buildings climb and mask the slopes of the Quirinal which were smoothed out to fit them without the aid of explosives such as the engineers of today have at their disposal. The proportions of these buildings have been so harmonized that all thought of their weight is forgotten in the satisfying perception of their perfect equilibrium. Here is a masterpiece indeed, which has survived successive ages without ceasing to stir each in turn to enthusiasm. The Romans of old were aware that neither their city itself nor the world outside offered anything finer to man's admiration. Ammianus Marcellinus has recorded that when the emperor Constantine, in company with the Persian

* *Congiaria* were public distributions of food or money.

ambassador Ormisda, made his solemn entry into Rome in 357 and for the first time trod the pavement of Trajan's Forum, he could not restrain a cry of admiration and the regret that he could never construct anything like it.[8] He stated, however, that he would and could copy the equestrian statue of Trajan which stood there. To this the Persian replied, 'First, Sire, command a like stable to be built, if you can, so that the steed which you intend to create may range as widely as this which you see.' The Romans of the later empire felt impotent before these monuments created by the genius of their ancestors.

The perfection of the prodigious ellipse of the Colosseum cannot counteract the uneasiness one feels at the thought of the carnage that took place there. The baths of Caracalla suffer from a certain excess which presages decadence. Nothing, on the other hand, disturbs the nobility of the impression created by the Forum and the market-place of Trajan. They impress without overwhelming. The grace of their curves tempers their immensity. On this high plane of art great artists of great epochs meet, and we find that something of this restrained and vital harmony flowed into Michelangelo's façade of the Farnese Palace and into the Colonne Vendôme which the architects of Napoleon Bonaparte cast from the bronze cannons of Jena. Rome at her greatest is reflected here.

It is a striking fact that Trajan obviously strove not alone to com-memorate the victory which had at one blow replenished the treasury of the Caesars and furnished this abundant wealth,[9] but also to justify it by the quality of the culture which his soldiers brought to the vanquished. The statues of his porticos unceasingly connect the glories of the intellect with those of arms. At the foot of the market where the people of Rome bought their daily food, beside the Forum where the consuls gave their audience and the emperors made their pronouncements – whether a Hadrian proclaimed re-mission of taxes or a Marcus Aurelius poured his private wealth into the public treasury – there swept the great hemicycle where, as M. Marrou has demonstrated, the masters of literature continued down to the fourth century to gather their students round them and impart instruction.[10]

The Basilica itself, for all its luxury, stood three steps lower than the two great libraries which were its neighbours. According to the interpretation recently revived by M. Paribeni, we may assume that the historic Column which rose between them represents the brilliant realization by Apollodorus of an original conception emanating from the emperor himself. No prototype has yet been discovered, although it may name among its posterity the Aurelian Column at Rome itself and the columns of Theodosius and Arcadius at Constantinople, to name only examples dating from antiquity. It is no accident that the Column of Trajan was erected in the very centre of the city of books. Trajan must have intended the spirals which clothe it to represent the unrolling of two scrolls (*volumina*) which formed a marble record of his warlike exploits and extolled to the skies his clemency as well as his might.[11] One relief, three times as large as the others, separates the two series of records and reveals their significance.[12] It represents a figure of Victory in the act of writing on her shield '*Ense et stylo*', which might be rendered, 'By the word and by the pen'. This is the eloquent symbol of the pacificatory and civilizing goal which Trajan in all sincerity set himself in his conquests. It throws light on the thought which dominated his ambitions and led him, while deprecating violence and injustice, to seek by all means to find spiritual justification for the imperialism of Rome.

In this spot which proclaims the ideal of the new empire we see the very heart of the metropolis which had grown with the empire's growth and which ended by vying in population with the greatest of our modern capitals. The inauguration of his Forum completed the renovation of the city which Trajan had undertaken in order to make the Urbs worthy of his hegemony and to bring relief to a population crushed by its own increasing numbers. With this in mind he had enlarged the circus, excavated a *naumachia*, canalized the Tiber, drawn off new aqueducts, built the largest public baths that Rome had ever seen, and subjected private building enterprise to rigorous and far-sighted control.[13] The Forum crowned his work. By levelling off the Quirinal he opened new roads to traffic, as well as added another immense open public space in the centre of the city to those created by his predecessors, Caesar, Augustus, the Flavians, and Nerva, who one after another had sought to relieve the congestion of the Forum proper. By adorning his Forum with *exedrae*, a Basilica and libraries, he dignified the leisure of the multitudes who daily frequented it; to improve the facilities for provisioning the teeming populace, he supplemented these buildings by markets, comparable in their spaciousness and the ingenuity of their design to those which Paris acquired only in the nineteenth century. These works of Trajan can, in fact, be fully understood only when we keep in mind the multitudes whose lot they alleviated and whose presence still haunts their ruins. We have other irrefutable evidence of their having existed, but even without that the works of Trajan alone would prove it.

## 2. The Precincts of Rome and the City's True Extent

No question has been more frequently discussed than the population of the capital of the Roman Empire, nor is there any whose solution is more urgent for the historian – especially if it is true, as the Berber sociologist Ibn Khaldun contended, that the level of a civilization can be in some degree estimated by the size and growth of its cities, an inevitable consequence of the development of human society. But there is no question which has provoked more polemics or given rise to more contradictory opinions. Since Renaissance days the scholars who have approached the problem have always been divided into two hostile camps. Some, hypnotized by the object of their study, are over-ready to ascribe to their beloved antiquity, which they dream of as an Age of Gold, the same range and vitality that the modern world owes to the progress of science. Justus Lipsius, for instance, among others, estimates the population of ancient Rome at about four millions.[14] Others, more inclined to underestimate past generations, refuse *a priori* to ascribe to them achievements equal to those of modern times, and Dureau de la Malle, who was the first French scholar to devote serious research to the distribution of populations in ancient times, considers a total of about 261,000 the highest figure which can plausibly be assigned to the city of the Caesars.[15] Both Dureau de la Malle and Justus Lipsius, however, started with rooted preconceptions, and an unprejudiced critic may perhaps find it possible to arrive at an approximation somewhere between these two extremes that is sufficiently near the truth.

Those who champion what I shall call the 'Little Rome' theory are invariably statisticians who first submit the question to an examination of the circumstantial evidence. They dismiss all indications, however explicit, given by ancient writers, and base their conclusions solely on a consideration of the terrain. They accept only one basis of calculation: the relation between the known area and the possible population inhabiting it. They consequently decide that Imperial Rome, which they hold to have been exactly delimited by the Aurelian Wall and to have very nearly coincided with the area of the present-day Rome they have visited, cannot have sheltered a population much larger than the present. At first sight this argument might appear convincing. Reflection shows, however, that it is based on the fallacy of supposing that the territorial aspect of ancient Rome was the same as at present, and on the false postulate that we are entitled arbitrarily to apply to this area the demographic coefficient derived from the most recent statistics.

In the first place this method makes the mistake of ignoring the elasticity of space or, more exactly, the compressibility of man. Dureau reached his figures by applying to the space enclosed by the Aurelian Wall the population density of Paris under Louis Philippe, say 60 persons to the acre. If he had been writing seventy-five years later, when the density of Paris had reached 160 persons to the acre, as it did in 1914, his result would have been nearly three times as large. M. Ferdinand Lot fell into the same *petitio principii* when he overhastily ascribed to the Rome of Aurelian the population density of the Rome of 1901, and estimated its inhabitants at 538,000.[16] Since then, post-war building has not nearly doubled the area of Rome, yet the census of January 1939 records a population of 1,284,600, considerably more than double. In both these cases it is not the population which Rome actually housed in former times that is computed, but the population which might have been contained within the space of ancient Rome, reckoned by the density of population at the time of the writer, a choice which is purely accidental and arbitrary. Even on an unchanging terrain, living conditions alter from one epoch to another, and it is evident that however ingenious the attempt to establish a proportion between an area which is conceived as a known quantity and a population which is an unknown quantity, this ratio must remain purely hypothetical.

If, moreover, as I myself believe, ancient Rome was not circumscribed within the limits that have been affirmed, a further unknown quantity is introduced which vitiates the above calculations. The Aurelian Wall, which is supposed to have formed its perimeter, no more represented the absolute limit of Imperial Rome than the *pomerium*, falsely ascribed to Servius Tullius, had earlier sufficed to circumscribe the Rome of the republic. This point demands some explanation.

Like all the Greek and Latin cities of antiquity, ancient Rome, from the dawn of her legend to the end of her history, had always consisted of two inseparable elements, a sharply defined urban agglomeration (*Urbs Roma*) and the rural territory attached to it (*Ager Romanus*). The Ager Romanus extended to the boundaries of the adjacent cities, which had preserved their municipal individuality in spite of political annexation; Lavinium, Ostia, Fregenae, Veii, Fidenae, Ficulea, Gabii, Tibur, and Bovillae. The Urbs proper was the home of the gods and their sanctuaries, of the king, and later of the magistrates who were heirs to his dismembered power, of the Senate and the *comitia* who, in cooperation first with the king and later with the magistrates, governed the City-State. Thus in its origins the city represented something greater and different from a more or less closely packed aggregate of dwelling houses: it was a *templum* solemnly dedicated according to rites prescribed by the discipline of the augurs, its precincts strictly defined by the furrow which the Latin founder, dutifully obeying the prescriptions of Etrurian ritual, had carved round it with a plough drawn by a bull and cow of dazzling white. The share had been duly lifted over the spots where one day the city gates would stand, and the clods of earth thrown up in its passage had been scrupulously lifted and thrown within the circuit. The sacred orbit thus described in anticipation of the fortifications and walls to come, formed the abbreviated ground plan, the prophetic image of the future city, and hence was known as the *pomerium* (*pone muros*). From the *pomerium* the Urbs derived its name, its original definition, and its supernatural protection, assured by the taboos which preserved its soil alike from the defilement of foreign cults, the threat of armed levies, and the interment of the dead.[17]

The position of the *pomerium* altered with the successive developments which produced the Rome of history. Although it preserved its religious character and continued to protect the citizens by remaining closed to gatherings of the legions, by classical times it had ceased to form the limit of the city. It remained a spiritual symbol, but its practical functions had been usurped by a concrete reality – the Great Wall, which false tradition ascribed to King Servius Tullius but which was in fact built by order of the republican Senate between 378 and 352 B.C.[18] This wall was constructed of blocks of volcanic rock so firmly dressed that entire sections of it are still extant in the Rome of the twentieth century, notably in the Via delle Finanze, in the gardens of the Palazzo Colonna, and in the Piazza del Cinquecento opposite the railway station; sufficient traces of it remain to enable us to reconstruct the whole. From the third century B.C., the urban area of Rome was no longer defined by the *pomerium*, but by the wall whose massive courses had withstood the assault of Hannibal; and the two areas were clearly distinguished from each other. Though both excluded the great plain, the Campus Martius, which lay between the Tiber and the hills and was dedicated to military exercises, the wall was nevertheless more extensive than the *pomerium*, and comprised many districts not included in the latter: the Citadel (*arx*) and the Capitoline, the north-western tip of the Esquiline, the Velabrum, and above all the two summits of the Aventine. The northern Aventine had been included from the first, the southern when the consuls of 87 prolonged the wall to strengthen the city against the attack of Cinna. In all, it is reckoned that the wall enclosed 1·6 square miles, a trifling area compared to the 27 square miles of modern Paris, but large beside the 295 acres of ancient Capua, the 290 of Caere, and the 80 with which Praeneste had to be content. Such comparisons, however, are idle. The calculation of the ground area of the Urbs gives no certain clue to the number of its inhabitants.

From the moment that the Romans, in a fair way to conquer the world, had ceased to dread their enemies, the walls which they had built for their protection with yesterday's Gallic terror fresh in mind had lost all military value, and the inhabitants of the city began to overflow their bounds, as they had earlier overflowed the *pomerium*. By virtue of the right of the *imperatores*, who had extended the frontiers of the empire, and also with a view to placating the urban plebs, Sulla in the year 81 B.C. released for dwelling-houses a portion of the Campus Martius between the Capitol and the Tiber – how large a portion we unfortunately do not know.[19] On this side then, the Urbs officially outgrew its boundaries, as it had in fact unofficially spread beyond them in other directions. When Caesar removed to a Roman mile beyond the walls the boundary marks assigned to Rome in accordance with the posthumous law preserved to us by the Table of Heraclea,[20] he merely gave legal recognition to a state of affairs which no doubt went back to the second century B.C.

Augustus in his turn only pursued and amplified the innovation initiated by his adoptive father, when in 7 B.C. he completed the identification of the Urbs with the fourteen regions into which he had re-divided the ancient and the newer quarters of the city: thirteen regions on the left bank of the Tiber, the fourteenth on the right or farther bank, the 'regio Transtiberina', whose memory is kept alive by the Trastevere of today.[21]

Augustus, who boasted that he had pacified the world and who solemnly closed the Temple of Janus,[22] had no hesitation in dismantling the ancient republican fortifications. And Rome, now freed – thanks to her glory and to her annexations – from all anxiety about her own security, proceeded to burst her bonds on every side. If five of the fourteen regions of Augustus were contained within the ancient circuit of the city, five others lay partly within and partly without, while the remaining four were completely outside: the fifth (Esquiline), the seventh (Via Lata), the ninth (Circus Flaminius), and the fourteenth (Transtiberina). As if to emphasize the emperor's intentions, popular usage presently gave the first of these the name of Porta Capena, and the gate which had originally been a point on the circumference now came to occupy the centre.

The fourteen regions of Augustus lasted as long as the empire, and their limits bounded the Rome of the first Antonines. Within this framework we must reconstruct the city of this period for ourselves. It is not possible to submit these regions to exact measurement, and it would be a grave error to identify them with those still marked by the brick wall with which Aurelian sought to protect the capital of the empire against the approach of the barbarians, and which, from A.D. 274 on, served at once as rampart and *pomerium*.[23] Even today, with its ruined curtains and succession of dilapidated towers, this impressive structure, whose brick masonry blazes in the rays of the setting sun, conveys to the least sensitive of tourists a vivid impression of the majesty that made Rome glorious even in her decadence.

The Aurelian Wall, which reached a length of 18·837 kilometres and enclosed an area of 5·354 square miles, was constructed in precisely the same manner as the almost contemporary enclosures with which Gaul bristled in defence against the Germanic hordes. These latter have been made the subject of an admirable study by M. Adrien Blanchet.[24] The Gallic fortifications never attempted to protect an entire town, but only its more vital parts, as a cuirasse protects the warrior's breast; similarly the Aurelian Wall did not aspire to encircle all the fourteen regions of Rome. Far from feeling bound by the configuration of the entire city, Aurelian's engineers gave their attention to linking together the main strategic points and to utilizing as far as possible such earlier constructions, like the aqueducts, as could more or less easily be incorporated in their system.

From the Pincian to the Salarian Gate in the seventh region, the toll-post marks (*cippi*) have been discovered as far as a hundred metres beyond the wall.[25] From the Praenestine to the Asinarian Gate, the fifth region must have extended 300 metres beyond it, for at this distance we find the obelisk of Antinoüs erected, according to the hieroglyphs of its inscription, 'at the boundary of the town'. Similarly, from the Metrovian to the Ardeatine Gate, the first region overshot the wall by an average of 600 metres, since the curtain runs in this sector one Roman mile (1,482 metres) to the south of the Porta Capena, and the region included the Aedis

Martis, a mile and a half away, and stretched as far as the River Almo (known today as the Acquataccio), whose course lies 800 metres farther on. Finally, and above all, it would be easy to demonstrate that the fourteenth region, whose total perimeter is double that of the wall on the farther bank of the Tiber, overshot the wall by 1,800 metres in the north and 1,300 in the south. In view of these facts, there can be no question of assuming that the fourteen regions which constituted Imperial Rome were confined within the area surrounded by the Aurelian Wall. It would be equally inadmissible to imagine them restricted to the 7¼ square miles delimited by the mobile cordon of the toll-posts, for from the time of Augustus the jurists had laid down the principle that Rome of the fourteen regions was not confined within an unalterable circumference, but in law, as in fact, was in a state of perpetual growth, and that her area was automatically extended as new dwellings were constructed prolonging the blocks of ancient buildings.[26] This essentially realistic legal ruling not only defeats at the start any attempt to calculate the population of Rome on so uncertain and changeable a basis as the area of the fourteen regions, but presupposes in the lawyers who enunciated it a faith in an indefinite future growth of the Imperial City.

## 3. The Growth of the City's Population

Available records bear convincing witness to the growth of the Roman population. It progressively increased from the time of Sulla till the principate, and was further accelerated under the prosperous government of the Antonines. To convince ourselves of this, we need only collate two sets of statistics, separated by an interval of three centuries, which have by a fortunate accident been preserved. They give a census of the *vici* of Rome, that is, the quarters within the fourteen regions separated from each other by the streets which bounded them. Augustus had granted each *vicus* a special administration presided over by its own *magister*, and protected by the Lares of the cross-roads.[27] On the one hand the elder Pliny informs us that in the lustrum of A.D. 73 conducted by the censors Vespasian and Titus, Rome was divided into 265 *vici*.[28] On the other, the

*Regionaries*, that invaluable compilation of the fourth century, records a total of 307 *vici*.[29] The oldest of the *Regionaries*, the *Notitia*, was begun in 334, and the latest, the *Curiosum*, covers the year 357. The year A.D. 345 might be taken as an intermediate date. So we find that between A.D. 74 and 345 the number of *vici* had grown by 42, which implies a territorial increase of 15 per cent in the area of Rome. At the same time, we observe that between the time of Caesar and that of Septimius Severus a corresponding increase of population must have taken place. We have, it is true, no direct evidence of this, but may unhesitatingly deduce it from the increase in the charges for public assistance to the Roman plebs. In the times of Caesar and Augustus, Annona, the mythological personification of the year's food supplies, had on her hands only 150,000 poor to whom she distributed free grain.[30] When Dio Cassius lauded the liberality of the *congiarium* of 203 in the reign of Septimius Severus, the number of recipients had risen to 175,000, an increase of 16·6 per cent.[31] The parallelism of these percentages is instructive. First of all it proves – what might *a priori* have been assumed – that the increase of population had gone hand in hand with the geographical extension of the fourteen regions. The second thing it indicates might also have been taken for granted because of the consolidation of the *Pax Romana* during the second half of the second century: the greatest increase to which the *Regionaries* of the fourth century bear witness – but of which we have indications before the largesse of 203 – dates from the *Pax Romana*. From this it follows – happily for us and our thesis – that we must estimate the population of Rome under the early Antonines, that is to say at a period of marked prosperity for which statistics are unfortunately lacking, at a higher figure than the epochs immediately preceding, and not far below the figure supplied by the later data of the *Regionaries*.

Now from the beginning of the first century B.C. to the middle of the first century A.D. we are in a position to follow the irresistible movement which swelled the population of Rome to a point where her cohesion was in danger of being undermined and her food supply of breaking down. As I have pointed out elsewhere, the outbreak of the Social War in 91 B.C. drove back on Rome in

27

chaotic confusion all Italians who refused to make common cause with the allied insurgents and sought a refuge from their reprisals.[32] The influx of these refugees caused a sudden leap in numbers similar to that of fifteen years before, when the flood of Greek refugees from Asia Minor raised Athens to the rank of a great European capital. Faced by provinces and an Italy torn between the democratic government of Rome and the armies mobilized against that government by the senatorial aristocracy, the censors of 86 B.C. were obliged to abandon the attempt to make the usual general census of all citizens of the empire, and proceeded instead to catalogue the different categories of population who were herded together in the city. Saint Jerome records in his *Chronicle* the result of this census, of 463,000 souls, made without regard to sex, age, status, or nationality: '*descriptione Romae facta inventa sunt hominum CCCCLXIII milia.*'[33] Thirty years later the figure was considerably higher, if it is true, as Lucan's commentator asserts, that when Pompey took charge of the Annona in September 57 B.C. he succeeded in getting the grain needed to feed a minimum of 486,000 mouths.[34] After the triumph of Julius Caesar in 45 B.C. the population made another upward bound. The fact itself cannot be doubted, though for lack of figures we cannot make an exact estimate of the increase; instead of the 40,000 whom Cicero mentions in his *In Verrem*[35] as receiving free grain in 71 B.C., Caesar in 44 B.C. admitted no less than 150,000 to the free distribution.[36] Moreover, as *Censor Morum*, he standardized the accidental procedure of the censors of 86 B.C. and ordered that the traditional *album* of the citizens of the empire should be supplemented by detailed statistics on the inhabitants of the Urbs, who should henceforth be tabulated street by street and building by building from information furnished by proprietors on their own responsibility.[37]

The advance in numbers continued under the principate of Augustus. The available data combine to force us to conclude that the inhabitants of Rome must have reached nearly a million. First, we note the quantity of grain which the Annona had to store each year for the support of the population: Aurelius Victor tells us that 20,000,000 *modii* (4,669,000 bushels) were supplied by Egypt, and Josephus records that Africa furnished twice that amount – in all, therefore, 60,000,000 *modii*.[38] Allowing an average yearly consumption of 60 *modii* (14·006 bushels) per head, this would represent 1,000,000 recipients. Secondly, we have Augustus' own declaration in his *Res Gestae* that when he was invested for the twenty-second time with the *tribunicia potestas* and for the twelfth time with the consular dignity, that is to say, in the year 5 B.C., he gave 60 *denarii* to each of the 320,000 citizens composing the urban plebs.[39] Now, according to the words which the emperor deliberately employed, this distribution was confined to adult males – the Latin text specifies *viritim*, the Greek translation κατ᾽ἄνδρα. It excluded, therefore, all women and girls and all boys under eleven. Taking the average proportion established in our time by the actuaries between men, women, and children, this yields a Roman population of at least 675,000 *cives*. To this we must add a garrison of 12,000 men who lived in Rome but did not partake in the *congiaria*, the host of non-citizens (*peregrini*), and another item, more important than either, the slaves. The words of Augustus himself thus lead us to calculate the total population of Rome at close to a million, if indeed it did not exceed that figure.

Lastly, we have the statistics included in the *Regionaries* of the fourth century A.D. These compel us to assess still higher the figure for the second century, a time when, as we have seen, the population of Rome vigorously increased. Adding up, region by region, the dwelling-houses of the Urbs as catalogued in the *Notitia*, we get the two totals: 1,782 *domus* and 44,300 *insulae*; but both the summary of the *Notitia* and Zacharias record 1,797 *domus* and 46,602 *insulae*. It is safe to assume that the discrepancy between these documents is due to the muddle-headedness of the copyist of the *Notitia*, who appears to have dozed over the detailed enumerations which he had to transcribe. In the course of his uncongenial task he frequently mangled or omitted items before his eyes, or simply duplicated them, as when he attributed the same number of *domus* to the tenth and eleventh regions and the same number of *insulae* to both the third and fourth and the twelfth and thirteenth regions. In other words, we are entitled to put our trust rather in the summary of the *Notitia* and Zacharias; and from the figures they give of the dwellings of Rome to deduce that other figure which they do not give – the total of the population which may be inferred from the 1,797 *domus* and the 46,602 *insulae* of their record.

Obviously the result can only be approximate, and the exaggerated scruples of contemporary criticism have wilfully complicated the conditions of calculation. In France, especially, M. Édouard Cuq[40] and M. Ferdinand Lot [41] have interpreted the plural form '*domus*' of the *Notitia* as embracing all the real estate of the Urbs, and the plural '*insulae*' as a synonym for '*cenacula*', denoting the sets of living quarters or 'flats' into which buildings were divided. They hold, therefore, that the two figures overlap. Taking an average of five persons per 'flat', they dogmatically apply it to the 46,602 *insulae* of the *Notitia*, and on this basis estimate the total population of the Urbs as 233,010. Their arithmetical calculations are, however, vitiated from the start by the evident falsity of their interpretation of the Latin words. To a Latin scholar the word *domus*, whose etymology implies a hereditary property, means a private house which is undivided and in which there live only the owner and his family; while the *insula*, as its name vividly suggests, is a large isolated building, an interest-bearing piece of real estate, a 'block' subdivided into a number of flats or *cenacula*, each of which houses a tenant or a family of tenants. Examples of these usages could be indefinitely multiplied: Suetonius recalls Caesar's order laying the duty of filling up the census forms on the owners of *insulae*: '*per dominos insularum*';[42] Tacitus shrinks from the task of compiling an exact list of the temples, the *domus*, and *insulae* which had fallen victims to the fire of A.D. 64;[43] the biographer who wrote the *Historia Augusta* records that during the reign of Antoninus Pius a fire in Rome consumed 340 dwellings in one day – apartment houses or private houses: '*incendium trecentas quadraginta insulas vel domus absumpsit.*'[44] In all these texts the *insula* never appears as an autonomous building. It is an architectural unit, but not a unit of dwelling. That it was used in this sense in the *Notitia* is proved beyond all possibility of doubt by the detailed description given there of the Insula of Felicula as one of the sights of the ninth region deserving the attention of tourists. The reference is to the apartment block of Felicula, of whose extraordinary dimensions we shall speak later. We are therefore not justified in dividing the 46,602 *insulae* among the 1,797 *domus* of our statistics. They must on the contrary be added together; and to estimate the inhabitants of the *insulae*, we must multiply not only by the average dwellers in a *cenaculum* but also by the number of *cenacula* or flats in each *insula*.

The total of 233,010 inhabitants at which MM. Cuq and Lot arrived by their wrong conception of the *insula* is less even than the total of adult male citizens alone who enjoyed the generosity of Augustus. The discrepancy is so obviously ludicrous that it suffices to condemn their theory. Are we then, in natural reaction against this sort of calculation, to reckon about 25 *cenacula* to each *insula*, which would result in the *Notitia* from the ratio between the 1,797 *domus* defined as so many *insulae*, and the 46,602 *insulae* defined as so many *cenacula*? This would be to fall into an error of exaggeration as reprehensible as the opposite. When we study the various types of Roman house in the following chapter, we shall soon be convinced that the average *insula* contained five or six *cenacula* or flats, each of which housed at least five or six occupants. We are hence obliged to conclude, from the evidence of the *Regionaries* of the fourth century, that in the second century (when the growth of Rome was probably completed, or at any rate her population had greatly increased) the city had 50,000 citizens, bond or free, living in at last 1,000 *domus*, and a further population, which must have varied between 1,165,000 and 1,677,000, in its 46,602 apartment blocks. Even taking the lower of these two figures, and limiting the total estimate to around 1,200,000 inhabitants for the Urbs of the Antonines,[45] it is clear that Rome's population approached that of our own capitals in size, without enjoying any of the benefits of improved technics and communications which facilitate life and intercourse in our modern towns.

The capital of the empire must have suffered all the distresses of over-population which we experience, but in a far worse degree. If Rome was as enormous for her day as New York is for ours; if Rome, Queen of the Ancient World,

*Terrarum dea gentiumque, Roma*
*Cui par est nihil et nihil secundum*[46]

(goddess of continents and peoples, O Rome, whom nothing can equal and nothing approach) became in the time of Trajan a colossal and devouring town which stupefied the stranger and the provincial as the American metropolis astonishes the Europe of today, she paid even more dearly for the dimensions which her dominating position had inflicted upon her.

# II

# HOUSES AND STREETS

*

EVEN assessing the area of the Urbs as nearly 8 square miles, the circuit of the Imperial City was too limited to accommodate 1,200,000 inhabitants, comfortably – especially since every part of it could not be used for housing. We must subtract the numerous zones where public buildings, sanctuaries, basilicas, docks, baths, circuses, and theatres were in the hands of public authorities, who permitted only a handful of persons to live in them, such as porters, bonders, clerks, beadles, public slaves, or members of certain privileged corporations. We must exclude the capricious bed of the Tiber and the forty or so parks and gardens which stretched along the Esquiline, the Pincian, and both banks of the river; the Palatine Hill, which was reserved exclusively for the emperor's enjoyment; and finally the Campus Martius, whose temples, porticos, *palestrae, ustrinae,* and tombs covered more than two hundred hectares, from most of which all human habitations were banished in deference to the gods.

Now we must remember that the ancient Romans had no access to the almost unlimited suburban space which overground and underground transport puts at the disposal of London, Paris, and New York. They were condemned to remain within closer territorial limits owing to a lack of technical skill which strictly limited the space at their command; and they were unable to increase the area of their city in proportion to the numerical increase of their population. They were driven to compensate for this lack of room by two contradictory expedients: narrow streets and tall houses. Imperial Rome was continually forced to juxtapose her splendid monuments to an incoherent confusion of dwelling-houses at once pretentious and uncomfortable, fragile and inordinately large, separated by a network of gloomy, narrow alleys. When we try to reconstruct ancient Rome in our imagination, we are ever and

33

again disconcerted by the contrast of modern spaciousness with primitive medieval simplicity, an anticipation of orderliness that is almost American with the confusion of an oriental labyrinth.

## 1. Modern Aspects of the Roman House[1]

At first sight the student is struck by the 'up-to-date' appearance of what was of old the prevailing type of Roman building. The plan, the dimensions, and the structure of these buildings, were revealed in the author's study of the docks of Ostia, published in 1910;[2] by the excavations which were resumed in 1907 on the site of this colony – suburb and faithful miniature of Rome herself – from which Guido Calza ten years later skilfully drew the necessary deductions;[3] by the unearthing in Rome itself of Trajan's market-place and of buildings bordering the Via Biberatica;[4] by the discovery of ruins surviving under the stairway of the Ara Coeli;[5] and finally by the study of buildings which existed on the slopes of the Palatine in the Via dei Cerchi,[6] and under the gallery of the Piazza Colonna.[7]

Thirty years ago when men tried, in imagination, to visualize ancient Rome, they transferred to the banks of the Tiber the various types of building which had been recovered from the lava and *lapilli* of Vesuvius and reconstructed an image of the Urbs to match those of Herculaneum and Pompeii. Today, on the other hand, no trained archaeologist would dream of applying this summary and completely illusory method. Certainly it may safely be admitted that the mansion known as the House of Livia on the Palatine,[8] and the House of the Gamala at Ostia, which later passed into the hands of a certain Apuleius,[9] had kinship with the country houses of Herculaneum and Pompeii; and it may at a pinch be assumed that the private mansions of the wealthy, the *domus* which are noted in the *Regionaries*, frequently borrowed the same features. But the *Regionaries* give the city only 1,797 *domus* against 46,602 *insulae*; that is to say, only one private house for every 26 blocks of apartment houses. Corroborating the evidence of the texts and the objective interpretation of the fragments of the survey register of the Urbs which Septimius Severus re-exposed on the Forum of Peace,[10] the most recent explorations have shown that there was as large a gulf between the predominant *insula* and the rare *domus* as between a Roman palace and a seaside villa, or between the *maisons* of the great Paris boulevards and the cottages of the Côte d'Émeraude. Paradoxical as it may seem at first sight, there is certainly a much closer analogy between the *insula* of Imperial Rome and the humble *casa* of contemporary Rome than between the *insula* and the *domus* of Pompeian type.

The Roman *domus* turned a blind, unbroken wall to the street and all its doors and windows opened on its interior courts. The *insula*, on the other hand, opened always to the outside and when it formed a quadrilateral around a central courtyard, its doors, windows, and staircases opened both to the outside and to the inside.

The *domus* was composed of halls whose proportions were calculated once for all and dictated by custom in advance. These halls opened off each other in an invariable order: *fauces*, *atrium*, *alae*, *triclinium*, *tablinum*, and peristyle. The *insula* combined a number of *cenacula*, that is to say, distinct and separate dwellings like our 'flats' or 'apartments', consisting of rooms not assigned in advance to any particular function. The plan of each storey was apt to be identical with that above and below, the rooms being superimposed from top to bottom of the building. The *domus*, influenced by Hellenistic architecture, spread horizontally, while the *insula*, begotten probably in the course of the fourth century B.C. of the necessity of housing a growing population within the so-called Servian Walls, inevitably developed in a vertical direction.

In contrast to the Pompeian *domus*, the Roman *insula* grew steadily in stature until under the Empire it reached a dizzy height. Height was its dominant characteristic and this height which once amazed the ancient world still astounds us by its striking resemblance to our own most daring and modern buildings. As early as the third century B.C. *insulae* of three storeys (*tabulata, contabulationes, contignationes*) were so frequent that they had ceased to excite remark. In enumerating the prodigies which, in the winter of 218–217 B.C., preluded the invasion of Hannibal, Livy mentions without further comment the incident of an ox which escaped from the cattle market and scaled the stairs of a riverside *insula* to fling itself into the void from the third storey amid the horrified cries of the onlookers.[11] By the end of the republic the average height of the *insulae* indicated by this anecdote had already been exceeded. Cicero's Rome was, as it were, borne aloft and suspended in the air on the tiers of its apartment houses: '*Romam cenaculis sublatum atque suspensam.*'[12] The Rome of Augustus towered even higher. In his day, as Vitruvius records, 'the majesty of the city and the considerable increase in its population have compelled an extraordinary extension of the dwelling houses, and circumstances have constrained men to take refuge in increasing the height of the edifices.'[13] This remedy proved so perilous that the emperor, alarmed by the frequent collapse of buildings, was forced to regulate it and to forbid private individuals to erect any building more than 20 metres high.[14] It followed that avaricious and bold owners and contractors vied with each other in exploiting to the full the freedom still left them under this decree. Proofs abound to show that during the empire period the buildings attained a height which for that epoch was almost incredible. In describing Tyre at the beginning of the Christian Era, Strabo notes with surprise that the houses of this famous oriental seaport were almost higher than those of Imperial Rome.[15] A hundred years later, Juvenal ridicules this aerial Rome which rests only on beams as long and thin as flutes.[16] Fifty years later Aulus Gellius complains of stiff, multiple-storeyed houses ('*multis arduisque tabulatis*');[17] and the orator Aelius Aristides calculates in all seriousness that if the dwellings of the city were all reduced to one storey they would stretch as far as Hadria on the upper Adriatic.[18] Trajan in vain renewed the restrictions imposed by Augustus and even made them more severe by imposing a limit of eighteen metres on the height of private houses.[19] Necessity, however, knows no law: and in the fourth century the sights of the city included that giant apartment house, the Insula of Felicula, besides the Pantheon and the Column of Marcus Aurelius. It must have been erected a century and a half before, for at the beginning of the reign of Septimius Severus (193–211) its fame had already spread across the seas. When Tertullian sought to convince his African compatriots of the absurdity of the heretical Valentinians, who filled the infinite space which separates the Creator from his creatures with mediators and inter-mediaries, he rallied the heretics on having 'transformed the universe into a large, furnished apartment house, in whose attics they have planted their god under the tiles' ('*ad summas tegulas*') and accuses them of 'rearing to the sky as many storeys as we see in the Insula of Felicula in Rome.'[20]

Despite the edicts of Augustus and Trajan, the audacity of the builders had redoubled and the Insula of Felicula towered above the Rome of the Antonines like a skyscraper. Even if this particular building remained an exception, an unusually monstrous specimen, we know from the records that all around it rose buildings of five and six storeys. Martial was fortunate in having to climb only to the third floor of his quarters on the Quirinal, for many other tenants of the house were worse lodged.[21] In Martial's *insula* and in the neighbouring blocks of flats there were many dwellers perched much higher up, and in the cruel picture Juvenal paints of a fire in Rome, he seemed to be addressing one unfortunate who, like the god of the Valentinians, lived under the tiles: 'Smoke is pouring out of your third-floor attic, but you know nothing of it; if the alarm begins on the ground floor, the last man to burn will be he who has nothing to shelter him from the rain but the tiles, where the gentle doves lay their eggs.'[22]

There are two types of these innumerable and imposing struc-tures, whose summits were invisible to the passer-by unless he stepped back some distance. In the more luxurious, the ground floor or most of it was let as a whole to one tenant. This floor had the prestige and the advantages of a private house and was often dignified by the name of *domus* in contrast to the flats or *cenacula* of the upper storeys.[23]

Only people of consequence with well-lined purses could indulge in the luxury of such a *domus*. We know for instance that in Caesar's day Caelius paid for his an annual rent of 30,000 sesterces ($1,200·00).[24] In the humbler *insulae* the ground floor might be divided into booths and shops, the *tabernae*, which we can visualize the better because the skeletons of many have survived to this day in the Via Biberatica and at Ostia. Above the *tabernae* lowlier folk were herded. Each *taberna* opened straight on to the street by a large arched doorway extending its full width, with folding wooden leaves which were closed or drawn across the threshold every evening and firmly locked and bolted. Each represented the storehouse of some merchant, the workshop of some artisan, or the counter and show-window of some retailer. But in the corner of each *taberna* there was nearly always a stair of five or six steps of stone or brick continued by a wooden ladder. The ladder led to a sloping loft, lit directly by one long oblong window pierced above the centre of the doorway, which served as the lodging of the storekeeper, the caretakers of the shop, or the workshop hands.[25] Whoever they might be, the tenants of *tabernae* had never more than this one room for themselves and their families: they worked, cooked, ate, and slept there, and were at least as crowded as the tenants of the upper floors. Perhaps on the whole they were even worse provided for. Certainly they frequently found genuine difficulty in meeting their obligations. To bring pressure to bear on a defaulter, the landlord might 'shut up the tenant' (*percludere inquilinum*), that is, make a lien on his property to cover the amount due.[26]

There were, then, differences between the two types of apartment house which are known by the common name of *insula*, but almost all resulted from the primary distinction between those houses where the ground floor formed a *domus* and those in which it was let out in *tabernae*. The two types might be found side by side, and they obeyed the same rules in the internal arrangement and external appearance of their upper storeys.

Let us for a moment consider the Rome of our own day. It is true that in the course of the last sixty years, and particularly since the parcelling out of the Villa Ludovisi, Rome has seen the separate development of 'aristocratic quarters'. But prior to that, an equalitarian instinct had always tended to place the most stately dwellings and the humblest side by side; and even today the stranger is sometimes surprised to turn from a street swarming with the poorest of the poor and find himself face to face with the majesty of a Palazzo Farnese. This brotherly feature of the living Rome helps us to reconstruct in imagination the Rome of the Caesars where high and low, patrician and plebeian, rubbed shoulders everywhere without coming into conflict. Haughty Pompey did not consider it beneath his dignity to remain faithful to the Carinae.[27] Before migrating for political and religious reasons into the precincts of the Regia, the most fastidious of patricians, Julius Caesar, lived in the Subura.[28] Later Maecenas planted his gardens in the most evilly reputed part of the Esquiline.[29] About the same period the ultra-wealthy Asinius Pollio chose for his residence the plebeian Aventine, where Licinius Sura, vice emperor of the reign of Trajan, also elected to make his home.[30] At the end of the first century A.D. the emperor Vespasian's nephew and a parasite poet like Martial were near neighbours on the slopes of the Quirinal,[31] and at the end of the second century Commodus went to dwell in a gladiatorial school on the Caelian.[32]

It is true that when they were laid waste by fire the various quarters of the city rose from their ashes more solid and more magnificent than before.[33] Nevertheless, the incongruous juxta-positions which persist to this day were repeated with a minimum of change after each renovation, and every attempt to specialize the fourteen regions of the Urbs was foredoomed to failure. Hypersensitive people, anxious to escape the mob, were driven to move to a greater and greater distance, to take refuge on the fringes of the Campagna among the pines of the Pincian or the Janiculum, where they could find room for the parks of their suburban villas.[34] The common people, meanwhile, driven out of the centre of the city by the presence of the court and the profusion of public buildings but nevertheless fettered to it by the business transacted there, overflowed by preference into the zones inter-mediate between the fora and the outskirts, the outside districts adjacent to the Republican Wall, which the reform of Augustus had with one stroke of the pen incorporated in the Urbs. The *Regionaries* record the number of *insulae* or apartment blocks in each region, and the number of *vici* or arteries serving the *insulae*; and separate averages may be obtained for the eight regions of the old city and the six regions of the new. The average for the older regions is 2,965 *insulae* with 17 *vici* and for the newer 3,429 *insulae* with 28 *vici*. We note that the largest number of *insulae* were massed in the new city; and that they attained the greatest size not in the old city where there were 174 *insulae* per *vicus*, but in the new where there were only 123 per *vicus*. The *Regionaries* also locate for us the insula of Felicula, the giant skyscraper in the ninth region, known as the region of the Circus Flaminius, in the very heart of the new city. Isolated soundings lead us to the same conclusion as do mass statistics: the successful experiments of imperial city planning caused the huge modern-style apartment blocks of ancient Rome to increase in number and grow to immoderate size.

Seen from the outside, all these monumental blocks of flats were more or less identical in appearance and presented a fairly uniform façade to the street. Piled storey upon storey, the large-bayed *cenacula* were superimposed one above the other; the first steps of their stone staircases cut through the line of the *tabernae* or the walls of the *domus*. Reduced to its governing essentials, the plan of these buildings is familiar. They might well be urban houses of today or yesterday. From a study of the best preserved of their ruins, the most competent experts have been able to reproduce on paper the original plan and elevation; and these drawings show such startling analogies with the buildings in which we ourselves live that at first sight we are tempted to mistrust them. A more attentive examination, however, bears witness to the conscientious accuracy of these reconstructions. M. Boethius, for instance, has brought together on one photographic plate such and such a section of Trajan's market or such and such a building at Ostia and an equivalent existing piece of building in the Via dei Cappellari at Rome or the Via dei Tribunali at Naples. By this means he has demonstrated a surprising resemblance – at moments approaching identity – between these plans, separated in time by so many centuries.[85] If they could rise from the dead, the subjects of Trajan or of Hadrian would feel they had come home when they crossed the threshold of these modern Roman *casoni*; but they might with justice complain that in external appearance their houses had lost rather than gained in the course of the ages.

Superficially compared with its descendant of the Third Italy, the *insula* of Imperial Rome displays a more delicate taste and a more studied elegance, and in truth the ancient building gives the more modern impression. Here wood and rubble are ingeniously combined in its facings and there bricks are disposed with cunning skill, all harmonized with a perfection of art which has been forgotten among us since the Norman mansions and the castles of Louis XIII. Its doorways and its windows were no less numerous and often larger. Its row of shops was usually protected and screened with the line of a portico. In the wider streets its storeys were relieved by a picturesque variety either of loggias (*pergulae*) resting on the porticos or of balconies (*maeniana*). Some were of wood, and the beams that once supported them may be found still embedded in the masonry; others were brick, sometimes thrown out on pendentives whose lines of horizontal impost are the parents of the parallel extrados, sometimes based on a series of cradle-vaults supported by large travertine consoles firmly embedded in the masonry of the prolonged lateral walls.

Climbing plants clung round the pillars of the loggias and the railing of the balconies, while most of the windows boasted miniature gardens formed of pots of flowers such as the elder Pliny has described. In the most stifling corners of the great city these flowers assuaged somewhat the homesickness for the countryside which lay heavy on the humble town dweller sprung from a long line of peasant ancestors.[36] We know that at the end of the fourth century the host of a modest inn at Ostia, like that in which Saint Augustine set his gentle and memorable discourse with Saint Monica,[37] always surrounded his guest house with green and shady trees. The Casa dei Dipinti, considerably older still, seems to have been completely festooned with flowers, and the highly plausible reconstruction of it which MM. Calza and Gismondi have made suggests a garden city in every respect like the most attractive ones that enlightened building societies and philanthropic associations are putting up today for the workmen and lower middle classes of our great towns.

Unfortunately for this *insula*, the most luxurious of those to which archaeology has so far introduced us, its external appearance belied its comforts. The architects had indeed neglected nothing in its outward embellishment. They had paved it with tiles and mosaics. By long and costly processes they had clothed it with colours

as fresh and living in their day as those of the frescoes of Pompeii,
though now three parts obliterated. To these it owes the name
by which learned Italians call it, Casa dei Dipinti, the House of
Paintings. I dare not assert that it was equipped with *laquearia*
enamelled on movable plaques of arbor vitae or carved ivory,
such as wealthy upstarts like Trimalchio fixed above their dining-
tables and worked by machinery to rain down flowers or perfume
or tiny valuable gifts on their surprised and delighted guests,[38]
but it is not improbable that the ceilings of the rooms were covered
with the gilded stucco which the elder Pliny's contemporaries
admired.[39] Be that as it may, all this luxury had its price, and the
most opulent of the *insulae* suffered from the fragility of their
construction, the scantiness of their furniture, insufficient light and
heat, and absence of sanitation.

## 2. Archaic Aspects of the Roman House

These lofty buildings were far too lightly built. While the *domus* of
Pompeii easily covered 800 to 900 square metres, the *insulae* of
Ostia, though built according to the specifications which Hadrian
laid down, were rarely granted such extensive foundations. As for
the Roman *insulae*, the ground plans recoverable from the cadastral
survey of Septimius Severus, who reproduced them, show that they
usually varied between 300 and 400 square metres.[40] Even if there
were no smaller ones (which is extremely unlikely) of which all
trace has been buried for ever in the upheavals of the terrain, these
figures are misleading: a foundation of 300 square metres is inadequate enough to carry a structure of 18 to 20 metres high,
particularly when we remember the thickness of the flooring which
separated the storeys from each other. We need only consider the
ratio of the two figures given to feel the danger inherent in their
disproportion. The lofty Roman buildings possessed no base
corresponding to their height and a collapse was all the more to be
feared since the builders, lured by greed of gain, tended to economize
more and more at the expense of the strength of the masonry and
quality of the materials. Vitruvius states that the law forbade a
greater thickness for the outside walls than a foot and a half, and in

order to economize space the other walls were not to exceed that.[41] He adds that, at least from the time of Augustus, it was the custom to correct this thinness of the walls by inserting chains of bricks to strengthen the concrete. He observes with smiling philosophy that this blend of stone-course, chains of brick and layers of concrete in which the stones and pebbles were symmetrically embedded, permitted the convenient construction of buildings of great height and allowed the Roman people to create handsome dwellings for themselves with little difficulty: '*populus romanus egregias habet sine impeditione habitationes.*'

Twenty years later Vitruvius would have recanted. The elegance he so admired had been attained only at the sacrifice of solidity. Even after the brick technique had been perfected in the second century, and it had become usual to cover the entire façade with bricks, the city was constantly filled with the noise of buildings collapsing or being torn down to prevent it; and the tenants of an *insula* lived in constant expectation of its coming down on their heads. We may recall the savage and gloomy tirade of Juvenal: 'Who at cool Praeneste, or at Volsinii amid its leafy hills, was ever afraid of his house tumbling down? . . . But here we inhabit a city propped up for the most part by slats: for that is how the landlord patches up the crack in the old wall, bidding the inmates sleep at ease under the ruin that hangs above their heads.'[42]

The satirist has not exaggerated, and many specific cases provided for in the legal code, the *Digest*, take for granted precisely the precarious state of affairs which excited Juvenal's wrath.

Suppose, for instance, that the owner of an *insula* has leased it for a sum of 30,000 sesterces to a principal tenant who by means of sub-letting draws from it a revenue of 40,000 sesterces, and that the owner presently, on the pretext that the building is about to collapse, decides to demolish it; the principal tenant is entitled to bring an action for damages. If the building was demolished of necessity, the plaintiff will be entitled to the refund of his rent and nothing further. On the other hand, if the building has been demolished only to enable the owner to erect a better and ultimately more remunerative building, the defendant must further pay to the principal tenant who has been compelled to evict his sub-tenants whatever sum the plaintiff has thus lost.[43]

This text is suggestive both in itself and in its implications. The terms in which it is couched leave no doubt as to the frequency of the practices of which it speaks, and they indicate that the houses of Imperial Rome were at least as fragile as the old American tenements which not so long ago collapsed or had to be demolished in New York.

The Roman houses, moreover, caught fire as frequently as the houses of Stamboul under the Sultans. This was because, in the first place, they were unsubstantial; further, the weight of their floors involved the introduction of massive wooden beams, and the movable stoves which heated them, the candles, the smoky lamps, and the torches which lighted them at night involved perpetual risk of fire; and finally, as we shall see, water was issued to the various storeys with grudging hand. All these reasons combined to increase both the number of fires and the rapidity with which they spread. The wealthy Crassus in the last century of the republic devised a scheme for increasing his immense fortune by exploiting these catastrophes.[44] On hearing the news of an outbreak, he would run to the scene of the disaster and offer profuse sympathy to the owner, plunged in despair by the sudden destruction of his property. Then he would offer to buy on the spot – at a sum far below its real value – the parcel of ground, now nothing but a mass of smouldering ruins. Thereupon, employing one of the teams of builders whose training he had himself superintended, he erected a brand new *insula*, the income from which amply rewarded him for his capital outlay.

Even later, under the empire, after Augustus had created a corps of *vigiles* or fire-fighting night watchmen, the tactics of Crassus would have been no less successful.[45] In spite of the attention Trajan paid to the policing of the Urbs, outbreaks of fire were an everyday occurrence in Roman life. The rich man trembled for his mansion, and in his anxiety kept a troop of slaves to guard his yellow amber, his bronzes, his pillars of Phrygian marble, his tortoise-shell inlays.[46] The poor man was startled from his sleep by flames invading his attic and the terror of being roasted alive.[47] Dread of fire was such an obsession among rich and poor alike that Juvenal was prepared to quit Rome to escape it: 'No, no, I must live where there is no fire and the night is free from alarms!'[48] He had hardly overstated the case. The jurists echo his satires, and Ulpian informs us that not a day passed in Imperial Rome without several outbreaks of fire: '*plurimis uno die incendii exortis.*'[49]

The scantiness of furniture at least reduced the gravity of each of these catastrophes. Granted that they were warned in time, the poor devils of the *cenacula* (like that imaginary Ucalegon whom Juvenal ironically saddled with the epic name of one of the Trojans of the Aeneid) were quickly able 'to clear out their miserable goods and chattels'.[50] The rich had more to lose and could not, like Ucalegon, stuff all their worldly possessions into one bundle. Apart from their statues of marble and bronze, their furniture, however, was sparse enough, for wealth displayed itself not in the number of items but in their quality, the precious materials employed, and the rare shapes which bore witness to their owner's taste.

In the passage of Juvenal quoted above,[51] the millionaire he pictures was taking precaution to save not what we nowadays would call 'furniture', but his curios and *objets d'art*. For every Roman, the main item of furniture was the bed (*lectus*) on which he slept during his siesta and at night and on which he reclined by day to eat, read, write, or receive visitors.[52] Humble people made shift with a shelf of masonry built along the wall and covered with a pallet. Those better off had handsomer and more elaborate couches in proportion to their means. Most beds were single ones (*lectuli*). There were double beds for married couples (*lecti geniales*); beds for three which graced the dining-room (*triclinia*); and those who wished to make a splash and astonish the neighbours had couches for six. Some were cast in bronze; most were simply carved in wood, either in oak or maple, terebinth or arbor vitae, or it might be in those exotic woods with undulating grain and changing lights which reflected a thousand colours like a peacock's tail (*lecti pavonini*). Some beds boasted bronze feet and a wooden frame, others again ivory feet and a frame of bronze. In some cases the woodwork was inlaid with tortoise-shell; in some the bronze was nielloed with silver and gold. There were even some, like Trimalchio's, of massive silver.

Whatever its nature and style, the bed was the major piece of furniture alike in the aristocratic *domus* and in the proletarian *insula*, and in many cases it deterred the Romans from seeking to provide themselves with anything else. Their tables (*mensae*) had little in common with ours.[53] They never developed into sturdy tables with four legs – those were introduced late in history through the intermediary of Christian rites. When the empire was in its glory, the *mensa* was a set of little shelves in tiers, supported on one leg, and used to display for a visitor's admiration the most valuable treasures of the house (*cartibula*). Alternatively, it might be a low table of wood or bronze with three or four adjustable supports (*trapezophores*) or a simple tripod whose folding metal legs usually ended in a lion's claw. As for seats, remains of these are – not without reason – more rarely found in the excavations than tables. The armchair with back, the *thronus*, was reserved for the divinity; the chair with a more or less sloping back, the *cathedra*, was especially popular with women.[54] Great ladies, whose indolence is a target for Juvenal's scorn,[55] would languidly repose in them, and we have literary record of their existence in two houses: the reception hall in the palace of Augustus[56] – Corneille's 'Be seated, Cinna' is derived directly from Seneca's account – and in the room (*cubiculum*) where the younger Pliny invited his friends to come and talk with him.[57] Also they appear in literature as the distinguishing property of the master who is teaching in a *schola*[58] or, in connexion with religious ceremonies, as the property of the *frater arvalis* of the official religion,[59] of the head of certain esoteric pagan sects, and later of the Christian presbyter. We speak with perfect right, therefore, of the 'Chair of Saint Peter' or the 'chair' of a university professor.

Ordinarily the Romans were content with benches (*scamna*) or stools (*subsellia*) or *sellae* without arms or back, which they carried about with them out of doors. Even when the seat was the magistrate's ivory *sella curulis*, or made of gold like Julius Caesar's, it was never more than a folding 'camp stool'.[60] The rest of the furniture, the essentials apart from beds, consisted of the covers, the cloths, the counterpanes, the cushions, which were spread over or placed on the bed, at the foot of the table, on the seat of the stool, and on the bench; and finally, the eating utensils and the jewellery. Silver table services were so common that Martial ridicules patrons who were too niggardly of their Saturnalian gifts to give their clients at least five pounds (a trifle over three pounds avoirdupois) of silverware.[61] Only the very poor used earthenware. The rich had vessels carved by a master hand, sparkling with gold and set with precious stones.[62] Reading some of the ancient descriptions, one seems to relive a scene out of the *Arabian Nights*, set in spacious, unencumbered rooms where wealth is revealed only by the profusion and depth of the divans, the iridescence of damask, the sparkle of jewellery and of damascened copper – and yet all the elements of that 'comfort' to which the West has grown so much attached are lacking.

Even in the most luxurious Roman house, the lighting left much to be desired: though the vast bay windows were capable of flooding it at certain hours with the light and air we moderns prize, at other times either both had to be excluded or the inhabitants were blinded and chilled beyond endurance. Neither in the Via Biberatica nor in Trajan's market nor in the Casa dei Dipinti at Ostia do we find any traces of mica or glass near the windows, therefore the windows in these places cannot have been equipped with the fine transparent sheets of *lapis specularis* with which rich families of the empire sometimes screened the alcove of a bedroom, a bathroom, or garden hothouse, or even a sedan chair. Nor can they have been fitted with the thick, opaque panes which are still found in place in the skylight windows of the baths of Herculaneum and Pompeii, where they provided a hermetic closure to maintain the heat without producing complete darkness.[63] The dwellers in a Roman house must have protected themselves, very inadequately, with hanging cloths or skins blown by wind or drenched by rain; or over-well by folding shutters of one or two leaves which, while keeping cold and rain, midsummer heat or winter wind at bay, also excluded every ray of light. In quarters armed with solid shutters of this sort the occupant, were he an ex-consul or as well known as the younger Pliny, was condemned either to freeze in daylight or to be sheltered in darkness.[64] The proverb says that a door must be either open or shut. In the Roman *insula*, on the contrary, the tenant could be comfortable only when the windows were neither completely open nor completely shut; and it is certain that in spite of their size and number, the Romans' windows rendered them neither the service nor the pleasure that ours give us.

In the same way, the heating arrangements in the *insula* were extremely defective.[65] As the *atrium* had been dispensed with, and the *cenacula* were piled one above the other, it was impossible for the inhabitants of an *insula* to enjoy the luxury common to the peasantry, of gathering round the fire lighted by the womenfolk in the centre of their hovels, while sparks and smoke escaped by the gaping hole purposely left in the roof. It would be a grave mistake, moreover, to imagine that the *insula* ever enjoyed the benefit of central heating with which a misuse of language and an error of fact have credited it. The furnace arrangements which are found in so many ruins never fulfilled this office. They consisted of, first, a heating apparatus (the *hypocausis*) consisting of one or two furnaces which were stoked, according to the intensity of heat desired and the length of time it was to be maintained, with wood or charcoal, faggots or dried grass; second, an exit channel through which the heat, the soot, and the smoke penetrated indiscriminately into the adjacent *hypocaustum*; third, the heat-chamber (the *hypocaustum*) characterized by piles of bricks in parallel rows, between and over which heat, soot, and smoke circulated together; and finally the heated rooms resting on, or, rather, suspended above the *hypocaustum* and known, therefore, as the *suspensurae*. Whether or not they were connected with it by the spaces within their partition walls, the *suspensurae* were separated from the *hypocaustum* by a flooring formed of a bed of bricks, a layer of clay, and a pavement of stone or marble. This compact floor was designed to exclude unwelcome or injurious exhalations and to slow down the rise of temperature. It will be noticed that in this device the heated surface of the *suspensurae* was never greater than the surface of the *hypocaustum* and its working demanded a number of *hypocauses* equal to, if not greater than, the number of *hypocausta*. It follows therefore, that this system of furnaces had nothing to do with central heating and was not applicable to many-storeyed buildings. In ancient Italy it was never used to heat an entire building, unless it was one single and isolated room like the latrine excavated in 1929 at Rome between the Great Forum and the Forum of Caesar.[66] Moreover, even in the buildings where such a furnace system existed, it never occupied more than a small fraction of the house: the bathroom in the best-equipped villas of Pompeii or the *caldarium* of the public baths. It need hardly be stressed that no traces of such a system have been found in any of the *insulae* known to us.

This was not the worst. The Roman *insula* lacked fireplaces as completely as furnaces. Only a few bakeries at Pompeii had an oven supplied with a pipe somewhat resembling our chimney; it would be too much to assume that it was identical with it, for, of the two examples that can be cited, one is broken off in such a way that we cannot tell where it used to come out, and the other was not carried up to the roof but into a drying cupboard on the first floor. No such ventilation shafts have been discovered in the villas of Pompeii or Herculaneum; still less, of course, in the houses of Ostia, which reproduce in every detail the plan of the Roman *insula*. We are driven to conclude that in the houses of the Urbs bread and cakes were cooked with a fire confined in an oven, other food simmered over open stoves, and the inhabitants themselves had no remedy against the cold but what a brazier could provide.[67] Many of these were portable or mounted on runners. Some were wrought in copper or bronze with great taste and skill. But the grace of this industrial art was scant compensation for the brazier's limited heating power and range. The haughtiest dwellings of ancient Rome were strangers alike to the gentle, equal warmth which the radiator spreads through our rooms and to the cheerfulness of our open fires. They were threatened moreover by the attack of noxious fumes and not infrequently by the escape of smoke which was not always prevented either by the thorough drying or even by the preliminary carbonization of the fuel (*ligna coctilia, acapna*).

To make matters worse, the *insula* was as ill supplied with water as with light and heat. I admit that the opposite opinion is generally held. People forget that the conveyance of water to the city at State expense was regarded as a purely public service from which private enterprise had been excluded from the first, and which continued to function under the empire for the benefit of the collective population with little regard for the needs of private individuals. According to Frontinus, a contemporary of Trajan, eight aqueducts brought 222,237,060 gallons of water a day to the city of Rome,[68] but very little of this immense supply found its way to private houses.

In the first place, it was not until the reign of Trajan and the opening on 24 June 109 of the aqueduct called by his name, *aqua Traiana*, that fresh spring water was brought to the quarters on the right bank of the Tiber;[69] until then, the inhabitants had to make their wells suffice for their needs. Secondly, even on the left bank access to the distributory channels connected by permission of the princeps with the *castella* of his aqueducts was granted, on payment of a royalty, only to individual concessionaires and to ground landlords;[70] and certainly up to the beginning of the second century these concessions were revocable and were, in fact, brutally revoked by the administration on the very day of the death of a concessionaire.[71] Finally, and most significantly, it seems that these private water supplies were everywhere confined to the ground floor, the chosen residence of the capitalists who had their *domus* at the base of the apartment blocks.

In the colony of Ostia, for instance, which, like its neighbour Rome, possessed an aqueduct, municipal channels, and private conduits, no building that has so far been excavated reveals any trace of rising columns which might have conveyed spring water to the upper storeys. All ancient texts, moreover, whatever the period in which they were written, bear conclusive witness to the absence of any such installations. Under the empire, the poet Martial complains that his town house lacks water although it is situated near an aqueduct.[72] In the *Satires* of Juvenal the water-carriers (*aquarii*) are spoken of as the scum of the slave population.[73] The jurists of the first half of the third century considered the water-carriers so vital to the collective life of each *insula* that they formed, as it were, a part of the building itself and, like the porters (*ostiarii*) and the sweepers (*zetarii*), were inherited with the building by the heir or legatees.[74] The praetorian prefect Paulus, in issuing instructions to the *praefectus vigilum*, did not forget to remind the commandant of the Roman firemen that it was part of his duty to warn tenants always to keep water ready in their rooms to check an outbreak: '*ut aquam unusquisque inquilinus in cenaculo habeat iubetur admonere.*'[75]

Obviously, if the Romans of imperial times had needed only to turn a tap and let floods of water flow into a sink, this warning would have been superfluous. The mere fact that Paulus expressly formulated the warning proves that, with a few exceptions to which we shall revert later, water from the aqueducts reached only the ground floor of the *insula*. The tenants of the upper *cenacula* had to go and draw their water from the nearest fountain. The higher the flat was perched, the harder the task of carrying water to scrub the floors and walls of those crowded *contignationes*. It must be confessed that the lack of plentiful water for washing invited the tenants of many Roman *cenacula* to allow filth to accumulate, and it was inevitable that many succumbed to the temptation for lack of a water system such as never existed save in the imagination of too optimistic archaeologists.

Far be it from me to stint my well-deserved admiration for the network of sewers which conveyed the sewage of the city into the Tiber. The sewers of Rome were begun in the sixth century B.C. and continually extended and improved under the republic and under the empire. The *cloacae* were conceived, carried out, and kept up on so grandiose a scale that in certain places a wagon laden with hay could drive through them with ease; and Agrippa, who perhaps did more than any man to increase their efficiency and wholesomeness by diverting the overflow of the aqueducts into them through seven channels, had no difficulty in travelling their entire length by boat.[76] They were so solidly constructed that the mouth of the largest, as well as the oldest of them, the *Cloaca Maxima*, the central collector for all the others from the Forum to the foot of the Aventine, can still be seen opening into the river at the level of the Ponte Rotto. Its semicircular arch, five metres in diameter, is as perfect today as in the days of the kings to whom it is attributed.[77] Its patinated, tufa voussoirs have triumphantly defied the passage of twenty-five hundred years. It is a masterpiece in which the enterprise and patience of the Roman people collaborated with the long experience won by the Etruscans in the drainage of their marshes; and, such as it has come down to us, it does honour to antiquity. But it cannot be denied that the ancients, though they were courageous enough to undertake it, and patient enough to carry it through, were not skilful enough to utilize it as we would have done in their place. They did not turn it to full account for securing a cleanly town or ensuring the health and decency of the inhabitants.

The system served to collect the sewage of the ground floor and of the public latrines which stood directly along the route, but no effort was made to connect the *cloacae* with the private latrines of the separate *cenacula*. There are only a few houses in Pompeii whose upstairs latrines were so designed that they could empty into the sewer below, whether by a conduit connecting them with the sewer or by a special arrangement of pipes; and the same can be said of Ostia and Herculaneum.[78] But since this type of drainage is lacking in the most imposing *insulae* of Ostia as in those of Rome, we may abide in general by the judgement of Abbé Thédenat, who thirty-five years ago stated unequivocally that the living quarters of the *insulae* had never at any time been linked with the *cloacae* of the Urbs.[79] The drainage system of the Roman house is merely a myth begotten of the complacent imagination of modern times. Of all the hardships endured by the inhabitants of ancient Rome, the lack of domestic drainage is the one which would be most severely resented by the Romans of today.

The very rich escaped the inconvenience. If they lived in their own *domus*, they had nothing to do but construct a latrine on the ground level. Water from the aqueducts might reach it and at worst, if it was too far distant from one of the sewers for the refuse to be swept away, the sewage could fall into a trench beneath. These cess trenches, like the one excavated near San Pietro in 1892, were neither very deep nor proof against seepage, and the manure merchants had acquired the right – probably under Vespasian[80] – to arrange for emptying them. If the privileged had their *domus* in an *insula*, they rented the whole of the ground floor and enjoyed the same advantage as in a private house. The poor, however, had

a longer way to go. In any case they were forced to go outside
their homes. If the trifling cost was not deterrent, they could
pay for entry to one of the public latrines administered by the
*conductores foricarum*.[81] The great number of these establishments,
which the *Regionaries* attest, is an indication of the size of their
clientele. In Trajan's Rome, as today in some backward villages, the
immense majority of private people had to have recourse to the
public latrine. But the comparison cannot be pushed further. The
latrines of ancient Rome are disconcerting on two counts; we need
only recall the examples of Pompeii, of Timgad, of Ostia, and that
already alluded to at Rome itself, which was heated in winter by a
*hypocausis*: the *forica* at the intersection of the Forum and the Forum
Iulium.[82]

The Roman *forica* was public in the full sense of the term, like
soldiers' latrines in war time. People met there, conversed, and
exchanged invitations to dinner without embarrassment.[83] And at
the same time, it was equipped with superfluities which we forgo and
decorated with a lavishness we are not wont to spend on such a
spot. All round the semicircle or rectangle which it formed, water
flowed continuously in little channels, in front of which a score or
so of seats were fixed. The seats were of marble, and the opening
was framed by sculptured brackets in the form of dolphins, which
served both as a support and as a line of demarcation. Above the
seats it was not unusual to see niches containing statues of gods or
heroes, as on the Palatine, or an altar to Fortune, the goddess of
health and happiness, as in Ostia;[84] and not infrequently the room
was cheered by the gay sound of a playing fountain as at Timgad.[85]
Let us be honest with ourselves: we are amazed at this mixture of
delicacy and coarseness, at the solemnity and grace of the decorations and the familiarity of the actors. It is like nothing but the
fifteenth-century *madrasas* in Fez, where the latrines were also
designed to accommodate a crowd, and decorated with exquisitely
delicate stucco and covered with a lacelike ceiling of cedar wood.
Suddenly Rome – where even the latrines of the imperial palace, as
majestic and ornate as a sanctuary beneath its dome, contained three
seats side by side[86] – Rome at once mystic and sordid, artistic and
carnal, without embarrassment and without shame seems to join

hands with the distant Haghrab at the epoch of the Merinids, so far removed from us in time and space.

But the public latrines were not the resort of misers or of the very poor. These folk had no mind to enrich the *conductores foricarum* to the tune of even one as. They preferred to have recourse to the jars, skilfully chipped down for the purpose, which the fuller at the corner ranged in front of his workshop. He purchased permission for this from Vespasian, in consideration of a tax to which no odour clung, so as to secure gratis the urine necessary for his trade.[87] Alternatively they clattered down the stairs to empty their chamber pots (*lasana*) and their commodes (*sellae pertusae*) into the vat or *dolium* placed under the well of the staircase.[88] Or if perhaps this expedient had been forbidden by the landlord of their *insula*, they betook themselves to some neighbouring dungheap. For in Rome of the Caesars, as in a badly kept hamlet of today, more than one alley stank with the pestilential odour of a cess trench (*lacus*) such as those which Cato the Elder during his censorship paved over when he cleaned the *cloacae* and led them under the Aventine.[89] Such malodorous trenches were extant in the days of Cicero and Caesar; Lucretius mentions them in his poem, *De rerum natura*.[90] Two hundred years later, in the time of Trajan, they were still there, and one might see unnatural mothers of the Megaera type, anxious to rid themselves of an unwanted child, surreptitiously taking advantage of a barbarous law and exposing a new-born infant there; while matrons grieving over their barrenness would hasten no less secretly to snatch the baby, hoping to palm it off on a credulous husband as their own, and thus with a supposititious heir to still the ache in his paternal heart.[91]

There were other poor devils who found their stairs too steep and the road to these dung pits too long, and to save themselves further trouble would empty the contents of their chamber pots from their heights into the streets. So much the worse for the passer-by who happened to intercept the unwelcome gift! Fouled and sometimes even injured, as in Juvenal's satire,[92] he had no redress save to lodge a complaint against the unknown assailant; many passages of the *Digest* indicate that Roman jurists did not disdain to take cognizance of this offence, to refer the case to the judges, to track down the offender, and assess the damages payable to the victim. Ulpian classifies the various clues by which it might be possible to trace the culprit.

If [he says] the apartment [*cenaculum*] is divided among several tenants, redress can be sought only against that one of them who lives in that part of the apartment from the level of which the liquid has been poured. If the tenant, however, while professing to have sub-let [*cenacularium exercens*], has in fact retained for himself the enjoyment of the greater part of the apartment, he shall be held solely responsible. If, on the other hand, the tenant who professes to have sub-let has in fact retained for his own use only a modest fraction of the space, he and his sub-tenants shall be jointly held responsible. The same will hold good if the vessel or the liquid has been thrown from a balcony.[93]

But Ulpian does not exclude the culpability of an individual if the inquiry is able to fix the blame on one guilty person, and he requests the praetor to set in equity a penalty proportionate to the seriousness of the injury. For instance:

When in consequence of the fall of one of these projectiles from a house, the body of a free man shall have suffered injury, the judge shall award to the victim in addition to medical fees and other expenses incurred in his treatment and necessary to his recovery, the total of the wages of which he has been or shall in future be deprived by the inability to work which has ensued.[94]

Wise provisions these, which might seem to have inspired our laws relating to accidents, but which we have failed to adopt in their entirety, for Ulpian ends with a notable restriction. In formulating his final paragraph he expresses with unemotional simplicity his noble conception of the dignity of man: 'As for scars or disfigurement which may have resulted from such wounds, no damages can be calculated on this count, for the body of a free man is without price.'

The lofty sentiment of this phrase rises like a flower above a cess pit and serves to accentuate our dismayed embarrassment at the state of affairs of which these subtle legal analyses give a glimpse. Our great cities are also shadowed by misery, stained by the uncleanness of our slums, dishonoured by the vice they harbour. But at least the disease which gnaws at them is usually localized and confined to certain blighted quarters, whereas we get the impression that slums invaded every corner of Imperial Rome. Almost everywhere throughout the Urbs the *insulae* were the property of owners who had no wish to be concerned directly in their management and who leased out the upper storeys to a promoter for five-year terms – in return for a rent at least equal to that of the ground-floor *domus*. This principal tenant who set himself to exploit the sub-letting of the *cenacula* had no bed of roses. He had to keep the place in repair, obtain tenants, keep the peace between them, and collect his quarterly payments on the year's rent. Not unnaturally he sought compensation for his worries and his risks by extorting enormous profits. Ever-rising rent is a subject of eternal lamentation in Roman literature.

In 153 B.C. an exiled king had to share a flat with an artist, a painter, in order to make ends meet.[95] In Caesar's day the humblest tenant had to pay a rent of 2,000 sesterces ($80) a year. In the times of Domitian and of Trajan, one could have bought a fine estate at Sora or Frusino for the price of quarters in Rome.[96] So intolerable was the burden of rent that the sub-tenants of the first lessee almost invariably had to sub-let in their turn every room in their *cenaculum* which they could possibly spare. Almost everywhere, the higher you went in a building, the more breathless became the overcrowding, the more sordid the promiscuity. If the ground floor was divided into several *tabernae*, they were filled with artisans, shopkeepers, and eating-house keepers, like those of the *insula* which Petronius describes.[97] If it had been retained for the use of one privileged possessor, it was occupied by the retainers of the owner of the *domus*. But whatever the disposition of the ground floor, the upper storeys were gradually swamped by the mob: entire families were herded together in them; dust, rubbish, and filth accumulated; and finally bugs ran riot to such a point that one of the shady characters of Petronius' *Satyricon*, hiding under his miserable pallet, was driven to press his lips against the bedding which was black with them.[98] Whether we speak of the luxurious and elegant *domus* or of the *insulae* – caravanserias whose heterogeneous inhabitants needed an army of slaves and porters under the command of a servile steward to keep order among them – the dwelling-houses of the Urbs were seldom ranged in order along an avenue, but jostled each other in a labyrinth of steep streets and lanes, all more or less narrow, tortuous, and dark, and the marble of the 'palaces' shone in the obscurity of cut-throat alleys.

## 3. Streets and Traffic

If some magic wand could have disentangled the jumble of the Roman streets and laid them end to end, they would certainly have covered a distance of 60,000 *passus*, or approximately 89 kilometres. So we learn from the calculations and measurements carried out by the censors Vespasian and Titus in A.D. 73.[99] And the elder Pliny, moved to pride by the contemplation of this immense extent of streets, compares with it the height of the buildings they served and proclaims that there existed in all the ancient world no city whose size could be compared to that of Rome.[100]

The size is not to be denied, but if, instead of admiring the imaginary and orderly perspective which Pliny plotted in a straight line on his parchment, we consider the actual layout of Roman streets, we find them forming an inextricably tangled net, their disadvantages immensely aggravated by the vast height of the buildings which shut them in. Tacitus attributes the ease and speed with which the terrible fire of A.D. 64 spread through Rome to the anarchy of these confined streets, winding and twisting as if they had been drawn haphazard between the masses of giant *insulae*.[101] This lesson was not lost on Nero; but if in rebuilding the burnt-out *insulae* he intended to reconstruct them on a more rational plan with better alignment and more space between, he failed on the whole to achieve his aim.[102] Down to the end of the empire the street system of Rome as a whole represented an inorganic welter rather than a practical and efficient plan. The streets always smacked of their ancient origin and maintained the old distinctions which had prevailed at the time of their rustic development: the *itinera*, which were tracks only for men on foot, the *actus*, which permitted the passage of only one cart at a time, and finally the *viae* proper,

which permitted two carts to pass each other or to drive abreast.[103]
Among all the innumerable streets of Rome, only two inside the
old Republican Wall could justly claim the name of *via*. They
were the Via Sacra and the Via Nova, which respectively crossed
and flanked the Forum, and the insignificance of these two thoroughfares remains a perpetual surprise. Between the gates of the
innermost enclosure and the outskirts of the fourteen regions, not
more than a score of others deserved the title: the roads which led
out of Rome to Italy, the Via Appia, the Via Latina, the Via
Ostiensis, the Via Labicana, etc. They varied in width from 4·80
to 6·50 metres, a proof that they had not been greatly enlarged
since the day when the Twelve Tables had prescribed a maximum
width of 4·80 metres.

The majority of the other thoroughfares, the real streets, or *vici*,
scarcely attained this last figure, and many fell far below it, being
simple passages (*angiportus*) or tracks (*semitae*) which had to be at
least 2·9 metres wide to allow for projecting balconies.[104] Their
narrowness was all the more inconvenient in that they constantly
zigzagged and on the Seven Hills rose and fell steeply – hence the
name of *clivi* which many of them, like the Clivus Capitolinus, the
Clivus Argentarius, bore of good right. They were daily defiled
by the filth and refuse of the neighbouring houses, and were neither
so well kept as Caesar had decreed in his law, nor always furnished
with the foot-paths and paving that he had also prescribed.[105]

Caesar's celebrated text, graven on the bronze tablet of Heraclea,
is worth rereading. In comminatory words he commands the
landlords whose buildings face on a public street to clean in front
of the doors and walls, and orders the aediles in each quarter to
make good any omission by getting the work done through a
contractor for forced labour, appointed in the usual manner of
state contractors, at a fee fixed by preliminary bidding, which the
delinquent will be obliged forthwith to pay.[106] The slightest delay
in payment is to be visited by exaction of a double fee. The command is imperative, the punishment merciless. But ingenious as
was the machinery for carrying it out, this procedure involved a
delay – of ten days at least – which must have usually defeated its
purpose, and it cannot be denied that gangs of sturdy sweepers

All communications in the city were dominated by this contrast between night and day. By day there reigned intense animation, a breathless jostle, an infernal din.[113] The *tabernae* were crowded as soon as they opened and spread their displays into the street. Here barbers shaved their customers in the middle of the fairway. There the hawkers from Transtiberina passed along, bartering their packets of sulphur matches for glass trinkets. Elsewhere, the owner of a cook-shop, hoarse with calling to deaf ears, displayed his sausages piping hot in their saucepan. Schoolmasters and their pupils shouted themselves hoarse in the open air. On the one hand, a money-changer rang his coins with the image of Nero on a dirty table, on another a beater of gold dust pounded with his shining mallet on his well-worn stone. At the cross-roads a circle of idlers gaped round a viper tamer; everywhere tinkers' hammers resounded and the quavering voices of beggars invoked the name of Bellona or rehearsed their adventures and misfortunes to touch the hearts of the passers-by. The flow of pedestrians was unceasing and the obstacles to their progress did not prevent the stream soon becoming a torrent. In sun or shade a whole world of people came and went, shouted, squeezed and thrust through narrow lanes unworthy of a country village; and fifteen centuries before Boileau sharpened his wit on the *Embarras de Paris*, the traffic jams of ancient Rome provided a target for the shafts of Juvenal.

It might have been hoped that night would put an end to the din with fear-filled silence and sepulchral peace. Not so; it was merely replaced by another sort of noise. Ordinary men had by now sought sanctuary in their homes, but the human stream was, by Caesar's decree, succeeded by a procession of beasts of burden, carts, their drivers, and their escorts.[114] The great dictator had realized that in alleyways so steep, so narrow, and so traffic-ridden as the *vici* of Rome the circulation by day of vehicles serving the needs of a population of so many hundreds of thousands caused an immediate congestion and constituted a permanent danger. He therefore took the radical and decisive step which his law proclaimed. From sunrise until nearly dusk no transport cart was henceforward to be allowed within the precincts of the Urbs. Those which had entered during the night and had been overtaken by the dawn must halt and stand empty. To this inflexible rule four exceptions alone were permitted: on days of solemn ceremony, the chariots of the Vestals, of the Rex Sacrorum, and of the Flamines; on days of triumph, the chariots necessary to the triumphal procession; on days of public games, those which the official celebration required. Lastly one perpetual exception was made for every day of the year in favour of the carts of the contractors who were engaged in wrecking a building to reconstruct it on better and hygienic lines. Apart from these few clearly defined cases, no daytime traffic was allowed in ancient Rome except for pedestrians, horsemen, litters, and carrying chairs. Whether it was a pauper funeral setting forth at nightfall or majestic obsequies gorgeously carried out in full daylight, whether or not the funeral procession was preceded by flute-players and horn-blowers or followed by a long cortège of relations, friends, and hired mourners (*praeficae*), the dead, enshrined in a costly coffin (*capulum*) or laid on a hired bier (*sandapila*), made their last journey to the funeral pyre or the tomb on a simple handbarrow borne by the *vespillones*.[115]

On the other hand, the approach of night brought with it the legitimate commotion of wheeled carts of every sort which filled the city with their racket. For it must not be imagined that Caesar's legislation died with him and that to serve their own customs or convenience individuals sooner or later made his Draconian regulations a dead letter. The iron hand of the dictator held its sway through the centuries, and his heirs, the emperors, never released the Roman citizens from the restraints which Caesar had ruthlessly imposed on them in the interests of the public welfare. On the contrary, the emperors in turn consecrated and strengthened them. Claudius extended them to the municipalities of Italy;[116] Marcus Aurelius to every city of the empire without regard to its own municipal statutes;[117] Hadrian limited the teams and the loads of the carts allowed to enter the city;[118] and at the end of the first century and the beginning of the second we find the writers of the day reflecting the image of a Rome still definitely governed by the decrees of Julius Caesar.

According to Juvenal the incessant night traffic and the hum of

noise condemned the Roman to everlasting insomnia. 'What sleep
is possible in a lodging?' he asks. 'The crossing of wagons in the
narrow, winding streets, the swearing of drovers brought to a
standstill would snatch sleep from a sea-calf or the emperor Claudius himself.'[119] Amid the intolerable thronging of the day against
which the poet inveighs immediately after, we detect above the
hurly-burly of folk on foot only the swaying of a Liburnian litter.
The herd of people which sweeps the poet along proceeds on foot
through a scrimmage that is constantly renewed. The crowd ahead
impedes his hasty progress, the crowd behind threatens to crush
his loins. One man jostles him with his elbow, another with a
beam he is carrying, a third bangs his head with a wine-cask. A
mighty boot tramps on his foot, a military nail embeds itself in
his toe, and his newly mended tunic is torn. Then, of a sudden, panic
ensues: a wagon appears, on top of which a huge log is swaying,
another follows loaded with a whole pine tree, yet a third carrying a
cargo of Ligurian marble. 'If the axle breaks and pours its contents
on the crowd, what will be left of their bodies?'

Thus, under the Flavians and under Trajan, just as a century and a
half earlier after the publication of Caesar's edict, the only vehicles
circulating by day in Rome were the carts of the building contractors. The great man's law had survived its author's death, and
this continuity is a symptom of the quality which guarantees to
Imperial Rome a unique position among the cities of all time and
every place. With effortless ease Rome harmonized the most incongruous features, assimilated the most diverse forms of past and
present, and, while challenging the remotest comparisons, she remains essentially and for all time incomparable. We have seen her
arrogant and fragile skyscrapers rise to heights which her engineer-
ing could scarcely justify, we have seen the most modern refinements of extravagant luxury existing side by side with preposterous
discomfort and medieval barbarity, and now we are faced with the
disconcerting traffic problems of her streets. The scenes they witness
seem borrowed from the *suqs* of an oriental bazaar. They are
thronged by motley crowds, seething and noisy, such as might
jostle us in the square Jama' Alfna of Marrakesh, and filled with a
confusion that seems to us incompatible with the very idea of

civilization. And suddenly in the twinkling of an eye they are transformed by a logical and imperious decree, swiftly imposed and maintained generation after generation, symbol of that social discipline which among the Romans compensated for their lack of techniques, and which the West today, oppressed by a multiplicity of discoveries and the complexities of progress, is for its salvation striving to imitate.

# III

## SOCIETY AND SOCIAL CLASSES

*

### 1. Romans and Foreigners

At first sight Roman society appears to be divided into water-tight compartments and to bristle with barriers between class and class. All free-born men (*ingenui*), whether citizens of Rome or elsewhere, were in principle in a distinct category, radically separated by their superiority of birth from the mass of slaves who were originally without rights, without guarantees, without personality, delivered over like a herd of brute beasts to the discretion of their master, and like a herd of beasts treated rather as inanimate objects than as sentient beings (*res mancipi*). Among the *ingenui*, again, there existed a profound distinction between the Roman citizen whom the law protected and the non-citizen who was merely subject to the law. Finally, Roman citizens themselves were classified and their position on this ladder of rank determined by their fortunes.

Whereas under the republic there had been equality for all citizens before the law, in the empire of the second and third centuries a legal distinction arose which divided the citizen body into two classes: the *honestiores* and the *humiliores*, also called *plebeii* or *tenuiores*.[1] To the first class belonged Roman senators and knights with their families, soldiers and veterans with their children, and men who held or had held municipal offices in towns and cities outside of Rome, with their descendants. All other citizens belonged to the second, and unless wealth or ability brought them into public office, they remained there.

The *humiliores* were subject to the most severe and humiliating punishments for infraction of the laws. They might be sent to the mines (*ad metalla*), thrown to the beasts in the amphitheatre, or crucified. The *honestiores*, on the other hand, enjoyed certain privileges. In case of grave misconduct, they were spared punishments which would tend to degrade their position in the eyes of the people and generally got off with banishment, relegation, or losing their property.

The two highest groups among the *honestiores* were known as 'orders' (*ordines*) and were composed respectively of senators and knights. The members of the lower or Equestrian Order had to possess a minimum of 400,000 sesterces ($16,000).[2] If they were honoured by the confidence of the emperor they were then qualified to be given command of his auxiliary troops or to fulfil a certain number of civil functions reserved for them; they could become domanial or fiscal procurators, or governors of secondary provinces like those of the Alps or Mauretania. After Hadrian's time they could hold various posts in the imperial cabinet, and after Augustus they were eligible for any of the praefectures except that of *praefectus urbi*.[3]

At the summit of the social scale was the Senatorial Order.[4] A member of this order had to own at least 1,000,000 sesterces ($40,000). The emperor could at will appoint him to command his legions, to act as legate or proconsul in the most important provinces, to administer the chief services of the city, or to hold the highest posts in the priesthood.[5] An ingenious hierarchy gradually established barriers between the different ranks of the privileged, and to make these demarcations more evident Hadrian bestowed on each variety its own exclusive title of nobility. Among the knights, 'distinguished man' (*vir egregius*) served for a mere procurator; 'very perfect man' (*vir perfectissimus*) for a prefect – unless he were a praetor, who was 'most eminent' (*vir eminentissimus*), a title later restored by the Roman Church for the benefit of her cardinals; while the epithet 'most famous' (*vir clarissimus*) was reserved for the senator and his immediate relatives.[6]

This exact and rigid system, whose ingenious variations anticipate the elaborate hierarchy devised by Peter the Great, is paralleled by Napoleon's system of graded precedence in the army and the Legion of Honour. In Rome, where officers and functionaries came and went, it established a sort of social pyramid on the summit of which, midway between earth and heaven, the princeps was poised in lonely, incomparable majesty.

As his title indicates, the princeps was, in one sense, only the First of the Senate and of the People. In another sense, however, this primacy implied a difference not only of degree but of nature between himself and the rest of humanity. For the emperor, as incarnation of the law and guardian of the auspices, was closer to the gods than to the ordinary human being, from whom he was separated after his accession by his sacred character of 'Augustus'. He was the offspring of the gods, and at death he would return to them after his apotheosis – to be proclaimed *divus* himself in due course. In vain Trajan repudiated with scorn Domitian's claim to be addressed by the double title of 'Master and God' (*dominus et deus*).[7] He could not free himself from the toils of the cult which worshipped the imperial genius as represented in his person and which bound the incongruous federation of cities in East and West together in the universal empire (*orbis Romanus*). He had to endure hearing his decrees publicly hailed as 'divine' by those whose wishes they fulfilled.

Thus Rome appears a world petrified under a theocratic aristocracy, an inflexible structure composed of innumerable separate compartments. On closer examination we find, however, that the partitions were by no means water-tight, and that powerful equalitarian currents never ceased to circulate, continually stirring up and renewing the elements of a society whose divisions were far from isolated. Not even the imperial house was proof against these currents. When the Julian family became extinct on the death of Nero, the principate was no longer the monopoly of one predestined clan or even of the city. As Tacitus expressed it, 'The secret of empire was now disclosed – that an emperor could be made elsewhere than at Rome.'[8]

Not the blood of Caesar or of Augustus henceforth conferred the principate, but the loyalty of the Legions. Vespasian, legate of the East, Trajan, legate of Germany, were carried to supreme power, the former by the acclamations of his troops, the latter by the fear his army inspired and the confidence he himself inspired. Both rose to the divine imperial throne because they had first seized the power which had the empire in its gift, differing in this from Caligula, Claudius, or Nero, whose claims to empire lay in their dynasty's divinity. The legionaries who proclaimed Vespasian, the senators who compelled Nerva to adopt Trajan, the general of the Rhine frontier, had carried through a revolution. Thenceforward just as every corporal of Napoleon's Grand Army carried a marshal's baton in his knapsack, so every army chief was felt at Rome to be a potential candidate for the imperial crown, the attainment of which was the ultimate promotion accorded to the greatest Roman warrior.

We need, therefore, feel no surprise that at the time when this new idea of merit and advancement came to be applied to the imperial dignity it should circulate through the whole body of the empire to quicken and rejuvenate. Intercommunication was established on every side between nations and classes, bringing fresh air among them, drawing them together, fusing them. In proportion as the *ius gentium*, that is to say, the law applying to foreign nations, modelled itself more and more on the *ius civile* or law of the Roman citizen, and at the same time as philosophy taught the *ius civile* to take heed of the *ius naturale* (natural law), the distance between Roman and foreigner, between the citizen and the *peregrinus*, was lessened. Whether by personal favour, by emancipation, or by mass naturalizations extended at one stroke either to a class of demobilized auxiliaries or to a municipality suddenly converted into an honorary colony, a new flood of *peregrini* acquired citizenship.[9] Never had the cosmopolitan character of the Urbs been so distinctly marked. The Roman proper was submerged on every social plane, not only by the influx of Italian immigrants but by the multitude of provincials bringing with them from every corner of the universe their speech, their manners, their customs, and their superstitions.

Juvenal inveighs against this mud-laden torrent pouring from the Orontes into the Tiber.[10] But the Syrians, whom he so greatly despised, hastened at the first possible moment to assume the guise of Roman civilians; even those who most loudly advertised their xenophobia were themselves more or less newcomers to Rome, seeking to defend their adopted home against fresh incursions. Juvenal himself was probably born at Aquinum.[11] In his house in 'Pear Street' on the Quirinal, Martial sighs for Bilbilis, his little home in Aragon.[12] Pliny the Younger, whether at Rome or in his Laurentine villa or on his estates in Tuscany, remains faithful to his

Cisalpine birthplace; distant Como, which his liberality embellished, was never absent from his heart.[13]

In the Senate House senators from Gaul, from Spain, from Africa, from Asia, sat side by side; the Roman emperors, Roman citizens but newly naturalized, came from towns or villages beyond the mountains and the seas.[14] Trajan and Hadrian were born in Spanish Italica in Baetica. Their successor, Antoninus Pius, sprang from bourgeois stock in Nemausus (modern Nîmes) in Gallia Narbonensis; and the end of the second century was to see the empire divided between Caesar Clodius Albinus of Hadrumetum (Tunis) and Septimius Severus of Leptis Magna (Tripoli). The biography of Septimius Severus records that even after he had ascended the throne he never succeeded in ridding his speech of the Semitic accent which he had inherited from his Punic ancestors.[15] Thus Rome of the Antonines was a meeting place where the Romans of Rome encountered those inferior peoples against whom their laws seemed to have erected solid ethnic barriers, or – to be more accurate – Rome was a melting pot in which, despite her laws, the peoples were continually being subjected to new processes of assimilation. It was, if you will, a Babel, but a Babel where, for better or for worse, all comers learned to speak and think in Latin.

## 2. Slavery and Manumission

Everyone learned to speak and think in Latin, even the slaves, who in the second century raised their standard of living to the level of the *ingenui*. Legislation had grown more and more humane and had progressively lightened their chains and favoured their emancipation. The practical good sense of the Romans, no less than the fundamental humanity instinctive in their peasant hearts, had always kept them from showing cruelty toward the *servi*. They had always treated their slaves with consideration, as Cato had treated his plough oxen; however far back we go in history we find the Romans spurring their slaves to effort by offering them pay and bonuses which accumulated to form a nest egg that as a rule served ultimately to buy their freedom. With few exceptions, slavery in Rome was neither eternal nor, while it lasted, intolerable;

but never had it been lighter or easier to escape from than under the Antonines.

From the first century of the republic it had been recognized that the slave had a soul of his own, and the free citizens had, in practice, permitted him to join them in the service of whatever cult he preferred. At Minturnae, for instance, as early as 70 B.C., the sanctuary of Spes, the Goddess of Hope, had been served by as many slave *magistri* as by free and freed *magistri* put together.[16] Later, as culture grew spiritually richer and the influence of philanthropic philosophies increased, slaves gathered in ever greater numbers round the altars of the gods. In the first century of our era epitaphs began openly to pay honour to the *manes* of dead slaves; and in the second century the mystic funeral *collegia*, such as that founded at Lanuvium in 133 under the double invocation of Diana and Antinoüs, brought *ingenui*, freedmen, and slaves together in brotherly communion.[17] In this particular case the slaves engaged, if they later gained their freedom, to regale their fellow members with an amphora of wine on the day of their liberation. The laws naturally kept pace with the progress of ideas. At the beginning of the empire a certain *Lex Petronia* had forbidden a master to deliver his slave to the beasts of the amphitheatre without a judgement authorizing him to do so.[18] Toward the middle of the first century an edict of Claudius decreed that sick or infirm slaves whom their master had abandoned should be manumitted;[19] and a short time afterwards an edict possibly drawn up by Nero under the inspiration of Seneca, who had vigorously championed the human rights of the slave, charged the *praefectus urbi* to receive and investigate complaints laid before him by slaves concerning the injustice of their masters.[20] In 83 under Domitian a *senatus-consultum* forbade a master to castrate his slaves, and fixed as the penalty for infringement of this decree the confiscation of half the offender's property.[21] In the second century Hadrian had to double the penalty for this offence, which he declared a 'capital crime', and he dictated to the Senate two decrees inspired by the same humanity: the first prevented masters from selling their slaves to either the *leno* or the *lanista*; that is, either to the procurer or to the trainer of gladiators; the second compelled a master who had condemned his slave to death to submit the sentence for the approval of the *praefectus vigilum* before carrying it into execution.[22] This humanitarian evolution culminated in the middle of the century when Antoninus Pius condemned as homicide any slaying of a slave by the sole order of his master.[23]

Altogether, at this time Roman legislation reflects rather than imposes the humanitarian attitude which manners and customs had adopted. Juvenal castigates with the lash of his satire the miser who 'pinches the bellies of his slaves';[24] the gambler who flings away a fortune on a throw of the dice and 'has no shirt to give a shivering slave';[25] the coquette who loses her temper, storms and takes out her ill humour on the unoffending backs of her maids.[26] The poet's indignation is but the echo of public opinion, which abhorred no less than he the abominable cruelties of that Rutilus whom Juvenal withered with his scorn.[27] In his day most masters, if they did not entirely abstain from corporal punishment of their slaves, at most visited their faults with rods such as Martial, without compunction, laid on his cook for a spoiled dinner. This did not prevent the master from caring for his slave and loving him even to the point of weeping for his death.[28]

In the great houses where many of the slaves were able specialists and some, like the tutor, the doctor, and the reader, had enjoyed a liberal education, they were treated exactly like free men. Pliny the Younger desires his cousin Paternus to choose slaves for him in the market with discernment.[29] He watches with anxiety over their health, going so far as to shoulder the expense of long and costly trips for them to Egypt or to Fréjus in the Provençal plain.[30] He accedes, with good grace, to their legitimate desires, obeying, as he says, their suggestions as if they were commands.[31] He relied with confidence more on their devotion than on his severity to stimulate their zeal when some relation turned up in his house, sure that they would endeavour to please their master by their attentions to his guest.[32] The same kindly attitude prevailed among Pliny's friends; they felt their slaves to be almost part of the family. When the old senator, Corellius Rufus, was ill in bed, he liked to have his favourite slaves with him in the room, and when he had to send them out in order to talk privately, his wife withdrew with them.[33] Pliny the Younger went even further, and did not disdain to discuss important matters with his slaves; when he was in the country he would invite the better educated among them to join with him in those learned discussions which at evening brightened his after-dinner walks.[34]

The slaves on their side were full of consideration for masters such as these. Pliny the Younger was stupefied by the news of the attack made on the senator Larcius Macedo by a party of his household slaves.[35] His amazement is an index of the rarity of such a crime. And the care – unfortunately useless – lavished on the victim by those of his slaves who had remained faithful proves that even in houses where they were the most severely handled, slaves could feel that their masters treated them like men. Indeed, a Greek who lived at Rome in the middle of the second century was struck by the levelling which had taken place between slaves and freemen, which to his amazement extended even to their clothes. Appian of Alexandria, writing under Antoninus Pius, remarks that even in externals the slave is in no way distinguished from his master, and unless his master donned the *toga praetexta* of the magistrate, the two were dressed alike.[36] Appian supplements this by recording a thing which astonished him even more: after a slave had regained his liberty he lived on terms of absolute equality with the Roman citizen.

Rome, alone of all cities of antiquity, has the honour of having redeemed her outcasts by opening her doors to them.[37] It is true that the freed slave remained bound to his former master, now his *patronus*, sometimes by services due or by pecuniary indebtedness, and always by the duties implied by an almost filial respect (*obsequium*). But once his emancipation or *manumissio* had been duly pronounced, whether by a fictitious statement of claim before the praetor (*per vindictam*) or by the inscription of his name on the censors' register (*censu*) at the solemn sacrifice of the *lustrum*, or more commonly in virtue of a testamentary clause (*testamento*), the slave obtained by the grace of his master, living or dead, the name and status of a Roman citizen. His descendants of the third generation were entitled to exercise the full political rights of citizenship and nothing further distinguished them from *ingenui*. In the course of time the formalities of manumission were relaxed, and custom, superseding law, substituted simpler and speedier methods of procedure for the manumission rites: a mere letter from the patron or a verbal declaration made, for instance, in the course of some festivity where the guests were requested to serve as witnesses. The caprice of fashion began to take a hand, and it seemed as if some masters took a pride in multiplying the number of manumitted slaves round them. This practice became finally so fashionable that Augustus, alarmed by such prodigality, made efforts to set some limit to its indulgence.[38] He fixed eighteen as the minimum age at which a master could exercise the right to free a slave, and thirty as the minimum age at which a slave could be manumitted. As regarded testamentary manumission, which was by far the most frequent form of legal emancipation, he laid down the rule that according to circumstances the number of slaves set free should bear a certain ratio to the total number of slaves possessed by the deceased master, and should in any case not exceed a maximum of a hundred.

He devised an inferior category of semicitizens, who were known as *Latini Iuniani*, to whom was granted the partial naturalization of the *Ius Latii*, which, however, debarred the holder from making or benefiting by a will. All slaves whom their masters had manumitted in violation of the imperial decrees or in any irregular fashion outside the formal legal procedure were flung pell-mell into the category of *Latini Iuniani*. But custom was stronger than the emperor's will and nullified his legislation. In an effort to counteract the falling birth rate, he released all *Latini Iuniani* who were fathers of families from the inferiority of second-class citizenship to which he had himself condemned them. Then Tiberius granted the same relaxation to former *vigiles* in order to stimulate enrolment in his cohorts; later, Claudius extended full rights to *liberti* of both sexes who employed their capital in outfitting merchant ships, Nero to those who invested it in building, and Trajan to those who used their money to set up bakeries.[39]

Ultimately all the emperors, out of love for their own freed slaves or those of their friends, took pains to obliterate the last trace of their servile origin, either by utilizing the legal fiction of the *natalium restitutio* or by slipping on to their finger the gold ring which might open the way to the equestrian status. Hence, in the period we are studying, the slaves who benefited by the ever-increasing numbers of manumissions were placed on a footing of complete equality with other Roman citizens, enabled to secure positions and fortunes and to purchase droves of slaves in their turn, as we see Trimalchio doing.

An epigraphist walking through the ruins of ancient Rome receives the impression that slaves and freedmen predominated in the life of the imperial epoch, for three times out of four they alone are mentioned in the inscriptions which are still to be read on the walls. In an article remarkable for the quantity and accuracy of its statistics, Tenney Frank points out that since in the majority of cases the form of a slave name betrays its owner's Graeco-oriental origin, it is easily proved that at least 80 per cent of the population of Imperial Rome had been emancipated from more or less ancient servitude.[40] At first sight the observer is filled with admiration for the strength which this constant rise seems to imply, both in a society which can unceasingly assimilate new elements and in an empire which can extend to the farthest horizon the area from which it draws new elements; and he is tempted to attribute to the Rome of the Antonines the free play and the deserved advantages of a perfect democracy.

## 3. The Confusion of Social Values

Unfortunately it is impossible not to perceive also the shadows which already darkened the brightness of this picture. In the reign of Nerva there survived in Rome only one half of the senatorial families which had been counted in A.D. 65, thirty-five years before; and thirty years later only one remained of the forty-five patrician families restored one hundred and sixty-five years before by Julius Caesar.[41] There was urgent need therefore for perpetual new blood from the humbler strata of the population to nourish and revivify the aristocracy of the Urbs. But, in drawing this new blood almost exclusively from the servile masses, Roman society and the Roman fatherland exposed themselves to great dangers in the future, and in the present to inevitable adulteration.

Indeed, if the slave classes were to be called on continuously to fill the gaps in the classes above, they must themselves be continuously replenished from without. Now the wars of Trajan – especially the second Dacian campaign, from which, according to his physician Crito, the emperor brought back fifty thousand prisoners who were promptly put up at auction – were the last wars in which the empire was victorious without difficulty and without disappointment.[42] After the two peaceful reigns of his successors Hadrian and Antoninus Pius, we reach the period of the semi-victories of Marcus Aurelius, victories dearly bought after overcoming exhausting resistance, and finally the period of reverses and invasions which dried up the main sources of slave supply. We can already foresee the moment when slavery will be driven back on itself, owing to the scarcity of new prisoners of war, and will cease to be able to support the rising column on which the Roman economy had depended during the preceding generations. Then Rome, if she is still to rule the world, must force it into that heartbreaking strait-jacket which came to govern the conditions of human life under the later empire.

This particular danger, it is true, had not yet shown itself under the Flavians or the earlier Antonines. There were, however, other more immediate ones which threatened the superficial prosperity of their reigns.

Inasmuch as the Caesars, under cover of legal fictions which had long ceased to deceive the most guileless, had seized and were exercising an absolute authority, their slaves and their freedmen took precedence of the rest of the city.[43] In theory they were still 'inanimate property', or at best semicitizens. In practice and in fact they had daily access to the sacred person of their master, they enjoyed his confidence, and to them he delegated some of his far-reaching prerogatives, so that they had undisguised command alike over nobles and plebeians. Up to the time of Claudius, the imperial 'cabinet' was composed almost exclusively of slaves.[44] They received the petitions of the empire, issued instructions both to provincial governors and to the magistrates of Rome, and elaborated jurisprudence of all the tribunals including the highest senatorial court. The emperors from Claudius to Trajan inclusive recruited their cabinet from their freedmen. Just as the French nobility of the seventeenth century chafed under the domination of '*la vile bourgeoisie*' of ministers and their clerks, so the senators of the empire with rage in their hearts silently bowed before the power of an ex-slave. Elevated at a bound to the steps of the throne, gorged with wealth and loaded with honours, men like Narcissus and Pallas in virtue of their mysterious services and sovereign power held authority in the emperor's name over the advancement, the property, and even the life of his subjects.

Nor was this all: even if the emperor went outside the circle of his household and chose confidants and friends from among members of the two great orders of the state, these friends and confidants in their turn had their slaves and freedmen to whom they were wont to delegate the labours and the conduct of their business, and the aristocrats who appeared to reign under the emperor governed in reality, like their master, through the medium of their domestic staff. Thus the slaves and freedmen of the emperor's court joined the slaves and freedmen of the emperor in the government of a city and an empire. How far their power and their collusion went was seen when those whom the suspicion-ridden despotism and insatiable cupidity of Domitian had permitted to live in the Curia resolved to save their skins by getting rid of him. The murder of the tyrant, desired and instigated by the senators, was plotted in the antechamber of his own palace and carried out by his 'people' and the 'people' of his entourage: the small choir boy of his *sacrarium*, the Greek Parthenius, his chamberlain (*praepositus a cubiculo*), and the Greek Stephanus, one of the stewards of his sister Domitilla.[45]

After his death the inscription '*Libertas Restituta*' was indeed stamped on the new coins, and the *patres conscripti* dreamed of resuscitating the republic by conferring the empire on one of the most self-effacing of their colleagues, the timid, sixty-year-old Nerva. But it is clear that this effort was nothing but a jingle of empty words and a parade of vain appearances. The republic, which is the Commonwealth of Citizens, and Liberty, who demands of her votaries a proud apprenticeship, could not be reborn of a conspiracy hatched by *peregrini* and *servi*, by outsiders and slaves; and the emperors began to see the threat to stable rule that lay in permitting men of such antecedents and of such a type to rear their heads so near the summit of the state. Hadrian took the initiative, which his successors respected, of reserving all places in his cabinet for members of the Equestrian Order.[46] If he had wished to carry this reform through with thoroughness, he should, however, have gone a step further and regulated also the tenure of secondary posts. For in order to command obedience and not to fear malpractices which they were powerless to stamp out, the emperors and their great men preferred to continue, as before, to select foreign slaves to be the *procuratores* and *institores* of the administration. They imagined these men to be in their power, while in fact, with the extension of the frontiers and the elaboration of the fiscal system, they themselves fell more and more into the power of their slave subordinates. It would be unjust to deny that there were among these *servi*, anxious to earn their manumission by their zeal, and among these *liberti* who felt a gratitude for their manumission exceeding their obligations, many conscientious servants, honest stewards, faithful and devoted agents; and the fact that the machinery of empire ran as smoothly as it did during the second century was due perhaps less to the vigilance of its supervising engineers than to the professional care and skill of its mechanics. The flock, however, was too large not to contain a proportion of black sheep: agents too harsh in their demands and exactions and too greedy of commissions and gratuities, administrators who were insolent, cruel, and untruthful. It was surely a fatal paradox for a government honestly concerned to improve its efficiency to delegate its functions to men born in chains and destined for slavery.

Instead of witnessing a logical and gradual evolution which would have demonstrated the value of imperial institutions, the Romans had continually to endure the civic degradation entailed by this arbitrary and drastic inversion of classes and of roles. Both in town and country it demoralized the citizens. Juvenal was infuriated to see the sons of free men in the Rome of Trajan constrained by self-interest to pay court to the slaves of the rich:

*Divitis hic servo claudit latus ingenuorum*
*Filius . . .* [47]

77

Under Commodus free citizens, as colonist volunteers, cultivated the African estate of Suq al Khmis (Thursday Market), and were mercilessly and unjustly flogged in the emperor's name by the slave steward of his *Saltus Burunitanus*.[48]

In Juvenal's day and after, it indeed seemed a happier fate to be a rich man's slave than a poor, freeborn citizen. Nothing more was needed to overturn the fair structure of imperial rule; and this pernicious disequilibrium was aggravated now and henceforward by the fact that in a society where rank was decided by wealth, this wealth, instead of circulating among hard-working families and yielding the fruits of toil and husbandry, tended more and more to become concentrated, through the favours of the emperor and by speculation, in the hands of a very few. While in the provinces and even in Italy there still survived a sturdy and numerous middle class who bore the burden of municipal government, the ranks of the middle class in the Urbs grew ever thinner, and there was nothing between the satellite plutocracy of the court and the mass of a plebs too poor to exist without the doles of an emperor and the charity of the rich, and too unoccupied to forgo the spectacles which, under Trajan, were provided every second day for its amusement.

## 4. Living Standards and the Plutocracy

Accurate figures are lacking, but certain comparisons in some degree supply the want. We saw in the first chapter that the number of persons receiving public assistance rose in the course of the second century from 150,000 to 175,000. We can without hesitation deduce from this that about 130,000 families, represented by their heads, were fed at the public expense. If we accept Martial's estimate of an average of five mouths per family,[49] the total number must have been between 600,000 and 700,000. If we reckon only three persons per family, the total would be 400,000. Directly or indirectly then, at least one-third and possibly one-half of the population of the city lived on public charity. But we should be wrong to conclude that two-thirds or one-half of the population were independent of it, for the total of the population includes three classes already

·mentioned as being ineligible for the distributions of free grain: the soldiers of the garrison – at the lowest computation some 12,000 men; the *peregrini* passing through Rome, whose numbers we cannot calculate; and finally the slaves, whose ratio to the free inhabitants may have been at least one to three, as was recorded for Pergamum about the same period.[50] If we suppose that Trajan's Rome had a population of 1,200,000 souls, we may deduct 400,000 slaves. This leaves less than 150,000 heads of Roman families who were sufficiently well off not to need to draw on the largesse of Annona.

The numerical inferiority of the haves to the horde of the have-nots, sufficiently distressing in itself, becomes positively terrifying when we realize the inequality of fortune within the ranks of the minority; the majority of what we should nowadays call the middle classes vegetated in semistarvation within sight of the almost incredible opulence of a few thousand multimillionaires. A yearly income of 20,000 sesterces ($800) was the 'vital minimum' for a Roman citizen to exist on. This is the income which a ruined reprobate whom Juvenal draws in one of his satirical scenes craves for his own old age.[51] In another passage the poet, speaking on his own behalf, limits a wise man's desire to a fortune of 400,000 sesterces ($16,000): 'If you turn up your nose at this sum,' he says to his imaginary interlocutor, 'take the fortune of two equites (or even three); if that doesn't satisfy your heart, neither will the riches of Croesus, nor all the treasures of the Persian kings!'[52] It is clear that in Juvenal's eyes a wise man ought to be happy with modest ease and comfort; clear also that modest ease presupposes a capital of 400,000 sesterces, the property qualification for a 'knight'. These two pieces of evidence corroborate and complement each other, since we know beyond possibility of doubt, thanks to the researches of Billeter, that in the poet's day the normal interest on money was 5 per cent.[53] It follows that in the Rome of Trajan the 'middle classes' began with the Equestrian Order, and unless a person was in a position to spend at least the 20,000 sesterces which this capital yielded annually, he could not maintain even the most modest standard of *bourgeois* life. Below this were the pauperized masses, to which the 'lower middle classes' approximated much more closely than to the wealthy capitalists with whom a legal fiction classed them.

What weight could their modest little fortune of 400,000 sesterces carry, compared with the millions and tens of millions that were at the disposal of the real magnates of the city? Senators from the provinces, whose estates and enterprises were so extensive as to procure them a place among the 'most illustrious' (*clarissimi*) and a seat in the Senate House, came to Rome not only to fulfil their civic functions or supervise the properties which they had been obliged to acquire in Italy, but first and foremost to render their name and the country of their origin illustrious by the magnificence of their Roman mansion and the distinction of the rank they had attained in the Urbs. Now how could the capitalist with 400,000 compete with them? – or with the *equites* who had reached the highest posts open to them and grown fat as they mounted the successive rungs of the administrative ladder, handling matters of finance and of supply? Or how even compete with those *liberti* who, in nursing the wealth of the emperor and his nobles, had amassed great fortunes for themselves? Rome, mistress of the world, drained all its riches. Making due allowance for the difference of time and manners, I cannot believe that the concentrations of capital in Rome from the principate of Trajan onwards can have been much less than they are in our twentieth century among the financiers of 'The City' or the bankers of Wall Street.

Some Roman capitalists owned many houses in different quarters of the metropolis. Martial directed this epigram against a certain Maximus:

You have a house on the Esquiline and another on the Hill of Diana; the Vicus Patricius boasts a roof of yours. From one you survey the shrine of widowed Cybele; from another the Temple of Vesta; from here the new, from there the ancient Temple of Jove. Tell me where I can call upon you or in what quarter I may look for you. The man, O Maximus, who is everywhere at home is a man without a home at all.[54]

Like the modern financier, the Roman fruitfully employed his capital in large and innumerable loans. Another epigram, for instance, shows us Afer enjoying himself by totting up the number of his borrowers and the total of their indebtedness: 'Coranus owes me 100,000 sesterces and Mancinus 200,000; Titius 300,000; Albinus twice as much; Sabinus a million and Serranus another million. . . .'[55] It may be that this Afer, like Maximus, was only an imaginary personage; they are all the more typical of the plutocracy which flourished in the Rome of Martial's time. In their narrow circle, gleaming with the gold of all the earth, we may be very sure that mortgagees were not lacking, like the fortune-hunter Africanus with his 100,000,000 sesterces to whom Martial alludes.[56] No one could reckon himself rich under 20,000,000. Pliny the Younger, the ex-consul and perhaps the greatest advocate of his day, whose will disclosed a sum closely approaching this, contended nevertheless that he was not rich, and makes the statement with evident sincerity. He writes in perfect good faith to Calvina, whose father owed him 100,000 sesterces, a debt which Pliny generously cancelled, that his means were very limited (*modicae facultates*) and that, owing to the way his minor estates were being worked, his income was both small and fluctuating, so that he had to lead a frugal existence.[57] It is true that a freedman like Trimalchio, whose estate Petronius estimated at 30,000,000, was better off than Pliny;[58] and the unknown Afer whom Martial caricatures, whose income from real estate alone amounted to 3,000,000, was three times as wealthy. Nevertheless Pliny's fortune – fifty times that of an *eques* – was in the same bracket as theirs, and there was really no common measure between it and the incomes of the 'middle classes'. The *petit bourgeois* was literally crushed by the great, and his sole consolation was to see even these enormous fortunes of the wealthy overborne in their turn by the incalculable riches of the emperor.

The emperor's wealth did not consist alone in the accumulated riches of his family or predecessors, or in the immense *latifundia* he inherited here and there in Africa or Asia, or in the fact that he everywhere annexed the bulk of all partial or total confiscations decreed by the judges. Over and above all this, nothing prevented his replenishing his private purse from the resources of the imperial Exchequer, into which poured the taxes levied for the maintenance of his soldiers, and none dared to suggest an audit of his accounts. He could dispose at will – with no need to render account to any man – of the revenues of Egypt, which was a personal possession of the Crown, and he could plunge open hands into the booty of war. To cite one instance: Trajan in 106 pounced on the entire treasure of Decebalus and made speed to reorganize for his personal benefit every source of profit in the recent conquests.[59] He became an authentic millionaire, whose authority was buttressed less on the loyalty of his legions than on the power of unlimited action conferred by an unrivalled private fortune, inexhaustible and uncontrolled. Almost as great a gulf separated him from the plutocrats of Rome as yawned between them and the 'middle classes', and the same disparity prevailed between his staff of slaves and theirs.

At the beginning of the second century B.C. houses in the Urbs which could boast of more than one slave were rare. This is proved by the custom of adding the suffix-*por* (= *puer*) to the genitive of the master's name to designate a slave: Lucipor, the slave of Lucius; Marcipor, the slave of Marcus. In contrast, during the second century A.D. there existed practically no masters of only one slave. People either bought no slave at all – for the belly of a slave took a lot of filling – or they bought and kept several together, which is why Juvenal in the verses already quoted uses the word 'belly' in the plural: '. . . *magno servorum ventres!*[60]

Two slaves to carry him to the circus was the very minimum with which the disillusioned old reprobate whose moderation we have appreciated above[61] could manage to get along. But the average was four or five times as many. The humblest householder could not hold his head up unless he could appear with a train of eight slaves behind him. Martial records that the miser Cimber arranged for eight Syrian slaves to carry the microscopic loads of his contemptible little gifts at the Saturnalia.[62] And according to Juvenal a litigant would have thought his case already lost if it had been entrusted to an advocate not accompanied to the bar by a train of slaves of at least this size.[63] A squad of eight was usually sufficient for a *petit bourgeois*. The man of the upper middle classes on the other hand commanded a battalion or more. Not to be completely swamped by the number of their retainers, they divided them into two parties, one of which they employed in the Urbs and one in the country; and they redivided the town staff again into two, those who served indoors (*servi atrienses*) and those who served without (*cursores, viatores*). Finally, these different batches were again divided into tens, each *decuria* being distinguished by a number. Even these precautions were unavailing. Master and slaves ended by not knowing each other by sight. In the very middle of his banquet Trimalchio fails to know which of his slaves he is giving orders to: 'What *decuria* do you belong to?' he asks the cook. 'The fortieth,' answers the slave. 'Bought or born in the house?' 'Neither,' is the reply. 'I was left you under Pansa's will.' 'Well, then, mind you serve this carefully, or I will have you degraded to the messengers' *decuria*.'[64] Reading such a dialogue, one can easily imagine that scarcely one slave in ten among Trimalchio's hordes really knew his master. One gathers that there were at least 400 of them, but the fact that Petronius alludes only to the fortieth *decuria* is no proof that there were not many more. Pliny the Younger – who, as we have seen, was at least poorer than Trimalchio by a matter of 10,000,000 sesterces – had at least 500 slaves, for his will manumitted 100; and the law *Fufia Caninia*, probably passed in 2 B.C. and still in force in the second century A.D. expressly permitted owners of between 100 and 500 slaves to set one-fifth free, and forbade owners of larger numbers to emancipate more than 100.[65]

It is impossible to repress our amazement in the face of figures so extravagant; yet it is known that in the second century they were often exceeded. The surprise felt by the jurist Gaius a century and a half after the passing of the law *Fufia Caninia* to think that it had not extended its scale of testamentary manumission beyond 100 per 500 slaves, is a sure indication that the scale no longer fitted the reality.[66] Toward the end of the first century A.D. under the Flavians the freedman C. Caelius Isidorus left 4,116 slaves, and while this figure for a private individual was sufficiently noteworthy to be judged worthy of mention by the elder Pliny,[67] there is no doubt whatever that the *familiae serviles* in the service of the great Roman capitalists often reached 1,000, and that the emperor, infinitely more wealthy than the richest of them, must easily have possessed a 'slave family' of 20,000.

This is the very high figure that we find in Athenaeus,[68] and from its size it could apply only to the household of the princeps. We must, of course, deduct from this army of slaves the groups which the *domus divina* of the Caesars kept dispersed throughout the world for the collection of their taxes, the supervision of their general farms, the administration of their immense country properties, their mines, and their quarries of marble and porphyry. But even on the Palatine at Rome, where modern research has discovered, along with the *graffiti* of the *paedagogium*, the traces of their places of punishment,[69] the imperial slaves must have been legion, if only to fulfil the incredible number of tasks which were entrusted to them, and which are revealed by their obituary inscriptions.

Reading these without prejudice, the student is dumbfounded by the extraordinary degree of specialization they reveal, the insensate luxury and the meticulous etiquette which made this specialization necessary. The emperor had as many categories of slaves to arrange and tend his wardrobe as he had separate types of clothes: for his palace garments the slaves *a veste privata*, for his city clothes the *a veste forensi*, for his undress military uniforms the *a veste castrensi*, and for his full-dress parade uniforms the *a veste triumphali*, for the clothes he wore to the theatre the *a veste gladiatoria*. His eating utensils were polished by as many teams of slaves as there were kinds: the eating vessels, the drinking vessels, the silver vessels, the golden vessels, the vessels of rock crystal, the vessels set with precious stones. His jewels were entrusted to a crowd of *servi* or *liberti ab ornamentis*, among whom were distinguished those in charge of his pins (the *a fibulis*) and those responsible for his pearls (the *a margaritis*). Several varieties of slaves competed over his toilet: the bathers (*balneatores*), the masseurs (*aliptae*), the hairdressers (*ornatores*), and the barbers (*tonsores*). The ceremonial of his receptions was regulated by several kinds of ushers: the *velarii* who raised the curtains to let the visitor enter, the *ab admissione* who admitted him to the presence, the *nomenclatores* who called out the name. A heterogeneous troop were employed to cook his food, lay his table, and serve the dishes, ranging from the stokers of his furnaces (*fornacarii*) and the simple cooks (*coci*) to his bakers (*pistores*), his pastry-cooks (*libarii*) and his sweetmeat-makers (*dulciarii*), and including, apart from the majordomos responsible for ordering his meals (*structores*), the dining-room attendants (*triclinarii*), the waiters (*ministratores*) who carried in the dishes, the servants charged with removing them again (*analectae*), the cupbearers who offered him drink and who differed in importance according to whether they held the flagon (the *a lagona*) or presented the cup (the *a cyatho*), and finally the tasters (*praegustatores*), whose duty it was to test on themselves the perfect harmlessness of his food and drink – and who were assuredly expected to perform their task more efficiently than the tasters of Claudius and Britannicus. Finally, for his recreation, the emperor had an embarrassing variety of choice between the songs of his choristers (*symphoniaci*), the music of his orchestra, the pirouettes of his dancing women (*salatrices*), the jests of his dwarfs (*nani*), of his 'chatterboxes' (*fatui*), and of his buffoons (*moriones*).

Even if the emperor had simple tastes, like Trajan, and hated ceremony and ostentation, he could not fulfil his sacred function in the eyes of his subjects without the pampered splendour which surrounded his existence in the capital. His official activity was hedged in a semi-mythological pageantry in which the 'King of Kings' would have felt at home. To make a straightforward although a halting comparison, the court of the Valois might have envied the delights, and the court of Versailles the pompous magnificence and the solemn ritual of the court of Imperial Rome. The Roman Caesar might have anticipated the Roi Soleil by taking for his motto the *nec pluribus impar* of Louis XIV. The mansions of the Roman magnates no doubt did their best to ape the emperor's palace. But they were left far behind, and vast as they were, and complex as was their organization – we can read it between the lines of the epitaphs of their freedmen and their slaves – they gave but a feeble, small reflection. Caesar overwhelmed even the mightiest of his subjects, and the feeling of his unchallengeable superiority, of which all were conscious, helped to reconcile the humbler of them to the great discrepancy between their own straitened and inferior state and the luxury of the dominant classes.

For the rest, the transition between the plebs and the middle classes was relatively easy. Prosperity had followed on the successful campaigns of Trajan; his victories and Hadrian's diplomacy had given an impulse to commerce by opening the routes to the Far East; the economic liberalism of which the first Antonines had set an example had tempered the evils caused through the accumulation of lands in the same hands, and created independently of – and when necessary in spite of – the great landowners the right of hereditary enjoyment for those who had the courage to clear their own fields. All these things gave stimulus to business and multiplied the opportunities for industrious and energetic men, farmers-general or tenant-partners of the great estates, shipowners or bankers, wholesale or retail merchants, honestly to acquire a comfortable fortune.

On the other hand the salutary changes which sovereigns at last worthy of their office had imposed on all branches of their administration, the re-establishment of a simple but vigorous discipline in the army, the care with which civil and military chiefs were chosen and promoted, coinciding with the larger salaries and increased pay which rewarded their services and preserved their independence, constituted a series of factors or of measures favourable to the rise and prosperity of a middle class of a new social standing. There was not a procurator who then drew less than 60,000 sesterces a year, not a centurion or a *primipilus* whose salary fell below the 20,000 to 40,000 range.[70] The former were in a position to double or treble the equestrian fortune they already possessed; and the others to acquire it, as so many inscriptions of the second century bear witness. The man who best incarnates the spirit of the middle classes at this period, Juvenal, is in fact himself one of these ex-officers who had been able to make his little pile and secure himself a respectable position in the bosom of the Roman *bourgeoisie*.

True, Juvenal sighs for the happier life which his limited means would have enabled him to enjoy in the country but denied to him in Rome. In this he is representative of his time. A man in his stratum of society found in fact his real home in the cities and provinces of Italy. In Rome people of his type were swamped by the superabundance of riches in which they had no share, and if a chain seemed to link them on the one hand to the plebs from which they had risen and on the other to the great magnates who had risen from their ranks, they were more conscious of the weight of the latter than the support of the former, and they lost all hope of shaking off the burden and rising to join the ranks above. The large fortunes on the plane above increased automatically or benefited from circumstances which profited the wealthy alone: from the exercise of the office and authority which they monopolized (a proconsulate for instance brought in a million sesterces per annum); from the arbitrary favour of an emperor who might delegate his powers indefinitely to the same favourite; from a gust of wind on the stock exchange, where speculation was all the more unbridled since at Rome, the banking house of the world, speculation was the life-blood of an economic system where production was losing ground day by day and mercantilism was invading everything. Work might still ensure a modest living, but no longer yielded such fortunes as the chance of imperial favour or a speculative gamble might bestow. Middlemen and entertainers, these parasites who feed on multitudes, raked in millions. Martial voices his indignation to see advocates accepting their fees in kind and the fairest mental gifts cultivated without adequate reward.

'To what master, Lupus, should you entrust your son? I warn you ... let him have nothing to do with the works of Cicero or the poems of Virgil. .... Let him learn to be a harpist or a player of the flute; or if he seems dull of intellect make him an auctioneer [*praeco*] or architect.'[71] In another place he exclaims: 'Two praetors, four tribunes, seven advocates, and ten poets recently approached an old father, suing for his daughter's hand. Without hesitation he gave the girl to Eulogus the auctioneer. Tell me, Severus, was that the act of a fool?'[72] Outside the city, the middle classes still found it worth while to believe in the value of work, but inside Rome they had lost all confidence in it.

Let us reread the charming epigram where the 'parasite' poet has graven what I should like to call the 'Plantin sonnet' of Latin literature, which assuredly served Plantin as a model:

The things that make life happier, most genial Martial, are these: means not acquired by labour but bequeathed; fields not unkindly, an ever-blazing hearth; no lawsuit, the toga seldom worn, a quiet mind; a free man's strength, a healthy body; frankness with tact, congenial friends, good-natured guests, a board plainly spread; nights not spent in wine but freed from cares, a wife not prudish yet pure; sleep such as makes the darkness brief: be content with what you are and wish no change; nor dread your last day nor long for it.[73]

This poem voices no cry of happiness; it utters a sigh in which resignation blends with content. It formulates no aspiration toward the unattainable. It places happiness in the negation of work, whose vanity it implies. The clouds of reality cast their shadow over this dreary ideal which breaths the fatigue of an ageing world. Society, at least in Rome, was beginning to become fossilized. The hierarchy, still fluid in the centre, was growing petrified toward the summit. The regular inflow which should have continuously renewed it gave way too often before accidental pressure and unexpected shocks. Slowed down and diverted from their course, the equalitarian currents tended to exaggerate essential inequalities. The democratic order tottered with the wavering of the middle classes, who had been its firm foundation; it was crushed under the double weight of the masses, from whom a crazed economic system had stolen all hope of normal betterment, and of corrupt bureaucracy which aggravated the absolutism of the monarch whose fabulous wealth it commanded and translated into acts of arbitrary omnipotence. Thus the brilliance of the Urbs of the second century was already shrouded in the shadows which under the later empire spread from Rome over the rest of the known world, and Rome lacked the courage to shake herself free of the sinister gloom that thickened round her. To struggle with success against the evils of their day, societies have need to believe in their own future. But Roman society, cheated of its hopes of gradual and equitable progress, obsessed alternately by its own stagnation and by its instability, began to doubt itself just at the time when the conscious unity of its established families was cracked and breaking.

# IV

## MARRIAGE, WOMAN, AND THE FAMILY

\*

### 1. *The Weakening of Paternal Authority*

IN the second century of our era the ancient law of the *gens* had fallen into disuse ('*totum gentilicium ius in desuetudienem abisse*'); and nothing but the memory – the 'archaeological memory' one might almost say – remained of the principles on which the patriarchal family of ancient Rome had been based: relationship through the male line (*agnatio*) and the unlimited power of the *pater familias*.[1]

Whereas in former days the only recognized relationship was that created by male descent (*agnatio*), relationship was now recognized through the female line (*cognatio*) and extended beyond legitimate marriage.

This is clearly illustrated by the laws governing inheritance. According to the ancient code of the Twelve Tables, a mother had no right of succession to a son who had died intestate. Under Hadrian, the *senatus consultum Tertullianum* admitted her as a legitimate heir on the condition that she possessed the *ius liberorum*, which rested on her having had three children (four, if she was a freedwoman). Then, by the *senatus consultum Orphitianum* passed under Marcus Aurelius, children were entitled to inherit from their mother, whatever the validity of the union from which they sprang, and to take precedence of other relatives in this matter.[2]

This completed the development which had undermined the ancient system of civil inheritance, wrecking the fundamental conception of the Roman family and recognizing instead the claims of 'blood' in the sense in which our modern societies have accepted them. The Roman family is henceforth based on the *coniunctio sanguinis*, because, according to the lofty conception of Cicero in the *De Officiis*, this natural tie was the best qualified to bind human beings in affection and mutual goodwill: '*et benevolentia devincit homines et caritate*'.[3]

During the same period the two essential weapons of the *patria potestas* were gradually blunted: the father's absolute authority over his children, and the husband's absolute authority over the wife placed 'in his hand' (*in manum*) as if she were one of his daughters (*loco filiae*). By the second century of our era they had disappeared completely. The *pater familias* had been deprived of the right of life or death over his children which had been granted him by the Twelve Tables and the sacred, so-called Royal Laws.[4] But until the beginning of the third century, when abandoning a child was considered the equivalent of murder,[5] he might expose his new-born child to perish of cold and hunger or be devoured by dogs on one of the public refuse dumps, unless it was rescued by the pity of some passer-by.[6] No doubt a poor man still had recourse as readily as heretofore to this haphazard form of legal infanticide, despite the isolated protests of Stoic preachers like Musonius Rufus.[7] We may assume that he continued remorselessly to expose his bastards and his infant daughters, since the records of Trajan's reign show the entries for public assistance given to young children for the same city and the same year as 179 legitimate children (145 boys and 34 girls) and only two bastards (*spurii*), a boy and a girl.[8] These discrepancies can best be explained by assuming that a large proportion of bastards and girl babies were victims of 'exposure'.

Having once spared the infant at its birth, however, the *pater familias* had no power afterwards to get rid of his child, either by selling him (*mancipatio*) into slavery – the *mancipatio* was now tolerated only as a legal fiction for the contradictory objects of adoption or manumission – or by putting him to death. A father's right to slay his child was still recognized in the first century B.C., as is proved by the case of Aulus Fulvius, an accomplice of Catiline;[9] but had later become a capital crime. Before Constantine equated with parricide the murder of a son by his father,[10] Hadrian had punished by banishment to an island a father who had slain his son in the course of a hunt, though the son was guilty of having committed adultery with his father's second wife;[11] and the emperor Trajan had compelled another father, guilty only of having maltreated his son, to emancipate the youth forthwith, and, when the boy died, did not allow the father to share in his estate.[12]

Similarly, after the end of the republic, the emancipation of a child had entirely changed in significance and effect. In ancient days it was a punishment, less drastic than death or slavery, but nevertheless severe enough, for in breaking the ties that bound the child to the family, it condemned him to an exclusion from the family which inevitably resulted in his being disinherited. Now, emancipation had become a benefit. Thanks to the praetorian legislation of the *bonorum possessio* introduced at the beginning of the empire, it enabled a son to acquire and administer his own property without being deprived of his paternal inheritance. Fathers were reluctant to have recourse to emancipation as long as it had the appearance of a punishment. But as soon as it became an advantage to the son, the cost falling only on the parent, fathers began to practise it as a matter of course. The laws had once more adapted themselves to public feeling which, condemning the atrocious severities of the past, asked in the days of Trajan and of Hadrian nothing more of paternal authority than that natural affection with which a jurist of the third century finally identified it: '*patria potestas in pietate debet non atrocitate consistere*'.[13]

This was enough completely to alter the atmosphere of the Roman home, and to imbue the relationship between father and son with a tenderness which was far removed from the coldness and rigorous discipline that Cato the Elder had maintained in his family. Reading the literature of the time, we find it full of examples of fathers of families whose *patria potestas* was betrayed only in the indulgence shown to their children; and of children who in their father's presence behaved as they pleased, as though they were completely their own masters. Pliny the Younger, whose own marriages were childless, claims for the children of his friends an independence of conduct and manners he would certainly not have denied to his own children, because these things had become accepted and were for 'the right sort of people' an element of seemly behaviour. 'A father', he writes, 'was scolding his son for somewhat excessive expenditure. ... As soon as the young man had gone I said: "Well, well, and did you never do anything yourself which might have deserved a reproof from your father?"[14]

Pliny the Younger preached a tolerance or, if the word is preferred, a liberalism which appeals to us. But, unhappily, the Romans failed to strike the happy mean. They were not content to lessen the old severity; they yielded to the impulse to become far too complaisant. Having given up the habit of controlling their children, they let the children govern them, and took pleasure in bleeding themselves white to gratify the expensive whims of their offspring. The result was that they were succeeded by a generation of idlers and wastrels like Philomusus, whose misadventure Martial recounts. This young man, having inherited his father's entire fortune, suddenly found himself much worse off than when he had enjoyed his generous monthly allowance: 'Your father, Philomusus, arranged to allow you 2,000 sesterces a month, and every day he handed you your allowance. . . . Dying, he left you every penny. Your father has disinherited you, Philomusus!'[15]

Unfortunately, it was not only in money matters that the price of over-individualism had to be paid. The fine edge of character had been blunted in the Rome of the second century. The stern face of the traditional *pater familias* had faded out; instead we see on every hand the flabby face of the son of the house, the eternal spoiled child of society, who has grown accustomed to luxury and lost all sense of discipline. Worse still, we see looming up the sinister face of the father who for love of gain does not hesitate to blight the hope of his race, and methodically to corrupt the adolescents whom it is his duty to bring up. Such was the case of the great advocate Regulus, the enemy and rival of Pliny the Younger.[16] He had yielded to every caprice of his son. He installed for him an aviary where parrots chattered, blackbirds whistled, and nightingales sang. He bought him dogs of every breed. He sent to Gaul for ponies for him to ride and drive. And at the death of the boy's mother, whose immense fortune had paid for these expensive gifts, the father hastened to emancipate his son, so that the young man might at once enjoy the full possession of his maternal inheritance. The youth abused it so indiscriminately that his foolish prodigality shortened his life. He died prematurely and what was left of his fortune reverted to his father. This is, no doubt, an extreme example, so singular and monstrous that Pliny is scandalized. That it should have been possible at all is enough. And it would not have been possible if the women had not been emancipated, as much or even more than the children, from the family solidarity which the exercise of the *patria potestas* had imposed of old; the two perished together.

## 2. *Betrothal and Marriage*

While the *patria potestas* of the father over his children grew progressively weaker, it also ceased to arm the husband against his wife. In the old days, three separate forms of marriage had placed the wife under her husband's *manus*: the *confarreatio*, or solemn offering by the couple of a cake of spelt (*farreus panis*) in the presence of the Pontifex Maximus and the priest of the supreme god, the *Flamen Dialis*; the *coemptio*, the fictitious sale whereby the plebeian father 'mancipated' his daughter to her husband; and finally the *usus*, whereby uninterrupted cohabitation for a year produced the same legal result between a plebeian man and a patrician woman.[17] It appears certain that none of these three forms had survived till the second century A.D. The *usus* had been the first to be given up, and it is probable that Augustus had formally abolished it by law. *Confarreatio* and *coemptio* were certainly practised in the second century A.D., but seem to have been rather uncommon. Their place had been taken by a marriage which both in spirit and in external form singularly resembles our own, and from which we may be permitted to assume that our own is derived.

This more modern form of marriage was preceded by a betrothal, which, however, carried no actual obligations. Betrothals were so common in the Rome of our epoch that Pliny the Younger reckons them among the thousand-and-one trifles which uselessly encumbered the days of his contemporaries.[18] It consisted of a reciprocal engagement entered into by the young couple with the consent of their fathers and in the presence of a certain number of relatives and friends, some of whom acted as witnesses, while the rest were content to make merry at the banquet which concluded the festivities. The concrete symbol of the betrothal was the gift to the girl from her *fiancé* of a number of presents, more or less costly, and a ring which was probably a survival of the *arra* or earnest money, a preliminary of the ancient *coemptio*.[19] Whether the ring consisted of a circle of iron set in gold or a circle of gold, the girl immediately slipped it, in the presence of the guests, on to that finger on which the wedding ring is still normally worn. The French speak of *le doigt annulaire* (*anularius*) with no recollection of the reason why this finger was originally chosen by the Romans. Aulus Gellius has laboriously explained it:

When the human body is cut open as the Egyptians do and when dissections, or ἀνατομαί as the Greeks phrase it, are practised on it, a very delicate nerve is found which starts from the annular finger and travels to the heart. It is, therefore, thought seemly to give to this finger in preference to all others the honour of the ring, on account of the close connexion which links it with the principal organ.[20]

This intimate relation established in the name of imaginary science between the heart and the betrothal ring he cites to emphasize the solemnity of the engagement and above all the depth of the reciprocal affection which contemporaries associated with it. The voluntary and public acknowledgement of his affection was the essential element not only of the ceremony itself but of the legal reality of the Roman marriage.

Numerous literary allusions have preserved for us the most minute details of the marriage ceremony.[21] On the day fixed for the wedding the bride, whose hair had been imprisoned the night before in a crimson net, put on the costume which custom dictated: a tunic without hem (*tunica recta*), secured round the waist by a girdle of wool with a double knot, the *cingulum herculeum*. Over this she wore a cloak or *palla* of saffron colour; on her feet sandals of the same shade; round her neck a metal collar. Her coiffure was protected by six pads of artificial hair (*seni crines*) separated by narrow bands, such as the Vestals wore during the whole period of their service; and over it she wore a veil of flaming orange – hence called the *flammeum* – which modestly covered the upper part of her face. On top of the veil was placed a wreath, woven simply of verbena and sweet marjoram in the time of Caesar and Augustus, and later of myrtle and orange blossom. After she was duly dressed she stood amid her own people and welcomed her groom, his family, and friends. Everyone then adjourned either to a neighbouring sanctuary, or into the *atrium* of the house to offer a sacrifice to the gods. After the animal sacrifice had been consummated – sometimes a ewe, rarely an ox, most often a pig – the *auspex* and the witnesses played their part. The witnesses, probably ten in number, selected from the circles of the two contracting parties, played a silent role and simply affixed their seal to the marriage contract. The drawing up of a contract was not obligatory, however. The *auspex*, on the other hand, was indispensable. His untranslatable title indicated that he fulfilled the functions of a personal, family augur without sacerdotal investiture and without official appointment. After examining the entrails, he gave his guarantee that the auspices were favourable. Without this, the marriage would have been disapproved by the gods and invalid. As soon as he had solemnly made his pronouncement amid respectful silence, the couple exchanged their mutual vows in his presence, in a formula which seemed to blend into one their wills as well as their lives: *Ubi tu Gaius, ego Gaia*. This concluded the marriage rite and the guests burst into congratulations and good wishes: *Feliciter!* May happiness wait upon you!

The subsequent festivities lasted until night fell and the moment had come to wrest the bride from her mother's embrace and bear her to her husband's home. The flute-players led the procession, followed by five torch-bearers. As it marched, the cortège indulged in cheerful and licentious singing. As they approached the house, nuts were thrown to the children who had flocked about. These nuts had been the playthings of the groom in his childhood and their rattle on the pavement was a merry prophecy of the happiness and fertility which the future promised him. Three boys, whose parents must still be alive, accompanied the bride. One brandished the nuptial torch composed of tightly-twisted hawthorn twigs. The other two held the bride by the hand. On reaching her new home, she was lifted across the threshold, which was spread with white cloth and strewn with luxuriant greenery. Three bridesmaids entered the house behind the *nova nupta*: one of them carried her distaff and a second her spindle, obvious emblems of her virtue and domestic diligence. After her husband had offered her water and fire, the third and most honoured bridesmaid, the *pronuba*, led her to the nuptial couch where her husband invited her to recline. He then removed her *palla* and proceeded to untie the *nodus herculeus* of her girdle, while the bridal party hastened to retire with the speed and discretion which propriety and custom demanded.

Except for the bleeding sacrifice and the flaming splendour of the bridal veil, might we not well imagine that this Roman ceremonial has survived till our own day, and that with trifling modifications it has formed the model for our modern weddings? As Monseigneur Duchesne recently remarked, with an insight all the more striking for being rare: 'Except for the taking of the auspices, Christian ritual has preserved entire the Roman nuptial rite. Everything is there down to the bridal wreaths. ... The Church is essentially conservative and in this type of ceremony has modified only such details as are incompatible with her teaching.'[22] Reduced to fundamentals, Christian marriage consists in the voluntary union of two souls. Apart from the rejoicings which follow and even the religious service which accompanies it, the sacrament consists in the affirmation of intimate union made by the bridal couple in the presence of the priest who attends simply to register their vows before God. This definition equally applies to the Roman marriage of classic times. The kernel of the rite is the moment when, fortified by the approval of the gods as guaranteed by the *auspex*, Gaius and Gaia simultaneously declare their solemn intention to bind themselves to one another. The essence of the ceremony is this joint declaration; all that precedes or follows is a superfluous and adventitious flourish. When toward the end of the republic Cato of Utica took Marcia as his second wife, they agreed to renounce all such accompanying ceremony. They exchanged their vows without empty pomp and circumstance. They summoned no witnesses, they invited no guests. They pledged themselves in silence under the auspices which Brutus took:

> *Pignora nulla domus; nulli coiere propinqui*
> *Iunguntur taciti contentique auspice Bruto.*[23]

No members of the family and no kinsmen assembled. Their hands were joined in silence and they were satisfied with the presence of Brutus as augur.

There is nobility in this conception that marriage is based on a union of hearts. There is no doubt that the progress of philosophy, especially of Stoicism, which lighted the path of Cato and Marcia, contributed to grafting on Roman law a modern ideal so foreign to its primitive development, an ideal which ultimately overturned the traditional legal economy.

The ancient Roman – whom Gaius already speaks of as a vanished type – condemned woman, in view of her natural frailty, to live in perpetual tutelage.[24] By the marriage *cum manu* she escaped the *manus* of her father and his male relations only to fall into the *manus* of her husband. The marriage *sine manu* made her the ward of a so-called 'legitimate guardian' who had to be chosen from among her male relations if the direct male line of her progenitors had died out. When, however, the marriage *sine manu* had completely supplanted the *cum manu* marriage, the 'legitimate guardianship' which had been its inseparable accompaniment began to lose its importance. By the end of the republic, a ward who chose to complain of the absence of her guardian – however short that absence might have been – was able to get another appointed for her by the praetor.[25] When, at the beginning of the empire, the marital laws which are associated with the name of Augustus were passed, the 'legitimate guardians' were sacrificed to the emperor's desire to facilitate prolific marriages, and mothers of three children were exempted from guardianship.[26] In Hadrian's day a married woman did not need a guardian even to draft her will, and a father no more dreamed of forcing his daughter to marry against her will than of opposing a marriage on which she had set her heart, for, as the great jurist Salvius Iulianus maintained, a marriage could not be made by constraint, but only by consent of the parties thereto, and the free consent of the girl was indispensable: *'nuptiae consensu contrahentium fiunt; nuptiis filiam familias consentire oportet.'*[27]

97

### 3. The Roman Matron

It can be understood that this new definition of marriage revolutionized its nature. There are certain causes which inevitably entail certain consequences. In our own days we have seen the French legislator first minimize and finally abolish all obstacles to the triumphant wishes of a marrying couple. All remnants of parental authority disappeared with the parents' right to oppose a match desired by their children. The same phenomenon occurred in the Roman empire. Having shaken off the authority of her husband by adopting the marriage *sine manu*, the Roman matron was freed from the leading strings of guardianship by the free choice the times allowed her in contracting a union. She entered her husband's home of her own free will and lived in it as his equal.

Contrary to general opinion – which colours the conditions existing under the empire with memories of the early days of the republic and of long-lapsed republican customs – it is certain that the Roman woman of the epoch we are studying enjoyed a dignity and an independence at least equal if not superior to those claimed by contemporary feminists. More than one ancient champion of feminism under the Flavians, Musonius Rufus for one, had claimed for women this dignity and independence on the ground of the moral and intellectual equality of the two sexes.[28] The close of the first century and the beginning of the second include many women of strong character, who command our admiration. Empresses succeeded each other on the throne who were not unworthy to bear at their husband's side the proud title of Augusta which was granted to Livia only after her husband's death. Plotina accompanied Trajan through the Parthian wars and shared alike his glories and responsibilities. When the *optimus princeps* lay at death's door, having only in secret appointed Hadrian to succeed him, it was Plotina who interpreted and reinforced his last wishes; and it was she who ensured that Hadrian enter in peace and without disturbance on the sovereign succession of the dead emperor. Sabina's character remains untouched by the ill-natured gossip of the *Historia Augusta*, which is refuted by a mass of inscriptions commemorating her kindnesses, and by the numerous statues which deified her even in her lifetime. Hadrian, who is wrongly supposed to have been on bad terms with her, carefully surrounded her with so much deference and gracious consideration that the *ab epistolis* Suetonius forfeited overnight his 'Ministry of the Pen' for having scanted the respect due to her.[29] The great ladies of the aristocracy in their turn were proud to recall as immortal models the heroines of past evil reigns who, having been the trusted confidantes of their husbands, sharing their commands and their politics, refused to be parted from them in the hour of danger and chose to perish with them rather than leave them to fall uncomforted under the tyrant's blow.

Under Tiberius, Sextia would not survive Aemilius Scaurus, nor Paxaea her Pomponius Labeo.[30] When Nero sent Seneca the fatal command, the philosopher's young wife Paulina opened her veins together with her husband; that she did not die of haemorrhage like him was solely because Nero heard of her attempt to commit suicide and sent an order to save her life at any cost; she was compelled to let them bandage her wrists and close the wounds. The record which the *Annales* have preserved for us of this moving scene, the portrait they paint of the sad and bloodless face of the young widow who bore to her dying day the marks of the tragedy, express the deep emotion which the memory of this drama of conjugal love still inspired in the Romans of Trajan's day after the lapse of half a century.[31] Tacitus felt the same admiration for the loyalty of Paulina that his friend Pliny the Younger felt for the courage of the elder Arria, to whom he does homage in the most beautiful of his letters.

I must be pardoned for once more borrowing at length from Pliny's celebrated pages.[32] Arria the Elder had married the senator Caecina Paetus. In tragic circumstances she showed of what stoic devotion her love was capable. Both Paetus and his son were ill, and it was believed that there was no hope for either. The young man died. He was endowed with rare beauty and with a moral purity rarer still, and his parents loved him even more for his qualities than because he was their son. Arria prepared her son's obsequies and herself arranged the funeral so that her sick husband should be spared the knowledge of it. Returning to Paetus' room she acted as if the boy were living still and were better, and when the father asked news of him again and yet again 'she would answer that he had rested well or had eaten with appetite'. Then feeling the pent-up tears coming in spite of her, she slipped away and gave herself to her sorrow. When she had cried her fill she dried her eyes, repaired the ravages to her face, and came in again to her husband, as though leaving every pang of bereavement on the threshold. By this superhuman effort of self-control Arria saved her husband's life.

But she could not save him from the imperial vengeance when in A.D. 42 he was implicated in the revolt of Scribonianus, and was arrested before her eyes in Illyricum where she had accompanied him. She begged the soldiers to take her too. 'You cannot do less than let a consul have slaves to serve him at table, to dress him, and to put on his shoes. All this I will do for him myself.' When her prayers proved vain she hired a fishing boat and in this frail craft followed the ship on which they carried Paetus. It was useless. At Rome Claudius proved adamant. Arria announced that she would die with her husband. At first her son-in-law Thrasea sought to dissuade her. 'What,' he said, 'should you agree, if I were one day to die, that your daughter should perish with me?' Arria would not allow her stern resolution to be weakened. 'If my daughter in her turn had lived as long with you and in the same happiness as I with Paetus, I should consent,' she said. To cut the argument short she flung herself headlong against the wall and fell unconscious to the ground. When she came to herself she said: 'I warned you that I should find some road to death, however difficult, if you refused to let me find an easy one.' When the fatal hour at last arrived she drew a dagger from her robe and plunged it in her breast. Then, pulling the weapon out again, she handed it to her husband with the immortal words: 'It does not hurt, Paetus.'

I have dwelt on these famous episodes because they show in a certain type of woman of Imperial Rome one of the fairest examples of human greatness. Thanks to such women, proud and free as Arria, ancient Rome, in the very years when she was about to receive the bloody baptism of the first Christian martyrs, scaled one of the loftiest moral heights humanity has conquered. Not only had their memory become a veritable cult in the second century of our era, but their example still from time to time found imitators. It is true that the justice of the emperors now spared matrons the sacrifices which the wrath of Claudius and the ferocity of Nero had inflicted on them; but the cruelty of daily life still left all too many opportunities for at least the aristocrats to prove that Roman woman had not degenerated.

Pliny the Younger mentions among his own acquaintance some whose love for their husbands prompted them to die with them.[33]

I was sailing in a boat [he writes] on the Lake of Como, when an older friend called my attention to a villa ... which projects into the lake. 'From that room,' he said, 'a woman of our city once threw herself and her husband.' I asked why. Her husband was suffering from an ulcer in those parts which modesty conceals. His wife begged him to let her see it for no one could give him a more honest opinion whether it was curable. She saw it, gave up hope, and tying herself to her husband she plunged with him into the lake.

No doubt such cases were exceptional, or if you prefer, these are extreme cases where courage was abnormally heightened and virtue itself began to suffer from an excess of stoicism. But side by side with these, how many cases were there of households tenderly united, of wives quite simply pure and noble! Even Martial gives us a portrait gallery of accomplished women. 'Although sprung from tattooed Britons,' Claudia Rufina had a truly Latin soul. Nigrina, happier than Evadne or Alcestis, 'thou hast earned by a sure pledge given in life – that death was not needed to prove thy love.'[34] The transparent soul of Sulpicia was poured out in her poems:

She claims not as her theme the frenzy of the Colchian dame; nor does she recount Thyestes' dreadful feast ... she describes pure and honest love. No maid was so roguish ... no maid so modest. ... Neither as the Thunderer's spouse, nor as Bacchus' or Apollo's mistress, were her Calenus taken from her, would she live.[35]

Similarly, the society which surrounded Pliny the Younger was filled with honour, distinction, and devotion. The wife of his old friend Macrinus 'would have been worthy to set an example, even if she had lived in olden times; she has lived with her husband thirty-nine years without a quarrel, or a fit of sulks, in unclouded happiness and mutual respect.'[36] Pliny himself seems to have tasted perfect happiness in his marriage with his third wife, Calpurnia. He lavishes praise on her, boasting in turn of her tact, her reserve, her love, her faithfulness, and the taste for literature which had sprung from her sympathy for him. 'How full of solicitude is she when I am entering upon any cause! How kindly does she rejoice with me when it is over!' She never wearies of reading and re-reading him and learning him by heart. When he gives a public reading she attends behind a curtain, 'and greedily overhears my praises. She sings my verses and sets them to her lyre with no other master but Love, the best instructor.'[37]

Thus Calpurnia at her literary husband's side foreshadows the modern type of wife who is her husband's partner. Her collaboration is wholly free from pedantry and enhances instead of impairs the charm of her youth, the freshness of the love she feels for her husband and which he returns. The shortest of separations seems to have caused actual pain to both. When Pliny had to go away, Calpurnia sought him in his works, caressed them, and put them in the places where she was accustomed to see him. And Pliny for his part when Calpurnia is absent takes up her letters again and again, as if they had but newly arrived. At night he sees her beloved image in waking dreams, and 'his feet carry him of their own accord' to the room where she usually lived, 'but not finding you there, I return with as much sorrow and disappointment as an excluded lover'.[38]

Reading these affectionate letters, we are tempted to rebel against the pessimism of La Rochefoucauld and to deny the truth of his maxim that there was no such thing as a delightful marriage. On reflection, however, we begin to suspect that a trace of convention pervades these somewhat self-conscious and literary effusions. In Pliny's world, marriages were contracted rather from considerations of their suitability than from strength of feeling. He cannot have chosen his wife in a spirit very different from that in

which he accepts the commission to look out for a suitable husband
for the niece of a friend: with an eye not only to the physical and
moral attributes of the young man, but also to his fortune and
family connexions; 'for,' he confesses, 'I admit that these things
certainly claim some notice: *Ne id quidem praetereundum esse videtur.*'[39]
What he seems most to have loved in Calpurnia was her admiration
for his writings, and we soon come to the conclusion that he was
readily consoled for the absences he complains of by the pleasure
of polishing the phrases in which he so gracefully deplores them.
For, after all, even when the couple were living under the same
roof they were not together. They had, as we should say, their
separate rooms. Even amid the peace of his Tuscan villa, Pliny's
chief delight was in a solitude favourable to his meditations, and it
was his secretary (*notarius*), not his wife, whom he was wont to
summon to his bedside at dawn.[40] His conjugal affection was for
him a matter of good taste and *savoir vivre*, and we cannot avoid
the conviction that, taken all round, it was gravely lacking in warmth
and intimacy.

Let us revert, for instance, to the embarrassed letters which he
wrote to Calpurnia's grandfather and aunt to tell them of the
hopes of paternity with which Calpurnia had rejoiced him and of
the sad event which had so cruelly dashed them.[41] He announces to
Calpurnius Fabatus:

Your concern to hear of your granddaughter's miscarriage will be proportionate, I know, to your earnest desire that we should make you a
great-grandfather. Calpurnia, in her inexperience, did not realize her pregnancy, and left undone those things she should in the circumstances have
done, and did those things she should have left undone. She has received a
severe lesson, paying for this mistake by the utmost hazard of her life.

For Calpurnia Hispulla he varies the form but not the matter of
these strange explanations:

Calpurnia has been in the utmost danger – be it said without ill-omen! –
not through her fault but the fault of her youth. To this must be imputed
her miscarriage and the sad result of a pregnancy she had not suspected.
Pray excuse this accident to your father, whose indulgence is always more
readily forthcoming when solicited by one of your sex.

Indeed, it is not the grandfather but we who fail to understand – or else understand all too well how gravely Pliny was lacking in interest in other sides of his young wife's life, while he attended so carefully to her intellectual education. These letters reveal a coldness which shocks us and a detachment which appears unnatural. Such is the price paid for a liberty which merges into indifference and an equality which sometimes leads even the best, whom it should have drawn more closely together, into a sort of selfish torpor, while it tempts others into fads and perversions.

## 4. Feminism and Demoralization

Alongside the heroines of the imperial aristocracy, the irreproachable wives and excellent mothers who were still found within its ranks, it is easy to cite 'emancipated', or rather 'unbridled', wives, who were the various product of the new conditions of Roman marriage. Some evaded the duties of maternity for fear of losing their good looks; some took a pride in being behind their husbands in no sphere of activity, and vied with them in tests of strength which their sex would have seemed to forbid; some were not content to live their lives by their husband's side, but carried on another life without him at the price of betrayals and surrenders for which they did not even trouble to blush.

Whether because of voluntary birth control, or because of the impoverishment of the stock, many Roman marriages at the end of the first and the beginning of the second century were childless. The example of childlessness began at the top. The bachelor emperor Nerva, chosen perhaps for his very celibacy, was succeeded by Trajan and then by Hadrian, both of whom were married but had no legitimate issue. In spite of three successive marriages, a consul like Pliny the Younger produced no heir, and his fortune was divided at his death between pious foundations and his servants. The *petite bourgeoisie* was doubtless equally unprolific. It has certainly left epitaphs by the thousand where the deceased is mourned by his freedmen without mention of children. Martial seriously holds Claudia Rufina up to the admiration of his readers because she had three children;[42] and we may consider as an exceptional case the matron of his acquaintance who had presented her husband with five sons and five daughters.[43]

If the Roman women showed reluctance to perform their maternal functions, they devoted themselves on the other hand, with a zeal that smacked of defiance, to all sorts of pursuits which in the days of the republic men had jealously reserved for themselves. In his sixth satire Juvenal sketches for the amusement of his readers a series of portraits, not entirely caricatures, which show women quitting their embroidery, their reading, their song, and their lyre, to put their enthusiasm into an attempt to rival men, if not to outclass them in every sphere. There are some who plunge passionately into the study of legal suits or current politics, eager for news of the entire world, greedy for the gossip of the town and for the intrigues of the court, well-informed about the latest happenings in Thrace or China, weighing the gravity of the dangers threatening the king of Armenia or of Parthia; with noisy effrontery they expound their theories and their plans to generals clad in field uniform (the *paludamentum*) while their husbands silently look on.[44] There are others who seek literary fame in preference to the conspiracies of diplomats or exercises in strategy; inexhaustibly voluble, they affect a ridiculous pedantry in Greek and Latin, and even at table confound their interlocutors by the accuracy of their memory and the dogmatism of their opinions. 'Most intolerable of all is the woman who ... pardons the dying Dido and pits the poets against each other, putting Virgil in the one scale and Homer in the other.' There is no appeal against her presumption. 'The grammarians make way before her; the rhetoricians give in; the whole crowd is silenced.'[45] Pliny the Younger would certainly have fallen under the spell of woman's erudition, if we remember the praise he bestows on Calpurnia and the enthusiasm he expresses for the education and good taste of the wife of Pompeius Saturninus, whose letters were so beautifully phrased that they might pass for prose versions of Plautus or Terence.[46] Juvenal, on the other hand, like Molière's good Chrysale, could not endure these 'learned women'. He compares their chatter to the clashing of pots and bells; he abhors these '*précieuses*' who reel off the Grammar of Palaemon, 'who observe all the rules and laws of language', and adjures his friend: 'Let not the wife of your bosom possess a style of her own. . . . Let her not know all history; let there be some things in her reading which she does not understand.'[47]

So much for the intellectuals. But the outdoor types arouse even more ridicule than the blue stockings. If Juvenal were alive today he would be pretty sure to shower abuse on women drivers and pilots. He is unsparing of his sarcasm for the ladies who join in men's hunting parties, and like Mevia, 'with spear in hand and breasts exposed, take to pig-sticking', and for those who attend chariot races in men's clothes, and especially for those who devote themselves to fencing and wrestling.[48] He contemptuously recalls the *ceroma* which they affect and the complicated equipment they put on – the cloaks, the arm-guards, the thighpieces, the baldrics and plumes. 'Who has not seen one of them smiting a stump, piercing it through and through with a foil, lunging at it with a shield and going through all the proper motions? . . . Unless indeed she is nursing some further ambition in her bosom and is practising for the real arena.' Some, perhaps, who today admire so many gallant female 'records' will shrug their shoulders and accuse Juvenal of poor sportsmanship and narrow-mindedness. We must at least concede that the scandal of his times justified the fears which he expressed in this grave query: 'What modesty can you expect in a woman who wears a helmet, abjures her own sex, and delights in feats of strength?' The feminism which triumphed in imperial times brought more in its train than advantage and superiority. By copying men too closely the Roman woman succeeded more rapidly in emulating man's vices than in acquiring his strength.

For three hundred years women had reclined with their husbands at the banquets. After they became his rival in the *palaestra*, they naturally adopted the regimen of an athlete and held their own with him at table, as they disputed the palm with him in the arena. Thus other women, who had not the excuse of sport, also adopted the habit of eating and drinking as if they took daily exercise. Petronius shows us Fortunata, the stout mistress of Trimalchio, gorged with food and wine, her tongue furred, her memory confused, her eyes bleared with drunkenness.[49] The great ladies – or the women who posed as such on the strength of their money-bags

- whom Juvenal satirizes, unashamedly displayed a disgusting gluttony. One of them prolongs her drinking bouts till the middle of the night and 'eats giant oysters, pours foaming unguents into her unmixed Falernian . . . and drinks out of perfume bowls, while the roof spins dizzily round and every light shows double.'[50] Another, still more degraded, arrives late at the *cena*, her face on fire,

and with thirst enough to drink off the vessel containing full three gallons which is laid at her feet and from which she tosses off a couple of pints before her dinner to create a raging appetite; then she brings it all up again and souses the floor with the washings of her insides. . . . She drinks and vomits like a big snake that has tumbled into a vat. The sickened husband closes his eyes, and so keeps down his bile.[51]

No doubt such cases were repulsive exceptions. But it is bad enough that satire should be able to draw such types and expect readers to recognize them. Moreover, it is evident that the independence which women at this time enjoyed frequently degenerated into licence, and that the looseness of their morals tended to dissolve family ties. 'She lives with him as if she were only a neighbour: *Vivit tamquam vicina mariti.*'[52]

Before long women began to betray the troth which they should have plighted to their husband, and which many of them in marrying had had the cynicism to refuse him. 'To live your own life' was a formula which women had already brought into fashion in the second century. 'We agreed long ago,' says the lady, 'that you were to go your way and I mine. You may confound sea and sky with your bellowing, I am a human being after all.

> *Ut faceres tu quod velles nec non ego possem*
> *Indulgere mihi. Clames licet et mare caelo*
> *Confundas! Homo sum!*'[53]

Not only the *Epigrams* of Martial and the *Satires* of Juvenal bear witness to the prevalence of adultery. In the chaste correspondence of Pliny the Younger a whole letter is dedicated to relating the ups and downs of a case which came before Trajan in his capacity as supreme commander-in-chief of the army. A centurion was convicted of having seduced the wife of one of his superior officers, a senatorial tribune in the same legion as himself. What amazes Pliny is certainly not the adultery itself, but the unusual set of circumstances which surrounded it: the flagrant breach of discipline it involved, which entailed the immediate 'breaking and banishing' of the centurion; the reluctance of the tribune to vindicate his honour by demanding the condemnation which his wife deserved and which the emperor was officially bound to pronounce.[54]

It is obvious that unhappy marriages must have been innumerable in a city where Juvenal as a matter of course adjures a guest whom he had invited to dinner to forget at his table the anxieties which have haunted him all day, especially those caused by the carryings on of his wife, who 'is wont to go forth at dawn and to come home at night with crumpled hair and flushed face and ears'.[55]

A hundred years before, Augustus had in vain tried stern measures against adulterers by passing a law which deprived them of half their fortune and forbade them marriage with each other for all time.[56] From a modern point of view this marked a distinct advance on the ancient law. In the time of Cato the Censor, for instance, a woman's adultery was recognized as a crime which her outraged husband was entitled to punish with death, but the man's adultery was considered negligible, and he got off scot free as if he were innocent.[57] The imperial legislation was both more humane, since it annulled the husband's right to take justice so cruelly into his own hand, and more equitable, since it dealt out equal punishment to both sexes. But the fact that the new law submitted the offence to a special court is an indication of the frequency with which adultery was committed, and we may be very sure that the law did little to curb it. By the end of the first century the *Lex Iulia de adulteriis* had been very nearly forgotten. Before applying it, Domitian was obliged solemnly to re-enact its provisions. Martial outdoes himself in sycophantic praise of the 'Greatest of Censors and Prince of Princes' who had passed this edict, which – if we are to believe him – Rome prized above triumphs, temples, spectacles, and cities: 'Yet more Rome owes thee, in that she is chaste [*Plus debet tibi Roma quod pudica est*].'[58]

But it seems that when Domitian was gone his edict mouldered along with the *Lex Iulia* under the dust of the archives and the indifference of the judges. A few years later Juvenal ventures to scoff at Domitian as 'the adulterer', who 'after lately defiling himself by a union of the tragic style, revived the stern laws that were to be a terror to all men, aye, even to Mars and Venus'.[59] And two generations after Juvenal, Domitian's law had fallen into so much discredit that Septimius Severus had to recast Domitian's work, as Domitian had endeavoured to recast that of Augustus.[60] To be frank, if the frequency of adultery had diminished in the second century, this was not due to the intermittent severities of the law but because facilities for divorce had, as it were, legitimized adultery by anticipation.

## 5. *Divorce and the Instability of the Family*

Classic Rome loved to recur in thought to the legendary days of old where she could see an ideal image of herself, an image which every day became less and less like the reality. But even in those times the Roman marriage had never been indissoluble.[61] In the marriage *cum manu* of the first centuries of Rome, the woman placed under the man's authority could in no wise repudiate her husband, while on the other hand the husband's right to repudiate his wife was inherent in the absolute power which he possessed over her. In the interest, no doubt, of the stability of the family, custom had, however, introduced some modifications into the application of this principle; and until the third century B.C. – as we see by specific examples which tradition has preserved – this repudiation was in fact confined to cases in which some blame attached to the wife. A council held by the husband's family then solemnly condemned her. The Twelve Tables have probably handed down a scrap of the formula of this collective sentence which permitted a husband to demand from his wife the surrender of the keys that had been entrusted to her as mistress of the house from which she was now to be ejected without appeal: *claves ademit, exegit.*[62] In 307 B.C. the censors deprived a senator of his dignities because he had dismissed his wife without first having sought the judgement of his domestic tribunal.[63] A century later, about 230 B.C., the senator Sp. Carvilius Ruga was still able to scandalize his colleagues by putting away a wife with whom he had no other fault to find than that she had given him no children.[64]

But soon men in his position no longer needed to fear such odium as he had incurred, and following generations of Roman husbands could shake off their wives on a trumpery pretext without arousing indignation or protest: one had perhaps gone out without her veil; one had stopped in the street to speak to a freedman of unsavoury reputation; another had attended the public games without express permission.[65] It was better to invoke no pretext at all than such mean and petty ones; and while the husband had usurped the right to dissolve at will the union he had entered into, it happened that, by the end of the republic, the marriage *sine manu* conferred the equivalent freedom on the woman. If she had embarked on marriage under the protection of her male progenitors or near relations, they needed only to say the word in order to break her bonds and take her home to them (*abducere uxorem*). If she had lost all male relations and depended solely on herself (*sui iuris*), it rested with her to pronounce the word that set her free.[66]

So far had things progressed that in the time of Cicero divorce by consent of the two parties or at the wish of one had become the normal course in matrimonial affairs. The ageing Sulla took a young divorced woman as his fifth wife, a certain Valeria, half-sister of the orator Hortensius.[67] Pompey, twice widowed, having lost both Aemilia and Julia, had been divorced before marrying Aemilia and was again divorced after the death of Julia. His first divorced wife was Antistia; he had asked her hand with the object of winning the favour of the praetor on whom depended the livery of seisin of her immense paternal fortune, but later this connexion threatened to hamper his political career. The second was Mucia, whose behaviour during his long absence on his overseas campaigns had left much to be desired.[68] Having lost his wife Cornelia, the daughter of Cinna, Caesar married Pompeia, but repudiated her for the simple reason that mere innocence was not enough: 'Caesar's wife must be above suspicion.'[69] The virtuous Cato of Utica, after being divorced from Marcia, felt no shame in taking her back when her private fortune was augmented by that of Hortensius, whom she had married and lost in the interval.[70] And the fifty-seven-year-old Cicero unblushingly discarded the mother of his children, after thirty years of married life with her, in order to replenish his bank account by taking to wife the young and rich Publilia.[71] Cicero's Terentia, however, seems to have borne this disgrace with fortitude, for she married again twice, first Sallust and later Messala Corvinus, and died a centenarian.[72]

From this time on, we witness an epidemic of divorces – at least among the aristocracy whose matrimonial adventures are documented – and in spite of the laws of Augustus, or perhaps rather on account of them, the disease tended to become endemic under the empire. Augustus had intended by his *Lex de ordinibus maritandis* only to check the fall of the birth rate among the upper classes. By the disability imposed on offenders he hoped to bring pressure to bear on divorced people to marry again; but he was far from intending to prevent ill-assorted couples from dissolving an unhappy marriage and speedily substituting a happier and more fruitful union. He forbade the breach of a betrothal because he had observed that hard-boiled bachelors took advantage of a series of engagements, capriciously cancelling one after the other, to postpone the wedding indefinitely. By continually announcing it but never celebrating it they evaded at once his commands and the punishment with which he threatened the refractory.[73] He could not prevent couples from divorcing each other, nor did he wish to do so. He contented himself with attempting to regularize the procedure. First, he conceded that the wish of the married pair should, as heretofore, suffice to dissolve a marriage, and insisted only that this wish should be publicly expressed in the presence of seven witnesses and announced by a message. This message was usually delivered by a freedman of the house. Later he thought wise to permit the divorced wife to take an action, known as the '*actio rei uxoriae*', to reclaim her dowry, even when from negligence or over-trustfulness she and her kin had omitted the precaution of stipulating for such restitution. The right of a wife to claim repayment of her dowry was henceforth undisputed except in the case of such dowry property as the judge allowed the husband to retain either for the maintenance of the children who remained in his care (*propter liberos*), or in compensation for damages caused by the wife by her extravagance (*propter impensas*), malversation (*propter res amotas*), or misconduct (*propter mores*).[74]

In passing these laws Augustus was prompted by the same impulse that had made him withdraw from the husband's administration any part of the dowry which was invested in land in Italy. In both cases his concern was to safeguard a woman's dowry – the unfailing bait for a suitor – so as to secure for her the chance of a second marriage. It turned out, however, as he ought to have foreseen, that his measures, comfortable though they were to his population policy and socially unexceptionable, hastened the ruin of family feeling among the Romans. The fear of losing a dowry was calculated to make a man cleave to the wife whom he had married in the hope of acquiring it, but nothing very noble was likely to spring from calculation so contemptible. In the long run avarice prolonged the wealthy wife's enslavement of her husband. As Horace puts it:

> . . . *dotata regit virum*
> *coniunx.*[75]

While progressively lowering the dignity of marriage, this legislation succeeded in preserving its cohesion only up to the point where a husband, weary of his wife, felt sure of capturing, without undue delay, another more handsomely endowed. In these circumstances, the vaunted laws of Augustus must bear part of the responsibility for the fact, which need surprise no one, that throughout the first two centuries of the empire Latin literature shows us a great many households either temporarily bound together by financial interest or broken up sometimes in spite of, sometimes for the sake of, money.

Thus the Roman matron, mistress of her own property in virtue of her *sine manu* status, was certain, thanks to the Julian laws, of recovering the bulk if not the whole of her dowry. Her husband was not free to administer it in Italy without her consent, nor to mortgage it anywhere even with her acquiescence.[76] Duly primed by her steward, who assisted her with advice and surrounded her with obsequious attention – this 'curled spark' of a procurator whom we see under Domitian always 'clinging to the side' of Marianus' wife[77] – the wealthy lady dispatched her business, made her dispositions, and issued her orders. As Juvenal predicts: 'No present will you ever make if your wife forbids; nothing will you ever sell if she objects; nothing will you buy without her consent.'[78] The satirist contends that there is nothing on earth more intolerable than a rich woman: '*intolerabilius nihil est quam femina dives*';[79] while Martial for his part explains that he could not endure to marry a wealthy woman and be stifled under a bridal veil by taking a husband to him instead of a wife:

> *Uxorem quare locupletem ducere nolim*
> *quaeritis? Uxori nubere nolo meae.*[80]

Prisoner not of his affections but of a dowry, the husband – if his sovereign lady did not give him his congé herself – sooner or later escaped from one gilded cage into another. In the city as at the court the ephemeral households of Rome were perpetually being disrupted, or rather were continually dissolving to recrystallize and dissolve again till age and death finally overtook them. The freedman whom Augustus' law charged with the duty of conveying the written order of divorce had never suffered so little from unemployment. Juvenal does not fail to leave us a picture of this busybody fussing on his errand: 'Let three wrinkles show themselves on Bibula's face', and her loving Sartorius will betake himself in haste to other loves. 'Then will his freedman give her the order: "Pack up your traps and be off! You've become a nuisance ... be off and be quick about it!"'[81] In such a case the outraged wife had no redress; there was nothing for her to do but to obey the order which the poet slightly paraphrases. Gaius has preserved the legal formula for us: '*Tuas res tibi agito* [take your belongings away!].'[82] She took care to take with her nothing that strictly belonged to her husband, whose right to his own goods she recognized in the parting formula she used to him: 'Keep your belongings to yourself! [*tuas res tibi habeto*].'

We must not imagine that it was always the man who took the initiative in these matters. Women in their turn discarded their husbands and abandoned them without scruple after having ruled them with a rod of iron. Juvenal points the finger of scorn at one of these: 'Thus does she lord it over her husband. But before long she vacates her kingdom; she flits from one home to another wearing out her bridal veil. . . . Thus does the tale of her husbands grow; there will be eight of them in the course of five autumns – a fact worthy of commemoration on her tomb!'[83] Martial's Telesilla was another such. Thirty days, or perhaps less, after Domitian had revived the Julian laws, 'she is now marrying her tenth husband . . . by a more straightforward prostitute I am offended less'.[84] In vain the Caesars now tried setting an example of monogamy to their subjects. But instead of following in the steps of Trajan and Plotina, Hadrian and Sabina, Antoninus and Faustina, imperial couples faithful to each other for life, the Romans preferred to ape the preceding emperors, all of whom, even Augustus, had been several times divorced.

Divorces were so common that – as we learn from the jurists of the time – a series of them not infrequently led to the fair lady and her dowry returning, after many intermediate stages, to her original bridal bed.[85] The very reasons which today would doubly bind an affectionate woman to her husband's side – his age or illness, his departure for the front – were cynically advanced by the Roman matron as reasons for deserting him.[86] It is an even graver symptom of the general demoralization that these things had ceased to shock a public opinion grown sophisticated and inhuman. Thus in the Rome of the Antonines Seneca's words were cruelly just: 'No woman need blush to break off her marriage since the most illustrious ladies have adopted the practice of reckoning the year not by the names of the consuls but by those of their husbands. They divorce in order to re-marry. They marry in order to divorce: *exeunt matrimonii causa, nubunt repudii.*'[87]

How far removed from the inspiring picture of the Roman family in the heroic days of the republic! The unassailable rock has cracked and crumbled away on every side. Then, the woman was strictly subjected to the authority of her lord and master; now, she is his equal, his rival, if not his *imperatrix*.[88] Then, husband and wife had all things in common; now, their property is almost entirely separate. Then, she took pride in her own fertility; now, she fears it. Then, she was faithful; now, she is capricious and depraved. Divorces then were rare; now they follow so close on each other's heels that, as Martial says, marriage has become merely a form of legalized adultery. 'She who marries so often does not marry; she is an adultress by form of law: *Quae nubit totiens, non nubit: adultera lege est.*'[89]

# V

## EDUCATION AND RELIGION

*

### 1. Symptoms of Decomposition

APART from legislation, other causes contributed to hasten this decadence or rather to determine this reversal of family values. Some were economic, and derived from the baleful influence of wealth ill-gotten and even worse distributed, about which we have already spoken. Some were social, and had their origin in the poisonous virus which slavery injects into a free population. Finally and above all, there were moral causes resulting from the spiritual disorders of a cosmopolis where crude indifference and gross superstition reigned together, both alike hampering the upward flight of new mystic theologies.

After the first quarter of the second century, rendered illustrious by the victories of Trajan, men and women captives in thousands – from Dacia, Arabia, and the distant shores of Tigris and Euphrates – flooded the markets and the mansions of the Urbs. The draw-backs inseparable from overabundance of slaves were forthwith intensified. The society of Imperial Rome supplied yet another proof of the natural law that, in every time and clime where it has been largely practised, slavery degrades and besmirches marriage if it does not wholly stamp it out. Even when he was not de-bauched, the wealthy Roman looked askance at a life in which every day he would have to contend or reckon with the wishes of a legitimate wife, and he often preferred the cosy concubinage which Augustus had recognized as a licit though inferior union, to which public opinion attached not the slightest stigma and in which even the imperial sage, Marcus Aurelius, was presently to take refuge from the loneliness of widowerhood.[1] He would, therefore, expressly manumit a favourite slave woman, convinced that the *obsequium* due from a freedman or woman to the *patronus* would keep her faithful and obedient, and knowing, further, that if children should bless their relationship he could wipe out all stain of bastardy by the simple process of adopting them. Or he might even omit the formality of the manumission, lest it weaken his authority. The host of epitaphs in which a husband and his *liberta* wife reserve access to their tomb not to their children but to their freedmen raises the suspicion that – unless the marriage had been without issue – these inferior wives had preferred for their offspring a simple manumission arranged for in their will to a formal act of regular adoption. Thus we find many of the best families of the city infected with an actual hybridization, similar to that which has more recently contaminated other slave-owning peoples; and this strongly accentuated the national and social decomposition that had set in everywhere as a consequence of the multitude of slave emancipations.

Where such things occurred, the better Romans at least saved their face by preserving a minimum of external decency in their conduct. But not a few thought even the light fetters of regular concubinage too rigid and too weighty. Preoccupied solely with their own ease and pleasure, as indifferent to the duties of their position as to the dignity of the honours they enjoyed, they held it preferable to rule as pashas over the slave harems which their riches permitted them to maintain. When the ex-praetor Larcius Macedo, one of the Younger Pliny's colleagues in the Senate, was assassinated by a group of discontented slaves, the whole swarm of his odalisques was seen rushing up to the body, howling with grief: '*concubinae cum ululatu et clamore concurrunt*'.[2]

It was not long before the presence of slaves introduced a seriously disturbing element into even legitimate households. Martial launches many a dart at home-keeping adulterers. He mocks the master who buys back the maidservant mistress he cannot bear to do without;[3] he makes merry over the great lady who has lost her heart to her hairdresser and having set him free pours an equestrian fortune into his lap;[4] he attributes Marulla's many offspring not to her husband Cinna but to Cinna's cook, his bailiff, his baker, his flutist, even to his wrestler, and to his buffoon.[5] No doubt these epigrams are aimed at the most crying scandals of the town. But the theme would have been less popular if scandals had been rarer, and the literature of the time gives us the impression that there must have been many Roman houses where the abusive dialogue which Martial's couplet presupposes might have taken place: 'Your wife calls you an admirer of servant maids, and she herself is an admirer of litter bearers. You are a pair, Alauda:

> *Ancillariolum tua te vocat uxor et ipse*
> *Lecticariola est. Estis, Alauda, pares.'*[6]

It is obvious that the abuses of slavery had introduced laxity of morals even into the houses where supplementary love affairs were taboo. The proximity of concubinage in even the best houses, and the atmosphere of licentiousness and irresponsibility created by so many slave liaisons on every side, had done more than the prostitution of the 'she-wolves' who stood around the circus and haunted the suburban roads at night, lurking behind the tombs,[7] to degrade marriage, until husband and wife in their turn considered it only a fleeting anodyne. To resist this contagion, the Romans would have needed an ideal such as – apart from a few powerful individual personalities, a few philosophic schools, and a few sects of genuine believers – their intelligence, weakened by a culture too elementary, too superficial, and too purely verbal, was no longer capable of conceiving or their feeble faith capable of realizing.

## 2. Primary Education

In the austere days of the republic, Cato the Censor claimed that he alone had the right to educate his son and boasted that he had himself taught the boy to read, write, fence, and swim.[8] This accords with Pliny's statement that in the past every parent was his child's teacher;[9] and although the father alone is expressly mentioned, we know from other sources of the important part played by certain Roman matrons in the education of their children. The outstanding example was, of course, Cornelia, the mother of the Gracchi, but in this connexion we also hear of Aurelia, the mother of Caesar, and Atia, the mother of Augustus.[10] Under the empire, however, we meet a far different set of circumstances.

In the first place, people of wealth and position were very little inclined to bother personally with their children's education. Women were left to a complete and fatal idleness. The weaker ones found their lack of occupation an incitement to or an excuse for licentious excesses. The better ones tried to combat their boredom by artificial enthusiasms, as we have seen, or passed the time in the amusements and gossip of the 'clubs'.[11] Some killed time at home, like old Ummidia Quadratilla who, till she died at eighty, had spent every day when there were no public spectacles to go to shifting about the men on a chess-board or watching the dumb show of the mimes with whom she had filled her house.[12]

A nurse, often Greek, was assigned to look after the child during its early years.[13] As Quintilian tells us, it was the ideal of the philosopher Chrysippus that she should be a philosopher.[14] Quintilian himself, more practical in his approach, stressed that she should speak correctly, since the child's first words will be in imitation of her speech.[15] The alphabet and simple reading were usually learned at home. In some cases this instruction seems to have been confided to the *paedagogus*, a slave who served as tutor, guardian, and servant of the child put in his care. Quintilian demanded that the *paedagogus* be well educated, or, failing that, that he recognize his own limitations.[16] Equipped with the ability to read, the child was ready for school, although we know of families in which the education was continued in the home until the preparation for rhetorical studies had been completed.[17]

The spoiled son of a wealthy family had a splendid time putting his so-called 'master' in his place, the place suited to a servant, whether he called himself a tutor or not. Already in the *Bacchides* Plautus portrays a precocious adolescent called Pistoclerus who, in order to drag his tutor Lydus with him to his light of love, needs only to remind him sharply of his servile state: 'Look here,' he says, 'am I your slave or are you mine?'[18] To such a question there was only one answer and – as Gaston Boissier points out – we need not imagine that Lydus was the only tutor in Rome to whom it was frequently addressed.[19]

Instruction in the elementary school, the *ludus litterarius*, was limited to three subjects: reading, writing, and arithmetic. The teacher (*magister*) had to depend entirely on the small fees paid him by the parents of his pupils and was often constrained to supplement his income as schoolmaster by other activities.[20] Though the State, in the person of the emperor, became increasingly interested in the support of distinguished teachers and scholars in the higher realms of learning, there is no evidence of any public contribution to elementary education during the classical period.

The Roman schoolmaster does not seem to have spoiled many children by sparing the rod.[21] Naturally discipline had to be preserved when boys and girls were crowded together in one inconvenient spot without distinction of age or sex. But Quintilian noted the hypocrisy and cowardice which an abuse of corporal punishment was apt to call forth in the pupil and spoke also of the brutal teacher.

Pain and fear [he sadly testifies] drive children into doing things which they cannot confess, and which soon cover them with shame. It is even worse where no one has taken the trouble to investigate the morals of the teachers and masters. I dare not speak of the abominable infamies to which men can be degraded by their right to inflict corporal punishment, nor of the assaults, for very fear of which the unfortunate children may sometimes provoke further assaults; I will have been sufficiently understood: *nimium est quod intellegitur*. . . . [22]

The primary school of Rome might thus debauch the children it was supposed to instruct; and on the other hand it rarely awoke in them any feeling for the beauty of knowledge. School opened at dawn and continued without a break till noon. It was held under the awning outside some shop, and invaded by all the noises of the street from which only a screen of tent cloth separated it. Its scanty furniture consisted of a chair for the master and benches or stools for the pupils, a blackboard, some tablets, and some calculating boards (*abaci*). Classes were continued every day of the year with exasperating monotony, broken only by the eighth-day pause (*nundinae*), the Quinquatrus, and the summer holidays. The master's sole ambition was to teach his pupils to read, write, and count; as he had several years at his disposal in which to accomplish this, he made no attempt to improve his wretched teaching methods or to brighten his dismal routine. Thus, he taught his hearers the names and the order of the letters before showing them their form – a method which Quintilian strongly condemns – and when the pupils had painfully learned to recognize the written characters by their appearance, they had to make a fresh effort to combine them into words and syllables.[23] They progressed as slowly as they liked, and when they passed on to writing they came up against a similar irrational and backward procedure. Without any preliminary training in holding or using a reed pen, they were suddenly faced with a pattern to copy. Their fingers had to be held by the master or guided by someone else to trace the outline of the letters placed before them, so that innumerable lessons were necessary before they acquired the necessary skill to make the simple copy for themselves.[24] The study of arithmetic required no more mental effort on their part and brought them no more pleasure than the process of learning to write. They spent hours counting the units, *one, two,* on the fingers of their right hand, and *three, four* on the fingers of their left, after which they set about calculating the tens, hundreds, and thousands by pushing little counters or *calculi* along the corresponding lines of their *abacus.*

It is known that the emperors of the second century, Hadrian in particular, favoured the extension of primary schools in the most distant provinces of the empire, and that by offering tax immunity they encouraged willing schoolmasters to set up schools in out-of-the-way villages, in a mining district like Vipasca in Lusitania, for example.[25] Undoubtedly the complaints of Quintilian were listened to in some quarters, and the example of certain illustrious teachers of good family proved contagious. Herodes Atticus had secured such a tutor for his son, a man who tried to make learning easier for his pupil by devising a procession of slaves, each of whom carried on his back an immense placard bearing in giant size one of the twenty-four letters of the Latin alphabet.[26] But for one master who made an effort to get out of the rut, how many remained impenitently stuck in it! How many of the *ludi litterarii* which multiplied in the second century completely failed in the educative mission which they were supposed to discharge toward the children of the citizens. On the whole we are compelled to admit that at the most glorious period of the empire the schools entirely failed to fulfil the duties which we expect of our schools today. They undermined instead of strengthened the children's morals; they mishandled the children's bodies instead of developing them; and if they succeeded in furnishing their minds with a certain amount of information, they were not calculated to perform any loftier or nobler task. The pupils left school with the heavy luggage of a few practical and commonplace notions laboriously acquired and of so little value that in the fourth century Vegetius could not take for granted that new recruits for the army would be literate enough to keep the books of their corps.[27] Instead of happy memories, serious and fruitful ideas, any sort of intellectual curiosity vital to later life, school children carried away the gloomy recollection of years wasted in senseless, stumbling repetitions punctuated by savage punishments. Popular education then in Rome was a failure; if there was any real Roman education we must look for it not among the elementary teachers, but among the grammarians and orators who to a certain extent provided the aristocracy and the middle classes of Imperial Rome with some equivalent of our secondary and higher education.

## 3. The Routine Teaching of the Grammarian

To listen to the initiated, swollen with pride in their knowledge and eloquence, we might imagine that the formalist teaching of the Roman grammarian attained perfection and led straight to the sovereign good. One of these fine speakers, Apuleius of Madaura, writing at the end of the second century, says:

At a banquet the first cup is for thirst, the second for joy, the third for sensual delight, and the fourth for folly. At the feasts of the Muses on the other hand, the more we are given to drink, the more our soul gains in wisdom and in reason. The first cup is poured for us by the *litterator* who begins to polish the roughness of our mind. Then comes the *grammaticus* who adorns us with varied knowledge. Finally it is the *rhetor*'s turn who puts in our hands the weapon of eloquence.[28]

No one could be better pleased with himself but, unhappily, there was many a slip between the cup and the lip and the reality in no wise justifies the lyric enthusiasm of Apuleius.

First and foremost, grammarians and rhetoricians addressed themselves to a very limited public and even in the second century their teaching retained the selective character which a distrustful oligarchy had imposed on it from the beginning. Early in the second century B.C. the Conscript Fathers, whose arms and diplomacy were now being turned against the Greeks, began to feel the necessity of not allowing their sons to be less cultivated than the subjects and vassals whom they were henceforth to govern. They therefore encouraged the foundation in Rome of schools of the Hellenistic type to rival those which flourished in the East, at Athens, at Pergamum, and at Rhodes, and they wished these schools to teach after the Greek manner everything known to the most learned Greeks. At the same time they were not unmindful of the political power which this superior education would confer; they had no wish to cede an inch of their political monopoly; they therefore contrived that these new educational advantages should be reserved for their own social caste. The first professors of grammar and rhetoric whom they permitted to set up in Rome were refugees from Asia and Egypt, victims of Aristonicus and of Ptolemy Physkon, to whom Rome offered sanctuary. All of them taught in Greek. When later these original teachers were superseded by Italians, the new grammarians and rhetoricians conformed to the Greek usage and borrowed the Greek language. The grammar classes were conducted in Greek and Latin, but the rhetoric classes almost exclusively in Greek, and in this language all further education was continued.[29]

There were, of course, a few attempts to break through this convention which made for isolation. At the time of the democratic revolution with which the name of Marius is linked, one of his clients, the orator Plotius Gallus, had the hardihood to address his pupils in Latin;[30] and a few years later the *Rhetorica ad Herennium* was published.[31] Interlarded with examples taken from recent history and crammed with references to the subjects debated in the *comitia*, it was evidently inspired by the same tendency toward the liberal, the concrete, and the popular. But the oligarchy was on the watch. It had no intention of letting itself be robbed of its hereditary right to govern; since eloquence dominated the assemblies which every year renewed the power of the oligarchs, these men were determined that none but their own sons should possess the secret of rhetoric and they set about persecuting these unwelcome innovators. The *Ad Herennium* had no imitators and we are still ignorant of its author's name. As for the *rhetores Latini*, the censors of 92 B.C. compelled them to stop giving lessons, affirming that their innovations were neither pleasing nor proper.[32] To see schools of Latin eloquence reopened, Rome had to wait till the dictatorship of Caesar, which was well served by the treatises of Cicero, and till the imperial Flavian regime, which generously subsidized Quintilian, most famous of professors.[33] But by that time the tradition had taken root and could not be eradicated; though rhetoric was now taught in Latin as well as Greek, it remained the privilege of the few. The better to sift out the students, the grammar class, which was the first step to rhetoric, remained bilingual till the end of the empire.

The most important consequence of this was that eloquence, the end and aim both of grammar and rhetoric, was emptied of all real content. Politics deserted the Forum at the approach of the praetorians. Legal controversies, more and more confined to groups of specialists, ceased to furnish matter for eloquence once the emperors made jurisprudence a monopoly of their councils – a process which Augustus began and Hadrian completed. Finally philosophy and science, both mathematical and natural, which had been linked with rhetoric in Greek antiquity, benefited only in their countries of origin, especially at the Museum of Alexandria and in Athens, from the generosity of Trajan and Hadrian. Vespasian had banished the philosophers from Rome and excluded them everywhere from the privileges reserved for grammarians and rhetoricians;[34] and the study of philosophy in Rome had never recovered from the ancient interdict pronounced against it by the Senate in 161 B.C. and repeated in 153 B.C., when, in defiance of the diplomatic immunity which they enjoyed, it expelled from the city the academician Carneades, the Stoic Diogenes, and the peripatetic Critolaus.[35] Philosophy had never ceased to excite suspicion and sarcasm at Rome. The citizen who wanted to might indulge in it in friendly conversations, in casual and private conferences, or in solitary meditations in his ivory tower, but if he wished to take it up more seriously he had either to be rich enough to maintain a master at his own cost in his own house, or to expatriate himself in some distant town where philosophers were allowed to air their speculations. Physics and metaphysics, politics and history were equally taboo in regular and public courses of instruction; and eloquence, denied action, divorced from pure thought and pure science, gyrated in a weary circle of literary exercises and verbal virtuosity. Thus it happened that despite their popularity with well-to-do youth, despite the protection granted them by the emperors, despite the place of honour which they occupied in the city, where Caesar had allotted them the *tabernae* of his Forum and Trajan a hemicycle of his,[36] the preparatory studies of grammar and rhetoric were sterilized by the incurable formalism to which eloquence herself had been reduced.

Young people began to attend the grammarian's at an age which naturally varied with their aptitude and family circumstances, but which at times, as we can see from the obituary inscriptions of the first centuries of our era, suggests the alarming precocity of infant prodigies.[37] They went to him to be initiated into literature, or rather into the two literatures whose professor he was. With the *grammaticus* Greek literature was not less but more important than Latin. In a remarkable recent book, M. Marrou states his belief that he has detected a weakening of the Hellenic influence in Roman culture from the days of Quintilian onward;[38] but I am convinced that he has been the victim of a preconception arising naturally from overconcentration on his subject, and I suspect that he has unduly extended to Italy findings which are true only for the Africa of Saint Augustine, who was born at Tagaste, educated at Madaura and Carthage, and who died as bishop of Hippo in A.D. 430.

A whole series of phenomena from the Rome of the second century can easily be cited which refute M. Marrou's thesis: the enthusiasm for Greek affected by the 'beauties' whom Juvenal and Martial turn to ridicule;[39] the successes which during the whole course of the second century in Gaul attended the itinerant Greek orators, of whom Lucian represents the most original type;[40] the publication in Greek of the treatises of the 'philosophers' from Musonius Rufus to Favorinus of Arles; the Greek epigrams of the emperor Hadrian and the *Meditations* of Marcus Aurelius; finally and above all the persistence of Greek in the liturgy and in the apologetic writings of the Roman Christians. The Christian Church did not adopt Latin until the great shock which, toward the middle of the third century, rent the empire asunder and shook the very foundations of ancient civilization.[41] It would indeed be strange if Greek had been in retreat in Rome at the moment when Latin literature in Italy was crumbling to give place to it in every sphere. The inscriptions bear witness to its vital and predominant place in the teaching curriculum – from the epitaph of young Q. Sulpicius Maximus, which tells us that he died at the age of eleven after winning the prize for Greek poetry over the heads of fifty-two competitors at the Capitoline games of A.D. 94,[42] to that of Delmatius' son who succumbed at the age of seven, and had followed the courses in Greek but only had time to learn the Latin alphabet.[43] It thus appears that the Roman grammarians never ceased to subordinate the study of Latin literature to that of Greek literature – much in the same way as under the *ancien régime* in France the study of French was always subsidiary to Latin.

What their lessons thus lost in life and reality they may well have gained in variety. While all the learning of the *magister* in the *ludus litterarius* was bound up in one book, a copy of the Twelve Tables, the letters of which his luckless little wretches had to spell out before trying to copy them, the *grammaticus* had a double library at his disposal. But the use he made of the two was unbalanced, showing a marked predominance of foreign writers and an over-whelming preference for the older ones. While Homer, the tragic and comic playwrights – above all Menander – the lyric poets, and Aesop provided him with an abundant choice of Greek texts, he soon limited his choice of Latin authors to the poets of earlier generations: Livius Andronicus, Ennius, and Terence; and he expounded in Greek the meaning of these authors whose works were more or less adapted from the Greek. It was not until the last quarter of the first century B.C. that a freedman of Atticus, Q. Caecilius Epirota, decided to make two revolutionary innovations in the grammar class he was conducting: he dared to talk Latin and to admit to the honour of his lessons Latin authors either still living or but recently dead – Virgil and Cicero.[44] His bold example was timidly followed, and during the first centuries of the empire we see the works of famous authors a generation or two after their death gradually added to the list of those included in the curriculum. The treatises of Seneca in prose, and in verse the *Epistles* of Horace, the *Fasti* of Ovid, the *Pharsalia* of Lucan, and the *Thebais* of Statius were successively accorded this honour. These intermittent attempts at being up to date were not in themselves sufficient, however, to modify the fundamental character of an education all the more justly described as 'classic' in that it clung more and more to the tradition of works whose success was already consecrated. It is even possible that the tendency toward classicism was strengthened by the renaissance of Attic art under Hadrian which has given us so many statues and bas-reliefs of frigid elegance and which was accompanied by a return of literary taste toward the archaism preached by an emperor more deeply in love with Cato the Elder and with Ennius than with Virgil or Cicero.[45] The school of grammar at Rome always fixed its eyes on the past – more or less, according to the moment – and the Latin there taught was never at any time a living language in the full sense of the term, but, like the Greek from which it was inseparable, a language which 'the classics' had employed and which had become fixed in the moulds they had poured it into once and for all. So much so, indeed, that the purely bookish teaching of the *grammatici* already showed symptoms of arterio-sclerosis, a disease which their futilely complicated methods of instruction further aggravated.

These methods consisted first in exercises of reading aloud, and in reciting passages learned by heart. With an eye on the ultimate though far-off evolution of the future orator, the grammar class began by a course of elocution which no doubt quickened the taste and widened the understanding of the pupils, but at the same time developed in them a tendency toward theatrical posing and bravura extremely damaging to genuine feeling. Next the professor introduced them to exegesis proper. As a preliminary they had to reconcile their various manuscript texts, into which the caprices of copyists had introduced divergencies from which our printed editions are fortunately free. Then the *emendatio*, or what we should nowadays call textual criticism, challenged the attention of the scholars. This might have proved a valuable mental discipline if it had not been perpetually blended with discussions of the qualities and faults of the passages examined, and falsified by the resulting aesthetic prejudices. Finally, the lessons usually closed with the commentary proper, the so-called *enarratio*, which aimed at a comprehensive judgement but was so long-drawn-out that its faults were later to spoil even the work of a great commentator like Servius.

The *grammaticus* hastily completed the analysis of the work he had chosen, then began the *explanatio*, phrase by phrase or verse by verse, dwelling with meticulous pedantry on the meaning of each word and defining the figures of speech to which they lent themselves and the diversity of the 'tropes' into which they entered: metaphor, metonymy, catachresis, litotes, syllepsis. The matter of the passage was considered wholly secondary to the function of the words which conveyed it, and the perception of reality to the form of the statements which vaguely allowed the meaning to peep out between the lines. Only by the digressions which occurred in his teaching did the *grammaticus* introduce the discipline of what the Romans called the liberal arts, the sum of which, far from embracing every branch of knowledge which has since become science, never included any but the twigs of knowledge; the Greeks called them the ἐγκύκλιος παιδεία, that is to say, not encyclopedic education, but the current, normal education such as antiquity bequeathed almost unaltered to the Middle Ages. The Roman grammarian had dipped into everything without studying any subject thoroughly, and his pupils in their turn did nothing more than flutter over the surface of the knowledge enshrined in Greek literature; mythology where this was necessary in order to understand poetic legend; music where the metres depended on the odes or the choruses; geography enough to follow Ulysses in the tribulations of his return home; history without which many passages of the Aeneid would have been unintelligible; astronomy when a star rose or set to the cadence of a verse; mathematics in so far as they bore on music and astronomy. Blinded by an excess of practical common sense, and with an eye always fixed on immediate profit, the Romans saw no long-term usefulness in disinterested research; they did not understand its value; they did not feel its attraction; they made a collection of the results research had achieved, and lifted science ready-made into their books, without feeling any need to increase it or even to verify it.

For instance, the Mauretanian state of King Juba II, who had been brought up in the household of Octavia, was infested by troops of elephants. He preferred to trust the rubbish he had read about them and imaginatively vulgarize it further in his own writings, rather than go out and study these monstrous beasts with his own eyes.[46] And fifty years earlier, when Caesar appointed Sallust governor of the new province of Africa, the historian took so little trouble to inform himself about the towns not subject to his authority that in his *De Bello Iugurthino*, wishing to localize Cirta (the future Constantine), the ancient capital of Numidia, which had just been raised to the rank of an autonomous colony, he calmly placed it – 'not far from the sea'.[47] If such was the apathy of the most eminent minds in Rome, we can understand that the average person did not rebel against a system of education which reduced science to the handmaid of literature, much as the Middle Ages reduced philosophy to the humble auxiliary of theology. Probably nothing contributed more to devitalize Roman education than this senseless subordination of science, unless it was the vanity of the goal the Romans set before literature itself, asking only that it should train orators for them at a time when the art of oratory had ceased to serve any useful purpose.

### 4. Impractical Rhetoric

Oratory had lost all practical value for, as Tacitus says, great eloquence (*magna eloquentia*), true eloquence which at need can dispense with oratory, 'is like unto flame; like flame she demands fuel to sustain her; like flame she is stimulated by movement and gives light only when she burns';[48] and as flame dies when deprived of air, there can be no healthy eloquence when liberty has perished. Now all the history which Tacitus had been able to study confirmed this opinion; Roman eloquence could no more survive the dissolution of the assemblies than Greek eloquence had been able to survive the coming of despotism to the states ruled by the Diadochi. Alexander's master, Aristotle, distinguished three types of eloquence: in the first the speaker sought to influence a decision yet to be taken; in the second he justified a resolution already acted on; and in the third he narrated past history or awarded praise which had nothing to do with the march of events or the conduct of men.[49] The philosopher had then recognized the superiority of the first over the second and of the second over the third. In the year 150 B.C. the rhetorician Hermagoras reversed this order of values and gave pride of place to the style which he called 'epideictic', that is to say, to purely formal eloquence; this was meritorious in his eyes in proportion as it moved on a wholly unreal plane of its own, and its ostentatious self-sufficiency implied a theory of 'art for art's sake' in a domain where this doctrine is indefensible.[50] Consciously or unconsciously, Hermagoras was affected by the consequences of the revolution which had taken place in the Hellenistic kingdoms; and the Romans willingly adopted his paradox when they themselves were saddled with a political regime similar to that of the Hellenistic monarchs, a regime in which the sovereignty of the imperator had swallowed up the independence of the republic. Less than a generation after Cato the Censor had subordinated eloquence to action, identifying the orator with 'a good man skilled in speaking' (vir bonus, dicendi peritus),[51] they had welcomed the treatises of Greek rhetoric in which eloquence and action were divorced; and when Caesar had bowed them to his monarchy they accepted naturally a state of affairs which condemned the eloquence they taught in their schools to exert itself in the void, fortified with an apparatus of stereotyped prescriptions and the tinkling of empty words, sonorous but echo-less.

The Roman professors of rhetoric uniformly forced every speech into a strait-jacket of six parts, from the exordium to the peroration.

Then they analysed the variety of combinations to which these could eventually be adapted. Next they devised a course of exercises by which perfection might be attained in each part; for example, the narration, the argument, the portrayal of character, the maxim, the thesis, the discussion. The most minute details were foreseen and provided for, and their development followed a series of invariable progressions leading to an almost automatic cadence. It seemed as if they took seriously the formula for turning out an orator complete from top to toe (*fiunt oratores*) and were convinced that by subjecting their pupils to these verbal acrobatics they could convert each and every one of them into a speaker deserving the fair name of orator.

Perhaps nothing is more characteristic of their cramped and crabbed method than the *chria*, this 'declension' not of the noun but of the thought, or rather of the phrase which expresses the thought and adds the weight of some high authority, as if the maxim of a wise man could be enriched and given new shades of meaning by being indefatigably 'declined' in various numbers and cases. For instance: 'Marcus Porcius Cato has said that the roots of science are bitter . . .' – 'this maxim of M.P.C., which says that . . .' – 'it appeared to M.P.C. that . . .' – 'the Marcus Porcius Catos have maintained that . . .' – and so on *ad infinitum*. In the same way, when Molière in the *Bourgeois Gentilhomme* was initiating M. Jourdain into the art of elegant speech, the poor man was invited to embroider his meaning with interminable variations, or *chriae*, which his instructor suggested: 'Lovely Marquise, your beautiful eyes cause me to die of love; – of love, lovely Marquise, your beautiful eyes cause me to die. . .' But whereas Molière was making merry over M. Jourdain and his teacher of literature, not a single rhetorician in Rome of the first and second centuries dreamed of laughing at the *chriae* whose boring variations have been solemnly recorded for us by Diomedes.[52] Quintilian also recognizes the practice in his *Institutio Oratoria*.[53]

When at last the professor of rhetoric considered his pupils sufficiently versed in these parrot-like repetitions and variations, he expected them to prove their accomplishments by delivering public harangues. In the time of Cicero these attempts were still known as *causae* – a word from which the French *chose* is derived –

but they lost the title under the empire. The orations now became either *suasoriae*, in which more or less thorny questions of conscience were discussed, or *controversiae*, which consisted in imaginary indictment or defence; in either case they were never anything but *declamationes*, a term which had not in those days the derogatory meaning our 'declamation' has since acquired. If only the masters of rhetoric could have shaken themselves free of their follies, this sort of test might have re-established contact between their schools and the concrete realities of life. But on the contrary they seemed determined to maintain as wide a gulf between the two as possible. The more far-fetched and improbable a subject was, the more eager they were to adopt it for discussion. The fact was that in origin the *grammaticus* and the *rhetor* were one.[54] Later, the schools of grammar and the schools of rhetoric were separated, but the traces of their original identity were never obliterated. The grammarian paved the way for the rhetorician's lessons, and the rhetorician for his part continued to mark time within the same narrow circle of ideas and images that had bounded the grammarian's vision. The pupil might change his class: the spirit of the teaching he received remained the same, and he was still the slave of an artificial literature and the prisoner of a narrow classicism.

Instead of directing the young men's thoughts to current problems, the subjects which Seneca the Elder set for the *suasoriae* of his pupils were always drawn from the past, and often from a foreign and distant past.[55] The most up-to-date which he has left us are borrowed from imaginary episodes of the last weeks of Cicero's life: in one, Cicero hesitates as to whether he will or will not ask mercy of Antony; in another he consents, in order to obtain it, to burn his works.[56] In all other cases, episodes of Roman history are neglected in favour of Greek; Alexander the Great debates whether he will venture to sail the Indian Ocean, or whether he will enter Babylon in defiance of the oracles;[57] the Athenians discuss whether they will surrender to the ultimatum of Xerxes, or the three hundred Spartans of Leonidas whether they will fight to the last man to hold up the Persians at Thermopylae.[58] Sometimes, however, even these singular and ancient subjects seem to the rhetorician too new and commonplace. He retraces history into the mists of prehistoric legend and bids his pupils write an essay in which Agamemnon ponders whether in order to secure a favourable wind for his fleet he will obey the prophetic injunctions of Calchas and sacrifice his daughter Iphigenia.[59]

It is obvious how artificial these *suasoriae* must have been. The *controversiae*, which might well have been made the means of preparing the future advocate for his profession, were no less far removed from real life. They deliberately turned away from current incidents of the day and went wandering in a dream world of weird hypotheses and monstrous events. The unnatural outlines which Suetonius has rescued from ancient manuals betray this morbid leaning toward the exceptional and the bizarre. In one of these preposterous cases, for instance, some men were strolling along one summer day to enjoy the sea air on the beach at Ostia. They met some fisher folk and agreed with one of them to buy the whole of his catch for a certain small sum. The bargain concluded, they claimed the ownership of an ingot of gold which an amazing chance brought up in the fisherman's net.[60] Another case deals with a slave merchant who, when unloading at Brindisi, wished to evade customs duty on the most valuable slave he had. He hit on the expedient of dressing up the handsome boy in the *toga praetexta*, the scarlet-bordered cloak of a young Roman citizen. Arrived at Rome the boy refused to lay his disguise aside and stoutly averred that it had been given him in token of his irrevocable manumission.[61]

Even these two fantastic lawsuits contain a grain of possible truth, which is systematically banished from the *controversiae* with which Seneca the Elder has dealt at such length.[62] Instead of basing these test pleadings on the substance of contemporary cases, the rhetorician labours ingeniously to multiply anachronisms and improbabilities. He takes the utmost care to devise his 'controversies' so that they will not fit into the framework of Roman civil law. In concocting them he invents imaginary, distorted, over-refined, and arbitrary facts which then in defiance of any logic he coordinates with some antiquated and foreign code of law, or even with some legislation manufactured solely in his own mental laboratory. Among all the subjects recorded by Seneca the Elder, I have discovered only one which was based with negligible alteration on an episode authenticated in the Latin annals: the prosecution of L. Quinctius Flamininus, who, when commanding in Gaul, had been guilty of giving orders during a banquet that the head of a prisoner should then and there be cut off to gratify the wishes of his mistress.[63] All the other sketches are barefaced outrages against truth. It is known, for instance, that during the proscriptions of 43 B.C. Cicero perished at the hand of a certain Popilius Laenas whose interests he had defended as advocate in some case, probably a civil suit, but certainly one of slight importance since none of our authorities has troubled to give details of it. The rhetorician seizes on this episode, but as the ingratitude revealed in it is not sufficiently black for his taste, he darkens it to his liking and unblushingly proposes to his pupils the following theme: 'Popilius, accused of parricide, was defended by Cicero and acquitted. Later, Cicero, proscribed by Antony, was slain by Popilius. Sustain an accusation against Popilius on the ground of evil morals.'[64] In this specific case an *actio de moribus* would not have lain, so it was invented to suit the needs of the rhetorical exercise.[65] No one has ever proved that Popilius Laenas committed any crime other than the legal execution of Cicero. The rhetorician cared not a whit that he was doing violence to history and confusing the legal issue so long as his wilful misrepresentations gave substance to the harangue which he asked of his pupils.

In this instance he condescends at least to choose a subject with a Roman background. For the most part he prefers one tinted with exotic colour and likes to transport his hearers to other countries. He goes off to the Greece of long ago to cull anecdotes which he spices to his taste. In one of them he starts from the hypothesis that in Elis the hands of sacrilegious persons were amputated according to law and on this fable bases the following *controversia*. The people of Elis had begged the Athenians to lend them Phidias to make a statue for them which they wished to dedicate to Olympian Jove. Athens lent the sculptor on condition that they should return the artist in due course or pay a fine of one hundred talents. When Phidias had finished his work they claimed that he had diverted to his own profit some of the gold entrusted to him for the divine statue, judged him sacrilegious, and cut off his hands before sending him back to Athens. The youth representing the Athenian advocate must claim the hundred talents, the Elidian advocate must refuse to pay them.[66] In a second example the rhetorician's hare-brained fictions blend the life histories of Iphicrates and Cimon, the son of Miltiades;[67] and the better to arouse terror and pity they defy all chronology in order to lodge an incredible indictment against Parrhasius, transforming him most unjustly into an infamous butcher.[68] The shocking accusation is that the painter, who was painting a picture of Prometheus for the temple of Athena, in order to render the sufferings of Prometheus with greater fidelity, put to the torture a slave prisoner of war from Olynthus who was acting as his model.

When the master of rhetoric refrained from falsifying history, he had recourse to little detective stories with too many characters and extravagant vicissitudes. His school of rhetoric knew nothing but tyrannies and conspiracies, kidnappings, reconnoitrings, obscenities, and horrors. One could hear plead there a husband who accused his wife of adultery because a rich merchant had made her his heir as a tribute to her virtue;[69] a father who wished to disinherit his son for refusing to be seduced by the prospect of an advantageous marriage and insisting on keeping as his wife the brigand's daughter who had saved his life and helped him to regain his liberty;[70] an impious but gallant soldier who, to arm himself for victory, had pillaged a tomb near the battlefield and robbed it of the arms that formed its trophy;[71] a virgin whom her kidnappers had forcibly compelled to practise prostitution, but who, loathing her hideous trade, slew a ruffian who approached her, succeeded in escaping from the house of ill fame and after regaining her liberty sought an honourable post as priestess in a sanctuary.[72]

The masters of rhetoric were proud of these imaginings. Obsessed by a desire for effect, they flattered themselves that their success varied with the improbable and complicated nature of the situations they invented and the remoteness of the characters from ordinary life. They estimated the value of an oration by the number and the gravity of the difficulties surmounted, and prized above all the eloquence which succeeded in expounding the inconceivable (*materiae inopinabiles*) and evolving as it were something out of nothing. Favorinus of Arles, for instance, aroused the enthusiasm of his audience one day by a eulogy of Thersites, brawler and demagogue, notorious as the ugliest man in the Greek camp before Troy, and on another occasion by an oration of thanksgiving to Quartan Fever.[73] In short, they systematically confused artifice with art, and originality with the negation of nature; the more we reflect on their methods, the more it seems clear that they were incapable of turning out anything but parrots or third-rate play actors. It cannot be denied that people have been found, and even recently among ourselves, to take up the cudgels to a certain extent in their defence, speciously arguing that their pedagogy had different aims from ours and that since they sought solely to stimulate their pupils' power of invention, they had every right to imagine that the more absurd a subject was the more credit a pupil deserved for handling it.[74] The absurdity lay in this conception itself, and such was the judgement of the last great writers of antiquity.

Seneca disapproved of teaching methods which do not prepare men for life, but only pupils for school: '*non vitae sed scholae discimus*'.[75] On the first page of his romance Petronius pokes fun at the sonority of pompous phrases which filled the classrooms of his day.[76] Tacitus sadly remarks that 'the tyrannicides, the plague cures, the incests of mothers which are so grandiloquently discussed in the schools bear no relation to the "forum" and that all this bombast hurls defiance at the truth'.[77] Juvenal scoffs at these would-be orators, these unmitigated asses, this Arcadian youth 'who feels no flutter in his left breast when he dins his "dire Hannibal" into my unfortunate head on every sixth day of the week', and these unhappy teachers of rhetoric who perish of 'the same cabbage served up again and again'.[78] We have no need to be more Roman than the Romans and to try to whitewash a system whose frenzied pedantry the best of them have reviled.

Reading just a few samples of these conventional extravaganzas, we can dismiss them with a shrug of the shoulders; but if we are condemned to read a whole series of them, one after the other, in the treatise of the elder Seneca, we fall a prey to unconquerable

boredom, not to say nausea. Reflecting that it was on these monotonous performances, these far-fetched and wilful exaggerations, these
false and unwholesome data, that the whole edifice of higher
education in Rome was reared, it is easy to understand that toward
the middle of the second century Latin letters began to perish
from such an abuse of literature. The decay of a civilization is
heralded by these laborious eccentricities, by the mental malnu-
trition to which the pick of Rome's youth was doomed, having no
other intellectual sustenance than this thin soup. For fear of being
accused of ignorance, the ambitious youth who wished to dazzle
and astonish his audience substituted memory for thought, affectation for sincerity, grimaces and contortions for natural expression,
and for a natural voice forced outbursts and calculated roars
practised in advance.

A morbid passion for the unusual and the extraordinary made
common sense seem a defect, experience of real life seem weakness,
and the sight of real life seem ugly. But Life herself inevitably took
revenge, and the Romans themselves began to weary of the fatuities
of their schools. The more impetuous among them failed to distinguish real learning from the parody of it which disgusted them,
and like Lucian resolved to doubt and make a mock of everything,
or like the common people turned their backs on every form of
culture and limited their thoughts to the satisfaction of their needs
and their desires.[79] The more inquiring and the nobler spirits,
deceived but not discouraged, turned aside to foreign religions to
seek an answer to the questions with which the mysteries of life
confronted them, to find a satisfaction for the aspirations of their
souls which neither bogus science nor the threadbare literature of
grammarians and rhetoricians had sufficed to fill.

## 5. The Decay of Traditional Religion

One great spiritual fact dominates the history of the empire: the
advent of personal religion which followed on the conquest of
Rome by the mysticism of the East. The Roman pantheon still
persisted, apparently immutable; and the ceremonies which had
for centuries been performed on the dates prescribed by the pontiffs

from their sacred calendars continued to be carried out in accordance with ancestral custom. But the spirits of men had fled from the
old religion; it still commanded their service but no longer their
hearts or their belief. With its indeterminate gods and its colourless
myths, mere fables concocted from details suggested by Latin
topography or pale reflections of the adventures which had overtaken the Olympians of Greek epic; with its prayers formulated in
the style of legal contracts and as dry as the procedure of a lawsuit;
with its lack of metaphysical curiosity and indifference to moral
values; with the narrow-minded banality of its field of action, limited to the interests of the city and the development of practical
politics – Roman religion froze the impulses of faith by its coldness
and its prosaic utilitarianism.[80] It sufficed at most to reassure a
soldier against the risks of war or a peasant against the rigours of
unseasonable weather, but in the motley Rome of the second
century it had wholly lost its power over the human heart.

The populace, it is true, still showed lively enthusiasm for the
festivals of the gods which were subsidized from public funds, but
Gaston Boissier is unduly optimistic when he attributes this enthusiasm to piety. Among the celebrations which were most eagerly
attended there were some which pleased the humbler people better
because 'they were gayer, noisier, and seemed to belong more
particularly to them'.[81] We need be under no misapprehension as
to the sentiments which underlay their devotion to these celebrations. In particular, to conclude from their taste for the drinking and
dancing on the banks of the Tiber which annually accompanied the
festival of Anna Perenna,[82] that they worshipped the ancient Latin
goddess of the circling year with enlightened sincerity would be as
rash as to measure the extent and vigour of Roman Catholicism in
Paris today by the crowds of Parisians who flock to the Reveillon.
It may be admitted that there is plenty of proof of the constancy
with which the *bourgeoisie* of Rome under the empire discharged its
duties toward the divinities recognized by the State. A 'conservative'
like Juvenal, who professedly execrates all foreign superstitions,
might at first sight appear to be devoted in every fibre to the national
religion; and reading the delightful opening of Satire XII, one
might well imagine that he still loved it profoundly. He paints with

charming freshness the preparations for one of the sacrifices to the Triad of the Capitol:

Dearer to me, Corvinus, is this day, when my festal turf is awaiting the victims vowed to the gods, than my own birthday. To the Queen of Heaven I offer a snow-white lamb; a fleece as white to Pallas, the goddess armed with the Moorish Gorgon; hard by is the frolicsome victim destined for Tarpeian Jove, shaking the tight-stretched rope and brandishing his brow; for he is a bold young steer, ripe for temple and for altar, and fit to be sprinkled with wine; it already shames him to suck his mother's milk and with his budding horn he assails the oaks. Were my fortune large, and as ample as my love, I should have been hauling along a bull fatter than Hispulla, slow-footed from his very bulk; reared on no neighbouring herbage he, but showing in his blood the rich pastures of Clitumnus, and marching along to offer his neck to the stroke of the stalwart priest, to celebrate the return of my still-trembling friend who has lately gone through such terrors, and now marvels to find himself safe and sound . . .[83]

But let us reread these exquisite verses. Their affectionate enthusiasm is not for the gods but for the country scene where the offerings are prepared, for the familiar beasts whom Juvenal has chosen from his flocks as worthiest of sacrifice, and whose beauty he appreciates both as connoisseur and poet; but above all for the friend whose unhoped-for return he celebrates and who in this clear description will savour in advance the joyous festival to which he is invited. As for the deities who occupy the obscure background of the picture, they must content themselves with a sketchy paraphrase like Minerva, or with their ritual adjective like Juno, Queen of Heaven, or with the purely geographical epithet attached to Jupiter, whose temple on the Capitol overhung, as everybody knows, the Tarpeian Rock. Juvenal would have been at a loss to throw any greater light on them. Their features were indeterminate to his eyes; the gods were to him no living personalities. He rejected the whole tissue of their mythology, for 'that there are such things as Manes and kingdoms below ground, and punt poles, and Stygian pools black with frogs, and all those thousands crossing over in a single bark – these things not even boys believe, except such as are not yet old enough to have paid their penny bath . . .'[84]

Juvenal's scepticism, moreover, was general. It had laid hold on

the humbler classes, the best-meaning of whom displayed, while
they deplored, the indifference felt by almost everyone for these
Roman gods with 'gouty' feet (*pedes lanatos*).[85] Great ladies (*stolatae*)
no longer climbed the Capitoline Hill to pray to Jupiter for rain.[86]
The most important and most orthodox contemporaries of Juvenal
shared the same feelings of scepticism. If great gentlemen like
Tacitus and Pliny the Younger 'practised' their religion as much
as or more than he, they 'believed' every whit as little. As praetor
Domitian, consul under Nerva, and pro-consul in Asia under
Trajan, Tacitus was compelled to officiate at the public ceremonies
of polytheism; and his aversion for the Jews was at least equal to
Juvenal's. So much for proof of his orthodoxy. But there are things
that make us doubtful of it; much as he abhors the Jews, he is not
afraid indirectly to praise their belief in one eternal and supreme
God, whose image must not be counterfeited and who cannot
pass away.[87] Similarly in his *Germania* he does not conceal his
admiration for the barbarous tribe who refuse to imprison their
gods within walls or to represent them in human form lest they do
outrage to their majesty; who prefer to consecrate to their worship
the woods and forests of their territory, and for whom the mysterious solitudes where they adore their unseen deities seem to
become identified with the Divine itself.[88] These two passages of
obvious though unformulated approval reveal Tactitus as a dis-
affected pagan.

Tacitus' friend, Pliny the Younger, shows no less detachment toward those religious forms to which he moulds his ways and
accommodates his acts. He respects their high antiquity and the
authority of the State which has consecrated them, but at the same
time he refuses them the intimate homage of his conscience. Gaston
Boissier quotes, in proof of the piety of Pliny, the letter in which
he describes to his friend Romanus the charm of the springs which
form the source of Clitumnus under the cypress shade and of the
old temple where the River God speaks his oracles.[89] It is certainly
a charming chapter, but in precisely the same vein as the Juvenal
verses just quoted. It has the same freshness, it also expresses the
gentle emotion which a friend of nature feels in gazing at a lovely
landscape. But it pays equally little heed to the devotions of which

this beautiful site is the theatre and the object, and it ends with a sly thrust at the pious folk who come here to perform them: 'You will also find food for study in the numerous inscriptions by many hands all over the pillars and walls, in praise of the spring and its tutelar deity. Many of them you will admire, others you will laugh at; but no, you are too kind-hearted to laugh at any. Farewell.'

In another passage in the letters Pliny writes to his architect Mustius that in compliance with the advice of the *haruspices* he is intending to repair and rebuild a temple of Ceres which stands on his estate.[90] The tone in which he announces this proposal indicates less veneration for the goddess than solicitude for the faithful. He anticipates that he will require a new Ceres, 'for age has maimed parts of the ancient wooden one which stands there at present'. His major concern, however, is the erection of a colonnade near the sanctuary: 'great numbers of people from all the country round assemble there, and many cows are paid and offered; but there is no shelter hard by against rain or sun'. Pliny is thus more set on winning the favour of his tenants than of Ceres, and the care he was expending on adding to the pleasures of their pilgrimages gives no more clue to his own religious convictions than Voltaire's similar activities as seigneur of Ferney.

There is still more convincing evidence, however, of the fundamental indifference Pliny felt toward the rites while he dutifully fulfilled the outward obligations. Let us look up the letter in which he announces his recent cooption into the College of Augurs.[91] His pleasure at the honour is wholly worldly. He barely alludes to the sacred power which this dignity confers (*sacerdotium plane sacrum*); he does not dwell on the incomparable privilege which is to be his of interpreting the signs of the Divine Will, of instructing the magistrates and the emperor himself in the value of their auspices. On the contrary, where a pious man would have welcomed the supernatural responsibilities with jubilation, what seems to him the most enviable feature of his new post is first that it is a life appointment (*insigne est quod non adimitur viventi*); secondly, that it has been bestowed on him on the recommendation of Trajan; thirdly, that he has succeeded 'so eminent a man as Julius Frontinus';

finally and above all, that the prince of orators, Marcus Tullius Cicero, had held the same preferment. There is no shadow of religious emotion in Pliny's self-gratulation. It is the pleasure of a courtier, a man of the world, a scholar – not of a believer. Pliny the Younger rejoiced to have been made an augur in much the same way that a modern author feels proud to be made a member of the French Academy; if we understand him aright the official priesthoods of the Romans had become for their dignitaries varying types of 'Academy'.

Even the enthusiasm which the imperial cult had awakened at the outset had in turn grown cold; it was now nothing more than another cog in the great official machine which functioned in virtue of its acquired momentum but had long since lost its soul.[92] The fall of Nero and the extinction with him of the family of Augustus had dealt a fatal blow by depriving the worship of the emperors of its dynastic sanctity. Vespasian, the upstart who had hoped to found a new dynasty, had posed in Egypt as a miracle worker, but had not deigned to attempt to increase his influence in Rome by such pretence. The courageous jest about his coming apotheosis which the dying man cracked on his deathbed is well known: 'I feel', he said laughing, 'that I am beginning to become a god.'[93] The murder of his son Domitian, who, forgetful of his origins, had insisted that even in Italy he should be addressed as 'Master and Lord' (*dominus et deus*), suddenly showed how well founded was his father's scepticism.[94] The worship of the emperors might perhaps have survived the crimes of 'Nero the Bald-head' if he had always handled enough wealth to enrich his Praetorian Guard and to pamper the populace of Rome. It was destroyed when people saw that if military revolutions sufficed to create an emperor, a palace conspiracy was enough to fell the master whom they were supposed to worship as a god. By the time of the Antonines, emperor worship had become no more than a pretext for revelry, a symbol of loyalty, a constitutional, stylistic phrase.

On the morrow of his accession Trajan proclaimed the divinity of his adoptive father Nerva (*divus*), but he was at pains to introduce a note of human probability into the transaction. Not only did he reserve the honours of apotheosis for the dead, but he saw therein the supreme reward which the State could bestow on its benefactors. He left it to his panegyrist to explain exactly the secular spirit in which he carried out this formality of general good administration; and he allowed Pliny the Younger to declare to the *Patres* that the most conclusive proof of the divinity of a dead Caesar lay in the excellence of his successor; '*Certissima divinitatis fides est bonus successor.*' In the formula of public prayer addressed to the gods for his life and his health he inserted the reservation that the gods should heed these prayers only if he governed the republic well and for the benefit of all: '*Si bene rem publicam et ex utilitate omnium rexerit.*'[95]

It would be wrong to undervalue the generous inspiration of such a policy. But at the same time it would be too ingenuous to imagine that it still provoked transports of enthusiasm. The days were gone when the conqueror of Actium, who had put an end to civil war and brought to Rome both peace and universal empire, was able to accept the homage and title of Augustus, at one bound place himself outside and above the condition of ordinary men, and raise himself, amid the enthusiasm of the masses and the song of the poets, to rank among the gods. The days were gone when popular credulity followed the march of the god Caesar across the firmament like the path of a comet in the Roman sky; the days when everyone from the humblest citizen to the princely heir attributed to the auspices of his son Tiberius the power to inspire the plans of generals and to guarantee their irresistible success. In much that way today a Japanese admiral can attribute to the spirit of his Mikado the victory of Tsushima. But in Rome the person and the history of the princeps had descended again to earth. If force of habit or the exigencies of ceremonial still led humble subjects to invoke the 'divine house' and the 'celestial decisions' of the emperor, the majority were perfectly aware that there was no longer an imperial 'house' properly so called; and in their gratitude the most truthful simply praised Caesar's indefatigable solicitude for the interests of humanity. In the same way, the emperors themselves, sovereign servants of the State, were conscious of ascending the throne as a last and final promotion.

Trajan made no effort to surround his acts with a supernatural halo, but boasted all the more of his achievement in overcoming the Germani before his accession, at a time when none could yet call him the son of a god: *'necdum de filius [erat]!'*[96] His *Panegyric* is worth reading: on every page the monarchy he had just inaugurated is depicted as the best of republics. While preserving the terminology of preceding reigns, a new regime had come into being in which for the first time, according to Tacitus, liberty and imperial rule were in harmony.[97] But by a fatal compensation it was also a time in which the imperial religion, at least in Rome and the neighbourhood of the Senate, was to lose its transcendence and to become secularized. In spite of a deliberate return to enlightened despotism, neither the jesting familiarity of Hadrian nor the self-effacement of Antoninus Pius nor the stoic resignation of Marcus Aurelius to the designs of Providence had power to rekindle in men's hearts the emotion which the cult of the emperor had ceased to evoke.

## 6. *The Progress of Oriental Mysticism*

Faith, however, had not entirely disappeared from Rome. Far from it. It had not even diminished. In proportion as the emptiness of an education which lacked every element of reason and reality had impoverished and disarmed men's intelligence, faith had extended its domain and increased in intensity. Roman faith had merely changed its object and direction. It had turned away from the official polytheism and taken refuge in the 'chapels' now formed by philosophic sects and by the brotherhoods that celebrated the mysteries of Oriental gods. Here believers could at last find an answer to their questionings and a truce to their anxieties; here were at once an explanation of the world, rules of conduct, release from evil and from death. Thus in the second century we observe the paradox that Rome has begun to possess a religious life, in the sense in which we understand the word today, at the very moment when her State religion had ceased to live in men's consciences.

This transformation of such infinite consequence had been long preparing. It was the product of Hellenistic influences to which Rome had been unconsciously subjected for two centuries, under which oriental revelation and Greek philosophy had interpenetrated each other and ended by fusing into one. At the period we are studying, the philosophies banished from the chairs had assumed the semblance and the force of religion for the teachers who became directors of men's consciences and for the disciples whose actions and ways of life they controlled, dictating even the cut of their beard and of their clothes. Even, if, like Epicureanism, these philosophies denied a future life and banished the immortals to the inaction of an intermediate world, they nevertheless proclaimed themselves saviours from death and its terrors. At the pious feats of their adherents the 'founders' were the 'heroes', and the same hymns and sacrifices were prescribed as for the ceremonies of the gods.[98] Whether the preachers were Greeks from Athens or Romans speaking and writing Greek, they could not conceal the fact that the ultimate foundations of their dialectic were oriental speculations. Joseph Bidez has demonstrated all that Stoicism owes not only to the Semites who spread it but also to the beliefs of Semitism;[99] and he is convinced that the Neo-Pythagoreanism professed by Nigidius Figulus at Rome was profoundly modified by Alexandrine thought.[100] On the other hand, the resemblances which Franz Cumont has noted between cults so diverse in origin as those of Cybele and of Attis, of Mithra and the Baalim, of the Dea Syra, of Isis and Serapis, are too numerous and too striking not to reveal the effects of a common influence. Whether they came from Anatolia or Iran, from Syria or from Egypt, whether they were male or female, whether they were worshipped with innocent or bloody rites, the 'oriental' divinities whom we meet in the Roman Empire present identical features and conceptions which overlap and seem even to interchange. These are deities who, far from being impassive, suffer, die, and rise from the dead; gods whose myths embrace the cosmos and comprehend its secrets; gods whose astral fatherland dominates all earthly fatherlands and who assure to their initiates alone, but to them without distinction of nationality or status, a protection proportionate to the purity of each.

We should seek in vain to find, behind the analogies which bind these religions together, an indefinable pre-established harmony between the oriental minds which gave them birth. The truth is that none of these 'oriental' religions reached Italian soil without a long sojourn in Greece or in some Graecized country. Hellenism imported them after the conquests of Alexander and they crossed the Greek frontiers only after having been relieved of their coarser baggage and laden instead with Greece's cosmopolitan philosophy. Hence the uniform colour with which they all are tinged, the adaptation of their individual myths to the idea of a universal divinity by a symbolism whose elements scarcely vary. Hence also their common subordination to an astrology which triumphs as obviously in the beamed diadem of Attis at Ostia as in the majority of our *mithraea* and on the ceiling of the sanctuary of Bel at Palmyra, where the eagle of Zeus spreads his wings within a circle of zodiacal constellations. Hence, above all, the ease with which the Romans were converted to the gods of the East, not only because the Orient was rich and populous but because the Hellenistic civilization in which Rome was steeped had moulded to one pattern cults derived from every quarter of the East – moulded them as it were in its own image and under the pressure of its own spiritual instincts.

In the second century of our era these cults were in process of submerging the city. The cults of Anatolia had been naturalized in Rome by Claudius' decree which reformed the liturgy of Cybele and of Attis.[101] The Egyptian cults, banished by Tiberius, were publicly welcomed back by Caligula; and the Temple of Isis in Rome which was destroyed by fire in A.D. 80 was rebuilt by Domitian with a luxury still testified to by the obelisks that remain standing in the Temple of Minerva or nearby in front of the Pantheon, and by the colossal statues of the Nile and of the Tiber which are now divided between the museums of the Louvre and the Vatican.[102] From the middle of the second century, Hadad and his consort Atargatis possessed a temple at Rome, which Paul Gauckler rediscovered in 1907.[103] It was situated on the right bank of the Tiber on the Janiculum below the Lucus Furrinae. Atargatis, or the Dea Syra, was the only deity to whom Nero, denier of all other gods, deigned to render homage.[104] Finally, it is certain that in Flavian times sanctuaries of Mithra had been established at Rome as at Capua.[105]

The numerous colleges devoted to these heterogeneous gods at

Rome not only coexisted without friction but collaborated in their recruiting campaigns. There was in fact more affinity and mutual understanding between these diverse religions than rivalry. One and all were served by priests jealously segregated from the crowd of the profane; their doctrine was based on revelation, and their prestige on the singularity of their costume and manner of life. One and all imposed preliminary initiation on their followers and periodical recourse to a more or less ascetic regimen; each, after its own fashion, indulged in the same astrological and henotheistic speculations and held out to believers the same messages of hope.[106]

Romans who had not been seduced by these exotic cults suspected and hated them. Juvenal, for instance, who could not repress his wrath to see the Orontes pour her muddy floods of superstition into the Tiber,[107] hit out with might and main against them all, without distinction. While Tiberius seized on the pretext of a case of adultery which had been abetted by some priests of Isis, to expel the lot,[108] the satirist raged indiscriminately against all oriental priests, charging them with roguery and charlatanism: Chaldean, Commagenian, Phrygian, or priest of Isis, 'who with his linen-clad and shaven crew runs through the streets under the mask of Anubis and mocks at the weeping of the people'.[109] Juvenal never wearies of exposing the shameless exploitation they practise, selling the indulgence of their god to frail female sinners 'bribed no doubt by a fat goose and a slice of sacrificial cake', or promising on the strength of their prophetic gifts and powers of divination 'a youthful lover or a big bequest from some rich and childless man'.[110] He declaims against their obscenity, attacking 'the chorus of the frantic Bellona and the Mother of the Gods, attended by a giant eunuch to whom his obscene inferiors must do reverence';[111] and 'the mysteries of Bona Dea, the Good Goddess, when the flute stirs the loins and the Maenads of Priapus sweep along, frenzied alike by the horn blowing and the wine, whirling their locks and howling. What foul longings burn within their breasts! What cries they utter as the passion beats within!'[112] He holds his sides with laughter at sight of the penances and self-mortifications to which the male and female devotees submit with sombre fanaticism: the woman 'who in winter will go down to the river of a morning, break the ice, and plunge three times into the Tiber'; then 'naked and shivering she will creep on bleeding knees right across the field of Tarquin the Proud'; and the other who 'at the command of White Io will journey to the confines of Egypt and fetch water from hot Meroe with which to sprinkle the Temple of Isis'.[113]

Juvenal's savage and inexhaustible anger need not surprise us. He expresses with all the force of his genius the natural reaction of the 'ancient Roman', hater alike of novelty and of the foreigner, to whom emotion and enthusiasm were a degradation, and who would gladly have disciplined the outpourings of faith by such ordinances as governed a civil or military parade. At this distance of time his prejudices necessarily appear to us gravely unjust, first, because he traced to the oriental religions alone superstitions whose origin goes back to prehistoric times long before Rome was invaded by the Orient, and in whose development oriental religion had no part; secondly, because he was so blinded by his loathing for them that he completely ignored the moral progress which – despite their excesses and their aberrations – they achieved by the sheer force of their fervour and sincerity.

It cannot be denied that their astrology brought renewed vitality to divination, but divination had always been practised in Rome. Divination was the natural offspring of a polytheism which from the days of Homer on had conceived even Jupiter as enslaved by the decrees of Fate; it was inextricably bound up with the taking of the auspices and the work of the haruspex which was performed in the name of Rome. The best minds of the second century, indifferent or hostile to foreign religions, had recourse to divination without embarrassment or scepticism, and the public authorities attached so much importance to it that they prosecuted unauthorized diviners. When Juvenal therefore makes mock of the Chaldean adepts who trembled with fear to learn of the conjunctions of Saturn, and of the sick woman 'who if she be ill in bed deems no hour so suitable for taking food as that prescribed to her by Petosiris',[114] he was deliberately turning his blind eye to the fact that in every stratum of Roman society the impious and the lukewarm were as much a prey to superstition and taboo as the pious whom he despised.

The upstart freedman Trimalchio sets his guests to dine round a table whose centre-piece represents the zodiac. He boasts to them that he was born under 'the sign of Cancer, the Crab', a sign so favourable that he needs only to stand firm on his two feet 'to possess property on land and sea'. Then he listens open-mouthed to tales of vampires and were-wolves, and finally, when he hears the cock crow in the midst of his midnight boozing, he trembles at the evil omen.[115] We find examples no less significant occurring higher in the social scale. In spite of discreet reserve and a few shafts of fugitive irony, Tacitus does not venture formally to deny the truth of the 'prodigies' which he records as scrupulously as did his predecessors, and he confesses that he dare not omit or treat as fables 'facts established by tradition'.[116] Most of his peers and contemporaries were harassed by the same preoccupations. Suetonius had a dream which upset him to such a point that he feared he was already losing a case in which he was engaged.[117] Regulus, the odious rival of Pliny the Younger at the bar, made use of horoscopes and the *haruspex* to increase his reputation and obtain legacies by undue influence.[118] As for Pliny himself, he was inclined to reject the puerilities of dream interpretation, quoting Homer to hold that:[119]

> *Without a sign, his sword the brave man draws,*
> *And asks no omen but his country's cause.*

At the same time he did not hesitate to write to the consul Licinius Sura, who to his fame as a warrior added the reputation of being a storehouse of science, asking what he ought to think about ghosts and apparitions, and minutely detailing a series of experiences which had led him hitherto to incline to believe in them.[120] Pliny's letters on this subject ought to put us on our guard against Juvenal's passionate attacks. Reading this tissue of childish credulity, we are suddenly filled with tolerance toward the Stoic attempt at least to legitimatize divination by assuming the immanent action of Providence, and toward the occultism and magic mongering which the oriental religions at least employed for the uplift of souls.

It is useless to attempt to deny that the oriental religions were superior to the more-dead-than-alive theology which they supplanted. Some of their rites no doubt, like the bull sacrifice of the Great Mother or the procession of the torn-up pine which accompanied the mutilation of Attis, have something both barbarous and indecent in them, 'like a whiff from slaughter-house or latrine'.[121] Nevertheless, the religions which practised them exercised a tonic and beneficent influence on individuals and lifted them to a higher plane. To convince ourselves that this was so we have only to consult the vigorous analysis made by Franz Cumont.[122] These oriental religions dazzled the faithful by the splendour of their festivals and the pomp of their processions; they charmed them by their languorous singing and their enervating music. Whether through the nervous tension induced by their prolonged mortifications and rapt contemplation, or through the excitement of dancing and the consumption of fermented drinks after long abstinence, they succeeded in provoking a state of ecstasy in which 'the soul delivered from the bondage of the body and set free from pain could lose itself in exaltation'. Cumont justly remarks that in mysticism it is easy to slip 'from the sublime to the depraved'. It is no less true, however, that under the combined influence of Greek thought and Roman discipline, oriental mysticism had been able to extract an ideal from the depravity of these naturalistic cults, and to rise toward those spiritual regions where perfect knowledge, flawless virtue, and victory over sin and pain and death appeared as the glorious fulfilment of divine promises. False as was the science incorporated in the 'gnosis' of each cult, it both stimulated and quenched the initiates' thirst for knowledge. The physical ablutions and lustrations which religion prescribed went hand in hand with the inward spiritual peace of renunciation and self-denial. Above all, by teaching that liturgy was nothing without personal piety, these religions acquired the right to prophesy for their disciples a future state of eternal happiness such as their ever-reborn deities enjoyed in the celestial sphere. Before long they set in motion a spiritual revival which drew to itself rebellious consciences.

On the one hand the best spirits in the Urbs, including those furthest removed from oriental mysticism, were vaguely conscious

that divine favours ought to be deserved rather than merely
snatched. While Juvenal vents his wrath, he cherishes the serene
conviction that 'the gods themselves know what is good for us
and what will be serviceable for our state; in place of what is
pleasing, they will give us what is best. Man is dearer to them than
he is to himself.'[123] Persius at the beginning of the second century
has no doubt but that the gods – whom he does not further specify
– ask of him in the first instance nothing save 'a soul where secular
and sacred law reign harmoniously side by side, a spirit purified
to its inmost recess, a heart filled with upright generosity'.[124] And
Statius under Domitian implicitly formulates a confession of faith
in the exclusive value of personal religion:

Poor as I am, how should I acquit myself towards the gods? I could not,
though Umbria should exhaust for me the richness of her valleys, though
the meadows of Clitumnus should furnish me with oxen white as snow;
yet the gods have frequently accepted the offering which I brought – a
handful of salt and flour on a little mound of grass.[125]

The poets, interpreting the minds of their countrymen, thus
conceived the divine favour as the reward of human virtue.

On the other hand, in the language of the second century the
Latin word *salus*, which originally had only the prosaic connotation
of physical health, began to take on a moral and eschatological
meaning implying the liberation of the soul on earth and its
eternal happiness in heaven; gradually the transcendental idea of
'salvation' spread from the oriental cults to all the truly religious
foundations of Roman antiquity. It animated the religion suddenly
founded under Hadrian in honour of Antinoüs, the handsome
Bithynian slave who had sacrificed his life in Egypt to save the
emperor's.[126] It gathered round it the brotherhoods in which the
tree-bearers of Cybele and Attis met under Antoninus Pius, notably
at Bovillae, and the simple funeral colleges which from the reign
of Hadrian on united in one family the plebeians and the slaves of
Lanuvium under the double invocation of Diana of the Dead and
of the saviour Antinoüs.[127] So much prestige had this idea of
salvation acquired that both the brotherhoods and the funeral
colleges took a name which of itself voiced this great hope:

'*collegium salutare*'. The emperors themselves did not escape the spell. The coins and statues of the second century show them eager to be assimilated to the Olympians – Augustus to Mars, progenitor of the founders of the Urbs, Augusta to Venus, common mother of the Caesars and the Roman people – or, again, to re-immerse their newfound holiness in the sacred flood of ancient Latin legend.[128] Nevertheless, they no longer believed that the apotheosis officially decreed them by the Senate would suffice to ensure them the eternal personal salvation which they craved like other men. After Hadrian had erected statues, temples, and towns to Antinoüs, and before Commodus had entered the congregation of Mithra, Antoninus Pius bore witness by the transparent language of the reverse of his coins that Faustina the Elder, the wife he had lost at the beginning of his reign and whose temple still rears its symbolic form above the Forum, had been able to mount to heaven only in the chariot of Cybele, by the favour of the Mother of the Gods, the Lady of Salvation (*Mater deum salutaris*).[129]

Thus, thanks to the collaboration of oriental mysticism and of Roman wisdom, new and fruitful faiths were born and flourished on the ruins of the traditional pantheon. In the bosom of outworn paganism a creed arose, or rather the sketch of a creed, which represented a genuine redemption of men by the double payment of their merit and of divine assistance. Thus by a coincidence, in which the agnostic sees only a function of historical determinism, but in which believers like Bossuet recognize the intervention of the Divine Providence they adore, Rome created an atmosphere favourable to Christianity at a moment when the Christian Church was sufficiently firmly established to excavate its first collective cemeteries, to show the example and lift up the prayers of its faithful as high even as the steps of the imperial throne.

## 7. The Advent of Christianity

Although Statius and Martial and Juvenal may perhaps not have suspected the fact; and though Pliny the Younger – who in Bithynia had himself been up against the Christians of his province[130] – lets fall no hint of its existence in his *Letters*; though Tacitus and Suetonius speak of it only from hearsay, the former in abusive language which excludes his having had any first-hand knowledge, the second with confusions which prove both the lacunae in his information and his own lack of insight[131] – it is nevertheless beyond all doubt that 'Christianity' in Rome goes back to the reign of Claudius (41–54), and that under Nero it had become so widespread that the emperor was able to throw the blame for the great fire of 64 on to the Christians. Using this as a pretext, he inflicted on them atrocious refinements of torture, the first of the persecutions which assailed without destroying the Church of Christ.[132] It is evident that its subterranean growth had progressed with astounding rapidity. This was perhaps due less to the importance of the Urbs in the world than to the existence in Rome of the Jewish colony which the goodwill of Julius Caesar had acclimatized there.[133] From the beginning of the empire members of the Jewish colony had proved so troublesome that in A.D. 19 Tiberius thought it necessary to take severe measures against them, and so numerous that he was able to ship off 4,000 Jews at one swoop to Sardinia.[134] It was through the Jewish colony that the first Christians coming from Jerusalem penetrated into Rome, breaking up the unity of the colony and ranging against each other the upholders of the ancient Mosaic law and the adherents of the new faith.

The Jewish religion had cast its spell over a number of Romans, attracted by its monotheism and the beauty of the Decalogue. The religion of the Christians, which dispensed the same light but offered in addition a splendid message of redemption and brotherhood, was not behind in substituting its own proselytizing. Seen from the outside and from a little distance, the two religions were at first easily confused with each other, and it is possible, for instance, that the invectives which Juvenal hurls at the Jews were really directed at the Christians whom he had not at this date learned to distinguish from them.[135] They also were obedient to the commandments of their God, and might well pass in the eyes of a superficial observer for being simply 'attached to Jewish customs'.[136] But after the destruction of the Temple of Jerusalem in A.D. 70, and under the early Antonines, 'the Church' inevitably began to be distinguished from 'the Synagogue'; and the Church's teaching, which made no distinction of race, soon began to supplant that of the Jews.

We have, naturally, no means of estimating the number of conversions which Christianity effected in those days in Rome, but it would be wrong to suppose that they were confined to the lower strata of the population. The Epistles of Saint Paul, saluting those of the brethren who are of the household of Caesar (*in domo Caesaris*), prove directly that the apostle had recruited some of his followers from among the retainers of the emperor, among those slaves and freedmen who, under a specious appearance of humility, included the most powerful servants of the empire.[137] A few years later a number of mutually corroborative indications point to the probability that the Christian Church was extending its conquests to the directing classes themselves. Tacitus tells us that Pomponia Graecina, wife of the consul Aulus Plautius, conqueror of the Britons, who lived under Nero and died under the Flavians, was suspected of belonging 'to a religion criminally foreign', because of her austerity, her sadness, and her mourning garments.[138] Dio Cassius and Suetonius both record that Domitian successively accused of the crime of atheism M. Acilius Glabrio, consul in 91, who was put to death;[139] then a pair of his own cousins-german, Flavius Clemens, consul in 95, who was condemned to death, and Flavia Domitilla who was banished to the island of Pandataria.[140] Finally Tacitus notes in his *Histories* that Vespasian's own brother, Flavius Sabinus, who was prefect of the Urbs when Nero turned the Christians into living torches to light his gardens, appeared toward the end of his life to be obsessed by the horror of the blood shed then.[141]

It is true that none of these texts formally names as Christians the illustrious personages of whom their authors speak, but it is permissible to wonder, with M. Emile Mâle, whether Flavius Sabinus in his humanity and his obsession may not have been won over to the new religion by the courage of the early Roman martyrs;[142] and it is still more probable that we may detect an allusion to Christianity both in the forbidden 'alien superstition' with which Pomponia Graecina was reproached and in the accusation of atheism brought against believers whose faith was bound to deter them from performing their duties toward the false gods of the official polytheism. In the case of Flavius Clemens and of Flavia Domitilla in particular, this probability is increased by the fact that their niece, called Flavia Domitilla after her aunt, was, according to the testimony of Eusebius, interned in the island of Pontia for the crime of being a Christian.[143]

Even if we adopt the calculations of certain radical critics and place in the second third of the second century the catacomb of Priscilla, where the memory of the Acilii Glabriones was preserved; the crypt of Lucina where a later Greek inscription had been discovered celebrating the name of a certain Pomponius Graecinus; and the tomb of Domitilla whose name irresistibly calls up memories of the victims of Domitian – we cannot get rid of the strong presumption, created by the convergent evidences to which De Rossi called attention, that there were notorious conversions to Christianity as early as the end of the first century.[144] It is proved beyond possibility of doubt that the retainers of many of the great men of Hadrian's world (117–138) had with the encouragement of their masters answered the call of Christ and swollen the ranks of his 'Roman Church'.

No doubt the Christians of Rome still formed a small minority of the population; a minority always exposed to the prejudice of the masses and the hostility of the authorities, not only because they abstained from taking part in the traditional practices, but even because, entranced by the vision of their celestial homes and oblivious of the city of their birth, they answered questions about their origin with the word 'Christian', and thus acquired the reputation of being deserters and public enemies.[145] But the penalties to which their refusal to compromise exposed them – and to which Bishop Telesphorus succumbed under Hadrian – were too intermittent to exterminate them, on the one hand, and on the other were too heroically endured not to command the admiration of their enemies. What contributed henceforth to increase their progress was not so much the series of their *Apologiae*, inaugurated by Quadratus in the reign of Hadrian, nor yet the heroism of their martyrs, as the power of their Credo and the Christian gentleness in which their life was steeped. Even those who dwell most on the analogies between Christianity and the pagan mysteries are at one in agreeing that Christianity towered above them all.[146] And to what a height! To the polytheism of the Graeco-Roman gods, reduced to mere symbols as they were, to the vague and diffuse monotheism of the oriental religions, the Christian opposed his doctrine of the One God, the Father Omnipotent. In contrast to the various idolatries, spiritualized though they might be by the divine ether and the eternal stars, he offered a worship solely of the spirit, purified of astrological aberration, of bleeding sacrifice, of mystery-ridden initiation; for all these he substituted a baptism of pure water, prayer, and a frugal common meal. Like the pagan religionists he gave answer in the name of his sacred books to every question about the origin of things and the destiny of man; but the Redeemer whose 'good tidings' he brought, instead of being an elusive and ambiguous figure lost in a mythological labyrinth, was revealed in miraculous reality in the earthly life of Jesus, the Son of God. Like the pagan religionists, the Christian guaranteed salvation after death, but instead of engulfing the believer in the silence of a starry eternity, he restored him to life in a personal resurrection foreshadowed by the resurrection of Christ himself. Like the pagan, the Christian laid down a rule of life for all believers, but while not excluding contemplation or asceticism or ecstasy, he did not abuse them and condensed his moral teaching into man's love of his neighbour which the gospels inculcated.

Herein lay beyond question the strongest attraction of the new religion. The Christians were brothers and called each other so. Their meetings were often called *agape*, which in Greek means 'love'. They constantly assisted each other 'without parade or patronage'. An unceasing interchange 'of counsel, of information, and of practical help' took place between one Christian and the other and, as Duchesne has said, 'all this was alive and active in a fashion wholly different from that of the pagan brotherhoods'. Many observers in those days were constrained to say of the Christians: 'How simple and pure is their religion! What confidence they have in their God and His promise! How they love one another and how happy they are together!'[147]

In the second century this evangelic happiness existed only in small isolated groups among the crowds of the overgrown city; but it was contagious and it had begun, unknown to the majority, to transform thousands of lives. This is a point of view which must not be overlooked if we are to understand the life of Rome at this epoch. The Church is still almost invisible, but she is there; she is at work; and if her beneficent doings are not seen in the full light of day, we must nevertheless take heed of the salutary influence she was widely and unobtrusively exerting. In secret she worked out a remedy for the gravest of the ills that were undermining the civilization of Rome. In the name of a new ideal she requickened ancient lost or half-forgotten virtues: the dignity and courage of the individual, the cohesion of the family, the value of moral truths in the conduct of adults and in the education of the young; and, above all, she imbued all relations between man and man with a humanity which the stern societies of ancient days had never known before. In this Rome whose outward grandeur ill concealed the internal distintegration which was in the long run to undermine her power and dissipate her wealth, what most strikes the historian of the time of the Antonines is the swarming of her crowds at the feet of the imperial majesty, her fever for riches, the mantle of luxury which cloaks her wretchedness, the prodigality of those spectacles which pander to her sloth and stir up her lowest instincts, the inanity of the intellectual gymnastics in which her scholars waste their time, and the frenzy of carnal indulgence in which others stupefy themselves. But we must not let either the dazzling splendour or the sombre shadow hide the little flame – pale and flickering though it be – which trembled in the souls of the elect, like a faint dawn.

# PART TWO

*

## THE DAY'S ROUTINE

# VI

## THE MORNING

*

In this Rome of the earlier Antonines, enormous, cosmopolitan, and heterogeneous, where the contrasts are both so numerous and so violent, it is nevertheless possible to get a fairly clear idea of the ordinary daily routine of an 'average Roman'. Obviously, in attempting such a reconstruction, a large degree of imagination and arbitrary hypothesis must always come in. But making allowance for varieties of profession and for individual idiosyncrasies created by the wealth of the multi-millionaires at the top and by the misery of the poor at the bottom of the social scale, there remains a minimum of cares, occupations, and leisure which with few variations composed the daily life of every inhabitant of the Urbs. It is all the easier to follow the development and mark the most important moments of the day, in that the general conformity of manners was not enforced like ours by the rigidity of a fixed time-table.

## 1. *The Days and Hours of the Roman Calendar*

After the Julian reform of 46 B.C. the Roman calendar – like ours, which is its offspring – was governed by the length of the earth's circuit of the sun.[1] The twelve months of our year retain the sequence, the length, the names which were assigned them by the genius of Caesar and the prudence of Augustus. From the beginning of the empire each of them, including February in both ordinary years and leap year, contained the number of days to which we are still accustomed. Astrology, moreover, had introduced, in addition to the old official division of the months by the Calends (first of each month), the Nones (the fifth or seventh) and the Ides (the thirteenth or fifteenth),[2] the division into weeks of seven days subordinate to the seven planets whose movements were believed to regulate the universe.[3] By the beginning of the third century this usage had become so firmly anchored in the popular consciousness that Dio Cassius considered it specifically Roman.⁴ With only one minor modification – the substitution of the day of the Lord, *dies Dominica* (*dimanche*), for the day of the Sun, *dies solis* – it has in most countries of Latin speech survived both the decadence of the astrologers and the triumph of Christianity. Finally, each day of the seven was divided into twenty-four hours which were reckoned to begin, not, as with the Babylonians, at sunrise, nor, as among the Greeks, at sunset, but as is still the case with us, at midnight.⁵ This ends the analogies between time as the ancients counted it and as we do; the Latin 'hours', late intruders into the Roman day, though they bear the same name and were of the same number as ours, were in reality very different.

Both word and thing were an invention of the Greeks deriving from the process of mensuration.⁶ Toward the end of the fifth century B.C. they had learned to observe the stages performed by the sun in its march across the sky. The sundial of Meton, which enabled the Greeks to register these, consisted of a concave hemisphere of stone (πόλος), having a strictly horizontal brim, with a pointed metal stylus (γνώμων) rising in the centre. As soon as the sun entered the hollow of the hemisphere, the shadow of the stylus traced in a reverse direction the diurnal parallel of the sun. Four times a year, at the equinoxes and the solstices, the shadow movements thus obtained were marked by a line incised in the stone; and as the curve of the spring equinox coincided with that of the autumn equinox, three concentric circles were finally obtained, each of which was then divided into twelve equal parts. All that was further needed was to join the corresponding points on the three circles by twelve diverging lines to obtain the twelve hours (ὧραι, *horae*) which punctuated the year's course of the sun as faithfully recorded by the dial. Hence the dial derived its name 'hour counter' (ὡρολόγιον), preserved in the Latin *horologium* and in the French *horloge*. Following the example of Athens, the other Hellenic cities coveted the honour of possessing sundials, and their astronomers proved equal to the task of applying the principle to the position of each. The apparent path of the sun varied of course with the latitude of each place, and the length of the shadow cast by the stylus was consequently different in one city and another. At Alexandria it was only three-fifths of the height of the stylus, at Athens three-quarters; it was nearly nine-elevenths at Tarentum and reached eight-ninths at Rome. As many different sundials had to be constructed as there were different cities. The Romans were among the last to appreciate the need. And just as they felt no need to count the hours till two centuries after the Athenians, so they took another hundred years to learn to do it accurately.[7]

At the end of the fourth century B.C. they were still content to divide the day into two parts, before midday and after. Naturally the important thing was then to note the moment when the sun crossed the meridian. One of the consul's subordinates was told off to keep a look-out for it and to announce it to the people busy in the Forum, as well as to the lawyers who, if their pleadings were to be valid, must present themselves before the tribunal before midday. The herald's instructions were to make his announcement when he saw the sun 'between the *rostra* and the *graecostasis*' – which clearly proves that his functions were of relatively recent date. For there could be no mention of the *rostra* until the speaker's tribune in the Forum had been adorned with the beaks (*rostra*) of the ships captured from the Antiates by Duilius in 338 B.C.; nor could there have been a *graecostasis* intended for the reception of Greek envoys until the first Greek embassy had been received in Rome, which would appear to have been that sent by Demetrius Poliorcetes to the Senate about 306 B.C.[8]

By the time of the wars against Pyrrhus some slight progress had been made by dividing the two halves of the day into two parts: into the early morning and forenoon (*mane* and *ante meridiem*) on the one hand; and on the other, into afternoon and evening (*de meridie* and *suprema*).[9] But it was not until the beginning of the First Punic War in 264 B.C. that the 'hours' and the *horologium* of the Greeks were introduced into the city.[10] One of the consuls of that year, M. Valerius Messalla, had brought back with other booty from Sicily the sundial of Catana and set it up as it was on the *comitium*, where for more than three generations the lines engraved on its πόλος for another latitude continued to supply the Romans with an artificial time. In spite of the assertion of Pliny the Elder that they blindly obeyed it for ninety-nine years,[11] we must be permitted to believe that they persisted in ignorance rather than in wilful error. They probably took no interest at all in Messalla's sundial and continued to govern their day in the old happy-go-lucky manner by the apparent course of the sun above the monuments of their public places, as if the *horologium* had never existed.

In the year 164 B.C., however, three years after Pydna, the enlightened generosity of the censor Q. Marcius Philippus endowed the Romans with their first *horologium* accurately calculated for their own latitude and hence reasonably accurate; and if we are to believe Pliny the Naturalist they welcomed the gift as a coveted treasure.[12] For thirty years their legions had fought in Greek territory, almost without ceasing, first against Philip V, then against the Aetolians and Antiochus of Syria, finally against Perseus; and they had gradually become familiar with the possessions of their enemies. At times, perhaps, they had toyed, without undue success, with a system of hours a trifle less erratic and uncertain than the one that had hitherto sufficed them. So they were pleased to have a sundial brought home and fitted up in their own country. Not to be behind Q. Marcius Philippus, the censors who succeeded him in office, P. Cornelius Scipio Nasica and M. Popilius Laenas, completed the work he had begun by flanking his sundial with a water-clock to supplement its services at night or on days of fog.[13]

It was more than a hundred years since the Alexandrians had equipped themselves with a ὑδρίον ὡροσκοπεῖον which Ctesibius had evolved from the ancient κλεψύδρα to remedy the inevitable failure of the *horologium* proper. This became known in Latin as the *horologium ex aqua*. Nothing could well have been simpler than the mechanism of the water-clock. Let us imagine the *clepsydra* – that is, a transparent vessel of water with a regular intake – placed near a sundial. When the *gnomon* casts its shadow on a curve of the *polos*, we need only to mark the level of the water at that moment by incising a line on the outside of the water-container. When the shadow reaches the next curve of the *polos*, we make another mark, and so on until the twelve levels registered correspond to the twelve hours of the day chosen for our experiment. This being granted, it is clear that if we give our *clepsydra* a cylindri-

cal form we can engrave on it from January to December twelve
vertical lines corresponding to the twelve months of the year. On
each of these verticals we then mark the twelve hourly levels registered for the same day of each month; and finally, by joining
with a curved line the hour signs which punctuate the monthly
verticals, we can read off at once from the level of the water above
the line of the current month the hour which the needle of the
sundial would have registered at that moment – if the sun had
happened to be shining.

Once the sundial had lent its services for grading the water-
clock, there was no further need to have recourse to the dial, and
it was a simple matter to extend the readings to serve for the night
hours. It is easy to imagine that the use of *clepsydrae* soon became
general in Rome. The principle of the sundial was still sometimes
applied on a grandiose scale: in 10 B.C., for instance, Augustus
erected in the Campus Martius the great obelisk of Montecitorio
to serve as the giant gnomon whose shadow would mark the daylight hours on lines of bronze inlaid into the marble pavement
below.[14] Sometimes, on the other hand, it was applied to more and
more minute devices which eventually evolved into miniature
*solaria* or pocket dials that served the same purpose as our watches.
Pocket sundials have been discovered at Forbach and Aquileia
which scarcely exceed three centimetres in diameter. But at the
same time the public buildings of the Urbs and even the private
houses of the wealthy were tending to be equipped with more and
more highly perfected water-clocks. From the time of Augustus,
*clepsydrarii* and *organarii* rivalled each other in ingenuity of construction and elaboration of accessories. As our clocks have their striking
apparatus and our public clocks their peal of bells, the *horologia ex
aqua* which Vitruvius describes were fitted with automatic floats
which 'struck the hour' by tossing pebbles or eggs into the air or
by emitting warning whistles.[15]

The fashion in such things grew and spread during the second
century of our era. In the time of Trajan a water-clock was as much
a visible symbol of its owner's distinction and social status as a
piano is for certain strata of our middle classes today. In Petronius'
romance, which represents Trimalchio as 'a highly fashionable

person' (*lautissimus homo*), his confederates frankly justified the admiration they felt for him: 'Has he not got a clock in his dining-room? And a uniformed trumpeter to keep telling him how much of his life is lost and gone?'[16] Trimalchio, moreover, has stipulated in his will that his heirs shall build him a sumptuous tomb, with a frontage of one hundred feet and a depth of two hundred, 'and let there be a sundial in the middle, so that anyone who looks at the time will read my name whether he likes it or not'.[17] This quaint appeal to posterity would have no point if Trimalchio's contemporaries had not been accustomed frequently to consult their clocks. It is clear that the hourly division of the day had become part and parcel of their everyday routine. On the other hand, it would be an error to suppose that the Romans lived with their eyes glued to the needles of their sundials or the floats of their water-clocks as ours are to the hands of our watches. They were not yet like us the slaves of time, for they still lacked both perseverance and punctuality.

In the first place, we may be very sure that the agreement between the sundial and the water-clock was still far from being exact. The gnomon of the sundial was correct only in the degree in which its maker had adapted it to the latitude of the place where it stood; and as for the water-clock, whose measurements lumped all the days of one month together though the sun would have lighted each differently, its makers could never prevent certain inaccuracies in its floats creeping in to falsify the corrections they had been able to make in the readings of the gnomon. If anyone asked the time, he was certain to receive several different answers at once, for, as Seneca asserts, it was impossible at Rome to be sure of the exact hour; and it was easier to get the philosophers to agree among themselves than the clocks: '*horam non possum certam tibi dicere: facilius inter philosophos quam inter horologia convenit.*'[18] Time at Rome was never more than approximate.

Time was perpetually fluid, or, if the expression is preferred, contradictory. The hours were originally calculated for daytime; and even when the water-clock made it possible to calculate the night hours by a simple reversal of the data which the sundial had furnished, it did not succeed in unifying them. The *horologia ex aqua* was built to reset itself, that is, to empty itself afresh for night and day. Hence a first discrepancy between the civil day, whose twenty-four hours were reckoned from midnight to midnight, and the twenty-four hours of the natural day which was officially divided into two groups of twelve hours each, twelve of the day and twelve of the night.[19]

Nor was this all. While our hours each comprise a uniform sixty minutes of sixty seconds each, and each hour is definitely separated from the succeeding by the fugitive moment at which it strikes, the lack of division inside the Roman hour meant that each of them stretched over the whole interval of time between the preceding hour and the hour which followed; and this hour interval instead of being of fixed duration was perpetually elastic, now longer, now shorter, from one end of the year to the other, and on any given day the duration of the day hours was opposed to the length of the night hours. For the twelve hours of the day were necessarily divided by the gnomon between the rising and the setting of the sun, while the hours of the night were conversely divided between sunset and sunrise; in proportion as the day hours were longer at one season, the night hours were, of course, shorter, and vice versa. The day hours and night hours were equal only twice a year: at the vernal and autumnal equinoxes. They lengthened and shortened in inverse ratio till the summer and winter solstices, when the discrepancy between them reached its maximum. At the winter solstice (December 22), when the day had only 8 hours, 54 minutes of sunlight against a night of 15 hours, 6 minutes, the day hour shrank to $44\frac{4}{5}$ minutes while in compensation the night hour lengthened to 1 hour, $15\frac{5}{9}$ minutes. At the summer solstice the position was exactly reversed; the night hour shrank to its minimum while the day hour reached its maximum.

Thus at the winter solstice the day hours were as follows:

| I. | Hora | prima | from | 7.33 | to | 8.17 a.m. |
|----|------|-------|------|------|-----|-----------|
| II. | „ | secunda | „ | 8.17 | „ | 9.02 „ |
| III. | „ | tertia | „ | 9.02 | „ | 9.46 „ |
| IV. | „ | quarta | „ | 9.46 | „ | 10.31 „ |
| V. | „ | quinta | „ | 10.31 | „ | 11.15 „ |

| | | | | | | |
|---|---|---|---|---|---|---|
| VI. | „ | sexta | „ | 11.15 | „ | 12.00 noon |
| VII. | „ | septima | „ | 12.00 | „ | 12.44 p.m. |
| VIII. | „ | octava | „ | 12.44 | „ | 1.29 „ |
| IX. | „ | nona | „ | 1.29 | „ | 2.13 „ |
| X. | „ | decima | „ | 2.13 | „ | 2.58 „ |
| XI. | „ | undecima | „ | 2.58 | „ | 3.42 „ |
| XII. | „ | duodecima | „ | 3.42 | „ | 4.27 „ |

At the summer solstice the day hours ran thus:

| | | | | | | |
|---|---|---|---|---|---|---|
| I. | Hora | prima | from | 4.27 | to | 5.42 a.m. |
| II. | „ | secunda | „ | 5.42 | „ | 6.58 „ |
| III. | „ | tertia | „ | 6.58 | „ | 8.13 „ |
| IV. | „ | quarta | „ | 8.13 | „ | 9.29 „ |
| V. | „ | quinta | „ | 9.29 | „ | 10.44 „ |
| VI. | „ | sexta | „ | 10.44 | „ | 12.00 noon |
| VII. | „ | septima | „ | 12.00 | „ | 1.15 p.m. |
| VIII. | „ | octava | „ | 1.15 | „ | 2.31 „ |
| IX. | „ | nona | „ | 2.31 | „ | 3.46 „ |
| X. | „ | decima | „ | 3.46 | „ | 5.02 „ |
| XI. | „ | undecima | „ | 5.02 | „ | 6.17 „ |
| XII. | „ | duodecima | „ | 6.17 | „ | 7.33 „ |

The night hours naturally reproduced in rigorous antithesis the equivalent fluctuations, with their maximum length at the winter solstice and their minimum at the summer solstice.

These simple facts had a profound influence on Roman life. For one thing, as the means of measuring the inconstant hours remained inadequate and empirical throughout antiquity, Roman life was never regulated with the mathematical precision which the above schedule, drawn up according to our methods, might suggest, and which tyrannizes over the employment of our time. Busy as life was in the Urbs, it continued to have an elasticity unknown to any modern capital. For another thing, as the length of the Roman day was indefinitely modified by the diversity of the seasons, life went through phases whose intensity varied with the dimensions of the daily hour, weaker in the sombre months, stronger when the fine and luminous days returned; which is another way of saying that even in the great swarming city, life remained rural in style and in pace.

## 2. The Roman Begins the Day

To begin with, Imperial Rome woke up as early as any country village – at dawn, if not before. Let us revert to an epigram of Martial's which I have already quoted, where the poet enumerates the causes of insomnia which in his day murdered sleep for the luckless city dweller. Before the sun was up, he was a martyr to the deafening din of streets and squares where the metal-worker's hammer blended with the bawling of the children at school: 'The laughter of the passing throng wakes me and Rome is at my bed's head. . . . Schoolmasters in the morning do not let you live; before daybreak, bakers; the hammers of the coppersmiths all day.'[20] To protect themselves against the clatter, the wealthy retired to the depths of their houses, isolated by the thickness of their walls and the garden shrubberies which shut them in. But even there they were assailed from within by the teams of slaves whose duty it was to clean the house. Day had scarcely broken when a crowd of servants, their eyes still swollen with sleep, were turned loose by the sound of a bell and flung themselves on the rooms, armed with an arsenal of buckets, of cloths (*mappae*), of ladders (*scalae*) to reach the ceilings, of poles (*perticae*) with sponges (*spongiae*) attached to the end, feather dusters, and brooms (*scopae*). The brooms were made of green palms or twigs of tamarisk, heather, and myrtle twisted together. The cleaners scattered sawdust over the floors; then they swept it off again with the accumulated dirt; they dashed with their sponges to attack the pillars and cornices; they cleaned, they scrubbed, they dusted with noisy fervour. If the master of the house was expecting an important guest, he would often rise himself to bring them into action and his imperious or fretful voice would pierce their hullabaloo, as, whip in hand, he shouted: 'Sweep the pavement! Polish up the pillars! Down with that dusty spider, web and all! One of you clean the flat silver, another the embossed vessels!'[21] Even if the master depended on a steward to carry out this supervision, he was none the less awakened by the racket of his servants, unless, like Pliny the Younger in his Laurentine villa, he had taken the precaution to interpose the silence of a corridor between his bedchamber and the commotion of the morning.[22]

In general, however, the Romans were early risers. In the ancient town the artificial light was so deplorable that the rich were as eager as the poor to profit by the light of day. Each man took the maxim of the elder Pliny as his motto – 'To live is to be awake: *profecto enim vita vigilia est.*'[23] Ordinarily no one lay in bed of a morning save the young roisterers or the drunkards who were forced to sleep off their overnight excesses.[24] Even some of these were up and about by noon, for 'the fifth hour', at which, according to Persius, they made up their minds to go out, normally finished about 11 a.m.[25] The 'late morning' when Horace betook himself in state to the Forum,[26] and which was a luxury Martial could allow himself only in his distant Bilbilis,[27] meant the third or fourth hour, which in summer ended at about 8 or 9 a.m.

The habit of getting up at dawn was so deeply ingrained that even if a person lay abed late he still woke before daybreak and took up the thread of his normal occupations in his bed by the flickering and indifferent light of the wick of tow and wax. From this light (*lucubrum*) came the words '*lucubratio*' and '*lucubrare*' which have given us the English '*lucubration*'.[28] From Cicero to Horace, from the two Plinys to Marcus Aurelius, distinguished Romans vied with each other in 'lucubrating' every winter; and the year round the Naturalist, having closed his night with his lucubrations, would wait upon Vespasian before daybreak, when the emperor likewise chose to transact business, in order to submit reports and open his master's correspondence.[29]

There was practically no interval between leaping out of bed and leaving the house. Getting up was a simple, speedy, instantaneous process. There is no denying that the bedchamber (*cubiculum*) had nothing seductive to tempt the occupant to linger. Its dimensions were habitually kept down to a minimum; its solid shutters when shut plunged the room into complete darkness, and when open flooded it with sun and rain or draughts. It was rarely adorned with works of art – Tiberius almost created a scandal by decorating his.[30] Normally it possessed no furniture but the couch (*cubile*) which gave it its name; possibly a chest (*arca*) in which materials and *denarii* could be stored; the chair on which Pliny the Younger would invite his friends and his secretaries to sit when they came to visit him and on which Martial would throw his cloak; and finally the chamber pot (*lasanum*) or the urinal (*scaphium*)[31] – the different models are minutely described in literature, ranging from vessels of common earthenware (*matella fictilis*) to others of silver set with precious stones.[32]

As for the bed – however sumptuous we like to picture its framework and its fittings – the comfort it offered was far from equalling its costliness. On a base of interwoven strips of webbing were placed a mattress (*torus*) and a bolster (*culcita, cervical*) whose stuffing (*tomentum*) was made of straw or reeds among the poor and among the rich of wool shorn from the Leuconian flocks in the valley of the Meuse, or even of swan's down.[33] But there was neither a proper mattress underneath nor sheets above. The *torus* was spread with two coverings (*tapetia*): on one (*stragulum*) the sleeper lay, the other he pulled over him (*operimentum*).[34] The bed was then spread with a counterpane (*lodix*) or a multicoloured damask quilt (*polymitum*).[35] Finally, at the foot of the bed, *ante torum* as the Romans put it, there lay a bedside mat (*toral*) which often rivalled the *lodices* in luxury.[36]

A *toral* on the pavement of the bedroom was almost obligatory. For the Roman, though he sometimes protected his legs by a sort of puttees (*fasciae*), wore nothing corresponding to our socks or stockings and went barefoot when he had taken off his sandals to go to bed. His normal footwear consisted either of *soleae*, a kind of sandal such as Capuchins wear, with the sole attached by ribbons over the instep, of *crepidae*, leather sandals held by a strap passing through their eyelets, of *calcei*, leather slippers with crossed leather laces, or of *caligae*, a type of military boot. On the other hand he was no more accustomed to undress completely before going to bed than the oriental of today. He merely laid aside his cloak, which he either threw on the bed as an extra covering or flung on the neighbouring chair.[37]

The ancients in fact distinguished two types of clothing: that which they put on first and wore intimately, and that which they flung around them afterwards. This is the difference between the Greek *endumata* and *epiblemata*; and similarly between the Latin *indumenta*, which were worn day and night, and the *amictus* which were assumed for part of the day only.[38]

First among the *indumenta* came the *subligaculum* or *licium*, not, as is sometimes supposed, a pair of drawers, but a simple loin cloth, usually made of linen and always knotted round the waist. In early days it was perhaps the only undergarment worn either by nobles or by labourers. Manual workers had no other. They flung their toga over it, as diehard conservatives continued to do even in the days of Caesar and Augustus, proclaiming thus their attachment to ancient custom.[39] By the second century none but the athletes were content to appear thus in public.[40] By this date even workmen had acquired the habit of putting on over the *licium* a *tunica* which became the most important of the *indumenta*.[41] The tunic was a kind of long shirt of linen or wool formed of two widths sewed together. It was slipped over the head and fastened round the body by a belt. It was draped to fall unequally, reaching only to the knees in front but somewhat below them behind.[42] Fashion had introduced some variations into a dress which had at first been uniform for both sexes and for every social rank. The woman's tunic tended to be longer than the man's and might even reach to the heel (*tunica talaris*).[43] The military tunic was shorter than the civilian's, the ordinary citizen's than that of the senator which was striped by a broad, vertical band of purple (*tunica laticlavia*). Under the empire the Romans not infrequently wore two tunics, one on top of the other; the under-tunic was called *subucula*, and the other, the tunic properly so called, was the *tunica exterior*. People sensitive to cold might wear two *subucalae* instead of one, or even go the length of wearing four tunics, as Augustus is supposed to have done, if we can believe the details which Suetonius supplies about the caprices of the emperor.[44] In winter as in summer the tunic had short sleeves, just covering the top of the arm, and it was not until the empire that this length could be exceeded with propriety.[45] This explains why even the slaves were allowed to wear warm gloves during the great cold,[46] and why it was necessary to have an *amictus* above the *indumenta*.

The specifically Roman *amictus* of the republic and the early empire was the cloak known as *toga*, a word related to the verb *tegere,* to cover. It consisted of a large circle of white woollen material 2·7 metres in diameter, which was distinguished by its circular shape from all the later varieties derived from the *himation* of the Greeks.[47] In a fine passage Léon Heuzey has recently pointed out the antagonistic attitudes of mind which found expression in these two different forms of dress.[48] With their natural love for rectilinear architecture, 'the Greeks retained the straight edges and the right angles which the cloth had originally had in the loom'; and they procured 'admirable effects from these elementary forms whose simplicity was pleasing to their taste and the clear-cut lines of their mind'. The Etruscans, on the other hand, and after them the Romans, who early adopted the arch as the basis of their building and who of choice made their temples on a circular plan, similarly rounded off the angles of their clothing. They thus achieved 'richer and more majestic adjustments, but a less straightforward and less really beautiful effect'. This toga of unalterable character and irreducible amplitude remained the national costume of the Romans throughout the heyday of the empire, the ceremonial dress inseparable from every manifestation of their civic activity. So unmistakable was it, that the Roman residents of Asia took off their togas in order to conceal their identity from Mithridates.[49]

The toga was a garment worthy of the masters of the world, flowing, solemn, eloquent, but with overmuch complication in its arrangement and a little too much emphatic affectation in the self-conscious tumult of its folds. It required real skill to drape it artfully. Adjusting the toga properly was such a business that even a magistrate as free from vanity as Cincinnatus could not hope to achieve success without some help, which this frugal hero demanded only of his wife Racilia.[50] It required unremitting attention if the balance of the toga was to be preserved in walking, in the heat of a discourse, or amid the jostlings of a crowd. The weight of it was an intolerable burden.[51] Laborious and frequent washings were necessary to preserve its immaculate whiteness, and repeated washing soon wore it threadbare and condemned it to be discarded.[52]

In vain the emperors signed decrees attempting to insist on the toga being worn:[53] Claudius decreed it obligatory for the tribunal,[54] Domitian for the theatre,[55] Commodus for the amphitheatre.[56] At the beginning of the second century at Rome everyone was trying to flee to the country where he could lay aside the toga for the *pallium*,[57] an imitation of the Greek *himation*, for the *lacerna*, which was a coloured *pallium*, or for the *paenula*, which was a *lacerna* completed by a hood (*cucullus*). Even in the Urbs itself the *synthesis* was substituted for the toga for dining in company; this was a garment combining the simplicity of the tunic above with the fullness of the toga below.[58] Even in the *municipia* the magistrates would no longer dignify their functions by wearing the toga, and ordinary citizens wore it only on their last bed on the day of their funeral.[59]

They took good care not to wear the toga when lying on their bed alive. Putting on the toga, or the *amictus* which had succeeded it in popular favour, was the sole operation which gave trouble on rising in the morning – scarcely less trouble then to the wearers than now to the archaeologists who try to reconstruct the process. If, like some of the provincial *aediles*, a man renounced every kind of *amictus*, or if he postponed till later in the day the bother of swathing himself artistically in one, his dressing could be accomplished in the twinkling of an eye. He needed only to slip on his footgear on the *toral*. The emperor Vespasian used to drape himself unaided in half a minute, and the moment he had put on his *calcei* he was ready to give audience and set about the performance of his imperial duties.[60] The Romans of this period were thus ready to attend to the business of their public life within a few minutes of getting out of bed.

Their breakfast consisted of a glass of water swallowed in all haste.[61] They did not waste time in washing for they knew they would be going to bathe at the end of the afternoon, either in their private *balneum* if they were rich enough to have had one installed in their own house, or else in one of the public *thermae*.

Only one single villa, that of Diomedes, has been excavated in Pompeii where the master's bedroom included a *zotheca* or alcove equipped with a table and a basin.[62] In the text of Suetonius where we are allowed to witness the rising of Vespasian, the subject of a morning wash is passed over in silence;[63] and though the same

Suetonius mentions it in telling of the last hours of Domitian, his allusion is too elliptic for us to attach much importance to it.[64] Terrified by the prophecy that the fifth hour of 18 September A.D. 96 – the hour at which in fact he died a bloody death – was to be inexorably fatal to him, the emperor had mewed himself in his room and had not quitted his bed the whole morning. He remained seated on the bolster beneath which he had a sword concealed. Then suddenly, at the false news that the sixth hour had come, when actually the fifth had but begun, he decided to get up and proceed to the care of his body (*ad corporis curam*) in an adjacent room. But Parthenius, his chamberlain, who was one of the conspirators, kept him back on the pretext that a visitor was insisting on making grave revelations to him in person. Suetonius unfortunately has not specified what were the cares which he was going to give his body when the assassins' plot prevented him. The brevity of the allusion, the readiness with which Domitian was turned aside from his intention, indicates that nothing very serious was intended. The word *sapo* in those days was used only for a dye, and the use of soap in our sense was still unknown, so that at most he may have meant to dip his face and hands in fresh water. This was the limit of the *cura corporis* of the fourth century which Ausonius versified in a charming little ode of his *Ephemeris*, the Occupations of a Day: 'Come, slave, up! Give me my slippers and my muslin mantle. Bring me the *amictus* you have got ready for me, for I am going forth. And pour out the running water that I may wash my hands, my mouth, my eyes –

> *Da rore fontano abluam*
> *Manus et os et lumina!*[65]

After which the poet enters his chapel and, having prayed, sets out to seek his friends.

### 3. The Barber

The real toilet of the Roman dandy was performed at the hairdresser's (*tonsor*), to whose care he confided the cut of his beard and the arrangement of his hair. This was already the essential *cura corporis* for Julius Caesar, whose fastidiousness as a dandy Suetonius has not failed to record for us in this connexion.[66] By the second century the barber-hairdresser had become a tyrant. The man who was rich enough to include *tonsores* in his household retinue put himself in their hands in the morning and again, if necessary, in the course of the day.

Those unable to face the considerable expense of keeping a private hairdresser would go at varying hours, as often as seemed necessary, to one of the innumerable barbershops in the *tabernae* of the city, or which did business in the open for their humbler customers.[67] Idlers went frequently and dawdled there. If we consider the time they spent and the anxieties which obsessed them, it is perhaps hardly fair to call 'idlers' men who were continually busy dividing their attention between the comb and the mirror: '*hos tu otiosos vocas inter pectinem speculumque occupatos?*[68] The crowd which assembled from dawn to the eighth hour[69] was so great that the *tonstrina* became a rendezvous, a club, a gossip shop, an inexhaustible dispensary of information, a place for arranging interviews and the like.[70] On the other hand, so motley and so composite was the crowd that few sights were more picturesque, and from the time of Augustus lovers of painting seized on it as a subject for *genre* pictures such as the Alexandrians had loved. The hairdresser's fee was so generous that we frequently find in Juvenal's *Satires* and Martial's *Epigrams* allusion to the ex-barber who has made his pile and has transmogrified himself into an *Eques* or a wealthy landed proprietor.[71]

The hairdresser's shop was surrounded with benches on which the waiting clients sat. Mirrors hung on the walls so that customers might give themselves a critical glance on leaving the chair.[72] In the centre, his clothes sometimes protected by a simple napkin, large or small (*mappa* or *sudarium*), sometimes by a wrap (*involucrum*) of cambric (*linteum*) or of muslin (*sindon*), the victim whose turn had come would seat himself on a stool while the barber, surrounded by his officious assistants (*circitores*), would cut his hair or, if it had not grown too much since his last visit, would merely dress it for him in the latest mode of the day. The fashion of hairdressing was determined by the mode affected by the sovereign. With the exception of Nero, who liked to mass his hair artistically,[73] the emperors appear from their coins and their busts to have conformed, at least down to Trajan, as much to the example of Augustus, who never granted more than a few hasty moments to his *tonsores*,[74] as to the aesthetic ideal expounded simultaneously by Quintilian and by Martial, both of whom were equally hostile to long hair and piled-up curls.[75] At the beginning of the second century the majority of Romans were therefore content with a simple haircut and a stroke of the comb. The comb was all the more necessary since the haircut was performed with a pair of iron scissors (*forfex*) whose two blades were as innocent of a common pivot as their base was of rings for the operator's fingers. Its efficiency, therefore, left much to be desired, and it would not avoid the irregularities which we call 'steps' and which according to Horace's *Epistles* exposed the victim to public derision:

> *Si curatus inaequali tonsore capillos*
> *Occurri, rides. . . .* [76]

The dandies presently began to prefer curls to the straight haircut. Hadrian, his son Lucius Caesar, and his grandson Lucius Verus are all shown in their effigies with artificially-curled hair, produced either by appropriate manoeuvres of the comb (*flexo ad pectinem capillo*)[77] or by the aid of a *calamistrum*, a curling-iron which the *ciniflones* had heated in its metal sheath under burning coals, and round which the *tonsor* twisted the hair with expert hand. At the beginning of the second century this practice had become current not only with young men, who could not be blamed for indulging in the practice, but also among older folk whose scantier hair lent itself badly to a treatment too flattering not to be ridiculous:

From one side and from the other [writes Martial] you gather up your scanty locks and you cover, Marinus, the wide expanse of your shining bald scalp with the hair from both sides of your head. But blown about they come back at the bidding of the wind, and return to themselves and gird your bare poll with big curls on this side and on that. . . . Will you please in simpler fashion confess yourself old, so as after all to appear so? Nothing is more unsightly than a bald head with dressed hair.[78]

It was part of the *tonsor*'s business to complete the youthful illusion which his clients sought by pouring dye on the curls so laboriously attained,[79] spraying them with perfume, spreading make-up cream on the cheeks, and gumming on little circles of cloth either to conceal the flaws of an unattractive skin or to enhance the brilliance of a poor complexion. These spots were known as *splenia lunata* or, as we should call them, 'patches'.[80] These more obvious refinements never ceased to bring down vigorous ridicule on their addicts, from the lampoons of Cicero on the damp fringes of certain fops among his enemies[81] to the epigrams launched by Martial against their later imitators: 'Constantly smeared darkly with cassia and cinnamon and the perfumes from the nest of the lordly phoenix, you reek of the leaden jars of the perfumer Niceros, and therefore you laugh at us, Coracinus, who smell of nothing. To smelling of scent I prefer to smell of nothing.'[82] Or again: 'There is about you always some foreign odour. This is suspect to me, your being always well-scented.'[83] Or: 'Rufus, whose greasy hair is smelt all over Marcellus' theatre . . . while numerous patches star and plaster his brow.'[84]

At the particular period with which we are dealing, however, the daily recurrent task of the *tonsor* was to trim or shave the beard. This was no doubt a custom which had become established only comparatively late. The Romans, like the Greeks, had for a long time worn beards as a matter of course. The Greeks cut theirs, following the example and obeying the command of Alexander. It was a hundred and fifty years before the Romans began to imitate them. At the beginning of the second century B.C. Titus Quinctius Flamininus on his proconsular coins and Cato the Elder in the literary allusions to his censorship and to his person are both represented as bearded.[85] A generation later the number of beards had decreased. Scipio Aemilianus liked to be shaved every day; and did not give it up even when he ought to have renounced it in protest against the unjust accusations which were being levelled at him.[86] Forty years later the fashion he had set had spread under the dictatorship, as if the spirit of Greek civilization – from which in its own despite the dictatorship drew its inspiration – had extended its ascendancy from the fundamentals of political government to the minutest details of everyday life. Sulla was clean-shaven; Caesar, his true successor, attached the greatest importance to appearing always freshly shaved.[87] After he became emperor, Augustus would not have dreamed of neglecting to submit daily to the barber's razor. By the end of the first century B.C. nothing but the gravest or most painful crisis would have induced the great men of the day to omit a formality which had become for them a state duty: Caesar, after the massacre of his lieutenants by the Eburones;[88] Cato of Utica, after the outbreak of the civil war;[89] Antony after his check at Modena;[90] Augustus after the fresh disaster of Varus.[91] Under the empire, from Tiberius to Trajan, the *principes* never failed to shave; and their subjects would have thought themselves unworthy of their imperial masters if they had not followed suit.

To tell the truth, shaving was for the Romans a sort of religious rite. The first time that a young man's beard fell to the barber's razor was made the occasion of a religious ceremony: the *depositio barbae*. The dates on which the emperors and their relations performed it have duly been recorded: Augustus himself, September 39 B.C.;[92] Marcellus while he was taking part in the expedition against the Cantabrians, 25 B.C.;[93] Caligula and Nero at the time that they assumed the *toga virilis*.[94] Ordinary citizens copied their doings with scrupulous exactitude. Mourning parents recorded in an epitaph that their dead son had just 'deposited his beard', in his twenty-third year, at the same age as Augustus;[95] and just as Nero had consecrated the hairs of his first beard sacrifice in a golden casket offered to Capitoline Jove, so Trimalchio exhibited to his guests a golden pyx, in which he had similarly deposited his *lanugo*, in his private chapel between the silver statuettes of his lares and a marble statuette of Venus.[96] Poor men for their part had to get along with a pyx of glass; and in Juvenal's days rich and poor made this solemnity a festival according to – and indeed often beyond – their means, with rejoicings and feastings to which all the friends of the family were invited.[97]

The barber used scissors to cut the beard which was to be offered as 'first fruits' to the divinity; and adolescents whose chins were still covered only with a more or less abundant down usually waited till their boyhood was well over before embarking on their first shave.[98] But once a certain age was passed, no one but a soldier or a philosopher could decently have ventured any longer to shrink from the razor.[99] Martial compares unshaven men to the African he-goats who feed by the shores of Cyniphs between the two Syrtes.[100] The very slaves were sent off to the *tonsores* who operated in the open air on humbler folk, unless their master for economy invited his own barber to try his hand on their skin.[101] For no one shaved himself. The clumsy instruments and awkward technique which were all they had at their disposal forced the Romans to place themselves in the hands of specialists.

The comment may be made that archaeologists have discovered numbers of razors in prehistoric and Etruscan ruins, but that by what at first seems a curious paradox they have found few or none in their Roman excavations. The explanation is simple. The razors of Terra Mare and of the Etruscans were of bronze, while the Roman razor, whether the razor properly so called (*novacula*) or the knife which served either for shaving or for cutting the nails (*culter* or *cultellus*), was of iron and has been eaten by rust.[102] These iron instruments, or *ferramenta*, to use the generic name applied to every variety of them, were both fragile and perishable tools. This, however, was their least serious demerit. In vain the *tonsor* whetted them on his bone or whetstone – a *laminitana* bought in Spain,[103] which he lubricated by spitting on it; do what he would, the edge of his razor passed ineffectively and dangerously over a skin which had not been softened beforehand either by soap-suds or by oil. There is, so far as I know, but one text which throws any light on these details, and in my opinion it establishes beyond question that the only lotion ever applied by the Roman barber to his client's face was water pure and simple. Plutarch tells a delightful anecdote of the prodigality of M. Antonius Creticus, father of Antony the Triumvir.[104] One day a friend came to beg a loan from him. Now money had a way of burning a hole in his pocket, and the unfortunate spendthrift had to confess that his wife held the purse-strings tightly drawn and had not left him a penny to bless himself with. In this predicament he thought of a ruse to defeat his impecuniosity and satisfy his friend. He called to a slave to bring him some water in a silver bowl, and proceeded to wet his beard as if he were going to be shaved. Then, making a pretext to dismiss the slave, he handed the silver basin to his friend, who went off well content. Obviously the stratagem of Antonius Creticus would have had no point unless the barber's sole preliminary was to pass clean water over his face.

In these circumstances it is clear that the barber needed to be an expert of no common dexterity. It was not until he had served a long apprenticeship to a master and had learned to handle the blunt razors of a beginner that he obtained the right to open a barber-shop on his own account.[105] Even then his trade bristled with diffi-culties and dangers. The virtuosos who excelled in it soon acquired a fame which poets did not disdain to commemorate in their verse. To the memory of such a one Martial composed the following delicate epitaph:

Within this tomb lies Pantagathus, snatched away in boyhood's years, his master's grief and sorrow, skilled to cut with steel that scarcely touched the straggling hairs, and to trim the bearded cheeks. Gentle and light upon him thou mayst be, O earth, as it behoves thee; lighter than the artist's hand thou canst not be.[106]

Pantagathus unfortunately belonged to the cream of his pro-fession; most of his colleagues were far from commanding equal skill. The *tonsores* of the cross-roads in particular exposed their humble customers to most disagreeable experiences. A moment of inattention on their part, an accident in the street, an unexpected push or shove from the crowd, the impact of a missile suddenly thrown, and the barber's hand might slip, inflicting a wound on his client for which the jurists of Augustus thought it well to de-termine the responsibility and assess the damages in advance.[107] At the beginning of the second century no progress had been made, and the barber's victims had usually to choose between a cautious but interminable treatment and the scars of a speedy but dangerous and bloody operation. The most famous barbers cultivated an in-credible leisureliness. Augustus outwitted this by unrolling a manu-script or resorting to his stylus and tablets while the *tonsor* was attending to him.[108] A hundred years later the barber's slowness was still the subject of jest: 'While nimble Eutrapelus goes round Lupercus' face and trims his cheeks a second beard grows.'[109]

A barber, young, but such an artist as was not even Nero's Thalamus to whom fell the beards of the Drusi, I lent on his request to Rufus once to smooth his cheeks. While at command he was going over the same hairs, guiding his hand by the judgement of the mirror, and smoothing the skin, and making a second thorough clip of the close-cut hair, my barber became a bearded man himself.[110]

At the hands of the average *tonsor* the torment did not last so long but was proportionately more painful:

He who desires not yet to go down to Stygian shades, let him, if he be wise, avoid barber Antiochus. White arms are mangled with knives less cruel when the frenzied throng, the votaries of Cybele, raves to Phrygian strains; with gentler touch the surgeon Alcon cuts the knotted hernia and lops away broken bones with a workman's hand. ... These scars, whate'er they are thou numberest on my chin, scars such as are fixed on some time-worn boxer's face – these a wife formidable with wrathful talons wrought not – 'tis Antiochus' steel and hand accursed. Alone among all beasts the he-goat has good sense: bearded he lives to escape Antiochus.[111]

These gashes were so frequent that Pliny the Elder has preserved for us the receipt for the plaster which was found suitable to staunch the bleeding, a receipt unpleasant enough: spider's webs soaked in oil and vinegar.[112]

To be honest, it required courage of no mean order to go to the barber's; inconvenience for inconvenience, suffering for suffering, the Romans often preferred to have recourse to other expedients, like Martial's Gargilianus: 'With salve you smooth your cheeks, and with hair-eradicator your bald pate: surely you are not afraid, Gargilianus, of a barber?'[113] Some went daily to the *dropacista*: 'You stroll about sleek with curled hair . . . you are smoothed with depilatory daily . . . . Cease to call me brother, Charmenion, lest I call you sister!'[114] The *dropax* used for these purposes was a depilatory liniment made of a resin and pitch; alternatively the face might be rubbed with *psilothrum*, an ingredient procured from the white vine, or some other of the pastes formed with a base of ivy gum, ass's fat, she-goat's gall, bat's blood or powdered viper, all of which Pliny lists for us.[115] Some preferred to take the Naturalist's advice and combine these applications with direct epilation, and like Julius Caesar before them, or like women nowadays, to have their hairs individually plucked out with tweezers (*volsella*).[116] Some dandies pushed endurance to the point of begging their *tonsor* to use simultaneously on their skin scissors, razor, and depilatory-pincers according to convenience, incurring the gibe of Martial as they left the *tonstrina:* 'Part of your jaw is clipped, part is shaved, part is plucked of hairs. Who would imagine this to be a single head?'[117]

By the middle of the century the bulk of Romans were beginning to revolt against their enslavement to the barber. When therefore the emperor Hadrian – either wishing, as his biographer says, to conceal an ugly scar, or simply hoping to shake off an intolerable yoke – decided to let grow the beard which on coins, busts, and statues decorates his chin, his subjects and successors hastily vied with each other in following his example.[118] From that moment, what had for two-and-a-half centuries been the essential *cura corporis* of men in Rome disappeared from the daily programme, leaving no trace and causing no regret.

## 4. *The Matron Dresses*

So much for the toilet of the Roman man. This covers, however, only half our subject. To tackle the other half and watch the Roman woman getting up, we must move over to her quarters and for the greater part of the time change the *mise en scène*.

We may recall the amusing chapter of the *Physiologie du mariage* which learnedly weighs the advantages and disadvantages of the various systems a couple must choose between if they are to maintain the harmony of their married life: one bed in one room, or two beds in the same room, or two beds in two separate rooms. Balzac tolerates the first, prefers the last, and absolutely bans the compromise of the twin beds. It so happens that the great French novelist has thus, without suspecting it, codified the customs which prevailed in Imperial Rome.

Only on the first floor of one house recently excavated at Herculaneum have we discovered some *cubicula* with two beds. And in this case it seems more than probable that they belonged to an inn, so there is nothing to prove that the two beds were designed for a married couple. Literary texts give no hint of several beds together in one room except in the overcrowded *cenacula* (or sub-let) apartments of the *insulae*. Everywhere they record either the community of the *lectus genialis* or two separate rooms for the married pair. The couple made their choice of one or the other arrangement according to the space available in their house, that is to say, in the last analysis, according to their social standing. Humble folk and the modest middle classes had no room to spare in their homes and did not expect anything but a shared bed. In one of his epigrams Martial poses as being willing to accept the hand of a rich old woman, on the condition that they need never sleep together: '*Communis tecum nec mihi lectus erit.*'[119] But on the other hand he enlarged tenderly on the mutual affection which Calenus and Sulpicia preserved during the fifteen years of their married life, and dwelt without undue prudery on the amorous ecstasies which were witnessed by their nuptial bed and by the lamp 'copiously sprinkled with the perfumes of Niceros'.[120]

The great aristocrats, however, organized their life in such a way that each of the married pair could enjoy independence in the home. Thus we always find Pliny the Younger alone in the room when he wakes 'round about the first hour, rarely earlier, rarely later'; in the silence and solitude and darkness which reign round his bed behind the closed shutters, he feels himself 'wonderfully free and abstracted from those outward objects that dissipate attention and left to my own thoughts.'[121] This was his favourite time for composition. We must, however, imagine that his beloved Calpurnia was sleeping and getting up in another room, where he would join her when she was under his roof, and toward which his steps would turn of their own accord when she was absent.[122]

It was evidently the right thing in the higher society of those days for man and wife to sleep apart, and the upstarts were not slow to copy the great in this matter. Petronius notes this eccentricity in his novel. Trimalchio swaggers in front of his guests, boasting the size of the house he has had built for himself. He has his own bedroom where he sleeps; his wife's he calls 'the nest of this she-viper'.[123] But Trimalchio is deceiving either himself or us. Nature and habit are too strong for him; they reassert themselves at the gallop. In practice, one of the rooms ordered from the architect remains unused. Whatever he may pretend, he does not sleep by himself in haughty isolation, but shares in another room the bed of Fortunata. Like the French husbands who punctiliously address their wives as *vous* in company, but let an occasional *tu* inadvertently escape them of a sudden, he ingenuously betrays himself in the passage where, while indulging liberally in smutty confidences, he blatantly attributes his insomnia to the unseemly noises emitted by the weighty 'better half' at his side: 'Why do you laugh, Fortunata? It is you who prevent my closing an eye the whole night.'[124]

It matters little either way. Whether she slept in a room of her own or shared a room with him, the Roman woman's morning toilet closely resembled her husband's. Like him, she kept on her undergarments in bed at night: her loin cloth, her brassière (*strophium, mamillare*) or corset (*capitium*), her tunic or tunics, and sometimes, to the despair of her husband, a mantle over all.[125] Consequently she, like him, had nothing to do when she got up, but to draw on her slippers on the *toral* and then drape herself in the *amictus* of her choice; and her preliminary ablutions were as sketchy as his. Pending the hour of the bath, the essential *cura corporis* for her as for him consisted of attentions which we should consider accessory. In matters of toilet the Roman lady of the empire resembled the oriental lady of today; she considered the superfluous thing the most necessary.

It is the jurists who, in laying down an inventory of female inheritance, best help us to arrange in order the unequal and successive planes on which the Roman woman's coquetry set up its batteries. The personal objects which a woman left behind her were legally divided into three categories; toilet articles (*mundus muliebris*), adornments (*ornamenta*), and clothes (*vestis*).[126] Under the heading *vestis* the lawyers enumerate the different garments which women wore. To the toilet belonged everything she used for keeping clean (*mundus muliebris est quo mulier mundior fit*): her wash-basins (*matellae*), her mirrors (*specula*) of copper, silver, sometimes even of glass backed not with mercury but with lead; and also, when she was fortunate enough to be able to disdain the hospitality of the public bath, her bathtub (*lavatio*). Her 'adornments' included the instruments and products which contributed to her beautification, from her combs and pins and brooches (*fibulae*) to the unguents she applied to her skin and the jewels with which she adorned herself. At bathing time her *mundus* and her *ornamenta* were both needed; but when she first got up in the morning it was enough for her to 'adorn' herself without washing: '*ex somno statim ornata non commundata*'.

She began by dressing her hair. At the period which is now engaging our attention this was no small affair. Women had long since given up the simplicity of the republican coiffure – restored to honour for a space by Claudius – in which a straight, even parting divided the hair in front and a simple chignon gathered it together at the back. They were no longer content with braids raised on pads above the forehead, such as we see in the busts of Livia and Octavia. With Messalina there came in those complicated and high-piled methods of hairdressing which are familiar to us from illustrations of women during the Flavian period. In later years, though the ladies of the court who set the fashion, Marciana, sister of Trajan, and Matidia, his niece, gave up these styles, they nevertheless preserved the custom of dressing their hair in diadems as high as towers. 'Behold,' says Statius in one of his *Silvae*, 'behold the glory of this sublime forehead and the stagings of her coiffure.' Juvenal makes merry in his turn about the contrast between the height of a certain fine lady and the pretentiousness of her piled-up hair to which there seemed no limit: 'So numerous are the tiers and storeys piled one upon another on her head! In front you would take her for an Andromache; she is not so tall behind; you would not think it was the same person.'[127]

Roman women were as dependent on their *ornatrix* as their husbands on the *tonsor*. The skill of the tire-woman was indispensable for erecting these elaborate scaffoldings, and the epitaphs of many *ornatrices* tell us the dates of their death and the families by whom they were employed.[128] The woman had to devote as much time to her *séance* with the *ornatrix* as her husband had to give to the barber; and she suffered as much on these occasions as he did, especially if like the Julia of whom Macrobius tells she bade her tire-woman pitilessly tear out the greying hairs.[129] The post of *ornatrix* was far from being a sinecure. Not infrequently the torturer became a martyr, if perchance her mistress, worn out by holding one pose everlastingly, suddenly decided that the result of so much suffering still left much to be desired. Epigrams and satires are full of the cries of angry matrons and the groans of serving women in distress.

If Madame has an appointment and wishes to be turned out more nicely than usual [writes Juvenal] . . . the unhappy Psecas who does her hair will have her own hair torn, and the clothes stripped off her shoulders and her breasts. 'Why is this curl standing up?' she asks, and then down comes a thong of bull's hide to inflict chastisement for the offending ringlet![130]

Martial for his part relates: 'One curl of the whole round of hair had gone astray, badly fixed by an insecure pin. This crime Lalage avenged with the mirror in which she had observed it and Plecusa, smitten, fell because of those savage locks!'[131] Happy, in these circumstances, was the *ornatrix* whose mistress was bald! With a minimum of risk she could adjust the artificial tresses (*crines, galerus, corymbium*), or at need an entire wig. Sometimes the false hair was dyed blond with the *sapo* of Mainz obtained by blending goat's fat with beech ash;[132] sometimes it was an ebony black, like the cut hair imported from India in such quantities that the imperial government entered *capilli Indici* among the commodities which had to pay customs duty.[133]

The *ornatrix*'s duties did not end there, however. She had still to remove her mistress's superfluous hair, and above all to 'paint' her: white on brow and arms with chalk and white lead; red on cheeks and lips with ochre, *fucus*, or the lees of wine; black with ashes (*fuligo*) or powdered antimony on the eyebrows and round the eyes.[134] The tire-woman's palette was a collection of pots and flagons, Greek vases and alabaster jars, of *gutti* and pyxes from which as ordered she extracted liniments, pomades, and make-up. The mistress of the house normally kept this arsenal locked in a cupboard in the nuptial room (*thalamus*). In the morning she spread out everything on the table beside the powdered horn which, following Messalina's example, she used to enamel her teeth.[135] Before calling her *ornatrices* to get to work, she took care to secure the door, for she knew from Ovid that art does not beautify a woman's face unless it be concealed.[136] When she set out for the bath she took all her apparatus with her, each pot and jar in its own compartment in a special little box, sometimes made of solid silver, which was called by the generic name of *capsa* or *alabastrotheca*; these various jars contained her daytime face, which she made up on rising, made up again after her bath, and did not un-make until after nightfall at the last moment before going to bed: 'You lie stored away in a hundred caskets, and your face does not sleep with you!'[137]

Once made up, the fashionable lady, always assisted by her *ornatrices*, chose her jewels, set with precious stones, and put them on one by one: a diadem on her hair, and ear-rings in her ears; a collar (*monile*) or trinkets (*catellae*) round her neck; a pendant on her breast; bracelets (*armillae*) on her wrists; rings on her fingers, and circlets on her ankles (*periscelides*) like those which the Arab women of the sheik's tent wear.[138] Next her chamberwomen (*a veste*) hastened to the rescue and helped to dress her. They slipped over her head her long upper tunic (the *stola*), sign of her exalted rank, round the hem of which was stitched a braid (*instita*) embroidered in gold. They tied her belt (*zona*), and finally enveloped her either in a long shawl which covered her shoulders and reached down to her feet (the *supparum*), or in the *palla* – the woman's counterpart of the man's *pallium* – a big square cloak with rhythmic folds and of some dazzling colour.

Woman's dress in Rome was not distinguished from man's by the cut, but rather by the richness of the material and the brilliance of the colour. To linen and wool she preferred the cotton stuffs that came from India after the Parthian peace, assured by Augustus and confirmed by the victories of Trajan, had guaranteed the security of imports; above all she loved the silks which the mysterious Seres exported annually to the empire from the country which we nowadays call China. Since the reign of Nero silk caravans had come by the land routes across Asia, then from Issidon Scythica (Kashgar) to the Black Sea, or else through Persia and down the Tigris and Euphrates to the Persian Gulf, or by boat down the Indus and then by ship to the Egyptian ports of the Red Sea. Silk materials were not only more supple, lighter, and iridescent, they also lent themselves better than all others to skilful manipulation. The *affectores* with their ingredients reinforced the original colours; the *infectores* denaturalized them; and the various dyers, the *purpurarii*, *flammarii*, *crocotarii*, *violarii*, knew cunning dyes equalling in number the vegetable, animal, and mineral resources at their disposal; chalk and soapwort and salt of tartar for white; saffron and reseda for yellow; for black, nut-gall; woad for blue; madder, archil, and purple for dark and lighter shades of red. Mindful of Ovid's counsels,[139] the matrons adapted their complexions to the colours of their dresses and harmonized them so skilfully that when they went into the city they lit the streets with the bravery of their multi-coloured robes and shawls and mantles, whose brilliance was often further enhanced by dazzling embroideries like those which adorned the splendid *palla* of black in which Isis appeared to Apuleius.[140]

It was the matron's business to complete her costume with various accessories foreign in their nature to man's dress, which further accentuated the picturesqueness of her appearance. While a man normally wore nothing on his head, or at most, if the rays of the sun were too severe or the rain beat too fiercely down, threw a corner of his toga or *pallium* over his head or drew down the hood (*cucullus*) of his cloak (*paenula*), the Roman woman, if not wearing a diadem or *mitra*, passed a simple bandeau (*vitta*) of crimson through her hair, no longer imprisoned in its net, or else a *tutulus* similar to the bandeau of the *flaminicae*, which broadened in the centre to rise above the forehead in the shape of a cone. She often wore a scarf (*focale*) knotted at the neck. The *mappa* dangling from her arm served to wipe dust or perspiration from her face (*orarium*, *sudarium*). We must, however, beware of assuming that the practice of blowing the nose came in early, for the only Latin word which can fairly be translated as handkerchief (*muccinium*) is not attested before the end of the third century.[141] In one hand she often flourished a fan of peacocks' feathers (*flabellum*), with which she also brushed away the flies (*muscarium*). In fine weather she carried in her other hand, unless she entrusted it to a serving woman by her side (*pedisequa*) or to her escort, a sunshade (*umbella, umbraculum*), usually covered in bright green. She had no means of closing it at will, as we can ours, so she left it at home when there was a wind.[142]

Thus equipped, 'the fair' could face the critical eye of their fellow women and challenge the admiration of the passers-by. But it is certain that the complexity of their array, combined with a coquetry not peculiar to their day, must have drawn out the time demanded by their morning toilet far beyond that needed by their husbands. This was, however, a matter of no account, for the women of Rome were not busy people like their men, and to confess the truth they took no part in the public life of Rome except in its hours of leisure.

# VII

## OCCUPATIONS

*

### 1. The Duties of a 'Client'

IN Trajan's Rome women spent most of their time indoors. If they were poor they attended to the work of the household, until the hour when they could go to the public baths which were reserved for them. If they were rich and had a large household staff to relieve them of domestic cares, they had nothing to do but go out when the fancy took them, pay visits to their women friends, take a walk, attend public spectacles, or later go out to dinner. The men on the other hand rarely stayed at home. If they had to earn their bread, they hurried off to their business, which in all trade guilds began at dawn. Even if they were unemployed they were no sooner out of bed than they were in the grip of the duties inseparable from being a 'client'. For it was not only the freedmen who were dependent on the good graces of a patron. From the parasite do-nothing up to the great aristocrat there was no man in Rome who did not feel himself bound to someone more powerful above him by the same obligations of respect, or, to use the technical term, the same *obsequium*, that bound the ex-slave to the master who had manumitted him.[1]

The *patronus* for his part was in honour bound to welcome his client to his house, to invite him from time to time to his table, to come to his assistance, and to make him gifts. To clients who were in actual want the patron distributed food (*sportula*) which they carried off in a basket; or more often, to avoid the trouble this entailed, he gave them small presents of money when they called. In Trajan's time these customs were so universal that the number of clients scarcely varied from one house to another, and a sort of *sportula* tariff had become established in the Urbs: six-and-a-quarter sesterces per head per day.[2] How many briefless barristers, how

191

many professors without pupils, how many artists without orders reckoned this meagre dole as their main source of revenue![3] Clients who also practised a trade supplemented their earnings by the patron's dole, and in order not to arrive too late at their workshop they ran round to their patron to fetch it before daybreak.[4] As the importance of a magnate depended on the size of his clientele, a man would have tarnished his reputation if he had preferred a long morning in bed to the pleasure of the mob at his morning receptions. Such relaxation might pass in the provinces, in a distant spot like Bilbilis, for instance; but in Rome the great man would not dare to be inattentive to the complaints of one, the demands of another, the salutations of all.[5]

A severe and meticulous code of etiquette regulated this obligatory attendance. First, though a client was free to come on foot rather than in a litter, he could not decently appear without a toga; and this strict insistence on ceremonial dress weighed so heavily on his budget that it would soon have eaten up his *sportulae* if it had not become the fashion for the patron to take advantage of some solemn occasion to present him with a new toga in addition to the five or six pounds of silverware which he reckoned on receiving each December, when the Saturnalian gift-giving came round.[6] Secondly, clients were bound to wait their turn patiently, and this depended not on the order of their arrival but on their social status; the praetor came before the tribune, the *eques* before the plain citizen, the freedman before the slave.[7] Finally, the client had to take great care in addressing his patron not to call the great man simply by his name but to give him the title of *dominus* – failure to observe this detail might cause him to return home empty handed: 'This morning I addressed you, as it chanced, by your own name, nor did I add "My Lord", Caecilianus. Do you ask how much such casual conduct has cost me? It has robbed me of a hundred farthings.'[8]

Each morning, therefore, Rome awoke to the coming and going of clients discharging these customary politenesses. The humblest of all multiplied their attendances to collect as many *sportulae* as possible; the richest were not exonerated from paying client calls because they had first received some. For however high a man might climb in the Roman hierarchy, there was always someone above him to claim his homage. There was in fact no one in Rome, save the emperor alone, who recognized none greater than himself.

The women were at least exempt from this merry-go-round of salaams. They neither held court nor received it. In the second century the only exceptions to this rule were widows anxious to carry in person their tale of woe or their requests to the patron of their dead husband, and the wives of certain rapacious beggars who hoped by ostentatious sycophancy to cadge some supplementary alms and therefore made their wives accompany them in a litter on their round of calls. Juvenal does not stint his scorn for these self-interested manoeuvres: 'Here is a husband going the round followed by a sickly or pregnant wife; another by a clever and well-known trick claims alms for a wife who is not there, pointing in her stead to a closed and empty chair, "My Galla's in there," says he; "let's be off quick" – "Galla, put out your head!" – "Don't disturb her, she's asleep!"'[9] The ruse is so clumsy that we wonder whether Juvenal has not merely invented it. Real or fictitious, however, it gives us an idea that the Roman matron may have been reluctant to follow her husband of a morning in his round of client visits.

## 2. Businessmen and Manual Labourers

The role of client played, everyone got busy with the day's work. The Imperial Rome where the court resided with the senators and the bureaucrats of a far-flung tentacular administration was assuredly the city of 'rentiers', people of means, which Rostovtzeff has called it.[10] Men of means were the large landlords whose land wealth in the provinces had gained them admission to the Curia and entailed their residence in Rome;[11] men of means, the scribes attached to the offices of the various magistrates, whose posts were bought and sold like those of the French monarchy under the ancien régime;[12] men of means, no less, the administrators and shareholders of the tax-gathering societies whose tenders were guaranteed by capital funds and whose profits swelled their revenues; men of means, again, the innumerable functionaries punctually paid by the

Exchequer, who impressed on every part of the imperial government the master's seal; men of means, the 150,000 paupers whom Annona fed at State expense, idlers chronically out of work and well satisfied to be so, who limited their toil to claiming once a month the provisions to which they had once for all established a right until their death.

But at the same time there was another aspect of Rome. The presence in the capital of these 'men of means', officials, bureaucrats, or proletarians, did not deprive the city of its character of economic metropolis. Rome's political supremacy, her gigantic urban development, condemned her to display intense and unremitting activity not only in speculation and trade but in varied manufactures and productive work. Let us reflect that all the roads of Italy led to Rome, and all the lines of Mediterranean navigation, and that Rome, Queen of the World, attracted the best of the earth's products. She arrogated to herself the financing and direction of the world's activities and claimed the right to consume the world's riches. It is obvious that she had to toil unceasingly after her fashion to maintain this domination.

The heart-breaking comprehensiveness of this systematic exploitation is attested by the Romans themselves, and breathes from the crumbled ruins of some of their monuments. At the very beginning of the poem which Petronius has linked to his romance, he has described it for us:[18]

The world entire was in the hands of the victorious Romans. They possessed the earth and the seas and the double field of stars, and were not satisfied. Their keels, weighed down with heavy cargoes, ploughed furrows in the waves. If there was afar some hidden gulf, some unknown continent, which dared to export gold, it was an enemy and the Fates prepared murderous wars for the conquest of new treasures. Vulgarized joys had no more charm, nor the pleasures worn threadbare in the rejoicings of the plebs. The simple soldier caressed the bronzes of Corinth. . . . Here the Numidians, there the Sœres, wove for the Roman new fleeces, and for him the Arab tribes plundered their steppes.

Such are the images which float before our eyes as we gaze on what remains to us of the Forum of Ostia, the port of Rome.

The Forum consists of a vast esplanade more than one hundred metres long and over eighty metres wide.[14] In the middle rises a temple which I was fortunate enough to identify with that of Annona Augusta, that is to say, the Divinity of Imperial Supplies.[15] Along the side which faces the entrance to the sanctuary runs a portico supported on columns of *cipollino*, which backs on to the stage of the town's theatre, and in its shade the spectators of long ago were wont to stretch their legs. The three other sides were enclosed by a wall fronted by a double colonnade of brick faced with stucco, on to which opened a series of sixty-one small rooms separated from each other by a wooden partition resting on a foundation of masonry. From their uniform appearance and identical dimensions (approximately four metres by four) these little rooms all served one and the same purpose. What this purpose was has been revealed by the series of mosaics – black cubes on a white ground – which paved the colonnade in front of each. These mosaics with their figures and inscriptions introduce us into the corresponding rooms and assign them to one or another of the various professional associations which were installed there by permission of the Roman authorities. At the eastern end the caulkers and the ropemakers had their *statio*; in the next room the furriers; next came the wood merchants, whose name is enclosed in a dovetail cartouche; then the corn measurers (the *mensores frumentarii*), one of whom is shown performing his duties, one knee on the ground, diligently trying to divide the contents of a *modius* or regulation bushel exactly with his scraping tool or *rutellum*. At the opposite end was the *statio* of the weighers or *sacomarii*, whose business was complementary to that of the *mensores*. In 124 B.C. the weighers here dedicated to the genius of their office[16] a charming carved altar which is now exhibited in the Museo Nazionale delle Terme. This leaves little doubt that this *statio* and the other similar ones were formerly dedicated to some cult. All the others belonged to the corporations of fitters (*navicularii*), who were further distinguished among themselves only by their city of origin. There were the fitters of Alexandria, for instance, the fitters of Narbonne and Arles in Gaul, those of Cagliari and Porto-Torres in Sardinia. There were those of celebrated or forgotten ports in northern Africa; Carthage, whose mercantile fleet the mosaic artist has stylized; Hippo-Diarrhytus, the modern Bizerta; Curbis, now Courba to the north of the Gulf of Hammamet; Missua, now Sidi Daud, south-west of Cape Bon; Gummi, now Bordj Cedria, at the base of the Gulf of Carthage. There were the fitters of Musluvium, now Sidi Rekane, between Zama and Bougie, whose somewhat complicated and yet highly instructive armorial bearings include fish, a cupid astride a dolphin, and two female heads, one of which is almost effaced while the other is crowned with ears of corn and has a harvest woman's sickle at its side. And finally there were the fitters of Sabratha, the port of the desert whence the ivory of Fezzan was exported, symbolized by an elephant below the name of its seamen. Incomplete though this enumeration is, it may seem over-detailed to the reader. But if, instead of merely reading through a list of place-names, you decipher them yourself at Ostia, and yourself step on these naïve pictures in which each of the corporations tried by a sly touch to define its business and evoke the memory of its distant home, you cannot fail to be seized with admiration before the spacious and impressive reality which these modest tokens represent. It is true that they explain to us the purpose of the rooms on the threshold of which they lie, little chapels of co-operative brotherhoods or, if we prefer so to interpret them, simple resting-places where the ideal procession of guilds continually passed round their goddess Annona and where the flame of their civic religion burned. But apart from the esplanade which they adorn, their lines embrace all the expanse of land and sea between the Isthmus of Suez and the Pillars of Hercules. And suddenly you see the throngs of people, strangers to each other, born in far distant lands, rowing to meet each other here in answer to the needs of Rome, and you feel that there gravitates for ever round this unforgettable enclosure not only the mass of goods which Rome appropriated for herself in every corner of the earth but the cortège of docile nations whom she had consecrated to her service.

Into her three ports of Ostia, Portus, and the emporium beneath the Aventine poured the tiles and bricks, the wines and fruits of Italy; the corn of Egypt and Africa; the oil of Spain; the venison, the timbers, and the wool of Gaul; the cured meats of Baetica; the dates of the oases; the marbles of Tuscany, of Greece, and of

Numidia; the porphyries of the Arabian Desert; the lead, silver, and copper of the Iberian Peninsula; the ivory of the Syrtes and the Mauretanias, the gold of Dalmatia and of Dacia; the tin of the Cassiterides, now the Scilly Isles, and the amber of the Baltic; the papyri of the valley of the Nile; the glass of Phoenicia and of Syria; the stuffs of the Orient; the incense of Arabia; the spices, the corals, and the gems of India; the silks of the Far East.[17]

In the city and its suburbs the sheds of the warehouses (*horrea*) stretched out of sight. Here accumulated the provisions that filled Rome's belly, the stores that were the pledge of her well-being and of her luxury. The excavations undertaken in 1923 by the late Prince Giovanni Torlonia have revealed the importance of the *horrea* of the Portus of Trajan; though only one-third of the area covered in Hadrian's day by the *horrea* of Ostia has so far been excavated, they already cover some twenty-five acres. The discovery of the ancient Roman *horrea*, the number and extent of which are indicated in the literature of the time, has in fact only been begun.[18] Some of these specialized in a single type of goods: the *horrea candelaria* stored only torches, candles, and tallow; the *horrea chartaria* on the Esquiline were consecrated to rolls of papyrus and quires of parchment; while the *horrea piperataria* near the Forum were piled with the supplies of pepper, ginger, and spices convoyed there by the Arabs.

Most of the *horrea*, however, were a sort of general store where all kinds of wares lay cheek by jowl. They were differentiated by the name of the place they occupied or the name they had inherited from their first proprietor and retained even when they had passed into the hands of the Caesars – the *horrea Nervae* flanked the Via Latina; the *horrea Ummidiana* lay on the Aventine; the *horrea Agrippiniana* between the Clivus Victoriae and the Vicus Tuscus on the fringe of the Forum; others were grouped between the Aventine and the Tiber. Then there were the *horrea Seiana*, the *horrea Lolliana*, and the most important of all – the *horrea Galbae*, whose foundation went back to the end of the second century B.C. The *horrea Galbae* were enlarged under the empire and possessed rows of *tabernae* ranged round three large intermediate courtyards which covered more than eight acres. In these *tabernae* were stocked not only wine and oil but all sorts of materials and provisions, at least if we are to judge by the inscriptions deciphered by the epigraphists indicating the merchants to whom these 'granaries' gave shelter: in one place a woman fish merchant (*piscatrix*), in another a merchant of marbles (*marmorarius*), farther off an outfitter with tunics and mantles for sale (*sagarius*).

It is clear that with such an immense extent of warehouse room – to which were added in the first years of the second century B.C. the central halls of Trajan's market[19] – the Rome of the Antonines where antiquity had both its bank and its stock exchange was also the centre of the world's commerce. If Rome did not know anything of what we call 'Great Industry', she at least mobilized alongside her general staff of financiers and large-scale merchants a whole army of employees in her offices, of retailers in her shops, of artisans in her workshops, of the labourers necessary for the maintenance of her buildings and monuments, and of dockers to unload, store, and handle her colossal imports. Finally skilled workmen were needed to submit heavy raw materials as well as more delicate merchandise to a final transformation before they were handed on to the consumer. For Rome's distant subject peoples and those still more distant with whom they traded both within and without the imperial frontiers exhausted or enriched themselves to provide the city with what she demanded from every corner of the earth.

Some idea of the extent and variety of Roman trade can be gained by merely reading through the list of the corporations of Rome, drawn up by Waltzing at the beginning of the fourth volume of his masterly work.[20] More than one hundred and fifty of them have been traced and accurately defined, and this is in itself enough to prove the mighty volume of business in which an aristocracy of patrons and a plebs of employees collaborated within one group, though it is impossible for us now always to distinguish the merchant from the financier, the trader from the master of industry, the manufacturer from the retailer. Among the wholesalers, the *magnarii* of corn, of wine, and of oil; among the shippers, the *domini navium*, who built, equipped, and maintained whole fleets, the engineers and repairers of boats (*fabri navales et curatores navium*), it is impossible to draw a hard and fast line between the middleman and the capitalist.

The organization of food supplies was split up in the course of its natural development into a multitude of different specialist lines. Some groups represented retailers who had nothing to do but distribute their wares: purveyors of lupins (*lupinarii*), of fruits (*fructuarii*), and of melons (*peponarii*). Others were composed of people who had taken the trouble to produce or procure the goods they sold: the *olitores*, who were at once greengrocers and market gardeners; the *piscatores*, both fishermen and fishmongers. The greater number of these lines involved the exercise of a real trade. The travelling *vinarii* went from *vicus* to *vicus* with a whole battery of barrels and jars (*amphorae*) piled on their carts. The tavern-keepers (*thermopolae*) offered in their bowls cunning blends of wine and water which they then brought to the required temperature. A mere glance at the bas-reliefs which decorate the famous tomb of Eurysaches shows that in a great bakery the baker or *pistor* was assisted by a miller (*molinarius*).[21] The pastry-cooks (*siliginarii*), the confectioners (*pastillarii*), and the inn-keepers (*caupones*) won customers for their counters or their tables only by the reputation they established for care and skill in carrying out their receipts.

Passing to the luxury trades, we observe the labour and technical skill which they exacted at every turn: the perfumers and druggists (*pigmentarii*) boasted of the mixtures they had prepared; the mirror sellers had polished the mirrors hung from their shop-fronts; the florists (*rosarii, violarii*) had arranged the bouquets on their stalls to please the passers-by and had woven the wreaths which were to be found at the *coronarii*'s; the ivory vendors (*eborarii*) knew the art of working the tusks received from the African hunter; the sellers of rings (*anularii*) and pearls (*margaritarii*), the goldsmiths (*brattarii inauratores*), and the jewellers (*aurifices*) had all their several skills. In the professions which had to do with dress, there was none where sale and manufacture were separate. The *lintearii*, for instance, stiffened their own lawns; the robemakers (*vestiarii*) and the cloakmakers (*sagarii*), the shoemakers (*sutores*), the makers of men's boots (*caligarii*) and of women's boots (*fabri soliarii baxiarii*), one and all manufactured the goods they sold. Nor must we overlook all the humbler, subsidiary industries which hung on the skirts of the clothing trade, employing the washermen (*fontani*), the fullers (*fullones*), the dyers (*tinctores, affectores, infectores*), the more finely-skilled embroiderers (*plumarii*) and manipulators of silk (*serarii*) who introduced threads of cotton into the silken tissues which, from the reign of Claudius on, China regularly sent with the monsoon.

There were a peculiarly large number of corporations in Rome whose members themselves produced the goods which they offered to the public; others had nothing to offer but their manual services (*operae*). Among the former we may reckon the tanners (*corarii*), the furriers (*pelliones*), the ropemakers (*restiones*), the caulkers (*stuppatores*), the carpenters and cabinet-makers (*citrarii*), the metal workers in bronze and iron (*fabri aerarii, ferrarii*). In the second category we may include the building corporations: the wreckers (*subrutores*), the masons (*structores*), the timber workers (*fabri tignarii*); the workers responsible for land transport: muleteers (*muliones*), those in charge of pack animals (*iumentarii*), wagoners (*catabolenses*), carters (*vectuarii*), drovers (*cisiarii*); those responsible for water transport: boatmen (*lenuncularii*), oarsmen (*lintrarii*), coasters (*scapharii*), raftsmen (*caudicarii*), towers (*helicarii*), ballast-loaders (*saburrarii*); and finally, the corporations on whom depended the administration and policing of the docks: the guardians (*custodiarii*), the porters (*baiuli*), the stevedores (*geruli*), the wharfmen (*saccarii*). By the time you have turned the last page of Waltzing's formidable catalogue you will assuredly have come to the conclusion that Rome of the Antonines contained far more workers than 'men of means'. The noise of the city, of which the satires complain, which deafened the ears from one end of the year to the other, was made up of the cadence of their tools, the rush and hustle of their toil, their panting, and their swearing.[22]

In two essential characteristics the Roman working man was nevertheless different from his fellow-workmen in the great cities of today.

With the possible exception of the principal dock quarter on the banks of the Tiber and the slopes of the Aventine, the Roman workers did not live congregated in dense, compact, exclusive masses. Their living quarters were scattered about in almost every corner of the city, but nowhere did they form a town within the town. Instead of being concentrated in an immense bazaar or a monster factory area, their dwellings formed indefinite series with a hundred interruptions, so that, in the Urbs, warehouses, workshops, and workmen's dwellings alternated oddly with private mansions and blocks of flats.[23]

Further, these humming hives of workshops were almost exclusively male. Feminism under the Antonines was an extraordinary and aristocratic phenomenon peculiar to the upper classes. The great ladies in vain took pride in emulating men in every sphere of life; they found no imitators or disciples among their humbler sisters, who had no mind at all to fling themselves into the struggle for existence. The ladies might devote themselves to music, literature, science, law, or philosophy, as they threw themselves into sport – as a method of passing the time; they would have thought it beneath them to stoop to working at a trade. Among the thousands of epitaphs of the Urbs collected by the editors of the *Corpus Inscriptionum Latinarum* I have found scarcely any women earners: one *libraria* or woman secretary,[24] three clerks (*amanuenses*),[25] one stenographer (*notaria*),[26] two women teachers[27] against eighteen of the other sex,[28] four women doctors[29] against fifty-one *medici*.[30] For the great bulk of Roman women the civil registers would have required the entry – less and less familiar in ours – 'no profession'. In the urban epigraphy of the empire we find women either simply fulfilling the duties for which man is by nature unfitted, of seamstress (*sarcinatrix*),[31] woman's hairdresser (*tonstrix*,[32] *ornatrix*),[33] midwife (*obstetrix*),[34] and nurse (*nutrix*);[35] or resigning themselves gradually to those occupations for which women have always been better qualified or more expert than men.

I have discovered only one fishwife (*piscatrix*),[36] one female costermonger (*negotiatrix leguminaria*),[37] one dressmaker (*vestifica*)[38] – against twenty men tailors or *vestifici*[39] – three women wool distributors (*lanipendiae*),[40] and two silk merchants (*sericariae*).[41] We need feel no surprise at the absence of women jewellers; for one thing, at Rome there was no clear demarcation between the *argentarii* who sold jewellery and the *argentarii* who took charge of banking and exchange; and for another, all banking operations had been forbidden to women by the same praetorian legislation that had deprived them of the right to sue on each other's behalf.[42] It is surely noteworthy that women never figure in the corporations for which the emperors tried to stimulate recruitment: naval armament in the time of Claudius[43] and baking under Trajan.[44] I could find no *pistrix* amongst the *pistores* of the city;[45] nor has any woman's name crept into the lists of shippers which have survived to our times. If any matrons yielded to the exhortations of Claudius, who had gone so far as to promise the privileges pertaining to the mother of three children (*ius trium liberorum*) to any wealthy woman, whether married or childless or single, who would consent to outfit a cargo boat at her own expense,[46] they can have done so only indirectly, through the intermediary of some man of straw, a *procurator*, or some other business agent. Nothing gives stronger proof that the Roman woman, despite all the moral and civil emancipation which had fallen to her under the empire, preferred to remain in the sheltered security of her own home, far from the hurly-burly of the Forum and the noise of trade.

The Roman woman of those days was so deeply rooted in indolence that she apparently was not much oftener seen in shops as a purchaser than as an employee. It was – beyond a doubt – the proletarian husband himself, not his wife, who went on the stated day to knock at the portico of Minucius and receive the card, or rather the little wooden tablet (*tessera*), which proved him entitled to the bounty of Annona.[47] A historical bas-relief in the Museo dei Conservatori, which in all probability commemorates the liberal distributions of Hadrian, shows the emperor standing on a dais announcing his largesse to the Roman people, who are typified by three figures representing citizens of various ages: a child, a youth, and a grown man. The relief suggests no female recipient, nor was there probably any in the actual distributions of the imperial largesse.[48] Women are equally absent from most of the paintings of Herculaneum and Pompeii, and from the funerary bas-reliefs where the sculptor has pictured scenes in the streets and represented to the life the animation of buyers and sellers. We find woman depicted only in scenes where her presence was more or less obligatory and inevitable: where the fuller brought back the clean clothes to the lady of the house;[49] when a widow came to the marble merchant (*marmorarius*) to order a tomb for her dead husband;[50] when the boot-maker tried on shoes one by one;[51] and lastly at the dressmaker's and in the novelty shops which the Roman lady of the time of Trajan appears to have frequented diligently and eagerly. Sometimes she is shown making her choice while her husband sits on a bench at her side – as in the bas-reliefs of the Uffizi Museum at Florence[52] – sometimes with a chosen companion or a whole train of women friends, as in certain frescoes from the Campagna.[53]

On the other hand, in the Saepta Iulia, which the lethargy of the Comitia had turned into a promenade where the bronze founders, the jewellers, and the antique dealers exhausted their ingenuity in fleecing the amateur, the bargainers and the passers-by were only men: Eros the collector, the miserly Mamurra, aged Auctus.[54] And in the bakery,[55] at the butcher's,[56] in the eating shop,[57] we find only men as buyers and sellers.

In the pictures of public places which the Pompeians have left us, the women pass in their finery, sometimes alone, sometimes – as in the famous painting from the house known as Livia's on the Palatine – accompanied by a child.[58] But their hands are empty, unencumbered by either shopping bag or basket; they are obviously idle, walking about for pleasure, without care and without responsibility. We must accept the facts. In Imperial Rome women mixed in outdoor affairs as little as the Moslem woman of today in the cities of Islam. It was the Roman husband's business, as it is today among middle-class Musulmans, to do the shopping and supply the provisions for the house.[59]

But if this idleness of the Roman woman lends the Urbs an exotic, oriental air, the conditions under which the Roman man worked recall the most advanced Western practices of today. The Romans were wide awake and well organized and not overwhelmed by their tasks. They were not wholly absorbed in work. They had learned to compress it within limits which were strictly observed. The system of their corporations, coordinated by

Augustus' legislation and the edicts of his successors, permitted each trade body to set up rules valid for all its members. The laws of Nature herself and the workings of the Roman solar calendar had prevented their extending the working day beyond eight of our hours in winter. Not only is it probable that they had contrived so to arrange matters that the eight-hour day would not be exceeded even in summer, but, in my opinion, by the second century of our era they had succeeded in shortening the working day even further. It would have been unjust if the transport workers whom the law compelled to work their convoys during the night had had a heavier nocturnal task than their daytime fellow-workers. And in fact dawn was still far off when Trimalchio's guests, reeling home after the over-generous supper which he had set before them, and incapable of finding their way in a darkness rendered thicker by the fumes of their own intoxication, were suddenly set on the right road by their host's carters who were returning at the head of their convoy, having evidently finished their night's work.[60] We possess further indications that at that same period the stalls and booths and shops which opened, it is true, before daybreak, used to close long before sundown. When, for instance, a starveling parasite came far too soon to Martial's house to get an invitation for dinner, the fifth hour was not yet gone, but 'unwashed slaves' were already off duty and on their way to the bath.[61]

The free artisans were certainly not worse off in such matters than the slaves. Apart from certain people like the tavern-keepers or the 'antiquaries' who wished to tempt the strollers in the Saepta Iulia until the last moment, and who therefore did not shut down till the eleventh hour,[62] or the *tonsores* who had to fit their work into their customers' leisure and who kept open till the eighth hour,[63] by far the greater number of Roman workers downed tools either at the sixth or the seventh hour; no doubt the sixth in summer and the seventh in winter:

> *In quintam varios extendit Roma labores*
> *Sexta quies lassis, septima finis erit.*[64]

If one bears in mind that the 'hour' at the winter solstice equalled forty-five minutes according to our reckoning and seventy-five minutes at the summer solstice, these data bring the Roman working day down to about seven hours in summer and less than six in winter.

Summer and winter alike, Roman workmen enjoyed freedom during the whole or the greater part of the afternoon, and very probably our forty-hour week with its different arrangement would have weighed heavily on them rather than pleased them. Their rural habits, in the first place, and in the second their sense of their incomparable superiority, guarded them against unremitting labour and harassing tasks. So much so that at the time when Martial was writing, the merchants and shopkeepers, the artisans and labourers of the imperial race, upheld by their vital professional unions, had succeeded in so organizing their work as to allow themselves seventeen or eighteen of our twenty-four hours for the luxury of repose and enjoyed what we may call if we care to the leisure of people of means.

## 3. Justice and Politics

The intellectuals, as far as we can judge, were the people who had the worst of it; they were far worse off than either the businessmen or the workers. I am not thinking only of such monomaniacs as the elder Pliny, who were at once the heroes and the victims of a morbid appetite for work.[65] It is notorious that the Naturalist toiled over his writing for sheer love of it twenty hours out of the twenty-four, beginning his work by candlelight even in the month of August, and sometimes at one o'clock in the morning. No sooner had he got back from paying his daily homage at court than he went at it hammer and tongs with prodigious energy, only allowing himself a moment's relaxation, as noon approached, to snatch a little food. Then he stretched himself in the sun while a secretary read some author aloud to him as the last item of the morning's work. After this, he took a cold and hasty bath, followed by a short siesta and a rapid meal. Then once more to work again, passionate and indefatigable, putting in a second day's obstinate, concentrated uninterrupted work till evening supper. Pliny the Elder was an exception, the unique specimen of Roman encyclopedist, devoured by a lust for knowledge purchased even at the cost of life itself – for he died at the age of fifty-six. The researches to which he devoted himself body and soul were entirely free and disinterested and were in Latin characterized by the fair name of 'leisure'. Obviously he cannot be taken as the measure of the normal activity of his contemporaries.

Though they could not be compared even from afar to Pliny, yet the learned bourgeois who practised what we should nowadays call the liberal professions in Imperial Rome were generally absorbed in the duties of public life. We lack information about the diligence demanded of the *officiales* who filled the administrative offices and we have no means of precisely assessing the output of the imperial ministries. We find, however, enough suggestive details scattered through the literature of the time to give some idea of the weight of the obligations which rested in particular on the judicial world, and the still heavier burden which at certain periods of the year lay on the shoulders of a senator who was conscientiously bent on fulfilling the duties of his high office.

A valuable hint of Martial's teaches us that on the *dies fasti* consecrated to civil suits the ordinary tribunals sat without a break from dawn to the end of the fourth hour.[66] At first sight this would seem to limit the hearings to three of our hours in winter and not more than five hours at a stretch in summer. But when we look into the question it is clear that the text does not exclude the possibility of any adjournment, and other testimony compels us to believe that the session was resumed after an interval. In the Twelve Tables it is already laid down that a case which had been taken up before noon might be continued, if both parties were present, until sunset.[67] In Martial's day it was not unusual for an advocate on one side to claim and obtain from the judges 'six *clepsydrae*' for himself alone.[68] We may fairly deduce from a passage of Pliny the Younger that these *clepsydrae*, the regularity of whose time-keeping indicates their close relation to the equinoctial time-table, took twenty minutes of our time to run out;[69] hence the claim was for a period of up to two hours. If it was the custom for one advocate to take up in winter almost the whole of one session, it is reasonable to suppose that at least one other session for the reply and the hearing of witnesses must have been necessary to complete the case.

There were advocates, moreover, who protested at the time limit of six *clepsydrae*. Martial has pilloried one of these windbags in an epigram:

Seven water-clocks' allowance you asked for in loud tones, Caecilianus, and the judge unwillingly granted them. But you speak much and long, and with the back-tilted head, swill tepid water out of glass flasks. That you may once for all sate your oratory and your thirst, we beg you, Caecilianus, now to drink out of the water-clock![70]

If this jesting suggestion had been adopted, twenty minutes would have been subtracted from the two hours and a half rashly granted by the judge to this insatiable talker. But they were granted only in the poet's imagination; on the other hand, if the advocate on the other side had demanded the same time, the case which Martial cited – or invented – would have lasted at least five of our hours, whether interrupted or not by an adjournment.

We may rightly admire the profundity and delicacy of the judicial powers possessed by the Romans who have taught the art of law to all the world. But let us not disguise the fact that this legal genius was saddled with an accompanying evil demon, and that the Romans, jurists and pettifoggers, like the Normans of France, fell an easy prey to their passion for litigation. This mania is already discernible in the astute law speeches of Cicero. It was disastrous that it got the Urbs in its grip just at a time when the Caesars had proscribed political discussion. From the reign of one emperor to another, litigation was a rising tide which nothing could stem, throwing on the public courts more work than men could master. To mitigate the congestion of the courts Augustus, as early as the year 2 B.C., was obliged to resign to their use the forum he had built and which bears his name.[71] Seventy-five years later congestion had recurred and Vespasian wondered how to struggle with the flood of suits so numerous that 'the life of the advocates could scarce suffice' to deal with them.[72] In the Rome of the opening second century the sound of lawsuits echoed throughout the Forum, round the tribunal of the *praetor urbanus* by the *Puteal*

*Libonis,*[73] and round the tribunal of the *praetor peregrinus* between the *Puteal* of Curtius and the enclosure of Marsyas;[74] in the Basilica Iulia where the centumviri assembled; and justice thundered simultaneously from the Forum of Augustus, where the *praefectus urbi* exercised his jurisdiction,[75] from the barracks of the Castra Praetoria where the *praefectus praetorio* issued his decrees, from the Curia where the senators indicted those of their peers who had aroused distrust or displeasure, and from the Palatine where the emperor himself received the appeals of the universe in the semicircle of his private basilica, which the centuries have spared.

During the 230 days of the year open for civil cases and the 365 days open for criminal prosecutions,[76] the Urbs was consumed by a fever of litigation which attacked not only lawyers, plaintiffs, defendants, and accused, but the crowd of the curious whose appetite for scandal or taste for legal eloquence held them immobile and spellbound hour after hour in the neighbourhood of the tribunals.

The hearings were not easy. They exhausted everybody: pleaders and witnesses, judges and advocates, not excepting the spectators. Let us attend for a moment a sitting of the centumviri who exercise their jurisdiction in the Basilica Iulia, their chosen domicile.[77] Leaving the Via Sacra, which flanks the building planned and erected by Julius Caesar and reconstructed by Augustus, we mount the seven steps leading to the marble portico which framed it. Then two further steps take us into the huge hall, divided into three naves by thirty-six brick columns faced with marble. The central nave, which was also the widest, measured eighteen metres by eighty-two. The tribunes on the first storey which dominated the nave and the side-aisles that flanked it accommodated the male and female spectators who had not been fortunate enough to find places closer to the parties and in the more immediate neighbourhood of 'the court'. The centumviri who composed the court were not 100 in number as their name might seem to imply, but 180, divided into four distinct 'chambers'.[78] They took their seats either in separate sections or all four together, according to the nature of the cases which were brought before them. In the latter case the *praetor hastarius* in person presided, on an improvised dais, with his ninety assessors seated on either side of his curule chair. On benches at their feet sat the parties to the suit, their sureties, their defenders, and their friends. These formed the *corona*, or, as we might call it, the 'dress circle'. Farther off stood the general public. When the four chambers worked separately each had forty-five assessors with a decemvir as president, and the same arrangement was repeated four times, each chamber in session divided off from its neighbour by screens or curtains.

In either case, magistrates and the public were closely packed and the debates took place in a stifling atmosphere. To complete the discomfort, the acoustics of the hall were deplorable, forcing the advocates to strain their voices, the judges their attention, and the public their patience. It frequently happened that the thunder of one of the defending counsel filled the vast hall and drowned the controversies in the other chambers. In one notorious instance Galerius Tracalus (who had been consul in A.D. 68), whose voice was extraordinarily powerful, was greeted with the public applause of all four chambers, three of which could not see him and ought not to have heard him.[79] Matters were made worse and the noise increased by the enthusiasm of 'a low rout of claqueurs', whom shameless advocates, following the example of Larcius Licinus, were in the habit of dragging round after them to the hearing of any case they hoped to win, as much to impress the jury as to enhance their own reputation.[80] In vain Pliny the Younger protested against this practice. One day when Domitius Afer was pleading in Quintilian's presence and rejoicing one chamber of the centumviri by his impressive speech and calm delivery, his ears were deafened by immoderate clamour from outside. He stopped speaking in surprise. When silence was restored he resumed the thread of his discourse. New cries. Renewed silence on his part. The same interruption came a third time. Finally he inquired who was pleading next door. 'Licinus,' was the answer. Then he gave up all attempt to continue and abandoned the suit. 'Centumviri,' he said, 'it is all over with our profession.' It was not all over with these bravo criers, these σοφοκλεῖς, as they were called in Greek, 'signifying that they were applauders by profession', or these 'supper praisers' (*laudiceni*) as the Romans called them.[81] Whether it was good or bad, the speech they acclaimed at command brought them their bread and butter; and they could, without breaking the terms of their contract, withdraw their attention from the case as soon as some counsel who had not hired them took the floor. They remained, on the chance of being further wanted, but returned to their favourite pastimes, such as the games for which crude 'boards' were scratched on the steps of the Basilica Iulia.[82] But the hired applauders were the only people in the hall who enjoyed themselves. It is easy to imagine the discomfort and annoyance which a case inflicted on an attentive judge and a conscientious counsel when it had to be conducted in the middle of this mob, to the accompaniment of a continual uproar and periodic outbursts of mechanical applause.

Pliny the Younger flatters himself that he had established his reputation by pronouncing before the centumviri the longest and best of his speeches.[83] But at what a price in mental and physical exhaustion! Recalling at the end of his career his early triumphs in the Basilica Iulia, he gives the impression that he remembered them with horror,[84] and that he would have said of them, as of his sojourn at Centumcellae (Città Vecchia) in attendance on the tribunal which Trajan had set up in his villa there – 'What honourable days! But what exhausting ones!: *Vides quam honesti, quam severi dies!*'[85]

When the emperor was obliged to summon before him the cases over which he had direct jurisdiction or those which had been appealed from the provinces, he was as much a victim of overwork as the ordinary judges. We get light on this from the session in which Pliny took part during one of the emperor's country visits to his Centumcellae villa.[86] It lasted only three days. The three cases on the list were of no great importance. The first was an unfounded accusation brought by jealous slanderers against a young Ephesian, Claudius Ariston, a 'nobleman of great munificence and unambitious popularity', who was honourably acquitted. The next day Gallitta was tried on a charge of adultery. Her husband, a military tribune, was on the point of standing for office when she disgraced both him and herself by an intrigue with a centurion. The third day was devoted to an inquiry 'concerning the much-discussed will of Iulius Tiro, part of which was plainly

genuine, while the other part was said to be forged'. Though
Trajan would call and hear only one case a day, it nevertheless
wasted the greater part of his time. The probate case in particular
gave him a great deal of trouble. The authenticity of the codicils
was challenged by Eurythmus, the emperor's freedman and one of
his procurators in Dacia. The heirs, mistrusting the local courts,
wrote a joint letter to the emperor petitioning him to reserve the
case to his own hearing. After this request had been granted, however, some of the heirs pretended to hesitate out of respect for the
fact that Eurythmus was the emperor's own freedman, and it was
only on Trajan's formal invitation that two of them appeared at
the bar to lodge accusations in their turn. Eurythmus asked leave to
speak to prove his charges. The two heirs who had received permission to state their case refused to take the opportunity of doing
so, pleading that loyalty to their co-heirs debarred them from representing the interests of all when only two were present. Delighted
by these manoeuvres and counter-manoeuvres, counsels played
hide-and-seek to their hearts' content amid the jungle of legal
procedure. Again and again the emperor recalled them to the
point at issue, which he was determined not to lose sight of. Finally,
worn out by their chicanery, he turned at last to his own counsel
and begged him to put an end to their cavilling, after which he
declared the session closed and invited his assessors to the delightful
distractions (*iucundissimae remissiones*) which he had prepared for
them, but which he could not offer them before the dinner
hour.

All the while none of the people concerned had overstepped the
deference due to the emperor's sovereign majesty. We cannot claim
that it was always so. Sometimes the accused did not hesitate to
abuse the Caesar, and the imperial judicial session ended with what
we may rightly call 'a scene'. One of the Oxyrhynchus papyri
records that an Egyptian of the name of Appianus, hymnasiarch
and priest of Alexandria, had the pride and audacity to stage such
a scene with Commodus who had just sentenced him to death.[87]
The emperor had barely pronounced the sentence when Appianus
rose in scandalous defiance: 'Do you realize whom you are addressing?' asked Commodus. 'Certainly; a tyrant.' 'Not so,'

retorted Commodus, 'you are speaking to the emperor.' 'Certainly not,' was the reply. 'Your father, the divine Marcus Aurelius Antoninus, had every right to call himself emperor, because he cultivated wisdom, despised money, and loved what was good. But you have no such right, for you are the antithesis of your father: you love tyranny, vice, and brutality.'

Thus the princeps was liable not only to be deafened and exhausted by the speechifyings and intrigues of his litigants like any simple centumvir, but to be abused by them into the bargain. While the court of the emperor recalls the magnificence and splendour of Louis XIV, his tribunal suggests more the familiarity and popular tumult which surround the justice of an Eastern pasha seated on his divan in the patio of his seraglio; but it is endlessly complicated in addition by the subtleties and sonorities of the long-drawn-out Roman procedure.

Absorbing and exacting as might be the duties of judges and counsel, however, there were times when a senator could even less call his soul his own. True, since the days of Augustus the number of ordinary sessions of the Senate (*dies legitimi*) had been greatly reduced. The months of September and October were decreed to be a compulsory vacation; during the rest of the year the Senate was normally convoked only twice a month on the Calends and the Ides;[88] and the legislative activity of the Caesars left the lawmaking functions of the Senate to lie dormant. But from time to time the Senate had to reckon with extraordinary sessions, all the more overladen with business for being infrequent, especially such as compelled or permitted the princeps to perform terrible acts of vengeance for political crimes, for which he preferred nominally to evade responsibility. At such moments the Fathers were condemned to forced labour, and they had no means of escaping the slavery of these sensational convocations unless they could find some pretext for absence that would be accepted as valid and would not cast doubt on their motives for abstention.

The Senate assembled in the Curia of Julius Caesar.[89] Its reconstruction under Diocletian has in all probability preserved the original plan and dimensions. It measured 25·5 metres in length and 67·6 in width. It could scarcely have provided space for more than

300 seats distributed in three rising tiers, as Professor Bartoli has recently discovered by his excavations beneath the floor of the ancient church of Sant' Adriano. On great occasions, when at least one-third of the total 900 members of the Senate responded to the summons, they must have been as tightly packed as the English Parliament in the House of Lords when the Commons attend to hear the Speech from the Throne. After a sacrifice and preliminary prayers, the senators entered the Curia at the first hour of the day, and did not escape till night was falling.[90] They sat again next day, and the day after, and the day after that again, and for several days more. They could not possibly have endured this penitential overcrowding if the rules of the assembly, or rather the customary practice which served instead, had not implicitly permitted them to come and go, vanish and reappear at will. In the hall there was an endless series of discussions, a continual deluge of eloquence and knavery.

Pliny the Younger gives accounts of several sessions of the Senate transformed into a High Court: those where Marius Priscus, proconsul of Africa, appeared with his rivals in the art of prevarication;[91] those which investigated and punished the extortions of Caecilius Classicus, ex-governor of Baetica.[92] These reports call forth our pity for the senator chained to his curule chair. The first of these cases, over which Trajan presided in his capacity of consul, lasted from dawn to dusk through three consecutive days. On one of them Pliny the Younger, who had been entrusted with the prosecution of one of Priscus' accomplices, spoke for five hours without intermission, and toward the close his fatigue became so manifest that the emperor sent him more than once the advice 'to spare his voice and breath'. When he had finished, Claudius Marcellinus replied for the accused in a speech of the same length. When this second orator had reached his peroration Trajan adjourned the court till next day for fear a third harangue 'might be cut in two by nightfall'.

In comparison with the impeachment of Priscus the case of Classicus, in which Pliny's role was confined to listening and offering an opinion, appeared much easier to endure and seemed really 'short and easy: *et circa Classicum quidem brevis et expeditus labor*'.

Easy it certainly was, for the Spaniards had broken the back of the business for the prosecution, and mined in advance all the positions of the defence by laying hands on the intimate and cynical correspondence of the accused; in particular on a letter in which, blending his love affairs and his extortions, he announced his return to Rome to one of his mistresses in terms which inculpated him beyond hope of salvation: 'Hurrah! Hurrah! I am coming back to you a free man, for I have raised four million sesterces by selling out the Baetici.' But short the Classicus case certainly was not, despite the overwhelming nature of the facts established by this damning evidence. Like the Priscus case it took up three sessions of the Senate, and though Pliny the Younger had played a less spectacular part in it, he came out exhausted, when it was over, just as after the Priscus affair: 'You will easily conceive', he writes to his dear friend Cornelius Minicianus, '. . . the fatigue we underwent in speaking and debating so long and so often, and in examining, assisting, and confuting such a number of witnesses; not to mention the difficulties and annoyance of the defendants' friends: *Concipere animo potes quam sinus fatigati!* '[93] We can indeed conceive it, but what seems inconceivable to us is that the Romans should have tolerated this exhausting system with no attempt to modify or lighten it. Are we to believe that their heads and nerves were more resistant to strain than ours? Or that, having been inured by a century of public readings, they had become case-hardened against exasperation, weariness, and boredom?

## 4. Public Readings

The habit of giving and hearing public readings and recitations, which was the absorbing occupation and perpetual distraction of cultivated Romans, is so foreign to our manners that it demands a few words of explanation.

Scholars and men of letters in Rome knew nothing for two centuries of what we mean by 'publishing'. Down to the end of the republic, they made copies of their works in their own houses or in the house of some patron, and then distributed the manuscripts to their friends. Atticus, to whom Cicero had entrusted his speeches and his treatises, had the inspiration of converting the copying studio he had set up for himself into a real industrial concern.[94] At the same time Caesar, no less a revolutionary in things intellectual than in things material, helped to procure him a clientele by founding the first State Library in Rome, on the model of the great library which existed in the museum at Alexandria. The completion of the Roman library was due to Asinius Pollio, and it soon begot daughter libraries in the provinces.[95] The multiplication of public and municipal libraries resulted in the rise of publishers (*bibliopolae*, *librarii*). The new profession soon had its celebrities: the Sosii, of whom Horace speaks, who had opened a shop for *volumina* at the exit of the Vicus Tuscus on the Forum, near the statue of the god Vertumnus, behind the Temple of Castor;[96] Dorus, to whom one went for copies of Cicero and Livy;[97] Tryphon, who sold Quintilian's *Institutio Oratoria* and Martial's *Epigrams*;[98] and rivals of Tryphon — Q. Pollius Valerianus; Secundus, not far from the Forum of Peace; and Atrectus in the Argiletum.[99]

These book merchants, who assembled and trained teams of expert slaves, sold their copies dear enough – 2 or 3 sesterces for a text which would correspond to about 20 pages of our duodecimo; 5 denarii or 20 sesterces for a *liber*, which would make somewhat less than 40 similar pages but had been elaborately gotten up.[100] They were often paid by unknown writers for carrying out the work to order, but even in the case of famous authors they did not buy the original manuscript which they condescended to 'publish'.[101] They were also exempt from making any subsequent payment to the author, for the jurists had vaguely extended to all writings on papyrus or on parchment the old legal principle that *solo cedit superficies*, that is to say, the ownership of every addition follows the ownership of the basis to which it is added.[102] Thus the publishers grew rich by dispatching all over the world, 'to the confines of Britain and the frosts of the Getae', the verses 'which the centurion hummed in his distant garrison', but the poet's 'money-bag knew nothing of it' as he starved in his poverty.[103]

In these conditions it was inevitable that literary beginners and impecunious authors should seize the opportunity given by a public recitation of their prose or of their poems either to escape the demands of the *librarius* or to force his hand. They had no hesitation in thus deflowering a subsequent edition which would never bring them in a penny. It was also natural that the imperial government, which hoped to control literary production but shrank from the scandal caused by the *autos-da-fé* decreed by Tiberius,[104] or the death sentence which Domitian had pronounced against Hermogenes of Tarsus and his publishers,[105] preferred to arrive unobtrusively at the same result by underground methods which had proved effective in the valley of the Nile. The prefects and procurators placed in charge of the public libraries already possessed the power to effect the slow but certain disappearance of dangerous or suspect books to which they had closed the doors of their bookcases.[106] They claimed the right to sow the good seed of writings favourable to the regime and compositions useful as propaganda. We need, therefore, feel no surprise if Asinius Pollio, who gave his name to the first library in Rome, was the first to recite his works before his friends.[107] This practice was too well suited to the conditions of writers and the desires of government not to become the fashion quickly. Thus the conjunction of omnipotent publishers and servile libraries gave birth to a monster, the public *recitatio*, which soon grew to be the curse of literature. The calculations of the politicians and the vanity of authors set the fashion. After that nothing could stop it.

From the very beginning of his reign, Augustus' enthusiasm for recitations helped their progress; he would listen 'with as much goodwill as endurance to those who read aloud to him not only verses or history but also speeches and dialogues.'[108] A few years later things had gone even further. Claudius, who at Livy's instigation had started to write history, delighted to declaim his chapters one by one as he finished them.[109] Since he was of the blood royal, he had no difficulty in getting a full house. But he was shy and a stammerer, and at one of his experimental readings a grotesque incident occurred – a bench collapsed under the weight of a fat member of the audience, provoking volleys of laughter that were not on the agenda. After this he gave up reading aloud himself. But he did not abandon the pleasure of hearing his lucubrations declaimed in the cultured voice of a freedman. Later, when he became emperor, he put his palace at the disposal of others for their readings, and was only too happy if he could find leisure to be present as an ordinary listener. He would suddenly appear among an audience startled at this unexpected honour, a trick he played one day on the ex-consul Nonianus.[110] Domitian in his turn affected a passionate love of poetry and on more than one occasion himself read his own verses in public.[111] It is probable that Hadrian followed suit; at least he set his seal on public readings by consecrating a building for this exclusive purpose: the Athenaeum, a sort of miniature theatre which he had built with his own money on a site which is unknown to us.[112] His subjects were as grateful to him for this as if he had at last decided to house the 'liberal arts' (*ludus ingenuarum artium*) in a building worthy of them.[113]

The building of the Athenaeum was merely an indication of the importance public readings had acquired in the Urbs, which was now submerged under a flood of talent. There was nothing new about its architecture; it simply added an official monument to the numerous other halls which had long been filled with the eloquent murmur of these recitals. Any well-educated man who was moderately well off cherished the ambition of having a room in his house, the *auditorium*, especially for readings. More than one friend of Pliny the Younger embarked light-heartedly on this considerable expense – Calpurnius Piso, for instance, and Titinius Capito.[114] The plan of these *auditoria* varied little from house to house: a dais on which the author-reader would take his seat after having attended to his toilet, smoothed his hair, put on a new toga, and adorned his fingers with all his rings for the occasion. He was then prepared to entrance his audience not only with the merit of his writing but by the distinction of his presence, the caress of his glances, the modesty of his speech, and the gentleness of his modulations.[115] Behind him hung the curtains which hid those of his guests who wished to hear him without being seen, his wife for example.[116] In front of the reader the public who had been summoned by notes delivered at their homes (*codicilli*) were accommodated, in armchairs (*cathedrae*) for people of the higher ranks and benches for the others. Attendants told off for the purpose distributed the programmes of the séance (*libelli*).[117]

All this *mise en scène* was not within the reach of everybody's purse. Poor writers depended on the goodwill and generosity of the rich. Great gentlemen like Titinius Capito, animated by the best spirit of good-fellowship, were very ready to lend their auditorium.[118] Rich men, less generous but more practical, hired theirs out for cash down. Juvenal pours contempt on these Harpagons wearing the mask of a Maecenas who exacted large sums for the brief enjoyment of a 'tumble-down house in some distant quarter ... with tiers of seats resting on hired beams and chairs in the front row which will have to be returned when done with.'[119]

An auditorium was, however, not indispensable to a public recital unless the author was anxious to cut a dash and influence opinion. The more fastidious author whose reputation was already well established preferred a select audience of connoisseurs like himself. Pliny the Younger, for instance, took pride in inviting only a handful of friends whom he could accommodate in his *triclinium*, or dining-room, some stretched on the couches which were the permanent furniture of the room, and the others in chairs carried in for the occasion.[120] As for the poor devils who had neither *triclinium* nor the money to hire a room, they contrived to find an audience all the same. As soon as they spied a group of people anywhere whose curiosity at least they might pique, they would mingle with them and unblushingly unroll their manuscript – in the forum, under a portico, or among the crowd at the baths.[121] The *recitatio* had invaded even the crossroads. Examining the contemporary literature, we soon get the impression that everyone was reading something, no matter what, aloud in public all the time, morning and evening, winter and summer.

If you were in search of a large audience it was wise to avoid the hot months when many Romans had withdrawn to their country villas. But if you attached more importance to the quality than to the quantity of your hearers, the summer months were perhaps the best. Pliny the Younger 'read' in July, because he hoped that the closing of the courts would allow him more freedom of mind and would permit his rivals at the bar to grace his performance with their presence.[122] For the same reason, most readings took place in the afternoon when busy men had leisure at their disposal. But there were some insatiables who did not find an afternoon enough to pour forth their masterpieces and flattered themselves that they could keep an audience spellbound for a whole day (*totum diem impendere*) without prejudice to the morrow and the days following.[123] Surely we need not continue to wonder at the compulsory overwork the Romans tolerated in their tribunals and in the Senate when we consider the docility with which the idlers of Rome submitted to the optional overwork of the *auditoria*.

It is true that the audience did not stand on ceremony with their host, and that their attention was often more or less politely casual and intermittent. Pliny the Younger in his letters tells a number of anecdotes that give us insight into the liberties in which the listening public indulged. In the course of a certain April, for instance, 'scarce a day has passed wherein we have not been entertained with the recital of some poem'.[124] The public was at its last gasp. People continued mechanically to attend the séances from force of habit, but they seat themselves in the antechambers; spend the time of the recitation in talk and send in every now and then to inquire whether the author has come in, whether he has read the preface or whether he has almost finished the piece. ... Then they just look in and withdraw again before the end, some by stealth and others without ceremony. On one occasion Pliny the Younger arrived late and found a crowd of younger men.[125] He noted with a mixture of pride and embarrassment that his entry recalled those present to a sense of courtesy, cut short the jests they had been interchanging and re-established silence as if by magic. At other times he came upon audiences who, though they strove to maintain the appearance of decent manners and refrained from making a noise, nevertheless showed a coolness and lack of interest which bordered on insolence, if they did not abandon themselves to the refreshment of a well-earned snooze. At one *recitatio* the celebrated jurist Javolenus Priscus, a friend of the reader, was among the audience.[126] The host unrolled his *volumen* and read the first line of his poem which happened to begin:

'*Priscus, thou dost command* ...'

Javolenus roused himself with a start from the daydream in which his thoughts had been wandering leagues away and hastily ejaculated: 'But I don't command anything!' 'Think,' says Pliny, 'what a peal of laughter and what numerous sallies this droll accident occasioned.'

In other cases the listeners pretended to devote their attention to the proceedings, but their behaviour roused Pliny to 'a little fit of anger'.[127] There were some 'men of eloquence in their own estimation' among the audience and although 'the work read to us was a highly finished performance . . . they sat like so many deaf-mutes, without so much as moving a lip or a hand or once rising to their feet, even by way of relief from a seated posture'. Pliny unleashed his wrath at 'this indolence, this arrogance, this gaucherie, nay idiocy, that will be at the expense of a whole day merely to affront and leave as your enemy the man you visited as a particular friend'.

But the power of concentration had its limits even for the Romans, and nothing is more exhausting in any language than continuous eloquence. It was surely unreasonable on the author's part to inflict on an audience a whole day's reading of any work, however excellent; its beauties were bound to wither under fatigue and boredom. A recitation continued without pause and without end could produce only nausea; the hearers' one escape was inattention. Instead of promoting a love of literature, these public readings produced mental indigestion and must more often have deadened than stimulated the love of letters. Their corrupting influence was only increased by the introduction of an incoherent variety of items to lessen the monotony. They became a chaos of defeaning sound. Lawyers re-edited their speeches for them, and politicians polished up their harangues.[128] Men of the world who had never written in their lives, save in the course of their professional duties or to keep up family and social relations, did not hesitate to reproduce the eulogy they had pronounced at the funeral of a relative.[129]

As for professional writers, they foresaw a future for their most trifling composition and proved themselves inexhaustible. When pleadings and speeches were used up, they read books of history, which were best received when they dealt with a past so distant that no one present need feel embarrassment – 'for men are ashamed to hear those actions repeated which yet they do not blush to commit!'[130] In verse, the audiences were treated to a medley of Pliny's banter, Calpurnius Piso's mythology of the constellations, the elegies of Passennus Paulus, the *Thebais* of Statius, and a rigmarole of banal epics compounded of echoes of Statius and reminiscences of Virgil, 'tales about Hercules or Diomedes, or the bellowing in the labyrinth, and the lad Icarus who crashed his flying machine into the sea'.[131] To these must be added tragedies without scenery and comedies without actors.[132] One sort of literary composition succeeded another on the tribunes of the *auditoria*, with little of taste or relevance.

In vain Pliny the Younger seeks to beguile himself by extolling the excellence and value of a type of performance in which he knew he excelled, and tries to convince himself that a public reading stimulates him to revise and perfect his speeches, and that its object is to evoke the criticisms which will enable him to polish away its flaws.[133] These are only the pretexts, albeit sincere, and the quibblings, albeit ingenious, of a spoiled child who would be inconsolable if his pet toy were lost or forbidden. These slender benefits and problematical advantages could not outweigh the inconvenience, the danger, and the harm that Horace from the outset had foretold.[134] How horrified the poet would have been if he could have returned to Rome a hundred years after his death when the disastrous practice of recitations had brought a rich crop of all the ills he had only dimly foreseen! By that time the *recitatio* was well on the way to become the last straw among the evils of a purely formal education. The habit of writing and then of reading from *volumina*, whose unrolling never permitted attention to more than one passage at a time, with as little heed to what had gone before as to what was afterwards to come, had already induced such fragmentary and scrappy composition that even the best of Roman authors, judged by our standards, more or less deserve the condemnation Caligula pronounced on Seneca: 'sand without mortar (*arena sine calce*)'.[135] These public readings in which the author aimed to dazzle his audience more by the brilliance of the detail than by the beauty of the general plan aggravated the evil influence of the *volumen* and hastened the disastrous evolution which culminated in a taste so perverted that it responded only to tirades aimed at effect and to epigrammatic conceits (*sententiae*). By detaching the works they seized on from their natural setting – pleadings from the law court, political speeches from the Curia, tragedy and comedy from the theatre – these public recitations completed the severance of such links as still existed between literature and life, and drained literature of that genuine human content without which no masterpiece is possible.[136] They were peculiarly noxious in a manner of their own, to which the moderns have hitherto been no less blind than the ancient, and which helped to kill literature itself. For one thing, the opportunity they gave the author of gratifying his vanity gradually turned writers aside from ambitions nobler than the attainment of immediate intoxicating success before an audience stimulated to artificial enthusiasm by the presence of complaisant friends and of colleagues hoping to secure reciprocal admiration. It may still be a matter of dispute how much harm has been or will be caused to literature by the extension of the radio, but there is no reason to doubt that when the public-reading mania was at its height it did enormous damage to the production of *volumina*. And it is equally undeniable that the disease devoured like a cancer hordes of people who had developed through it a false belief in their literary vocation.

When once the public reading became an established fashion in Rome, and was recognized as the main and almost exclusive occupation of people of letters, literature lost all dignity and all serious purpose. The fashionable world adopted a currency which became more and more alloyed as the circle of amateurs was enlarged. Those who were invited wished to be the inviters in their turn, and when everybody mounted the dais in rotation, it ended by every listener becoming an author. This was in appearance the triumph of literature. But it was a Pyrrhic victory, an insensate inflation which foreshadowed bankruptcy. When there were as many writers as listeners, or, as we should say, as many authors as readers, and the two roles were indistinguishable, literature suffered from an incurable, malignant tumour.

# VIII

## SHOWS AND SPECTACLES

*

### 1. 'Panem et Circenses'

EVERYBODY knows by heart Juvenal's tirade against his degenerate contemporaries, 'the mob of Remus', a laconic indictment which throbs more with scorn than anger: 'Now that no one buys our votes, the public has long since cast off its cares; the people that once bestowed commands, consulships, legions, and all else, now meddles no more and longs eagerly for just two things – bread and circuses.

> *. . . duas tantum res anxius optat,*
> *panem et circenses.'*[1]

Famous though they are, it is well to recall these verses at the beginning of the chapter which explains them. Their vehement invective, which scorches like a branding iron, voices the noblest republican protest that was raised under the empire. They state an incontestable and dominant fact; they note a historic truth which Fronto was to record forty years later with the calm objectivity of the historian faced by irrefutable evidence: 'the Roman people is absorbed by two things above all others, its food supplies and its shows [*populum Romanum duabus praecipue rebus, annona et spectaculis teneri.*]'[2]

The Caesars had in fact shouldered the dual task of feeding and amusing Rome. Their monthly distributions at the Portico of Minucius assured the populace its daily bread. By the shows and spectacles they provided in various public places, religious or secular, in the Forum, at the theatres, in the Stadium, in the Amphitheatre, in mock sea fights (*naumachiae*), they occupied and disciplined its leisure hours. They kept the plebs expectantly awaiting the ever-renewed entertainments, and even in lean years, when treasury shortages compelled them to ration their expenditure, they exhausted their ingenuity to provide the public with more festivals than any people, in any country, at any time, has ever seen.

Let us examine the calendars deciphered for us by the epigraphists which note the dates of the Roman festivals.[3] In the first place we should keep in mind that the Roman year in general was divided into two kinds of days, the *dies fasti* and the *dies nefasti*.[4] On the former, civil and judicial business might be transacted without fear of offending the gods; on the latter such business was suspended. Here we need not take into account the fourteen days of a mixed nature when civil affairs might proceed normally after certain rites had been performed or during a certain limited part of the day.

Among the *dies nefasti*, we find a certain number characterized as *feriae* or public holidays, as well as another group set apart for *ludi* or public games. Such days are usually marked in surviving calendars with the letters NP and scholars do not agree as to the difference, if any, between the days marked with these two letters and those characterized by the single letter N, meaning *nefas*.[5] Yet it is certain that *feriae* and days set aside for games were public holidays in the present sense of the word, when work was relaxed or suspended altogether, and men gave themselves over to rest and pleasure. It is with these days that we are primarily concerned.

Let us begin with the days on which performances were held at public expense in the circus or the theatre, carrying our computations down to the time of Claudius, when the evidence of stone calendars breaks off. There were, first of all, the games which the republic at grave crises in its history had decreed in honour of the gods, and which were destined to minister to the ambition of the dictators and the policy of the Caesars: the *Ludi Romani*, instituted in 366 B.C. and ultimately lasting from 4 to 19 September; the *Ludi Plebei*, which made their appearance somewhere between 220 and 216 B.C. and were then held from 4 to 17 November; the *Ludi Apollinares*, which dated from 208 B.C. and went on from 6 to 13 July; the *Ludi Ceriales*, consecrated to Ceres in 202 B.C., which fitted in between 12 and 19 April; the *Ludi Megalenses*, in honour of the Great Idaean Mother of the Gods, Cybele, whose sanctuary was dedicated on the Palatine in 191 B.C., and whose games had since been held every year from 4 to 10 April; the *Ludi Florales*, whose homage the goddess Flora seems regularly to have enjoyed only after 173 B.C., and whose celebration was attended by special ceremonies from 28 April to 3 May. All in all, then, we find 59 days devoted to these traditional games of the Roman Republic before the time of Sulla.[6]

The first addition to this group is connected with his name. It is the *Ludi Victoriae Sullanae* – in the title we can detect Sulla's pretensions to divinity – which for two hundred years after his death continued to be held from 26 October to 1 November. Next, we learn of the *Ludi Victoriae Caesaris*, which from 20 to 30 July continued to recall to Roman memory the exploits of the conqueror of Gaul; and the *Ludi Fortunae Reducis*, which Augustus instituted in 11 B.C. and which lasted for ten days from 3 to 12 October. To these we must add the three days of the *Ludi Palatini* instituted by Livia in memory of Augustus;[7] the two days of the *Ludi Martiales* celebrated on 12 May and 1 August in connexion with the dedication of the shrine and temple of Mars Ultor; and the day of games celebrating the birthday of the emperor. The sum total for this post-Sullan group is 34 days, which, added to the 59 days of pre-Sullan games, gives us 93 public holidays when the Roman was entertained at spectacles at the expense of the State.

But this is not all. Our calendars also record the forty-five *feriae publicae*, the origins of which are lost in the mists of early Latin history but which were kept up under the empire: among others, the Lupercalia in February; the Parilia, Cerialia, and Vinalia in April; the Vestalia and Matronalia in June; the Volcanalia in August; and the Saturnalia in December. Ceremonies having the nature of games were connected with some of the holidays in this ancient group: for instance, the dance of the Salii which took place on the festival of the Quinquatrus (19 March) and the Armilustrium (19 October), the foot races of the Robigalia (25 April), the races on foot and muleback of the Consualia (21 August and 15 December). But since these festivals were essentially religious and their chief purpose was not the entertainment of the people, we may conveniently set them aside from the days devoted primarily to games. Allowing, then, for overlapping, in that six of these ancient festivals were celebrated on days when games were being held, we have 39 new holidays to add to the previous 93 game days, making a total of 132 days in all.

Finally, in the time of Caesar, we meet a new kind of public holiday, decreed by the Senate to commemorate a significant event in the life of the emperor. The first of these to appear were Caesar's birthday and the anniversaries of five of his most important military victories. The precedent was followed under Augustus and 18 new holidays were proclaimed commemorating secular and religious events of his reign or connected with his memory after death.[8] To these we must add six more days pertaining to events extending into the reign of Claudius. But of these 30 new holidays, only 18 do not coincide with days otherwise celebrated, so that our sum total of all holidays reaches an even 150. Finally, eight of the Ides dedicated to Jupiter and one of the Calends dedicated to Mars do not fall on other holidays and must be added to our list.[9]

In other words, at the time of Claudius the Roman calendar contained 159 days expressly marked as holidays, of which 93 were devoted to games given at public expense. The list does not include the many ceremonies for which the State took no responsibility and supplied no funds, but which were much in favour among the people and took place around the sanctuaries of the quarters, in the chapels of foreign deities whose worship was officially sanctioned, and in the *scholae* or meeting places of the guilds and colleges. Even less does it take account of the *feriae privatae* of individuals or family groups.

After Claudius, we have very little precise information as to public holidays. To be sure, a number of *ferialia* are still extant – lists giving a selected number of days which were celebrated with religious ceremonies by a limited group of people.[10] But in many cases it is difficult to conjecture whether these days were designated as public holidays in the city of Rome. Naturally the list of holidays changed from reign to reign, but the additions seem to have outnumbered the subtractions, for we know that Claudius,[11] Vespasian,[12] and Marcus Aurelius[13] all found it necessary to cut down the number of holidays. Marcus Aurelius, his biographer tells us, restored the business year to 230 days; and from later evidence it has been reasonably conjectured that most of the remaining 135 were devoted to public spectacles. For the manuscript Calendar of Philocalus, written in A.D. 354 and reflecting conditions of the third century, records 175 days of games out about of 200 public holidays, as against 93 out of 159 for the early empire, an increase from about 59 per cent to 87 per cent in the proportion of game days.[14]

We have, moreover, been speaking of ordinary years during which nothing remarkable had happened and the normal programme was not combined with the recurrence of quadrennial cycles such as the earlier Actiaca and the later Agon Capitolinus, and at longer intervals with the return of the 'renewal of the century' prolonged over a series of days, such as took place in 17 B.C. and in A.D. 88 and 204, or of the 'centenaries' of the Eternal City as in 47, 147, and 248.[15] Above all, we must not overlook the festivals which defy exact computation because they were dependent on imperial caprice and might be suddenly inserted in the calendar at any moment. These the Caesars decreed in quantities. They grew in importance with the prosperity of an emperor's reign, and their unexpectedness greatly intensified the interest they aroused. They were the triumphs which an emperor made the Senate decree for him; the *munera* or gladiatorial combats which he decreed on some arbitrary pretext. These gladiatorial displays soon came to equal the *ludi* in frequency, and in the second century they sometimes went on for months.[16] The reality, therefore, far exceeded our statistics; and in attempting to analyse it, we are driven to conclude that in the epoch we are studying Rome enjoyed at least one day of holiday for every working day.

## 2. The Employment of Leisure

At first sight the discovery of this proportion is almost stupefying. On reflection, however, it is obvious that it was the inevitable consequence of the political and social evolution which had led the masters of the empire to make use of and extend the old religious festivals as a means of consolidating their power over the masses

227

who crammed the city and swarmed round their palace on every side.

Religion presided at the birth of every one of these Roman 'holidays', and was more or less inseparably bound up with each. An outcrop of the religious substratum is visible on the surface of the ancient ceremonies which the Romans never omitted to perform though they had long since forgotten their significance. Thus the fishing contest of 7 June, over which the city praetor presided in person, ended on the Vulcanal rock with a fish fry for the prize winners.[17] But a note of Festus which cannot be challenged indicates that this offering of fried fish represented a sacrifice in which the god Vulcanus accepted the substitution of fish for human victims: *pisciculi pro animis humanis*.[18] Similarly, there was a horse-race in the Forum on 15 October, the result of which betrays its primitive origin.[19] Woe to the winner! The *flamen* of Mars sacrificed the luckless race-horse immediately after it had won the victory. Its blood was collected in two vessels, and the contents of one were straightway poured over the hearth of the Regia – the traditional palace of Numa and home of the Pontifex Maximus – while the other was sent to the Vestals who kept it in reserve for the year's lustrations. As for the horse's head, which had been severed by the knife of the sacrificing priest, the dwellers by the Sacred Way and the inhabitants of the Subura fought savagely to decide which of their respective quarters should have the honour of exhibiting on the wall of one of its buildings the trophy of the 'October Horse'. The significance of these strange customs is revealed at once when we turn back to the distant past in which they had their origin. Each year on their return from the annual military campaigning, which began in spring and continued until autumn, the Latins of ancient Rome offered a horse-race to the gods by way of thanksgiving; and they sacrificed the winning horse that the city might be purified by the shedding of its blood and protected by the fetish of its skeleton.

These two immemorial usages at once disclose the ancestral rituals. But religion is not less present for being less evident in the more recent games of the republic. The games designed to call Olympus to the rescue in hours of crisis had been instituted suc-

cessively in honour of Jupiter, of Apollo, of Ceres, of Cybele, and
of Flora. When, later, the dictators lengthened the list of games in
honour of their military victories, they designed to raise these
victories, and therewith themselves, to a more than human plane.
In the combats as in the races, in the dramatic representation as in
the imperial purple, the underlying idea was not merely to appease
the gods but to capture something of their strength, momentarily
incarnate in the magistrate celebrating his triumph, in the actors of
the drama, and in the victors of the contests. When, in 105 B.C., the
State for the first time inaugurated on its own behalf gladiatorial
combats such as private individuals had been wont to hold beside
the graves of their relations, it gave these displays the name of
*munera*, which they retained through the ages following.[20] This
word, implying a favour, gift, or funeral honours, connotes the
sinister function of these shows: to appease the wrath of the gods
by the death of men and to assuage the unrest of the dead by fresh
slaughter of the living. Festus defined them in the time of Augustus
as 'an oblation dictated by duty.'[21] 'An honour we are bound to
render to the spirits of the dead,' declared Tertullian at the end of
the second century.[22] 'Blood poured on the ground to calm the
scythe-bearing god in the heavens,' Ausonius was to call it, under
the later empire.[23]

It would almost seem that this horrible conception of human
sacrifice, inherited by the Romans from the sombre Etruscan
genius, had survived the centuries unaltered and unweakened. This
is only apparently the case. In imperial times any such erudite
explanation would have passed over the head of a public which in
its heart and for its own pleasure had completely secularized its
sacred games. No doubt the public went to the circus as to a service
and put on its festal toga for the occasion, for an edict of Augustus
had made the wearing of a toga obligatory.[24] No doubt, again, the
public was bound under pain of expulsion to observe the proprieties
and to refrain, for instance, from eating or drinking during the
races.[25] But in these matters the Romans had the feeling not of
following a liturgy but of complying with a rule of etiquette.
When, in compliance with the rule, they rose to their feet to
acclaim the inaugural procession in which the statues of the *Divi*

accompanied the official gods, they were demonstrating not their religious fervour but their fidelity to the dynasty, their attachment to their professional group under the patronage of this god or that goddess, and their admiration for the organization of so magnificent a parade.[26] If there chanced to be anyone among the crowd so ingenuously pious as to imagine that the divinity dear to his heart had made a sign of understanding or a protective movement in his direction, his unwonted credulity attracted the curiosity of his neighbours and excited the humour of the gossips.[27]

The ancient religion of Rome was still able to lend the hallowed association of its traditions to the splendour of the imperial spectacles and shows. But the public knew little of it and cared less; if they respected it at all, it was unconsciously. In this domain as in others, new beliefs had driven the old into the background, if they had not entirely eradicated them. If any living faith made the spectators' hearts beat faster it was a faith in astrology. They would gaze entranced at the accidental patterns formed in the sand of the arena; in the moat (*euripus*) which surrounded it they would read symbols of the seas; in the obelisk or *spina* they would see an emblem of the sun darting his rays to highest heaven; in the twelve stalls (*carceres*) from which the chariots started the constellations of the Zodiac; in the seven tracks of the race courses the circuit of the seven planets in the heavens and the succession of the seven days of the week; in the circus itself a miniature projection of the universe and, as it were, an epitome of its destiny.[28] If any enthusiasm exalted the public soul it was that evoked by the passing of the sacred cortège with the sculptured images of dead emperors, and the simultaneous appearance in his *pulvinar* or couch of the living emperor, to whose benevolence they owed the number and the splendour of their entertainments.

A salutary contact was thus established between the princeps and the mob, which prevented him on the one hand from shutting himself off in dangerous isolation and prevented them on their part from forgetting the august presence of the Caesar. The moment he entered the circus or the theatre or the amphitheatre, the crowd leapt spontaneously to their feet and greeted him with a waving of handkerchiefs, as the faithful today greet the Holy

Father in the basilica of the Vatican, offering a moving salutation that had the modulation of a hymn and the accent of a prayer.[29] This sort of adoration did not, of course, exclude more human sentiments, at once stronger and more intimate. The immense concourse had the happiness, as Pliny says in his *Panegyric*, not only 'of perceiving the princeps in the midst of his people',[30] but also of feeling drawn to him by the vicissitudes of the race, the fight, or the drama, sharing his emotions, his wishes, his pleasure, and his fears. Authority relaxed in the familiarity engendered by emotions felt in common, and at the same time drew new strength from bathing again in the waves of popularity which broke around its feet. At a time when the Comitia were silent and the Senate merely repeated the lesson prescribed to it, it was only amid the merriment of the *ludi* and the *munera* that public opinion could take shape and express itself in petitions suddenly echoed by thousands of voices demanding from Tiberius the Apoxyomenus of Lysippus,[31] and obtaining from Galba the death of Tigellinus.[32] The emperors developed skill in canalizing this mass emotion and directing its currents, and often succeeded in transferring to the multitude the responsibility for acts of vengeance which they had already planned but preferred to execute under an appearance of popular duress.[33] Thus the spectacles of Rome, though not forming an integral part of the governmental system of the empire, helped to sustain its structure, and without becoming incorporated in the imperial religion, fanned whatever flame still burned in it.

Nor was this all: they formed a barrier for autocracy against revolution. In the city there were 150,000 complete idlers supported by the generosity of the public assistance, and perhaps an equal number of workers who from one year's end to the other had no occupation after the hour of noon and yet were deprived of the right to devote their spare time to politics. The shows occupied the time of these people, provided a safety valve for their passions, distorted their instincts, and diverted their activity. A people that yawns is ripe for revolt. The Caesars saw to it that the Roman plebs suffered from neither hunger nor ennui. The spectacles were the great anodyne for their subjects' unemployment, and the sure instrument of their own absolutism. They shrewdly buttressed their power by surrounding the plebs with attentions and expending fabulous sums of money in the process.

Dio Cassius records that Augustus one day reproached the pantomime actor Pylades for deafening Rome with the noise of his quarrels and rivalries.[34] Pylades had the audacity to reply: 'It is in *your* interest, Caesar, that the people should keep their thoughts on us!' The artist's witty retort voiced the unspoken thought of Augustus and penetrated one of the secrets of his government. Games were the great preoccupation of his reign at home. He never failed to take a share in them, with ostentatious zeal and deliberate seriousness. He took his seat in the centre of his *pulvinar* between his wife and children. If he had to withdraw before the end, he excused himself and designated someone else to preside. If he stayed to the end, he was never seen to let his attention wander, whether he really enjoyed the performances for their own sake as he frankly confessed, or whether he wished to avoid the murmurs which his father Caesar had called forth by starting to read reports and to reply to them while the spectacle was in progress. He wanted to enjoy himself with his people, and he spared nothing to give them pleasure, so that the spectacles of his reign surpassed in splendour and in variety anything which had been admired before.[35] In his own *Res Gestae* he recalls with gratification that he had four times given games in his own name, and twenty-three times in the name of magistrates on whom the expense should have fallen, but who either were absent at the time or were not in a financial position to undertake them.[36]

Consuls and praetors were crushed under the burden of the expenditure entailed by their honourable promotion, and Martial has invented an amusing anecdote of a young woman, Proculeia, who as soon as her husband was appointed to the praetorship announced her intention of divorcing him:

What, I ask, is the matter, Proculeia? What is the reason of this sudden resentment? Do you answer me nothing? I will tell you: your husband was praetor. The purple robe of the Megalesian festival was like to cost a hundred thousand sesterces, even if a man gave a penurious show, and the plebeian festival would have run off with twenty thousand. This is not divorce, Proculeia: it is good business.[37]

The princeps was driven more and more to come to the rescue of his magistrates, and as each Caesar succeeded the last he bettered the example of Augustus, in order that it might not be said that the spectacles of his reign were less brilliant than those of former emperors. If we except Tiberius – this crowned republican whose incurable misanthropy extended alike to plebeian and patrician – all the emperors vied with each other to enlarge the programme of the traditional games, lengthening them sometimes till sunrise, and duplicating them with innumerable extra shows not in the calendar. Even the niggardly did not dare to shirk this expenditure. Under Claudius, who was economical, the Roman games cost 760,000 sesterces; and the Apollinarian games, which had cost their founder in his day 3,000 sesterces, ran to 380,000.[38] Even under the upstart Vespasian, son of a clerk, whose reputation for economy is well established, the building of the Flavian amphitheatre began. The magnitude of its own dimensions even more than its proximity to the colossal statue of the sun earned it eventually the name of the 'Colosseum'. The wiser emperors vied with the worst in this debauchery of pleasure and squandering of money; and the most ostentatious, the most apparently foolish in the matter was perhaps Trajan, the model emperor (*optimus princeps*) whose perfection was held to be worthy of Jupiter. In reality, as Fronto saw it, 'his wisdom never failed to pay attention to the stars of the theatre, the circus, or the arena, for he well knew that the excellence of a government is shown no less in its care for the amusements of the people than in serious matters, and that although the distribution of corn and money may satisfy the individual, spectacles are necessary for the contentment of the masses.'[39]

These last words give us the key to the problem. The policy of the Caesars was prescribed by the necessity which compels those who would govern the masses. We have recently seen the same principles being applied in Germany by the Kraft durch Freude, in Italy by the Dopo Lavoro, in France by the Ministry of Leisure. But these contemporary attempts to cater to men's leisure do not approach the scale of those undertaken by the Roman Empire. By means of them the empire preserved its existence, guaranteed the good order of an over-populated capital, kept the peace among more than a million men. The zenith of its greatness at the beginning of the second century coincides with the maximum magnificence of its races and its games, the performances in its theatre, the real combats of its arena, the artificial battles, the literary and musical competitions of its *agones*.

## 3. The Races

The games par excellence at Rome were those of the circus (*circenses*).[40] They cannot be considered apart from the building they took place in and drew their name from. The circuses were built expressly for them, and whatever their dimensions their plan was uniform, consisting of a long rectangle, rounded off at one end into a semicircle. The Circus Flaminius, built in 221 B.C. by the censor Flaminius Nepos on the site corresponding to the present Palazzo Caetani, was 400 metres by 260;[41] the Circus Gai which Caligula built on the Vatican was 180 metres by 90; its central obelisk now adorns the Piazza San Pietro;[42] the oldest and the largest of all was the Circus Maximus, which served as a model for the other two.[43] Nature had almost laid it out herself in the depression of the Vallis Murcia lying between the Palatine on the north and the Aventine on the south. The successive embellishments which it received mark the growing passion of the Romans for the *circenses*; the site was used for the exhibitions of Mussolini's Rome.

The track was originally formed by the low ground of the valley, and its soft, swampy nature eased the competitors' falls; the part containing the spectators' seats (*cavea*) was at first formed simply by the slopes of the adjacent hills, to which groups of the onlookers clung. In the centre of the field itself two wooden posts (*metae*) were staked, the more westerly one, the *meta prima*, rising in front of the trench which sheltered the subterranean altar of the god Consus, which was uncovered only during the games.[44] In 329 B.C. stables of *carceres* (for a long time simply removable stalls) were installed to the west of and facing the *meta prima*.[45] The two *metae* were joined by a longitudinal embankment which indicates that the valley bottom had dried out. The Romans considered this embankment the 'backbone' (*spina*) of the arena, and broke up its

monotony first with statues of divinities supposed to look with
favour on competitive sports – such as that of Pollentia, Goddess
of Might, which was accidentally knocked down in 189 B.C.[46]
– and later, in 174 B.C., with the *septem ova*, seven large wooden
eggs which were moved so as to indicate to the spectators which
of the seven laps of the race was now in progress.[47] It was not,
however, until the last century B.C. and the first century A.D. that
the Circus Maximus began to be honoured with the magnificent
monuments which made it famous in the ancient world, and of
which archaeology has unearthed only the remains.

For the protection of the public at the games which he celebrated
in 55 B.C., Pompey erected iron barriers round the arena where
twenty elephants were pitted against armed Gaetulians. But to the
terror of the spectators the iron bars buckled in many places under
the impact of the terrified monsters. To avoid a similar panic in
future, Caesar in 46 B.C. enlarged the arena to the east and west
and surrounded it with a moat filled with water.[48] At the same time
he built, or rebuilt, the *carceres* in volcanic tufa stone, and carved out
the face of the hillsides so as comfortably to accommodate in tiers
150,000 spectators, seated at their ease.[49] His adopted son was to
complete the work. In consultation with Octavius, Agrippa in
33 B.C. doubled the system of signals by alternating seven bronze
dolphins (*delphini*) with the seven eggs along the *spina*, and having
them reversed at each fresh lap.[50] Later Augustus bought from Heliopolis the obelisk of Rameses II, which today graces the Piazza del
Popolo, to occupy the centre of the circus.[51] And above the *cavea*
on the Palatine side he set up for himself, his family, and his guests
the 'royal enclosure' (the *pulvinar*) which he mentions in his *Res
Gestae*.[52] From the beginning of the empire the *pulvinar* showed the
Romans, overwhelmed by the sight of so much imperial majesty,
a sort of first sketch of the future *kathisma* from which the kings
would one day command the Hippodrome of Constantinople.[53]

It seems to have been Claudius who first introduced stone seats
for the senators, at the same time replacing the wooden *metae* by
posts of gilded bronze and the tufa of the *carceres* by marble.[54]
More stone seats were erected by Nero, this time for the Equites,
when he rebuilt the circus after the great fire of 64 and took the

opportunity to enlarge the track by filling in the *euripus*.[55] Later Trajan completed the enlargement of the *cavea* by deepening the excavations into the hills, a work which Pliny the Younger claimed in his *Panegyric* had increased the number of spectator's seats by 5,000.[56]

By this time the Circus Maximus had reached the colossal dimensions of 600 by 200 metres, and had achieved its final imposing form. Its curving exterior displayed three arcades faced with marble, superimposed like those of the Colosseum. Under these arcades wine merchants, caterers and pastry-cooks, astrologers and prostitutes had their place of business. Inside, the track was now covered with a bed of sand which sparkled with bright mineral grain. The most striking thing, however, was the *cavea*, whose triple tiers faced each other along the Palatine beneath the imperial *pulvinar* and along the Aventine. The lowest tier of seats was of marble; the second of wood; while the third seems to have offered standing places only. The *Regionaries* of the fourth century compute 385,000 places in all.[57] We must perhaps allow for some exaggeration in their estimate, but it is safe to pin our faith to the 255,000 seats which we can deduce from the testimony of the elder Pliny for the Flavian period, plus the additional 5,000 attributed to Trajan by Pliny the Younger.

Even with these allowances the figure is staggering. Like the Olympic Stadium at Berlin, the Circus Maximus when in use seemed a city in itself, ephemeral and monstrous, set down in the middle of the Eternal City. The most surprising thing about the giant structure was the ingenuity of the details which fitted it to perform its functions. At the two ends were two corresponding arched enclosures. That on the east, toward the Mons Caelius, was broken by the three-bayed triumphal arch which the Senate and the Roman people consecrated in A.D. 81 to the victory of Titus over the Jews,[58] and beneath which filed the procession of the *Pompa Circensis*. That on the west, toward the Velabrum, contained, on the ground floor, the twelve *carceres* where chariots and horses waited to begin the race as soon as the rope that was stretched between the two marble Hermes outside each of the twelve doors should fall; the storey above was occupied by the tribune reserved for the curule magistrate who was presiding over the games, and for his imposing suite.

The truth is that the Roman crowd revelled in these spectacles where everything combined to quicken their curiosity and arouse their excitement: the swarming crowd in which each was carried off his feet by all, the almost incredible grandeur of the setting, the perfumes and gaily-coloured toilets, the sanctity of the ancient religious ceremonies, the presence of the august emperor, the obstacles to be overcome, the perils to be avoided, the prowess needed to win, the unforeseen vicissitudes of each of the contests which brought out the powerful beauty of the stallions, the richness of their accoutrements, the perfection of their training, and above all the agility and gallantry of drivers and riders.

As the size of the circus had been increased and its equipment perfected, the series of contests had become extended and enriched. Every *ludus* had enlarged its programme; and games lasting one day gave place to those of seven or nine or fifteen days. Each race consisted of seven laps. But the number of races held in one day was increased in the early empire. Under Augustus it was customary to have a dozen a day. Under Caligula the number was doubled and a day of twenty-four races became the most common after that.[59] Let us reckon it up: seven laps or *spatia* for each race (*missus*) makes seven times 568 metres, or 3,976 metres per chariot per race. Twenty-four races covered a distance of 85 kilometres (about 55 miles)! When we remember that rest at noon and the pause which necessarily intervened between the *missus*, we must admit that the circus day was filled to overflowing.

But the Romans could never have too much, and moreover the variety of the *ludus* prevented any feeling of satiety. The interest of the horse-races was heightened by all sorts of acrobatic tricks. In the *desultores* the jockeys guided two horses at once and leaped from one to the other; again they flourished weapons and made mimic warfare on horseback; now they sat astride, knelt, and lay down on their horses at the gallop; now snatched a piece of cloth from the track or jumped over a chariot harnessed to four horses. As for the chariot races, they were diversified by the teams of horses; sometimes two horses (*bigae*) drew them, sometimes three (*trigae*), most commonly four (*quadrigae*), occasionally even six or eight or ten (*decemiuges*). Each race was enhanced by the solemnity of its start and its brilliant equipment. The signal for the trumpet to sound the start was given by the presiding consul, praetor, or aedile, who threw a white napkin from the height of his tribune into the arena. The gesture was critical and the great personage in himself was a sight worth seeing. Over a tunic, scarlet like Jupiter's, he had draped an embroidered Tyrian toga. Like a living statue, he held in his hand an ivory baton surmounted by an eagle on the point of flight, and on his head he wore a wreath of golden leaves so heavy that a 'slave or player at his side had to help him to hold it up'.[60]

At the president's feet, the chariots came to take up the place which the draw had allotted to them for the start, ranging themselves in perfect order and shining trim. Each upheld the honour of the party or *factio* to which it belonged.[61] The *factiones* had been founded to defray the enormous cost entailed by the selection and training of the competitors, man and beast, and the magistrates who gave the games had to contract with them for the performers. It may well be questioned whether the dimensions of the track could conveniently permit the management of more than four *quadrigae* at a time; it is certain that there were normally only four *factiones*, and that these – at any rate after the beginning of the second century – were usually allied in pairs. On the one hand were the Whites (*factio albata*) and the Greens (*factio prasina*), and on the other the Blues (*factio veneta*) and the Reds (*factio russata*). The stables of all four factions were in the ninth region; that of the Greens seems to have been near the spot now occupied by the Palazzo Farnese.[62] Each *factio* maintained a numerous staff of stableboys and trainers (*doctores et magistri*), veterinary surgeons (*medici*), tailors (*sarcinatores*), saddlers (*sellarii*), grooms (*succunditores*), stableguards (*conditores*), dressers and waterers (*spartores*), who accompanied the animals into the *carceres*, and of *iubilatores* whose duty it was to rouse their teams to eagerness by joyous cries. As for the chariot-drivers (*aurigae*, *agitatores*), the various *factiones* vied with each other to secure the best at whatever cost.

While the horses pawed the ground, branches on their heads,

tail held in air by a tight knot, mane starred with pearls, breastplate studded with plaques and amulets, neck bearing a flexible collar and a ribbon dyed with the colours of their party, the *auriga* among his servants was the cynosure of all eyes. He stood upright in his chariot, helmet on head, whip in hand, leggings swathed round calf and thigh, clad in a tunic the colour of his *factio*, his reins bound round his body, and by his side the dagger that would sever them in case of accident.

The public was tense even before the contest began. Each scanned with anxious eye the turn-out to which he had pinned his faith. In the packed *cavea* conversation hummed; neighbours of both sexes, piled on top of each other, animatedly compared their prophecies. This crowded gathering, seated according to the chance order of their entry, was not lacking in attraction either for women in search of a husband or for a libertine in search of adventure. It once happened under the republic that a beautiful young divorcée, Valeria, sister of the orator Hortensius, surreptitiously plucking a thread from the toga of Sulla in the hope of participating in his infallible good fortune, attracted the attention and won the last affections of the great dictator.[63] And Ovid, love poet of the empire, advised his disciples to learn to enjoy attendance at the circus, where the pleasant conversations which preceded the races and the fever of excitement which they roused offered so many opportunities for gallantry.[64]

Excitement seized the public the moment dust began to fly beneath the chariot wheels, and until the last lap was ended the spectators panted with hope and fear, uncertainty and passion. What anguish at the slightest hitch, and thrills when the posts were turned without mishap! As the *metae* were always on the left of the chariots, the success of the turning manoeuvre depended on the strength and handiness of the two outside horses called *funales*. They were not harnessed to the shaft like the two middle ones but more loosely attached by a trace (*funis*), the off-*funalis* swinging out on the right and the still more vital near-*funalis* acting as pivot on the left. If the chariot hugged the turning post too closely, it ran the risk of crashing into it; if, on the other hand, it swung out too far, it either lost position or was run into by the chariot following and again ran the risk of being wrecked. The *agitator* was subjected to a double strain: looking ahead, he must encourage and guide his horses; looking behind, avoid the impact of the chariot which was trying to pass him. He could breathe freely again only when he had safely reached the goal, after having fourteen times steered clear of the turning posts, kept or improved his place, escaped the snares of the track, and outwitted the stratagems of his competitors. The inscriptions which commemorate his victories conceal none of the difficulties he had overcome in achieving them – he had kept the lead and won: *occupavit et vicit*; he had passed from second to first place and won: *successit et vicit*; he had been the 'dark horse' whom no one expected to win and who in a supreme moment had triumphed: *erupit et vicit*.[65] The winner was greeted with a storm of applause and the winning driver and his beasts were overwhelmed by the outburst of the crowd's enthusiasm.

Purchased in the stud farms of Italy, Greece, Africa, and more especially of Spain, put into training at the age of three and making their first appearance in the races at five, the chariot racehorses included mares which were harnessed to the shaft and stallions which were usually attached by traces. Each of them possessed its pedigree, its list of victories, its individual fame, so widespread that its name was heard from one end of the empire to the other, so imperishable that the echo of it has come down to us. The famous names were incised on the rim of the earthen lamps the potters turned[66] and on the mosaic pavements discovered by moderns in provincial houses, like those in the Numidian *thermae* whose proprietor Pompeianus confessed his affection for the horse Polydoxus: 'Winner or not, we love you, Polydoxus! *Vincas, non vincas, te amamus, Polydoxe!*'[67] They can still be read, carved in stone like the name of the immortal Tuscus, who won the prize 386 times,[68] and Victor,[69] who on 429 occasions justified his surname of good augury; or engraved on sheets of bronze which the losing betters loaded with curses and consigned to the vengeance of the infernal gods in the bottom of the tombs which have yielded them up to us.[70]

The charioteers knew glory too – and more. Though they were

of low-born origin, mainly slaves emancipated only after recurrent success, they were lifted out of their humble estate by the fame they acquired and the fortunes they rapidly amassed from the gifts of magistrates and emperor, and the exorbitant salaries they exacted from the *domini factionum* as the price of remaining with the colours.[71] At the end of the first century and in the first half of the second, Rome prided herself on the presence of her star charioteers, whom she called *miliarii*, not because they were millionaires, but because they had won the prize at least a thousand times: Scorpus 2,048 times, Pontius Epaphroditus 1,467, Pompeius Musclosus 3,559, and lastly Diocles who, after having competed 4,257 times and won 1,462 victories, had the wisdom to retire from the arena in A.D. 150 with a fortune of 35 million sesterces.[72] Friedländer compares these performances and these gains with those of the Epsom jockeys at the end of the nineteenth century:[73] for example, Fred Archer, who won 1,172 prizes during six years' racing and died at 29 a millionaire. But while the Roman charioteer equalled the modern jockey in the number of his successes and the sums he won, he far excelled him in prestige and honour.

In the city their escapades were admired rather than deplored, and if one day, for instance, a charioteer had a mind to trounce or rob a passer-by, the police turned a blind eye.[74] On the walls of the streets, in the flats of the *insulae*, innumerable copies of their portraits were exhibited, and the golden nose of Scorpus twinkled everywhere: *Aureus ut Scorpi nasus ubique micet.*[75] Their names flew from lip to lip,[76] and if one of the champions happened to die, the poets of the court, skilled in grinding out praises of the emperor, did not think it beneath their dignity to dedicate a pathetic and well-turned farewell to the dead charioteer:

Let Victory sadly break her Idumaean palms; beat, Favour, with cruel hand thy naked breast; let Honour change her garb; and do thou, sorrowful Glory, cast on the cruel flames the offering of thy crowned locks. Ah, crime of Fate! Robbed, Scorpus, of thy first youth, art thou fallen, and so soon dost yoke Death's dusky steeds! That goal whereto thy car sped ever in brief course, and swiftly won, why to thy life also was it so nigh?[77]

The extraordinary honour which the charioteers enjoyed at

Rome was evidently due to the physical and moral qualities their calling demanded: their strength and imposing presence, their agility and coolness; also to the severe and early training to which they had been subjected; still more perhaps to the dangers implicit in their calling – these bloody 'shipwrecks' which they faced with such light hearts and which so often cut them off in the flower of their youth. Fuscus was killed at 24 after 57 victories; Crescens at 22 after having earned 1,558,346 sesterces; M. Aurelius Mollicius at 20 after 125 victories.[78] But the passionate devotion which they inspired in a whole people was fed also from more tainted sources. It was related to the passion for gambling for which the race course gave the opportunity and of which the charioteers were the masters. The shows of which they were the heroes and the arbiters were inseparable from the *sponsio* or wager. Martial exhorts his book: 'Make for Quirinus' Colonnade hard by ... there are two or three who may unroll you ... but only when the bets on Scorpus and Incitatus are disposed of.'[79] 'All Rome today is in the circus,' writes Juvenal, 'such sights are for the young, whom it befits to shout and make bold wagers with a smart damsel by their side.'[80]

The victory of one chariot enriched some, impoverished others; the hope of winning unearned money held the Roman crowd all the more tyrannically in its grip in that the larger proportion was unemployed. The rich would stake a fortune, the poor the last penny of their *sportula*, on the colours of a stable, the *factio* of their choice. Hence these explosions of exuberant joy, the outbursts of rage when the victor was proclaimed. Hence this chorus of obtrusive praise and of stifled imprecation round the favourite horses and the trusted charioteers. Hence also the banquet, *epulum*, served at the close of the day's show to mitigate too vivid disappointments and nip in the bud any inclination toward rioting; hence also these *sparsiones* and these *missilia*, the hail of eatables, of filled purses, of 'raffle tickets' for a ship, a house, a farm, which were rained down on the spectators in the circus at the bidding of Agrippa, of Nero, and of Domitian, and brought the more resourceful some requital and some consolation.[81] Hence too that intense partiality for one *factio* or another which the abandoned gamblers among the Caesars manifested – notably that of Vitellius and Caracalla for the 'Blues'.[82]

At the period we are studying, neither Trajan nor Hadrian had succumbed to this criminal mania; and the day was at hand when the philosopher Marcus Aurelius would congratulate himself on his indifference to 'gaming'.[83] But the multitude of their subjects was possessed by the passion for gambling, and even the best of the emperors turned it to his own advantage. The excitement which people had sought in politics they sought now in the races. Their stakes were laid no longer in the Forum but in the circus, whose 'factions' had become a substitute for the ancient political parties. This mania was unquestionably the symbol of a moral decline, and we can well understand that it cast a cloud on the patriotic pride of a Juvenal and the lofty wisdom of a Marcus Aurelius. At the same time we must recognize that it sprang from the need of the masses for something to stir their blood, and that the imperial regime showed skill in diverting it to the maintenance of its own stability and the preservation of the public peace.

## 4. The Theatre

If we are to believe certain scholars, the great cycles of games included under the republic more theatrical representations than races.[84] It is by no means easy to draw the line between them, and even if we accept this relative proportion as having obtained at the start, we must admit that it was reversed under the empire. By that time the *circenses* had surpassed in popularity the tragedies, comedies, and the other types of drama which succeeded them. Pliny the Younger, who says nothing about his contemporaries' passion for the theatre, deplores their craze for the circus: 'Such favour, such weighty influence, hath one worthless [charioteer's] tunic – I say nothing of the vulgar herd, more worthless than the tunic – but with certain grave personages. When I observe such men thus insatiably fond of so silly, so low, so uninteresting, so common an entertainment, I congratulate myself that I am insensible to these pleasures.'[85]

If in his day the races had won such popularity among the better educated classes, it is not hard to imagine the attraction they had for the man in the street, who aspired only to possession of an income sufficient to support 'a couple of stout Moesian porters on whose hired necks I may be taken comfortably to my place in the bawling circus'.[86] There is no doubt that Trajan understood the wishes of the majority of his subjects when in 112, to gratify them with some extra *ludi*, he paid the expenses of the circus for thirty days running, but of the theatre for only a fortnight.[87] It is true that the Ostian *Fasti*, to which we owe this piece of information, add that the theatrical performances were given on three stages at once. But huge as the Roman theatres were, the audiences of all three could have been accommodated five times over in the *cavea* of the Circus Maximus alone.

To the north-west of the Flaminian Circus, where the curves of the Piazza di Grotta Pinta still sketch the ground plan, was the semi-circle of the theatre of Pompey, dedicated in 55 B.C. It was 160 metres in diameter, and it was reckoned that its hemicycle provided 40,000 *loca*, which probably limits its seating capacity to about 27,000.[88] The hemicycle of the theatre of Balbus, laid out in 13 B.C. under the present Monte dei Cenci, contained only 11,510 *loca*, or perhaps 7,700 seats.[89] Finally, there was the theatre of Marcellus, designed by Julius Caesar's architects, and finished in 11 B.C. by those of Augustus, on the site now occupied by the Palazzo Ser-moneta. The remarkable excavations of the Via del Mare have shown that it was an imposing mass of travertine, harmoniously designed in a semicircle 150 metres in diameter; yet it had only 20,500 *loca*, or some 14,000 seats.[90] At the very most, therefore, these three theatres together could have accommodated about 50,000 spectators, an insignificant number as compared with the 255,000 of the Circus Maximus but impressive when set beside the largest theatres of the modern world: the Opera in Paris with 2,156 seats, the San Carlo in Naples with 2,900, the Scala in Milan with 3,600, or even the 5,000 seats of the Colon at Buenos Aires. The smallest theatre of Imperial Rome was still twice the size of the largest modern American theatre; and these dimensions would bear witness – if nothing else did – to the fact that the Roman's love of the theatre, though less consuming than his passion for the races, was still manifest. To satisfy it, the emperors commissioned or financed the construction of stone theatres, a significant undertaking in view of the fact that the 'season', which fell between the *ludi Megalenses* and the *ludi Plebei*, lasted only from April to November, and that during it performances could take place only on certain days. And since, despite its rapid decline, this passion for the theatre survived the empire, the Theatre of Pompey, restored under Domitian, under Diocletian, under Honorius, was once again restored, for the last time, by the benevolence of Theodoric the Ostrogoth between 507 and 511.

At first sight we feel tempted to admire this persistence and to deduce from it that the Roman people had a natural vocation for this art which had been the glory of ancient Greece and which the names of Accius and Pacuvius and the works of Plautus and Terence had made illustrious in Latin. But in reality the same fate which overtook the Athenian drama lay in wait for the Roman. Permanent theatres, whose ample dimensions and perfect curves still amaze us, were erected throughout the empire – not only in Italy and Gaul but in Lycia, in Pamphylia, at Sabratha in Tripoli.[91] But the art to which they were dedicated was already on its deathbed, as if the drama was by nature unsuited to the attendance of the masses. Competitive performances filled the days, but they pitted against each other only the leaders of the troupe, *domini gregis*. Production had dried up. The last writer of tragedy whose plays we know for certain were acted on the stage was P. Pomponius Secundus in the principate of Claudius.[92]

From the time of Nero, authors who persisted in writing plays wrote them most probably only to be read in an auditorium, to an audience of fellow-authors. After the first century B.C. the public battened almost exclusively on its old repertoire. In the immense open-air theatres, moreover, amid the confusion and hubbub of a huge crowd, the spectator could not conceivably follow a delicate intrigue in verse unless he knew every detail of it in advance – he had to have seen it played many times before, and his memory of the plot had to be jogged by the hints supplied in the prologue and the stereotyped symbols which assisted his understanding. The brown or white colour of the tragic and comic masks indicated the sex of the actor, while costumes draped in Greek or Roman fashion gave an immediate clue to the nationality and social status of the *dramatis personae*: white for an old man, multicoloured for a youth, yellow for a courtesan, purple for the rich, red for the poor, a short tunic for the slave, a chlamys for the soldier, a rolled *pallium* for the parasite, and a motley one for the go-between.[93] Because of these stereotyped fictions, however, the play lost most of its interest and the public, who either remembered or gave up hope of understanding, concentrated their attention on the by-play of the actors or some subsidiary detail of the *mise en scène*. The theatre was, in fact, too big for the play. Drama perished in the classic form which it had worn for nearly three centuries and which circumstances over which it had no control rendered no longer tolerable. It persisted, after undergoing a radical transformation, in a new form which banished it from literature.

At the end of the first century, probably under the influence of the Hellenistic theatre,[94] tragedy had evolved in a manner leading inescapably to ballet forms. From the earliest antiquity, Roman tragedy had been divided into dialogues (*diverbia*) and recitatives or lyrics (*cantica*), which the Roman public welcomed for variety's sake.[95] The producers of republican days placed the orchestral choirs on the stage, so that they might take more share in the action. The empire producer did not hesitate to incorporate the choir completely, thereby running the risk of submerging the play under the lyrical chanting and the fantastic scenic decoration. He mercilessly cut the traditional texts of the plays he produced each year and clipped the dialogue, so that after his scissors had done their worst a tragedy consisted of little but lyrics more or less skilfully punctuated by scraps of dialogue. If we imagine Corneille's *Cid* or Racine's *Athalie* reduced to their poems and choruses, we get some idea of the metamorphosis which drama had suffered on the stage of Imperial Rome.

Naturally, the more famous of these *cantica* were known to everyone, from repetition by generation after generation. At Caesar's funeral, the crowd sang a verse from a *canticum* of the *Armorum Iudicium* of Pacuvius, which seemed to have been composed two centuries before expressly to voice their present sorrow:
'Have I saved them only to perish at their hands?

*Men' servasse ut essent qui me perderent?*'[96]

246

And it was by means of a *canticum* that Britannicus evaded the trap
Nero laid for him during the Saturnalia of A.D. 55.[97] The emperor
had invited the young prince to a banquet with several of his
riotous companions, and suddenly commanded him to step into
the centre of the dining-hall and sing a song, hoping in this way to
discomfit him. Britannicus was unruffled. Instead of keeping an
embarrassed or resentful silence, he countered with a poem in tune
with his own tragic position, in that its hero was supposed to sing
it after the theft of his paternal throne and royal rank. Justus Lipsius
conjectures that it was a *canticum* from the *Andromache* of Ennius,
whose most beautiful lines have been preserved for us in Cicero's
*Tusculan Disputations:*

> *O Pater! O Patria! O Priami domus!*[98]

The effect was irresistible, and even at the emperor's table it evoked
'an emotion all the more sincere in that night and merry-making
had banished pretence'.

This was the sort of emotion that was produced by the *cantica* of
the plays. By modulating the chants which had so long stirred or
soothed the hearers, accompanying them with the blended music of
many instruments, emphasizing their salient features with a wonder-
ful setting, and above all by bringing them to life through pathetic
intonation and passionate gesture, the spectacle roused the audience
from its apathy. The power of these songs was multiplied by the
presence of thousands of men and women remembering them
together, vibrating to them in unison, hearing a universal echo
which moved or soothed them and ended by awaking in them
feelings sad and strong and eternal. Born of the incomparable
Greek tragedy, the Roman drama lay shattered to fragments amid
the marble of scenic decoration. But as these operatic airs rose
above the ruins of great tragedy, the pure intoxication which the
ancient masterpieces had inspired once again touched the listening
masses.

By a disastrous blunder this Roman opera, however, cast off
every bond which still linked it to true poetry. From of old the
law of this genre demanded that the actor of the *cantica* should be a
soloist.[99] The *cantica* were more and more trimmed to the measure

of the star singer on whom fell the burden of the effort and the honour of success. More and more he refused to have any but supernumeraries round him, the 'pyrrhicists' who swayed to his cadence and to his command, the *symphoniaci* who replied to him and took up his motifs, the instrumentalists of the orchestra who relieved or accompanied him; zither players, trumpeters, cymbalists, flutists, and castanet-players (*scabellarii*). All were but satellites revolving round one sun. It was the soloist alone who filled the stage with his movement and the theatre with his voice. He alone incarnated the entire action, whether singing, miming, or dancing. He prolonged his youth and preserved his slimness by a strict diet which banned all acid foods and drinks and which called for emetics and purgatives the moment his waistline was threatened. Faithful to the most severe training, he exercised unremittingly to preserve the tone of his muscles, the suppleness of his joints, and the volume and charm of his voice. Skilled in personifying every human type, in representing every human situation, he became '*the* pantomime' par excellence, whose imitations embraced the whole of nature, and who created a second nature with his fantasy.[100]

Though the law still called him an 'actor' and labelled him 'infamous',[101] the star of the Roman stage inevitably became the hero of the day and the darling of the women. In Augustus' time the city was full of the fame, pretensions, and squabbles of the pantomime Pylades.[102] Under Tiberius the mob came to blows over the comparative merits of rival actors and the riot became so serious that several soldiers, a centurion, and a tribune were left dead on the streets.[103] Dearly as Nero envied their notoriety, he had nevertheless to issue a decree of banishment against them, to put an end to the bloody affrays caused by their rivalries.[104] But neither emperor nor public could do without them. Soon after exiling them, he recalled them and admitted them to the intimacy of his court,[105] thus providing the first example of what Tacitus called *histrionalis favor*,[106] this incurable idolatry which toward the end of the first century drew the empress Domitia into the arms of the pantomime Paris.[107]

It cannot be denied that there were some great artists among these actor-idols of the Roman populace. Pylades I, for instance, certainly

ennobled 'the pantomime', a genre which he introduced into
Rome. Several anecdotes illustrate his conscientiousness and the
thought he gave to his art.[108] One day his pupil and rival, the
pantomime Hylas, while rehearsing before him the role of Oedipus,
was displaying a fine self-confidence. Pylades chastened him by
saying simply: 'Don't forget, Hylas, you are blind.' Another day
Hylas was playing a pantomime whose last line, 'Great Agamemnon', was in Greek. Wishing to give full force to his final verse,
he drew himself up to his full height as he delivered it. Pylades,
seated among the stalls of the *cavea* as an ordinary spectator, could
not refrain from calling out: 'Ah, but you are making him tall,
not great!' The audience, catching the comment, insisted on his
mounting the stage to re-enact the scene; when Pylades came to that
passage he merely assumed the attitude of a man sunk in meditation
– for it is the duty of a chief to think beyond his fellows and for
everyone.

Pylades' successors were not worthy of him. Most of them
abandoned all attempts to excel equally in the arts of singing and
dancing. Livius Andronicus, who played in his own tragedies in
the early days of Roman drama, gave up delivering the lyrics
because the strain had cracked his voice, and confined himself
thereafter to making the gestures appropriate to his part while a
singer sang the words to the sound of a flute.[109] And so the pantomime-actors of Domitian's and Trajan's day were content for the
most part to be dancers, leaving it to the choir to chant the *cantica*
which their steps, their attitudes, and their gestures were intended to
interpret. Though song had come to dominate tragedy, in pantomime it became subservient to the dance, the actors' talent was
displayed only in the mute language of their movements. Everything about them spoke, except their voice – head, shoulders, knees,
legs, and, above all, hands. Their eloquence commanded the admiration of Quintilian: 'Their hands', he said, 'demand and
promise, they summon and dismiss; they translate horror, fear, joy,
sorrow, hesitation, confession, repentance, restraint, abandonment,
time, and number. They excite and they calm. They implore and
they approve. They possess a power of imitation which replaces
words. To suggest illness, they imitate the doctor feeling the

patient's pulse; to indicate music they spread their fingers in the fashion of a lyre.'[110] By the second century, a pantomime had reached such a state of perfection that he was able without words to represent, amid the applause of a public capable of appreciating every point, Atreus and Thyestes in turn, or Aegisthus and Aërope, in the same day.[111]

Terpsichore is assuredly one of the Muses. But the breathtaking performances of Fregoli were far from inspired by Terpsichore, and we cannot doubt that the extravagant acrobatics of the Roman pantomimes killed the art of dancing.

In the first place, they unwisely reversed the order of values. At first they used their miming as a commentary on the *cantica*, but they went on to subordinate the *cantica* to their miming. They thought not of serving a work of art, but of exploiting it. Thereafter, the leaders of the troupe, musicians, and librettists were reduced to the level of artisans. The Roman poet thought himself lucky if the dancer give him an order, and he was privileged to 'sell his virgin *Agave* to Paris'[112] but this piece of good fortune cost him his creative freedom. The pantomimes laid down the law, dictated the *mise en scène* and the verses, prompted the music, and chose the subjects with an eye to exploiting their own talents and disguising their defects from a public too numerous to be discriminating. Finally, and worst of all, they aimed more and more at catching the eye and gratifying the senses rather than at touching the heart. The plays were either stark tragedies or sensual productions guaranteed to titillate an audience quickly responsive to their eroticism. Lucian has recorded most of the elements in the repertory of both categories.[113] In the first, *The Banquet of Thyestes*; *Niobe*, distraught with grief for her massacred children; the *Wraths* of mythology and epic legend – the *Wrath of Ajax* and the *Wrath of Hercules*, in which Pylades already displayed exaggeration.[114] As for the second category, the list is inexhaustible: the hapless or guilty loves of Dido and Aeneas, of Venus and Adonis, of Jason and Medea; the ambiguous stay of Achilles, dressed as a woman, among the daughters of Lycomedes at Scyros. There were tales of incest, like *Cinyras and Myrrha*, a story of father and daughter, which was first produced in Rome, Josephus records, the night before

Caligula was murdered;[115] or like *Procne and Tereus*. Tereus had ravished his sister-in-law, Philomela, and cut out her tongue to ensure her silence. His wife Procne avenged her by serving him at table the body of Itys, his legitimate son. Nero himself, in one of his scandalous exhibitions, did not blush to play the role of the sister, Canace, in *Macaris and Canace*, although she was confined on the stage and her incestuous bastard was flung to the hounds.[116] And last of all the bestial Pasiphae in the play of that name offered herself to a bull in the Cretan labyrinth.

Such subjects could not but brutalize or corrupt the spectators now shuddering with a terror purely physical, now feeling a sterile desire flow through their veins. These shocking dumb shows threw women into ecstasy. Lascivious gestures moved them: 'Tuccia cannot contain herself; your Apulian maiden heaves a sudden and longing cry of ecstasy as though she were in a man's arms; the rustic Thymele is all attention, she learns her lesson.'[117] It is easy to see why Trajan, out of respect for the sanctity of his own office, should have forbidden the actors on a stage given over to lasciviousness to interrupt their obscene ballets in order to dance, after their fashion, the praises of the reigning emperor;[118] yet it was rumoured that Trajan cherished only too much affection for Pylades II, the great pantomime of his time.[119] Tragedy, by transforming herself first into opera and then into ballet, had ended by degrading the Roman theatre to the level of a music hall.

The decadence of comedy, though perhaps somewhat less rapid, was no less complete. In the second century people still went to see Plautus and Terence played, but rather out of deference to tradition than for pleasure. If, as Roberto Paribeni has put it, the Romans had turned from tragedy because 'to their palates accustomed to burning curries' *Oedipus Coloneus* and *Iphigenia in Tauris* would have 'tasted like a draught of camomile tea',[120] it is obvious that the temperate spicing of the *Menaechmi* or the *Andria* would have seemed equally insipid. Bathyllus' attempt to rejuvenate comedy in Augustus' day by introducing music and dancing[121] did not survive the dramatist himself. Unable to regenerate comedy, the theatres replaced it by the mime, which had already proved a success in Eastern capitals. The Romans brought it home in the first century

B.C. and soon discovered how to adapt it to the taste of their mass public.

Mime (Greek μῖμος, Latin *mimus*) is a word used to denote both a type of show and the actor in it. It was a farce, modelled as closely as possible on reality. It was, properly speaking, a 'slice of life' which was transported hot and spicy on to the stage, and its success depended on its realism, or naturalism, if the term is preferred, which grew steadily more and more marked.

In the mime, conventions were abolished. The actors had no masks and wore the contemporary dress of the town. Their number varied with the play, and they formed a homogeneous troupe. Women's roles were taken by actresses whose reputation for light virtue was well established by the time of Cicero. He himself was not insensible to the talent of Arbuscula or the charms of Cytheris, and was prepared to take up the defence of a citizen of Atina guilty of abducting a *mimula*, in the name of a right consecrated by the custom of the *municipia*.[122] The subjects of the mimes were taken from the commonplace events of daily life, with a distinct leaning toward the coarser happenings and the lower human types: '*a diurna imitatione vilium rerum et levium personarum*'.[123] The treatment was usually caricature, which was pushed, as we shall see, to the limit of accuracy and impudence. Politics were permitted. Under the republic the mime was often critical of the government, and Cicero expected to gauge from its comments the reaction to the murder of Caesar.[124] Under the empire, however, the mime had no option but to range itself on the side of the princeps, lampooning those who were in bad odour at court. The mime-actor Vitalis boasted of being particularly successful in this sort of target practice: 'The man whom I took off and who saw his own image doubled under his very eyes was horrified to see that I was more truly he than he himself.'[125] In my opinion it is no accident that the mime most often played from A.D. 30 to 200, the *Laureolus* of Catullus, which was staged under Caligula and well known to Tertullian, demonstrated by the fate which overtook the brigand hero that under a good government the wicked are punished and the police always have the last word.[126]

The whole conception of the mime, with its flaunting of convention and its aiming at simplicity, certainly contained fertile seeds of theatrical reform. Two at least of the authors of mimes at the end of the first century B.C., Decimus Laberius and Publilius Syrus, lifted their pieces to the dignity of literature. But the more popular the mime became, the smaller was the part the text played in it. The great mimes I have quoted were those in which the authors played their own plays. The imperial mime actors brought to their sketchy plot words and action which they had mentally pieced together, and according to the mood of the moment and the temper of the public embroidered them with improvisations on the theme announced.

The Urbs delighted in the mimes acted by Latinus and Panniculus, which were filled with stories of kidnappings, cuckolds, and lovers hidden in convenient chests.[127] In these plays the actresses were permitted to undress entirely (*ut mimae nudarentur*) which had formerly been tolerated only during the midnight games of the Floralia.[128] The alternative was rough-house, where loud words resounded and actual blows were exchanged, until finally the scrapping became serious and blood was shed copiously. The fact that the *Laureolus* remained popular for nearly two centuries is explained by the ferocity of its brigand murderer and incendiary and by his hideous punishment. Domitian allowed the play to end with a scene in which a criminal condemned under the common law was substituted for the actor and put to death with tortures in which there was nothing imaginary. The spectators were not revolted by the ignoble spectacle of a pitiable Prometheus derided, torn by the nails which pinned his palms and ankles to the cross, or seared by the claws of the Calydonian bear to which he had been flung as prey; in fact, Martial sings the praises of the prince who made these things possible.[129] So performed, the mime seemed to the Romans of the time to reach the highest perfection attainable by the means and the effects at its disposal; and indeed, this slice of life cut from the living flesh leaves far behind the most graphic horrors portrayed today. As the mime reached the height of its achievement, it drove humanity as well as art off the Roman stage. It plumbed the depths of a perversion which had conquered the masses of the capital. They were not sickened by such exhibitions because the ghastly butcheries of the amphitheatre had long since debased their feelings and perverted their instincts.

## 5. *The Amphitheatre*

Revisiting the arenas of Rome after nearly two thousand years of Christianity, we feel as if we were descending into the Hades of antiquity. The amphitheatre demands more than reproach. It is beyond our understanding that the Roman people should have made the human sacrifice, the *munus*, a festival joyously celebrated by the whole city,[130] or come to prefer above all other entertainment the slaughter of men armed to kill and be killed for their amusement. As early as 160 B.C. the public deserted the theatre where the *Hecyra* of Terence was being performed, for one of these gladiatorial combats.[131] By the first century B.C. the populace had grown so greedy for these sights that candidates sought to win votes by inviting the people to witness spectacular scenes of carnage. In order to put an end to corrupt practices the Senate in 63 B.C. passed a law disqualifying for election any magistrate who had financed such shows for the two years preceding the voting.[132] It was natural that aspirants for the imperial throne should play on the people's passion to promote their own ambitious aims. Pompey even sated his fellow-citizens with combats;[133] Caesar freshened their attraction by the luxury with which he surrounded them.[134] Finally the emperors, deliberately pandering to the murderous lust of the crowds, found in gladiatorial games the most sure, if also the most sinister, of their instruments of power.

Augustus was the first. Outside the city itself, he adhered to the posthumous laws of Julius Caesar and continued to limit the municipal magistrates to offering one annual *munus*.[135] Within the city, he ordered the praetors to give annually two *munera* limited to 120 gladiators.[136] In A.D. 27, Tiberius forbade any private person with a fortune less than an 'equestrian capital' of 400,000 sesterces to give a *munus*.[137] Claudius transferred the duty of providing the public gladiatorial shows from the praetors to the more numerous quaestors, at the same time again limiting them to 120 gladiators per spectacle.[138]

This restriction aimed less at curbing the passion of his subjects than at enhancing the prestige of their sovereign. For while thus regulating the giving of the public *munera*, Augustus recognized no limit save his own caprice to the number of 'extraordinary' *munera*, which he offered the people three times in his own name and five times in the names of his sons and grandsons.[139] By the incomparable splendour of these private gladiatorial spectacles, he practically monopolized the right to provide 'extraordinary' *munera*, which was accomplished later by the formal prohibitions of the Flavians.[140] Thus the decrees of Augustus made the *munera* the imperial show par excellence, as official and obligatory as the *ludi* of the theatre and the circus. At the same time the empire provided grandiose buildings specially suited to their purpose. The design of these buildings, improvised more or less by chance, and repeated in hundreds of examples, seems to us today a new and mighty creation of Roman architecture – the amphitheatre.

Up to the time of Caesar those providing *munera* had either used the circus or hastily rigged up in the Forum palisades which were removed on the morrow.[141] In 53 or 52 B.C. Curio the Younger, whose candidature for the office of tribune Caesar surreptitiously supported with Gaulish money, hit upon a new campaigning scheme.[142] On the pretext of rendering honour to the *manes* of his lately deceased father, he announced that he would give scenic games supplemented by a *munus*. Ingeniously he ordered not one but two wooden theatres to be constructed, both very spacious and identical in shape but set back to back with their curves touching, and mounted on a swivel. Up to noon they were left in this back-to-back position, so that the noise of the one representation should not disturb the other. The *munus* was scheduled to take place in the afternoon – an arrangement of the programme which indicates that people who had been at work in the morning would forgo their afternoon comedy for a gladiatorial show. Suddenly the two theatres turned on their axes and came face to face to form an oval, while their respective stages vanished to give place to one arena. This ingenious manoeuvre roused the curiosity of the public, more thrilled by taking part in such a magic transformation than disturbed by any possible incidental danger to themselves. A century later Pliny the Elder was still exasperated by the imprudence of the proceeding: 'Behold this people, conquerors of the earth and masters of the universe, poised in a machine and applauding the danger they incur.'[143] The form, however, was not new, for the amphitheatre at Pompeii probably goes back to the time of Sulla and may originally have come from Capua.[144]

When Caesar offered a *munus* to the plebs in 46 B.C. to celebrate his quadruple triumph, he adopted the plan of the wooden double theatre.[145] It was reserved to the Augustan Age to translate it into the more durable medium of stone and to coin the word which was to denote this new type of monument – *amphitheatrum*.[146]

The first permanent amphitheatre was that built in 29 B.C. at Rome by a friend of the princeps C. Statilius Taurus. It was situated to the south of the Campus Martius and was destroyed in the great fire of A.D. 64.[147] The Flavians decided almost at once to replace it by a larger one of the same design.[148] It was started by Vespasian, completed by Titus, and decorated by Diocletian. Since A.D. 80 neither earthquakes nor the Renaissance plunderers who carried off its blocks of stone to build the Palazzo Venezia, the Palazzo Barberini, and the Palazzo Capitolino have seriously damaged it. Though scarred a little its beauty still reigns over the ancient site where it first rose more than eighteen-and-a-half centuries ago. It stands between the Velia, the Caelius, and the Esquiline, near the colossus of the sun within the domain of the Golden House, *Domus Aurea*, where one of the costly fish-ponds of Nero (*stagnum Neronis*) was expressly filled in for the purpose. This is the Flavian amphitheatre, better known since the Middle Ages as the Colosseum. By the year 2 B.C. Augustus, after much costly labour on the right bank of the Tiber, had supplemented the amphitheatre of Taurus, which had been built only for land combats, by a *naumachia* intended for the representation of naval battles.[149] Its exterior ellipse, with axes of 557 and 536 metres, enclosed not an arena of beaten earth covered with sand, but a sheet of water cut by an artificial island and curving through thickets and gardens. Though the *naumachia* of Augustus covered an area almost treble that of the Colosseum, which itself might have served at first either as an arena or a *naumachia*, the public soon became dissatisfied, and

Trajan was forced to build first the supplementary Amphitheatrum Castrense, not far from the present site of the Church of the Holy Cross of Jerusalem,[150] and then the supplementary Naumachia Vaticana, to the north-west of the Castle of S. Angelo.[151] Of the two *naumachiae* and of the Amphitheatrum Castrense almost nothing but the memory remains. But the ruins of the Colosseum suffice to show the typical arrangement of the Roman amphitheatre in its most perfect form.

The Colosseum was built of blocks of hard travertine stone extracted from the quarries of Albulae near Tibur (the modern Tivoli) and brought to Rome by a wide road specially constructed for the purpose. The building forms an oval, 527 metres in circumference, with diameters of 188 and 156 metres, and rears its four-storeyed walls to a height of 57 metres. Obviously modelled on the rotunda of the theatre of Marcellus, the first three storeys are formed of three superimposed tiers of arcades, originally ornamented with statues. The three storeys differ from each other only in the style of their columns, which are Doric, Ionic, and Corinthian, respectively. The fourth storey, which did not exist in Marcellus' theatre, consists of a plain wall, divided by half-engaged pilasters into compartments alternately pierced by windows and fitted with shields of bronze which Domitian set up and which have naturally disappeared. Above each of the windows were fastened three projecting corbels corresponding to three holes in the cornice. These corbels supported the bases of the masts to which on days of strong sun a detachment of sailors from the fleet of Misenum was detailed to attach the strips of giant awning (*velaria*) which sheltered the fighters in the arena and the spectators in the *cavea*. The seats began four metres above the arena with a terrace or *podium* protected by a bronze balustrade. On the *podium* were ranged the marble seats of the privileged, whose names have been handed down to us. Above these were the tiers for the ordinary public, divided into three zones or *maeniana*. The lower two were separated from the *podium* and from each other by circular horizontal corridors (*praecinctiones*) running between low walls. Vertically the circle of seats was divided by *vomitoria* or sloping corridors which 'disgorged' the floods of spectators. The first zone of seats contained twenty rows, the second sixteen. The second was separated from the third by a wall five metres high, pierced by doors and windows. The women were seated here below the terrace which linked it with the outer wall, while on the terrace stood the *peregrini* and slaves who, excluded from the distribution of entrance tokens, or *tesserae*, had not been able to secure places on the tiers.

While the *Regionaries* reckon that the Colosseum contained 87,000 *loca*, it is calculated that the number of sitting places was 45,000 and of standing places 5,000. It is still possible to trace in the architecture of the building the ingenious devices by which the comings and goings of this multitude were facilitated. There were 80 entrance arches in the circuit of the building; of these, the four at the extremities of the two axes were forbidden to the public and not numbered. The others were numbered I to LXXVI. Each guest of the emperor or the magistrates had only to direct his steps to the entrance corresponding to the number on his *tessera*, then to the corresponding *maenianum*, the section and row. Between the *cavea* and the outer wall two concentric walls formed a colonnade on the ground floor and on the upper storeys a gallery. These walls buttressed and supported the *cavea*, gave entrance to the staircases which led to the *vomitoria*, served as a 'foyer' where the crowd could walk about before the show and between the acts, and gave shelter against sun and shower. The best places on the level of the *podium* were, of course, those which faced the two ends of the shorter axis: the *pulvinar* of the emperor and the imperial family on the northern side, and on the southern the seats of the *praefectus urbi* and the magistrates. But it is certain that even the *pullati*, that is to say the poor people, clad in brown stuffs, who rubbed elbows in the top gallery, were able to follow the vicissitudes of the mortal dramas which succeeded each other in the arena.

The arena, 86 by 54 metres in diameter, enclosed an area of 3,500 square metres. It was surrounded by a metal grating, 4 metres in front of the base of the *podium*, which protected the public from the wild beasts which were loosed into the arena. Before the gladiators entered through one of the arcades of the longer axis, the animals were already imprisoned in the underground chambers of the arena. This basement was originally fitted with a water system which in A.D. 80 could flood the arena in a twinkling and transform it into a *naumachia*. Later – no doubt at the time when Trajan built his *Naumachia Vaticana* – it was provided with cages of masonry, in which the animals could be confined, and also with a system of ramps and hoists, so that they could either be quickly driven up or instantaneously launched into the arena. It is impossible not to admire the Flavian architects who, after draining the *stagnum Neronis*, had the skill to raise on the site of the old lake a monument so colossal and so perfect. Every detail of its internal arrangement is a triumph of technical ingenuity. Its solidity has defied the centuries and it still inspires the beholder with the sense of utter satisfaction that one feels in gazing on the Church of Saint Peter – the sense of a power so great as to be overwhelming, an art so sure that the infallible proportions blend into perfect harmony. But if its charm is to hold us, we must forget the inhuman ends for which this monument was raised, the spectacles of unpardonable cruelty for which the imperial architects of old created it.

At the period which we are studying, the organization of these bloody games left no room for improvement.[152] In the Italian *municipia* and in the provincial towns, the local magistrates whose duty it was annually to provide the *munera* called in the expert advice of specialist contractors, the *lanistae*. These contractors, whose trade shares in Roman law and literature the same infamy that attaches to that of the pander or procurer (*leno*), were in sober fact Death's middlemen.[153] The *lanista* would hire out his troupe of gladiators (*familia gladiatoria*), at the best figure he could command, to *duumvir* or aedile for combats in which about half were bound to lose their lives. He maintained his 'family' at his own expense, under a system of convict discipline which made no distinction between the slaves he had purchased, starving wretches whom he had recruited, and ruined sons of good family. These young ne'er-do-wells were lured by the rewards and fortune they would win from the victories he would ensure them, and by the certainty of being well and amply fed in his 'training school', the *ludus gladiatorius*. They discounted the premium which he was to pay them if they survived the term of their contract, and hired themselves out to him body and soul, abandoning all their human rights (*auctorati*) and steeling themselves to march at his command to the butchery.

At Rome on the other hand there were no longer any *lanistae*. Their functions were performed exclusively by the *procuratores* of the princeps. These agents had special official buildings on the Via Labicana at their disposal – the barracks of the *ludus magnus* probably erected under Claudius, and those of the *ludus matutinus* constructed by Domitian.[154] They were also in charge of the wild and exotic animals which subject provinces and client kings, even to the potentates of India, sent to fill the emperor's menagerie, or *vivarium*, just outside the Praenestine Gate.[155] Their gladiators, constantly recruited from men condemned to death and from prisoners taken in war, formed an effective army of fighters.

The body of gladiators was divided into pupils and instructors, who were assigned according to their physical aptitudes to the different 'arms':[156] the Samnites carried the shield (*scutum*) and sword (*spatha*); the Thracians protected themselves with a round buckler (*parma*) and handled the dagger (*sica*); the *murmillones* wore a helmet crowned with a sea fish; the *retiarii*, who were usually pitted against the *murmillones*, carried a net and a trident.

Like the games, the *munera* usually lasted from dawn to dusk, although sometimes, as under Domitian, they were prolonged into the night. It was, therefore, all important to vary the fighting, and the gladiators were trained to fight on water in a *naumachia* as readily as on the firm arena of the amphitheatre. They were not, however, pitted against wild animals; such contests were reserved for the *bestiarii*.

Writers and inscriptions on monuments tell of several types of animal contests or hunts (*venationes*).[157] There were some relatively innocent ones to break the monotony of massacre – tame animals doing incredible circus turns which surprised and amused Pliny the Elder and Martial:[158] teams of panthers obediently drawing chariots; lions releasing from their jaws a live hare they had caught; tigers coming to lick the hand of the tamer who had just been lashing them; elephants gravely kneeling before the imperial box or tracing Latin phrases in the sand with their trunks. There were terrible spectacles, in which ferocious beasts fought duels to the

death: bear against buffalo, buffalo against elephant, elephant against
rhinoceros. There were disgusting ones in which the men, from
the safe shelter of iron bars or from the height of the imperial
box – like Commodus later – let fly their arrows at animals roaring
with baffled rage, and flooded the arena with the blood of butchery.
Some were given a touch of beauty by living greenery planted in
the arena which ennobled the courage and the skill of the fighters.
They risked their lives, it is true, in battle with bulls, panthers and
lions, leopards and tigers; but they were always armed with hunting spears and glowing firebrands, with bows, lances and daggers,
and often accompanied by a pack of Scotch hounds, so that they
were exposing themselves no more than the emperor himself in
the hunts, which were in those days a kind of minor war. They
made it a point of honour to redouble the danger by their daring,
stunning the bear with their fists instead of their weapons, or
blinding the lion by flinging over his head the folds of their cloak;
or they would quicken the spectators' pleasure by waving a red
cloth in front of the bull, as the Spanish toreadors still do, or by
eluding his charge with deft feints and skilful ruses. Sometimes to
escape the beast's attack they would scale a wall or leap on to a
pole, slip into one of the partitioned turnstiles (*cochleae*) which had
been prepared beforehand in the arena, or hastily disappear into a
spherical basket fitted with spikes which gave it the forbidding
appearance of a porcupine (*ericius*).

Such *venationes*, however, usually provided an added attraction to
the main spectacle of gladiators.[159] They were but a slight exaggeration of the stern reality of ancient hunting, and can hardly be held a
reproach to the amphitheatre, for the Praetorian cavalry sometimes
took part in them as in military manoeuvres.[160] What revolts us is
the quantity of victims, the bath of animal blood: 5,000 beasts were
killed in one day of the *munera* with which Titus inaugurated the
Colosseum in A.D. 80,[161] 2,246 and 443 in two *munera* of Trajan.[162]
The extent of this carnage nauseates us today, but it served at least
one practical purpose. Thanks to this large-scale slaughter the
Caesars purged their states of wild beasts; the hippopotamus was
driven out of Nubia, the lion out of Mesopotamia, the tiger from
Hyrcania, and the elephant from North Africa. By the *venationes*

of the amphitheatre the Roman Empire extended to civilization the
benefit of the labours of Hercules.

But the Roman Empire also dishonoured civilization with all
the forms of *hoplomachia* and with a variety of *venatio* as cowardly as
it was cruel.

*Hoplomachia* was the gladiatorial combat proper. Sometimes the
battle was a mimic one, fought with muffled weapons, as our
fencing matches are staged with buttons on the foils. In such cases
it was called *prolusio* or *lusio*, according to whether it was merely
the prelude to a real fight or whether it filled the entire programme
or even several days. These mock battles were only a foretaste of
the *munus*, a sequence or simultaneous performance of serious duels
in which the weapons were not padded or the blows softened, and
in which each gladiator could hope to escape death only by
dealing it to his opponent. The night before, a lavish banquet,
which was destined to be the last meal of many, united the combatants of the morrow. The public was admitted to view this
*cena libera*, and the curious circulated round the tables with
unwholesome joy. Some of the guests, brutalized or fatalistic,
abandoned themselves to the pleasures of the moment and ate
gluttonously. Others, anxious to increase their chances by taking
thought for their health, resisted the temptations of the generous
fare and ate with moderation. The most wretched, haunted by a
presentiment of approaching death, their throats and bellies already
paralysed by fear, gave way to lamentation, commended their
families to the passers-by, and made their last will and testament.[163]

On the following day the *munus* began with a parade. The
gladiators, driven in carriages from the *ludus magnus* to the Colosseum, alighted in front of the amphitheatre and marched round the
arena in military array, dressed in chlamys dyed purple and embroidered in gold. They walked nonchalantly, their hands swinging
freely, followed by valets carrying their arms; and when they arrived opposite the imperial *pulvinar* they turned toward the emperor, their right hands extended in sign of homage, and addressed
to him the justifiably melancholy salutation: 'Hail, Emperor, those
who are about to die salute thee! *Ave, Imperator, morituri te salutant!*'[164]
When the parade was over, the arms were examined (*probatio*

*armorum*) and blunt swords weeded out, so that the fatal business might be expedited. Then the weapons were distributed, and the duellists paired off by lot. Sometimes it was decided to pit against each other only gladiators of the same category, while at other times gladiators were to oppose each other with different arms: a Samnite against a Thracian; a *murmillo* against a *retiarius*; or, to add spice to the spectacle, such freak combinations as Negro against Negro, as in the *munus* with which Nero honoured Tiridates, king of Armenia; or dwarf against woman, as in Domitian's *munus* in A.D. 90.

Then at the order of the president the series of duels opened, to the cacophonies of an orchestra, or rather a band, which combined flutes with strident trumpets, and horns with a hydraulic organ. The first pair of gladiators had scarcely come to grips before a fever, like that which reigned at the races, seized the amphitheatre. As at the Circus Maximus the spectators panted with anxiety or hope, some for the Blues, others for the Greens, the spectators of the *munus* divided their prayers between the *parmularii* (men armed with small shields) whom Titus preferred, or the *scutarii* (men armed with large shields) whom Domitian favoured. Bets or *sponsiones* were exchanged as at the *ludi*; and lest the result be somehow prearranged between the fighters, an instructor stood beside them ready to order his *lorarii* to excite their homicidal passion by crying 'Strike! [*verbera*]'; 'Slay! [*iugula*]'; 'Burn him! [*ure*]'; and, if necessary, to stimulate them by thrashing them with leather straps (*lora*) till the blood flowed. At every wound which the gladiators inflicted on each other, the public – trembling for its stakes – reacted with increasing excitement. If the opponent of their champion happened to totter, the gamblers could not restrain their delight and savagely counted the blows: 'That's got him! [*habet*]'; 'Now he's got it! [*hoc habet*]'; and they thrilled with barbaric joy when he crumpled under a mortal thrust.

At once the attendants, disguised either as Charon or as Hermes Psychopompos, approached the prostrate form, assured themselves that he was dead by striking his forehead with a mallet, and waved to their assistants, the *libitinarii*, to carry him out of the arena on a stretcher, while they themselves hastily turned over the blood-stained sand. Sometimes it happened that the combatants were so well matched that there was no decisive result; either the two duellists, equally skilful, equally robust, fell simultaneously or both remained standing (*stantes*). The match was then declared a draw and the next pair was called. More often the loser, stunned or wounded, had not been mortally hit, but feeling unequal to continuing the struggle, laid down his arms, stretched himself on his back and raised his left arm in a mute appeal for quarter. In principle the right of granting this rested with the victor, and we can read the epitaph of a gladiator slain by an adversary whose life he had once spared in an earlier encounter. It professes to convey from the other world this fiercely practical advice to his successors: 'Take warning by my fate. No quarter for the fallen, be he who he may! *Moneo ut quis quem vicerit, occidat!*'[165] But the victor renounced his claim in the presence of the emperor, who often consulted the crowd before exercising the right thus ceded to him. When the conquered man was thought to have defended himself bravely, the spectators waved their handkerchiefs, raised their thumbs, and cried: '*Mitte!* Let him go!' If the emperor sympathized with their wishes and like them lifted his thumb, the loser was pardoned and sent living from the arena (*missus*). If, on the other hand, the witnesses decided that the victim had by his weakness deserved defeat, they turned their thumbs down, crying: '*Iugula!* Slay him!' And the emperor calmly passed the death sentence with inverted thumb (*pollice verso*).[166]

The victor had, this time, escaped and he was rewarded on the spot. He received silver dishes laden with gold pieces and costly gifts, and taking these presents in his hands he ran across the arena amid the acclamations of the crowd. Of a sudden he tasted both wealth and glory. In popularity and riches this slave, this decadent citizen, this convicted criminal, now equalled the fashionable pantomimes and charioteers. At Rome as at Pompeii, where the *graffiti* retail his conquests, the butcher of the arena became the breaker of hearts: '*decus puellarum, suspirium puellarum*'.[167] But neither his wealth nor his luck could save him. He usually had to risk his own life again and sacrifice other lives in new victories before he could win, not the palms which symbolized success, but the more coveted wooden sword, the *rudis*, which signified his liberation and was granted as a title of honour.

At the period which we have reached, the emperors inclined to cut short the period of service which delayed the liberation of the best duellists. Martial praises the magnanimity of the invincible Domitian:

> *O dulce invicti principis ingenium*

because he had cried a halt to a fight between two gladiators who had reached a deadlock, and handed to both the *rudis* of liberty along with the palm of victory.[168] Similarly Trajan – if I have not misinterpreted the *Fasti* of Ostia – displayed his generosity by ordering that all the combatants who had not fallen by the end of the performance in his *naumachiae* and *munera* of A.D. 109 should be released.[169]

There are therefore occasional gleams of humanity in this business of wholesale butchery. At first the gladiator often begged leave to decline the emperor's clemency; he had fallen so low morally that he preferred to resume his trade of slayer rather than renounce the luxurious life of his barracks, the thrill of danger, and the intoxication of victory. We possess the epitaph of such a one, Flamma by name, who, after bearing off the palm twenty-one times, had four times received the *rudis* and each time 'signed on again'.[170] Later the *munera* developed to astounding proportions. I shall quote only the figures in the recently discovered fragment of the *Fasti Ostienses* which covers the period extending from the end of March A.D. 108 through April A.D. 113. There we find mention of two minor shows, one of 350 pairs of gladiators, the other of 202, while the major event was a *munus* lasting 117 days in which 4,941 pairs of gladiators took part.[171] Even the assumption that Trajan granted the survivors their liberty *en bloc* does little to assuage the memory of a field strewn with corpses. Cicero indeed assures us that although there may be other methods of teaching contempt for pain and death, there is assuredly none which speaks more eloquently to the eye than a *munus*;[172] and later Pliny the Younger contended that these massacres were essentially calculated to engender courage by showing how the love of glory and the desire to conquer could lodge even in the breast of criminals and slaves.[173] These are specious excuses. The thousands of Romans who day after day, from morning until night, could take pleasure in this slaughter and not spare a tear for those whose sacrifice multiplied their stakes, were learning nothing but contempt for human life and dignity.

These feigned combats, moreover, were often made the cloak of sordid murders and ruthless executions. Rome and even the *municipia* retained until the end of the third century the practice of proclaiming *munera sine missione*, that is to say, gladiatorial combats from which none might escape alive. No sooner had one of the duellists fallen than a substitute, *tertiarius* or *suppositicius*, was produced to fight the conqueror, until the entire body of combatants was exterminated. Then, too, there were moments in the normal full-day programme at Rome when exceptional atrocities were committed. The *gladiatores meridiani*, whose account was squared at the noon pause, were recruited exclusively from robbers, murderers, and incendiaries, whose crimes had earned them the death of the amphitheatre: *noxii ad gladium ludi damnati*. Seneca has described this shameful procedure for us.[174] The pitiable contingent of the doomed was driven into the arena. The first pair was brought forth, one man armed and one dressed simply in a tunic. The business of the first was to kill the second, which he never failed to do. After this feat he was disarmed and led out to confront a newcomer armed to the teeth, and so the inexorable butchery continued until the last head had rolled in the dust.

The morning massacre was even more hideous. Perhaps it was Augustus who unintentionally invented this spectacular punishment when he erected in the Forum a pillory which collapsed and dropped the victim, the bandit Selurus, into a cage of wild beasts.[175] Later the idea was taken up and made general. Criminals of both sexes and all ages, who by reason of their villainy – real or supposed – and their humble status had been condemned *ad bestias*, were dragged at dawn into the arena to be mauled by the wild animals loosed from the basement below. This spectacle in which the victims were thrown defenceless to savage animals is graphically represented in a Tripolitan mosaic.[176]

This was the kind of torture heroically undergone by the virgin Blandina in the amphitheatre at Lyons, by Perpetua and Felicitas in Carthage, and in the Eternal City itself by so many Christians, anonymous or canonized, of the Roman Church. In memory of these martyrs a cross now rises in the Colosseum in silent protest against the barbarism which cost so many of them their lives before the spirit of Christianity succeeded in abolishing it. Today we cannot see this emblem without a shudder.

In vain we seek to find some shadow of extenuation in the fact that the amphitheatre had scarcely begun to fill in time for the dawn *venatio*, and that the hour assigned to the *gladiatores meridiani* was the moment when the theatre was three parts empty (*dum vacabat arena*) because the workers had not yet come to take their seats and the idlers had already gone to snatch a bite at home. If this arrangement of the programme shows on the part of the Romans a sort of shamed apology for these nightmare scenes, there were among them all too many connoisseurs of horror who would not for the world have missed them. Rather than lose a moment of either they preferred, like Claudius, to make a rule of arriving before dawn and going without midday lunch.[177] Despite all the extenuations we may urge, the Roman people remain guilty of deriving a public joy from their capital executions by turning the Colosseum into a torture-chamber and a human-slaughter house.

## 6. Late Opposition

We must, however, credit the flower of Rome with terror at the progress of this dread disease and more than one attempt to reduce its virulence.

Augustus, for example, following the distant precedents of the great-hearted Philhellenes of the second century B.C., and resuming the spasmodic attempts of Sulla, of Pompey, and of Caesar, tried to acclimatize Greek games at Rome. These contests strengthened the body instead of destroying it, and included artistic as well as physical competitions. Both to commemorate his victory over Antony and Cleopatra and to give thanks for it to Apollo, Augustus founded the Actiaca, which were to be celebrated every fourth year both at Actium and Rome.[178] But by A.D. 16 the Actiaca are no longer recorded. Nero wished to revive them in his Neronia, which were to be periodic festivals comprising tests of physical endurance and competitions of poetry and song.[179] The senators deigned to take part in the former; but in the latter none dared to dispute the crown with the emperor, who believed himself an unrivalled artist. Despite their august patronage, however, the Neronia fell quickly into abeyance, and it was Domitian who at length succeeded in endowing Rome with a lasting cycle of games in the Greek style. In A.D. 86 he instituted the *Agon Capitolinus*, whose prizes the emperor awarded alternately for foot races and for eloquence, for boxing and Latin poetry, for discus-throwing and Greek poetry, for javelin-casting and for music.[180] He built the Circus Agonalis, on the site of the Piazza Navona, especially for his sports; and for the more 'spiritual' contests erected the Odeum, whose ruins are now hidden beneath the Palazzo Taverna on Monte Giordano.[181] In his reign the Greek games which his bounty maintained enjoyed an ephemeral popularity, and Martial sang the praises of the prize-winners.[182] The games survived their founder, but though we have proof that they were celebrated in the fourth century and that the jurists never ceased to emphasize the high honour they deserved they never seriously rivalled the *munera* in favour.[183] For one thing the *Agon Capitolinus* recurred only once in four years. Furthermore, Domitian designed them to appeal to a select and limited public, for his Odeum provided only 10,600 *loca* and his Circus Agonalis only 30,088 – say 5,000 and 15,000 seats respectively – so that the two together were less than half the size of the Amphitheatrum Flavium alone.

There is no denying the fact that the Greek games were never very popular. The crowd, addicted to the thrills of the Colosseum, looked on them as colourless and tame; and they enjoyed no greater favour among the upper classes, who professed to detect an exotic degeneracy and immorality in their nudism.

Pliny the Younger applauds the Senate's decision under Trajan to forbid the scandal of the gymnastic games at Vienne in Gallia Narbonensis and complacently quotes his colleague Junius Mauricus, 'who in resolution and integrity has no superior', as saying, 'and

I would that they could be abolished in Rome, too!' for 'these games have greatly infected the manners of the people of Vienne, as they have universally had the same effect among us'.[184] The incompatibility between the eurhythmy of Greek games and the brutality of gladiatorial combats was bound to be irreconcilable. It is significant that while the majority of provincial towns imitated Rome by building amphitheatres, whose ruins have been found in South Algeria and on the banks of the Euphrates,[185] Greece herself fought tooth and nail against the contagion, and in Attica, at least, apparently succeeded. This one exception is a poor make-weight to the general infatuation. In Italy the Greek games took refuge in Naples and Pozzuoli,[186] but were crushed to death by the *munera* in Rome.

It seemed indeed that the *munus* was not to be eradicated. Good emperors, therefore, sought to humanize it. While Hadrian forbade impressment of slaves into gladiatorial troupes,[187] Trajan and Marcus Aurelius exerted themselves to the utmost to extend the part played in their festivals by the mimic combats (*lusiones*), at the expense of the *munus* proper. On 30 March 108, Trajan finished a *lusio* which had lasted thirty days and involved 350 pairs of gladiators.[188] Marcus Aurelius, obeying the dictates of his Stoic philosophy, exhausted his ingenuity in reducing the regulations and budgets of the *munera* and in this way lessening their importance, and wherever it fell to him to offer entertainment to the Roman plebs he substituted simple *lusiones*.[189] But philosophy lost the round in this struggle against spectacles where, as Seneca phrased it, man drank the blood of man: '*iuvat humano sanguine frui*'.[190]

After Marcus Aurelius, whose son Commodus himself aspired to gladiatorial fame,[191] the Romans, not contented with the discontinuance of *lusiones*, inclined to desert the theatre for the amphitheatre. From the second century on we find the theatre architects in the provinces, notably in Gaul and Macedonia, modifying their building plans to accommodate gladiatorial duels and *venationes*. At Rome the representation of sinister drama was transferred to the arena, and it became usual to play the most terrifying mimes at the Colosseum – *Laureolus*, who was crucified alive for the amusement of the public,[192] *Mucius Scaevola*, who plunged his right hand into the burning coals of a brazier,[193] and the *Death of Hercules*, whose hero in the last act writhed in the flames of his pyre.[194] As the amphitheatre henceforth sufficed for the more lurid dramatic representations, no attempt was made to repair the ruined theatres, and in the reign of Alexander Severus (A.D. 235) the theatre of Marcellus was abandoned.[195]

It might have been predicted that the *munera* would be ever-lasting and that nothing henceforward could stop their invading growth. But where Stoicism had failed the new religion was to succeed. The conquering Gospel taught the Romans no longer to tolerate the inveterate shame. Racing continued as long as the races of the circus were maintained, but the butcheries of the arena were stopped at the command of Christian emperors. On 1 October 326, Constantine decreed that condemnation *ad bestias* must be commuted to forced labour *ad metalla*, and dried up at one blow the principal source of recruitment for the gladiatorial schools.[196] By the end of the fourth century gladiatorial shows had disappeared from the East. In 404 an edict of Honorius suppressed gladiatorial combats in the West.[197] Roman Christianity thus blotted out the crime against humanity which under the pagan Caesars had disgraced the amphitheatre of the empire.

# IX

## AFTERNOON AND EVENING

*

ON days when no spectacles or shows were provided, the Roman filled up the time until supper with strolling or gambling, exercise, or a bath at the *thermae*.

### 1. Strolling, Gaming, and Pleasure

At first sight the crowded streets of Imperial Rome might seem ill suited for walking. The pedestrian was hampered by the outspread stalls of 'audacious hucksters',[1] jostled by passers-by, spattered by riders on horseback; harassed by 'hoarse-throated beggars' who stationed themselves along the slopes, under the arcades, and on the bridges;[2] trampled by the military who held the middle of the road and advanced as if marching in conquered territory, planting the hobnails of their boots on the foot of any civilian rash enough not to have made way for them.[3] But this never-ending and motley crowd was interesting in itself. The flow of traffic which bore the Roman along bore with him all the nations of the habitable globe: 'the farmer of Rhodope ... the Sarmatian fed on draughts of horse's blood, the Egyptian who quaffs at its spring the stream of first-found Nile ... the Arab, the Sabaean, the Cilician drenched in his own saffron dew ... the Sygambrian with knotted hair, the Ethiopian with locks twined otherwise';[4] and even if he had no use for their cheap-jack wares the 'tramping hawker's' readiness of tongue delighted him, and so did the conjurers and snake charmers with their uncanny skill.[5] The general prohibition against carriages held good by day, but if he had the good luck to be mounted he could enjoy this welter of activity without being inconvenienced by it. He might prance along on his own mule or one lent him by the kindness of a friend or hired from a Numidian muleteer, part of whose duty was to lead it by the bridle.[6] Or he might prefer to loll in the depths of an

271

immense litter (*lectica*), panelled with 'transparent stone' through which he could see without being seen as his six or eight Syrian porters cut their way through the crowd. He might be borne in a carrying chair (*sella*), such as matrons were wont to use for paying calls; in this he could read or write as he went along.[7] Or again he might be content with a sort of wheelbarrow (*chiromaxium*) like the one Trimalchio had presented to his favourite.[8]

But if his aim was to escape the hurly-burly of the street, the Roman had only to seek the quiet regions which were the 'promenades' of the city: the fora and the basilicas, when once the judicial hearings were over; the gardens belonging to the emperors, which were left open to the public, even though they were not all, like Caesar's, bequeathed to the people. These he sought out 'when on the threshold of the city so rich was the beauty of spring and the charm of fragrant Flora, so rich the glory of Paestan fields; so ruddy, where'er he turned his footsteps, or his eyes, was every path with twining roses.'[9] And the Campus Martius with its marble enclosures (the Saepta Iulia), its sacred halls and porticos, provided a shelter from the sun, a refuge from the rain, and in all weathers, as Seneca puts it, a 'place where the most wretched could take his ease: *cum vilissimus quisque in campo otium suum oblectet.*'[10]

We still possess the entrance to one of these porticos which Augustus dedicated in the name of his sister Octavia and which enclosed within its marble columns a space 118 by 135 metres containing the twin temples of Jupiter and Juno.[11] But there were many other porticos to the north, and Martial mentions some of them in describing the route taken by the parasite Selius in quest of a friend who might be induced to ask him to dinner: the Portico of Europa, the Portico of the Argonauts, the Portico of a Hundred Pillars with its alley of plantains, the Portico of Pompey with its two groves.[12] These *saepta* were not only set amid refreshing shade and grass, but filled with works of art: frescos covered their inner walls, statues adorned the spaces between their columns and their interior courts. In the Portico of Octavia alone Pliny the Elder enumerates, apart from a certain number of command pieces executed by Pasiteles and his pupil Dionysius, the group of Alexander and his generals at the battle of the Granicus by Lysippus, a

Venus of Phidias, a Venus of Praxiteles, and the Cupid which Praxiteles had destined for the town of Thespiae.[13]

The walks of the imperial people were indeed set amid prodigious collections of booty. But among the Romans who stopped to contemplate these masterpieces, there were some who sought only to draw amusement from the familiar rarities. Martial tells an illuminating little anecdote.[14] Among other statues of wild beasts in the Portico of a Hundred Pillars stood a bronze bear, which one day attracted the attention of the idlers: 'While Hylas was in play challenging its yawning mouth he plunged his youthful hand into its throat. But an accursed viper lay hid in the dark cavern of the bronze, alive with a life more deadly than that of the beast itself. The boy perceived not the guile, until he felt the pang and died.' This was the folly of a mischievous lad, but we shall see that it was not only boys who played under the porticos in the gardens, the fora, and the basilicas.

In the shadow of their colonnades the idle Romans loafed or gathered to gossip. They ogled the passers-by, both men and women. When a sale was being held in the *saepta*, they leisurely attended, assessed the value of the objects offered, and haggled over the price. Everywhere they eagerly inquired the latest news, and everywhere they found some boastful busybody ready to satisfy their curiosity. Martial vividly describes such a braggart who invents as he goes along the 'secrets' with which he regales his auditors:

By such arts as these, Philomusus, you always earn your dinner; you invent much and retail it as truth. You know what counsel Pacorus, king of Parthia, takes in his Arsacian palace; you estimate the Rhenish and Sarmatian armies... you know how many ships set sail from Libya's shores... for whom Capitoline Jupiter designs his chaplets.[15]

But the best of conversations palls at last; and at this point they turned to gaming.

The Romans frankly confessed to their passion for gambling. They had always been possessed by it; but never before had the mania held them in so tyrannical a grip. In the second century Juvenal writes: 'When was gambling so reckless? Men come not now with purses to the hazard of the gaming table, but with a treasure chest beside them. What battles will you there see waged with a steward for armour bearer!'[16] And he sadly continues: 'Is it a simple form of madness to lose 100,000 sesterces and not have a shirt to give a shivering slave?' In the attempt to put a brake on this suicidal passion, the Caesars had kept up the prohibitions of republican days. Except during the Saturnalia, which Martial expressly mentions, and which Juvenal implies in the above-quoted passage (for 'shivering slave' suggests the cold of *Bruma* or the winter solstice at the end of December, which was the season of the Saturnalia), games of chance were forbidden under penalty of a fine fixed at four times the value of the stakes; and a *senatus consultum* of uncertain date confirming the *Lex Titia*, the *Lex Publicia*, and the *Lex Cornelia* renewed the prohibition of betting (*sponsiones*), except in the case of wagers laid on physical exercises.[17] We saw in the last chapter the popularity which this curious privilege won for the chariot races of the circus and the gladiatorial combats. It left a breach in apparently repressive legislation, through which many games of chance and *sponsiones* managed to slip.

Playing dice games with *tali* or *tesserae* which were thrown from the dice-box (*fritillus*) on to the ground or gaming table (*alveus*) would certainly have been an imprudent thing to do in public.[18] Neither would it, probably, have been acceptable for two friends to play *navia aut capita* (heads or tails) or *par impar* (odd or even) under the porticos. Yet Augustus used to invite his family to play *par impar* in the palace, alloting them 250 denarii apiece so that they might throw themselves into the fun of the game without anxiety or bitter afterthoughts.[19] As played by the imperial family, the game consisted only of a monotonous series of bets on the odd or even number of pebbles, nuts, or knuckle-bones hidden in the other player's hand.

There was another variety of game derived from 'Odd or Even' in which the element of mere chance was somewhat corrected, limited by the quickness of sight and speed of the player, a calculation of probabilities, and a certain psychological flair. This was *micatio* – the still popular *morra* of southern Italy today. The two players 'each raise the fingers of the right hand, varying each time the number raised and the number kept down and call aloud the total of the fingers raised by both', until one or other wins the round by guessing right.[20] *Micatio* could certainly be played openly in the Rome of the Antonines. From Cicero through the times of Petronius and Frontinus down to Saint Augustine, Latin tradition unanimously used to indicate a man of integrity by the phrase, 'You could play *micatio* with him in the dark'.[21] Not until the fourth century did the *praefectus urbi* feel compelled to banish *micatio* from the Forum.[22]

While the Roman game of backgammon (*duodecim scripta*), in which the moves of the men (*calculi*) were determined by numbers thrown with dice or bones as in our game, may have fallen under the ban of the law, chess (*latrunculi*) was exempt, since the moves depended only on the foresight and skill of the players.[23] This game of calculated combinations, which in the first century delighted both the Stoic Julius Canus and the consul Piso,[24] and in which in Martial's day intellectuals took pride in competing for the championship,[25] never lost honour with the public; it absorbed both those who played and the idlers who stood around commenting on their moves. When the players felt chess to be too complicated or the necessary apparatus for it too cumbersome – a chess-board of sixty squares and men of different colour and shape – they would fall back on an elementary game of draughts, whose *tabulae lusoriae* could be improvised anywhere with lines scratched in the ground or cut into the pavement.[26] Many *graffiti* of such draught-boards have been excavated under the arcades of the Basilica Iulia and the forum.

Nor were these the sum of the games: a number of bas-reliefs show children apparently playing 'nuts', the ancient equivalent of our marbles.[27] This would explain the Saturnalian custom of presenting grown-ups with bags of nuts for the festival; and it is tempting to suppose that adults often amused themselves in the squares and porticos with trying either to split a nut without crushing it, to throw one on to a heap without knocking the rest down, or as in our game of marbles to hit the opponent's men, or shoot the nut into a hole.

Such harmless relaxations brought a whiff of fresh air into the feverish atmosphere of the Imperial City. Yet in the course of time these pastimes must have lost much of their innocence, and often been made the pretext for clandestine bets. In any case there is no doubt that the idler had but to make a slight detour in his daily walk to find an opportunity of secretly indulging the vice to which the emperor thought he had given sufficient rein in the circus and the amphitheatre. Not infrequently the inns (*cauponae*) and taverns (*popinae* and *thermopolia*), whose front counters served cooling draughts or hot wine, concealed in their back premises gambling dens where year in and year out, not only during the Saturnalia, bets could be exchanged and dice and knuckle-bones rattled. The imperial laws which bore as hard on gamblers (*aleatores*) as on thieves could not reach out an arm long enough to catch the *susceptor*, the keeper of the den who sheltered them; the most the law could do was to deny him the right to sue for any violence done him or the furnishings of his tavern by clients in the excitement of their gaming or despair at their losses.[28] With this relative impunity, the keeper was all the more tempted to equip his shop for seductive, forbidden parties, and by installing prostitutes as barmaids, to convert his gambling den into a bawdy-house.[29]

A frequently quoted inscription from Aesernia tells of a passing traveller who, settling with the hostess of the local inn, acquiesces in an item of eight asses (about twelve cents) charged for the favours accorded him by the maid-servant during his one-night stay.[30] We might also cite the *popina*, recently unearthed in the Via dell' Abbondanza at Pompeii, which bears a suggestive poster notifying the passer-by that the establishment boasts three young ladies (*asellae*) on its staff.[31] It would be an illusion to imagine that Rome itself was in any way behind the Italian *municipia* in such conveniences.[32] There, as elsewhere, the *cauponae*, the *popinae*, and the *thermopolia* were currently equated with 'dives' (*ganeae*); and while the authorities out of consideration for the young Roman's morning exercise decreed that brothels should remain closed until the ninth hour,[33] the Roman tavern offered its attractions to every comer both morning and afternoon. The shady bar was perhaps not quite so omnipresent in Rome as in modern capitals, but it was common, winked at by the aedile police, and freely open to passers-by. Seneca records how many wastrels turned into these dens instead of finding their way to the *palaestra* to spend their leisure: '*Cum illo tempore vilissimus quisque . . . in popina lateat.*'[34]

## 2. The Baths

Happily for the Roman people, there was a more wholesome way for a man to enjoy his liberty, and the Caesars, in building *thermae* for the citizens, had provided them with 'recreation' in the full and best sense of the word. The word for baths is Greek; but it represented a specifically Roman reality – the association for the first time of the sports of the *palaestra* which exercised the body and the *thermae* which cleansed it. The baths are one of the fairest creations of the Roman Empire. They not only benefited civilization, after their fashion, but also served art, which has been permanently enriched by monuments whose spaciousness, proportions, and technical perfection command our profound admiration even in their decay. In building the *thermae* the emperors put personal hygiene on the daily agenda of Rome and within reach of the humblest; and the fabulous decoration lavished on the baths made the exercise and care of the body a pleasure for all, a refreshment accessible even to the very poor.

Since the middle of the third century B.C. wealthy Romans had built bathing halls in their town houses and country villas.[35] But this luxury was for the very rich and the republican austerity which forbade Cato the Censor to take a bath in the presence of his son[36] prevented the building of baths outside the family domain. In the long run, however, the love of cleanliness triumphed over false pruderies. In the course of the second century B.C. public baths – the men's and women's separate, of course, unlike later times – made their appearance in Rome; the feminine plural *balneae* denoting the public, as opposed to the neuter *balneum*, or private, bath.[37] Philanthropists endowed baths in their quarter of the city. Contractors built others as a speculation and charged entrance fees. In 33 B.C. Agrippa had a census of baths taken; there were 170 and the number grew steadily as time went on.[38] Pliny the Elder gave up trying to count those of his time,[39] and later they approached a thousand.[40] The fee charged by the owner or by the operator to whom he had leased the place was microscopic: a *quadrans*, quarter of an as, or roughly half a cent, and children entered free.[41] In 33 B.C. Agrippa was aedile and one of his duties was to supervise the public baths, test their heating apparatus, and see to their cleaning and policing. In order to mark his term of office by a sensational act of generosity he undertook to pay all entrance fees for the year of his aedileship.[42] Not long after, he founded the *thermae* which bear his name, and these were to be free in perpetuity.[43] This was a revolutionary principle in keeping with the paternal role which the empire had assumed toward the masses. It brought with it a revolution both in architecture and in manners; and buildings modelled on Agrippa's grew ever larger with succeeding reigns.

After the baths of Agrippa, the *thermae* of Nero were erected on the Campus Martius.[44] Then Titus built his beside the ancient *Domus Aurea*, with an external portico facing the Colosseum.[45] The brick cores of several columns of this portico are standing to this day. Next Trajan built on the Aventine the *thermae* which he dedicated to the memory of his friend Licinius Sura; and to the north-west of those of Titus, on the site of part of the Golden House which had been destroyed by fire in 104, he erected others to which he gave his own name and which he was able to inaugurate on the same day as his aqueduct, 22 June 109.[46] Later there came the *thermae* which we call the baths of Caracalla, but which ought to be known by their official designation of 'Thermae of Antoninus', for while Septimius Severus laid the foundations in 206, and they were prematurely inaugurated by his son Antoninus Caracalla, they were completed by the last Antonine of the dynasty, Severus Alexander, between 222 and 235.[47] The ruins of the baths of Diocletian today house the National Roman Museum, the Church of Saint Mary of the Angels, and the Oratory of Saint Bernard;[48] and the plan of their giant *exedra* can be traced by the curves of the piazza which preserves the name. Last of all, in the fourth century the *thermae* of Constantine were built on the Quirinal.[49] The best preserved of these great baths are those of Diocletian, covering an area of thirty-two acres, and those of Caracalla, spreading over twenty-seven acres, both of which belong to the

wonders of ancient Rome. These grandiose, bare ruins impress even
the most insensitive tourist. Both, however, lie outside the limits
of the chronological framework within which we are striving to
keep our attention. But the ruins of the baths of Trajan have
within the last few years been sufficiently excavated to allow us to
follow the master lines of their plan and establish the fact that it
corresponds to the plan of the baths of Caracalla.[50] There is only
a difference of scale between the two. It is comparatively simple,
therefore, to divine the typical arrangement of these monumental
buildings in the day when Martial grew enthusiastic over them,
and take stock of the innovations they had introduced.[51]

The primary feature of these *thermae* was every type of bath that
ingenuity could devise: hot, cold, and hot-air baths, the swimming
bath, and the tub bath. Externally the enormous quadrilateral was
flanked by porticos full of shops and crowded with shopkeepers and
their customers; inside it enclosed gardens and promenades, stadia
and rest rooms, gymnasiums and rooms for massage, even libraries
and museums. The baths in fact offered the Romans a microcosm
of many of the things that make life attractive.

In the centre of the *thermae* rose the buildings of the baths proper.
None of the *balneae* could rival them, either in the volume of water
led from aqueducts into their reservoirs, which in the baths of
Caracalla occupied two-thirds of the south side with their sixty-
four vaulted chambers; or in the complex precision of their system
of furnaces, of *hypocauses* and *hypocausta*, which conveyed, distributed, and tempered the warmth of the halls. Near the entrance
were the dressing-rooms where the bathers came to undress (the
*apodyteria*). Next came the *tepidarium*, a large vaulted hall that was
only gently warmed, which intervened between the *frigidarium*
on the north and the *caldarium* on the south. The *frigidarium*, which
was probably too big to be completely roofed in, contained the
pool into which the bathers plunged. The *caldarium* was a rotunda
lit by the sun at noon and in the afternoon, and heated by vapour
circulating between the *suspensurae* laid beneath its pavement. It
was surrounded by little bathing boxes where people could bathe
in private; and a giant bronze basin of water in the centre was kept
at the required temperature by the furnace immediately below in

the middle of the *hypocausis* that underlay the entire hall. To the south of the *caldarium* lay the *sudatoria*, or *laconica*, whose high temperature induced a perspiration like the hot room of a Turkish bath. Finally the whole gigantic layout was flanked by *palaestrae*, themselves backing on recreation rooms, where the naked bathers could indulge in their favourite forms of exercise.

This was not all: this imposing group of buildings was surrounded by an esplanade, cooled by shade and playing fountains, which gave space for playing grounds and was enclosed by a continuous covered promenade (the *xystus*). Behind the *xystus* curved the *exedrae* of the gymnasiums and the sitting-rooms, the libraries, and the exhibition halls. This was the truly original feature of the *thermae*. Here the alliance between physical culture and intellectual curiosity became thoroughly Romanized. Here it overcame the prejudice which the importation of sports in the Greek style had aroused.[52] No doubt conservative opinion continued to look askance at athletics, as encouraging immorality by exhibitionism and diverting its devotees from the virile and serious apprenticeship required by the art of war, teaching them to think more of exciting admiration for their beauty than of developing the qualities of a good foot soldier.[53] But opinion presently ceased to be offended at nudism in the baths, where it was obligatory, and admitted almost all athletic games to equal honour, as long as they were practised not as a spectacle but for their own sake and served the same salutary purpose as the baths themselves. Games prefaced and reinforced the tonic effect of the baths on bodily health and fitness.

In the last chapter we had to record the partial failure of the *Agon Capitolinus*. In vain Augustus, Nero, and Domitian had tried to effect a revolution in manners by transplanting to Rome a copy of the Olympic games. It was reserved to the *thermae* to succeed where the emperors had failed, for at the period of which we are writing the Roman people had contracted the habit of attending the baths daily and spending the greater part of their leisure there.

Our authorities unanimously state or imply that the *thermae* normally closed at sunset;[54] but the only indications we have as to when they opened seem at first to contradict each other. A line of Juvenal's suggests before noon, as early as the fifth hour;[55] and this is confirmed by an epigram of Martial's in which the poet, choosing the most opportune moment for his bath, decides on the eighth hour which 'tempers the warm baths; the hour before breathes heat too great, and the sixth is hot with excessive heat'.[56] On the other hand, the *Historia Augusta* in the Life of Hadrian records that a decree of the emperor forbade anyone, except in case of illness, to bathe in the public baths before the eighth hour;[57] while the Life of Severus Alexander recalls that in the preceding century bathing was not permitted before the ninth hour.[58] Finally, several of Martial's *Epigrams* seem to imply that many people took their bath at the tenth hour or later,[59] and that whatever might be the hour formally fixed for the opening of the baths and announced by the *tintinnabulum* of the bell, people were allowed to enter the exercise grounds before it sounded.[60] One thing only can in my opinion help to clear up this confusion and reduce or even reconcile the discrepancies in our data: the consideration of the plan of the *thermae* and the administrative regulations which governed the segregation of the sexes.

In the days of Martial and Juvenal, under Domitian, and still under Trajan, there was no formal prohibition of mixed bathing. Women who objected to this promiscuity could avoid the *thermae* and bathe in *balneae* provided for their exclusive use. But many women were attracted by the sports which preceded the bath in the *thermae*, and rather than renounce this pleasure preferred to compromise their reputation and bathe at the same time as the men.[61] As the *thermae* grew in popularity, this custom produced an outcropping of scandals which could not leave the authorities undisturbed. To put an end to them, sometime between the years 117 and 138 Hadrian passed the decree mentioned in the *Historia Augusta* which separated the sexes in the baths: '*lavacra pro sexibus separavit*'.[62] But since the plan of the *thermae* included only one *frigidarium*, one *tepidarium*, and one *caldarium*, it is clear that this separation could not be achieved in space, but only in time, by assigning different hours for the men's and women's baths. This was the solution enforced, at a great distance from Rome, it is true, but also under the reign of Hadrian, by the regulations of the procurators of the imperial mines at Vipasca in Lusitania.[63] The instructions issued to the *conductor* or lessee of the *balnea* in this mining district included the duty of heating the furnaces for the women's baths from the beginning of the first to the end of the seventh hour, and for the men's from the beginning of the eighth hour of day to the end of the second hour of night. The dimensions of the Roman *thermae* made impossible the lighting which an exactly similar division of times would have required. But there is in my opinion not the slightest doubt that Rome adopted the same principle, modifying the detail to suit the conditions imposed by the size of her *thermae*. We need only take account of the plan of the Roman *thermae*, with the baths proper in the centre and the huge annexes surrounding them, and coordinate this with the scattered indications found in the writers of the time, to be able to reconstruct a likely picture of the procedure.

From the statements of Juvenal we know that the doors of the annexes were opened to the public, irrespective of sex, from the fifth hour of the morning. At the sixth hour the central building was opened, but to women only after Hadrian's decree.[44] At the eighth or ninth hour, according to whether it was winter or summer, the bell sounded again. It was now the men's turn to have access to the baths, where they were allowed to stay till the eleventh or twelfth hour. From this division of the time, it is permissible to assume that women and men undressed successively inside the central baths, and that the *palaestrae* within their confines were the only places where nude athletics were permitted. This conclusion need not surprise us; and it tallies with the deductions we draw from texts describing the games in which the Romans indulged in their *thermae*.

We may, for instance, recall Trimalchio's encounter with the shady characters whom he was presently to invite to dine. It took place at bath time in the *thermae* – the *thermae* of a Campanian village, it is true, but copied from those of the capital. Encolpius and his companions begin by mingling with the groups which had gathered here and there in the *palaestra*. Suddenly they spy 'a bald old man in a reddish shirt playing at ball with some long-haired boys. ... The old gentleman, who was in his house shoes, was busily engaged with a green ball. He never picked it up if it touched

the ground. A slave stood by with a bagful and supplied them to
the players.'[65] This was a ball game for three, called a *trigon*, in
which the players, each posted at the corner of a triangle, flung the
balls to and fro without warning, catching with one hand and
throwing with the other.[66] The Romans had many other kinds of
ball games, including 'tennis' played with the palm of the hand
for a racquet (as in the Basque game of *pelote*);[67] *harpastum*, in which
the players had to seize the ball, or *harpastum*, in the middle of the
opponents, despite the shoving, bursts of speed, and feints[68] – a
game which was very exhausting and raised clouds of dust; and
many others such as 'hop-ball', 'ball against the wall', etc.[69] The
*harpastum* was stuffed with sand, the *paganica* with feathers; the
*follis* was blown full of air and the players fought for it as in basket
ball, but with more elegance.[70] Sometimes the ball was enormous
and filled with earth or flour, and the players pommelled it with
their fists like a punching bag,[71] in much the same way that they
sometimes lunged with their rapiers against a fencing post.[72] These
were some of the games which formed a prelude to the bath.
Martial alludes to them in an epigram addressed to a philosopher
friend who professed to disdain them: 'No hand-ball, no bladder-
ball, no feather-stuffed ball makes you ready for the warm bath,
nor the blunted stroke upon the unarmed stump; nor do you
stretch forth squared arms besmeared with sticky ointment, darting
to and fro, snatch the dusty scrimmage-ball.'[73]

This enumeration is far from complete and we must add simple
running, or rolling a metal hoop (*trochus*).[74] Steering the capricious
hoop with a little hooked stick which they called a 'key' was a
favourite sport of women; and so was swinging what Martial
called 'the silly dumb-bell' (*haltera*), though they tired at this more
quickly than the men.[75] When playing these games both men and
women wore either a tunic like Trimalchio's, or tights like those
of the manly Philaenis when she played with the *harpastum*[76] or a
plain warm cloak of sports cut like the *endromis* which Martial
sent to one of his friends with the gracious message: 'We send you
as a gift the shaggy nursling of a weaver on the Seine, a barbarian
garb that has a Spartan name, a thing uncouth but not to be despised
in cold December, . . . whether you catch the warming hand-ball,

or snatch the scrimmage-ball amid the dust, or bandy to and fro the featherweight of the flaccid bladder-ball.'[77]

For the wrestling match, on the other hand, the wrestlers had to strip completely, smear themselves with *ceroma* (an unguent of oil and wax which made the skin more supple), and cover this with a layer of dust to prevent their slipping from the opponent's hands. Wrestling took place in the *palaestrae* of the central building near some rooms which in the baths of Caracalla archaeologists have identified with the *oleoteria* and the *conisteria*.[78] Here not only wrestler but wrestleress – whose perverse complaisance under the masseur's attentions roused the wrath of Juvenal[79] – came to submit to the prescribed anointings and massage.

The bath which followed the games or the wrestling match was thus closely linked with sport. The bath itself usually consisted of three parts. First, the bather, drenched in sweat, went off to undress – if he had not already done so – in one of the dressing-rooms or *apodyteria* of the baths. Then he entered one of the *sudatoria* which flanked the *caldarium*, and encouraged the sweating process in this hothouse atmosphere: this was 'the dry bath'. Next he proceeded to the *caldarium*, where the temperature was almost as warm and where he could sprinkle hot water from the large tub known as the *labrum* on his sweating body and scrape it with the strigil. Cleansed and dried, he retraced his steps to the *tepidarium* to cool off gradually, and finally he ran to take a plunge in the cold pool of the *frigidarium*. These were the three phases of the hygienic bath as recommended by Pliny the Elder,[80] as experienced by the bathers in Petronius' novel,[81] and as suggested in the *Epigrams* of Martial.[82] Martial, however, allows his imaginary interlocutors the option of cutting out one of the bathing processes: 'If Lacedaemonian methods please you, you can content yourself with dry warmth and then plunge in the natural stream.'[83]

It was in practice impossible for the bather to rub himself down properly with the strigil. An assistant of some sort was indispensable, and if he had not taken the precaution of bringing some slaves of his own with him, he discovered that such assistance was by no means furnished gratis. An anecdote recorded in the *Historia Augusta* proves that people thought twice before they embarked on this expense.[84]

Hadrian's biographer relates that the emperor often bathed in the public baths with everyone else. One day he saw there an old soldier whom he had known in the army, busily rubbing himself against the marble with which the brick walls of the *caldarium* were faced, and asked why he was doing this. The old man replied that you had to have money to keep slaves, whereupon the princeps provided him with both slaves and money. Not unnaturally, the next day when the emperor's presence was announced a number of old men set to rubbing against the marble. Hadrian merely advised them to rub each other down.

We are safe in assuming that only the poor took the emperor's advice. Rich people could afford to have themselves served, rubbed, massaged, and perfumed as they would. When Trimalchio's future guests left the *frigidarium*, they found their accidental host inundated with perfumes and being rubbed down not with an ordinary cloth but with napkins of the finest wool, by three masseurs who, after quarrelling for the honour of grooming him, 'rolled him up in a scarlet woollen coat and put him in his litter'.[85] Trimalchio, duly dried by these specialists, was hoisted on the shoulders of his retainers and carried straight home where his dinner was awaiting him.

The majority of the bathers, however, especially those whose house was less luxurious and whose tables was less well set than Trimalchio's, lingered in the *thermae* and enjoyed their amenities until closing time. Groups of friends gathered in the public halls and *nymphaea* for conversation, or perhaps went to read in the libraries. The sites of the two libraries of the baths of Caracalla have been rediscovered at the two extremities of the line of cisterns. They are at once recognizable from the rectangular niches hollowed in the walls for the *plutei*, or wooden chests, which contained the precious *volumina*.[86] Others walked quietly to and fro in the ambulatories of the *xystus* among the masterpieces of sculpture with which the emperors had systematically peopled the *thermae*. We must not forget that modern excavation has rescued from the baths of Caracalla the Farnese Bull, Flora, and Hercules; the Belvedere Torso, and the two basins into which Roman fountains play in the square of the Palazzo Farnese. All of these stood of old on the mosaic pavements beneath the coffered vaults, between the marble-covered walls and the colonnades with capitals decorated with heroic figures which graced the baths.[87] The *thermae* of Trajan were not less richly endowed, and from them was retrieved, among other treasures, the famous group of the Laocoön, now in the Vatican.[88] It is impossible not to believe that the Romans, in the physical well-being and pleasant lassitude induced by exercise and bath, felt the beauty which surrounded them sink quietly into their souls.

It is true that the Romans themselves found evil to say about their *thermae*, and that many abuses flourished there. It is all too well established that there lurked under the stately porticos vendors of food and drink and procurers of both sexes;[89] that many congregated there to overeat and drink and indulge other disreputable tastes;[90] that many heated themselves merely in order 'to raise a thirst',[91] and found bathing a stimulant for other excesses: 'You will soon pay for it, my friend, if you take off your clothes, and with distended stomach carry your peacock into the bath undigested! This leads to death and an intestate old age!'[92] Such overindulgence in bathing as Commodus practised, who took up to eight baths a day, could only soften the muscles and exasperate the nerves.[93] We may fairly condemn abuses which the victims cynically acknowledged: 'Baths, wine, and women corrupt our bodies – but these things make life itself [*balnea, vina, Venus corrumpunt corpora nostra sed vitam faciunt*].'[94]

Nevertheless I am convinced that the imperial baths brought immense benefit to the people. In their dazzling marble grandeur the *thermae* were not only the splendid 'Palace of Roman Water',[95] but above all the palace of the Roman people, such as our democracies dream of today. In them the Romans learned to admire physical cleanliness, useful sports, and culture; and thus for many generations they kept decadence at bay by returning to the ancient ideal which had inspired their past greatness and which Juvenal still held before them as a boon to pray for: 'a healthy mind in a healthy body [*orandum est ut sit mens sana in corpore sano*].'[96]

### 3. Dinner

After the fatigue of the sports and tonic of the bath came dinner. The sun is sloping toward its setting and still we have not seen the Romans eat. Yet we know that some among them demanded four ample meals a day.[97] and our texts frequently mention three daily meals, whose names vary with the centuries. Just as our own names for meals – lunch, dinner, supper – have tended to shift, so the Roman *jentaculum*, *cena*, and *vesperna* became and remained throughout the classic period the *jentaculum*, *prandium*, and *cena*, while the *vesperna* disappeared.[98] In the period which concerns us, some Romans had kept the habit of all three – Pliny the Elder, for instance, among them, though he was anything but a great eater.[99] Old men tended also to keep up the three, as contemporary doctors prescribed.[100] But some people took a drink of water on rising,[101] and omitted one or other of the first two meals on the advice of their 'hygienists'. Galen notably took a *jentaculum* only about the fourth hour,[102] while the Roman plebs enjoyed its *prandium* at noon.[103] In any case, neither the *jentaculum* nor the *prandium* was a very nourishing or formidable meal. Martial's *jentaculum* consisted of bread and cheese;[104] *prandium* was often nothing more than a piece of bread,[105] but was more usually accompanied by cold meat, vegetables, and fruits washed down with a little wine.[106] Pliny the Elder's *jentaculum* was a very slight affair: '*cibum levem et facilem*'.[107] His *prandium* was merely a snack (*deinde gustabat*). Both *jentaculum* and *prandium* were so quickly disposed of that there was no need to set a table beforehand (*sine mensa*) or to wash the hands afterwards: '*post quod non sunt lavandae manus*'.[108] They were both evidently cold meals unceremoniously taken; the only serious meal, worthy of the name, was for everyone the evening dinner, the *cena*. In reading the lives of Vitellius and his like, it would be easy to imagine that the Romans passed their whole life at table. When we look more closely at the facts, however, we see that for the most part they did not sit down to table till their day was done, anticipating the practice of that connoisseur, the Prince of Beneventum, at the French Embassy in London a century ago.[109] They have been misrepresented as insatiable gourmands, when in fact they ate rather lightly until evening.

It is true that they then made up for lost time by doing full justice to their victuals. But here again it is prudent to avoid hasty generalizations and distrust superficial judgements. To picture the *cenae* of the Romans as so many eating orgies would be like imagining an Arab's feast the measure of his usual fare, or supposing that the long, lavish, hospitable meal offered at a country wedding represented the peasant's normal standard of living. The truth is that in similar settings and with identical customs and etiquette, there was a great difference between one *cena* and another according to the circumstances, personal tastes, and moral standards of individuals. The Romans might make their one and only proper dinner a vulgar eating contest or a dignified meal of delicacy and distinction.

Apart from such historic monsters as Vitellius and Nero who sat down to table at noon,[110] the hour of dinner was approximately the same for all; after the bath, that is to say, at the end of the eighth hour in winter and of the ninth in summer. This was the usual time in Pliny the Younger's circle for their 'elegant and frugal repast'.[111] It is the time suggested by Martial to his friend Iulius Cerialis whom he invites to meet him at the eighth hour at the baths of Stephanus, the nearest to his house, proposing to take him home for dinner afterwards.[112] On the other hand the time the *cena* ended depended on whether it was an ordinary meal or banquet, on whether the host was temperate or a glutton. When Pliny the Elder rose from table it was still light in summer and in winter the first hour of the night was not yet past.[113] Nero's *cena* lasted until midnight,[114] and Trimalchio's till the small hours;[115] the revellers to whom Juvenal addresses his reproaches 'began their sleep with the rise of Lucifer, the morning star, at an hour when our generals of old would be moving their standards and their camps'.[116]

Whatever the length of the dinner, well-to-do people always served it in a special room of their house or flat, the *triclinium*, whose length was twice its breadth.[117] The dining-room took its name from the couches with three reclining places each (*triclinia*) on which the guests reposed. This is an important detail of procedure to which we should have difficulty in adapting ourselves, and one nearer to the oriental custom of using cushions and divans, than to our practice. Nothing would have induced the Romans of the empire to eat otherwise. They considered the reclining position indispensable to their physical comfort, but also a mark of elegance and of social distinction. In the old days it was good enough for a woman to eat seated at her husband's feet.[118] But now that the Roman matron took her place beside the men on the *triclinia*, to eat sitting was suitable only for children, who sat on stools in front of their parents' couch,[119] or for slaves, who received permission to recline like their masters only on holidays;[120] for village rustics or provincials from distant Gaul,[121] or the passing customers of inns or taverns.[122] Whether or not they had donned for dinner the correct loose *synthesis* of light muslin which was suited to the warmth engendered by a ceremonial meal and was sometimes changed between the courses,[123] the Romans would have thought it unseemly not to dine reclining, men and women side by side. Opinion approved the austerity of Cato of Utica who, in mourning the rout of the senatorial army, made on the eve of Pharsalus a vow which he kept to the day of his suicide: to eat seated as long as the tyranny of Julius Caesar should be triumphant.[124]

Three sloping couches were ranged around a square table, one side of which was left free for the service.[125] The slope of the couches was so contrived that the edges came slightly above the level of the table. Each couch, more or less luxurious in its equipment, was spread with a mattress and with coverings, while cushions divided the central place from the other two. The ill-bred host who was not minded to put himself out for his guests sometimes occupied the central couch alone, or tolerated only one companion beside or rather 'below' him. For the places had a sort of hierarchic precedence, and their allotment was dictated by punctilious etiquette. The couch of honour was that opposite the empty side of the table (*lectus medius*); and on it the most honourable position was the right hand one, 'the consular' (*locus consularis*). Next in honour came the couch to the left of the central one (*lectus summus*), and last that on the right (*lectus imus*). On each of these couches the most privileged position was that to the left nearest the fulcrum or head of the couch. The other places were filled later. The guests reclined crosswise on the couches, their left elbow resting on a cushion, their feet, which they had freed from shoes or slippers and washed on entering,[126] at the foot of the couch. Not infrequently a round table was preferred to a square one, and the three couches replaced by one (*stibadium*) forming an arc of a circle or, as the phrase was, in the form of a '*lunar sigma*'. The most important personages occupied the two ends of the *stibadium*, on which nine people could recline at a pinch, but which normally accommodated only seven or eight.[127] If more than nine persons were to dine, other *stibadia* or *triclinia* had to be brought (*triclinia sternere*) into the dining-room, usually planned for thirty-six guests around four tables or for twenty-seven around three.[128]

An usher (*nomenclator*) announced the guests and showed them to their couch and place. Several waiters (*ministratores*) brought in the dishes and the bowls and placed them on the tables. Since the time of Domitian it had been the fashion to cover the table with a cloth (*mappa* or *mantile*);[129] before this it had been the custom merely to wipe the marble or wooden table top after each course.[130] The guests were provided with knives and toothpicks and spoons of various shapes:[131] the ladle or *trulla*; the *ligula*, holding rather more than a centilitre (quarter of a *cyathus*); and a little pointed spoon or *cocleare* with which eggs and shell-fish were eaten.[132] The Romans knew no more of forks than the Arabs of today or the Europeans at the beginning of modern times. They ate with their fingers, and this entailed frequent hand washings – before the meal began, and after each course. Slaves went round the couches with ewers and poured fresh perfumed water over the diners' hands, wiping them with the towel they carried over their arm.[133] Each guest was provided with a napkin for his personal use, which he spread in front of him so as not to stain the covering of the couch. A man had no hesitation in bringing his own napkin with him, for good manners permitted him to carry it away filled with titbits (*apophoreta*)[134] which he had not had time to consume.

It would certainly have required a Gargantuan appetite to polish off some of the menus recorded in literature. The full dress *cena* consisted of at least seven courses or *fercula* – 'which of our grandfathers dined by himself off seven courses?' asks Juvenal, *quis fercula septem secreto cenavit avus?*'[135] – the *hors d'œuvre*, or *gustatio*, three entrées, two roasts, and the dessert or *secundae mensae*. We see the procession of courses pass, with a supplementary roast thrown in, at Trimalchio's feast – a 'ridiculous meal', not because of the excess of food, which is scarcely more horrifying than the menu of certain official banquets Macrobius records for us three centuries later,[136] but for the complacent folly of the master, his childish excitement over his inventions, and the pretentious eccentricities of his dishes.

A donkey in Corinthian bronze stood on the sideboard with panniers holding olives, white in one side, black in the other. Two dishes hid the donkey; Trimalchio's name and their weight in silver was engraved on their edges. There were also dormice rolled in honey and poppy seed, and supported on little bridges soldered to the plate. Then there were hot sausages laid on a silver grill, and under the grill damsons and seeds of pomegranate.[137]

The guests were still busy with the *hors d'œuvre* 'when a tray was brought in with a basket on it, in which there was a hen made of wood, spreading out her wings as they do when they are setting. . . . Two slaves came up and began to hunt in the straw. Peahens' eggs were pulled out and handed to the guests.' Each egg was found to contain a 'fat beccafico rolled up in spiced yolk of egg'.[138] The second entrée arrived on a dish of monumental and puerile design.

Its novelty drew every eye to it. There was a round plate with the twelve signs of the Zodiac set in order, and on each one the artist had laid some food fit and proper to the symbol; over the Ram, ram's head pease, a piece of beef on the Bull, kidneys over the Twins, over the Crab a crown, an African fig over the Lion, a barren sow's paunch over Virgo, over Libra a pair of scales with a muffin on one side and a cake on the other, over Scorpio a small sea fish, over Sagittarius a bull's eye, over Capricorn a lobster, over Aquarius a goose, over Pisces two mullets.[139]

Underneath the top part of the dish 'we saw in the well of it fat fowls and sows' bellies and in the middle a hare got up with wings to look like Pegasus', while at the corners of the dish 'four figures of Marsyas also caught the eye; they let a spiced sauce run from their wine skins over the fishes which swam about in a miniature Euripus'.[140] After this the roasts came in, in corresponding style:

A tray was brought in with a wild pig of the largest size upon it wearing a cap of freedom, with two little baskets woven of palm twigs hanging from its tusks, one full of dry dates, the other of fresh. Round it lay sucking pigs made of simnel cake with their mouths to the teats, thereby showing that we had a sow before us.

A bearded man came who drew a hunting knife which he plunged into the pig's side, whereupon 'a number of thrushes flew out'.[141] Presently the slaves who were dressed up as Homeric heroes stood back

to let a boiled calf on a presentation dish be brought in. There was a helmet on its head. Ajax followed and attacked it with his sword drawn as if he were mad; and after making passes with the edge and the flat he collected slices on the point, and divided the calf among the astonished company.[142]

Finally came the dessert: 'A Priapus made by the confectioner standing in the middle, holding up every kind of fruit and grapes in his wide apron.'[143] Between the *cena* proper and the *secundae mensae* or dessert, the tables were taken away and replaced by others, and while the dining-room attendants were engaged on this task, others 'sprinkled about sawdust coloured with saffron and vermilion and what I had never seen before – powdered talc'.[144]

It might have seemed that at this point the satiated guests would think of nothing but taking their leave and going home to bed. But just as the banquet seemed about to close, it began afresh. Trimalchio made his guests take a red-hot bath, and led them into a second dining-room where wine flowed in rivers, and where those weary of eating could at least continue to drink according to the rites of the *commissatio*, the popular conclusion of such dinners.[145]

A first libation inaugurated the meal. After the *hors d'œuvre* a honey wine (*mulsum*) was served. Between the other courses the *ministratores*, while replenishing the guests' supply of little hot rolls, solicitously filled their drinking cups with every sort of wine, from those of Marseilles and the Vatican – not highly esteemed – up to the 'immortal Falernian'.[146] Wine blent with resin and pine pitch was preserved in amphorae whose necks were sealed with stoppers of cork or clay and provided with a label (*pittacium*) stating the vintage.[147] The amphorae were uncorked at the feast, and the contents poured through a funnel strainer into the mixing-bowl (*cratera*) from which the drinking-bowls were filled. Anyone who drank these heavy wines neat was considered abnormal and vicious, a mark for contumely.[148] It was in the *cratera* that the wine was mixed with water and either cooled with snow or in certain circumstances warmed. The proportion of water was rarely less than a third and might be as high as four-fifths.[149] The *commissatio* that followed dinner was a sort of ceremonial drinking match in which the cups were emptied at one draught. It was the exclusive right of the master of ceremonies to prescribe the number of cups, imposed equally on all, and the number of *cyathi* that should be poured into each, which might vary from one to eleven.[150] He also determined the style in which the ceremony should be performed: whether a round should be drunk beginning with the most distinguished person present (*a summo*), whether each in turn should empty his cup and pass it to his neighbour with wishes for good luck, or whether each should drink the health of a selected guest in a number of cups corresponding to the number of letters in his *tria nomina* of Roman citizen.[151]

We may well wonder how the sturdiest stomachs could stand such orgies of eating, how the steadiest heads could weather the abuses of the *commissationes*!

Perhaps the number of victims was sometimes smaller than the number of invited guests. There were often, in fact, many called but few chosen at these ostentatious and riotous feasts. Out of vanity, the master of the house would invite as many as possible to dine; then from selfishness or miserliness he would treat his guests inhospitably. Pliny the Elder criticizes some of his contemporaries who 'serve their guests with other wines than those they drink themselves, or substitute inferior wine for better in the course of the repast'.[152] Pliny the Younger condemns severely a host at whose table 'very elegant dishes were served up to himself and a few more of the company; while those placed before the rest were cheap and paltry. He had apportioned in small flagons three different sorts of wine,' graduated according to the social status of his friends.[153] Martial reproaches Lupus because his mistress 'fattens, the adulteress, on lewdly shaped loaves, while black meal feeds your guest. Wines of Setia are strained to inflame your lady's snow; we drink the black poison of a Corsican jar.'[154]

Finally Juvenal devotes more than a hundred lines to the kind of dinner Virro would offer a poor client.[155] This low-born upstart 'himself drinks wine bottled from the hills of Alba or Setia whose date and name have been effaced by the soot which time has gathered on the aged jar'; for him 'a delicate loaf is reserved, white as snow and kneaded of the finest flour,' for him

the huge lobster, garnished with asparagus . . . a mullet from Corsica . . . the finest lamprey the Straits of Sicily can purvey . . . a goose's liver, a capon as big as a house, a boar piping hot, worthy of Meleager's steel . . . truffles and delicious mushrooms . . . apples whose scent would be a feast, which might have been filched from the African Hesperides.

Round him the while his humble guests must be content with the coarse wine of this year's vintage, 'bits of hard bread that have turned mouldy', some 'sickly greens cooked in oil that smells of the lamp', 'an eel, first cousin to a water-snake . . . a crab hemmed in by half an egg . . . toadstools of doubtful quality . . . and a rotten apple like those munched on the ramparts by a monkey trained by terror of the whip'. In vain Pliny the Younger protested against 'this modern conjunction of self-indulgence and meanness . . . qualities each alone superlatively odious, but still more odious when they meet in the same person'.[156] Evidence from many sources places it beyond doubt that these practices were widespread. They had at least the advantage of limiting the damage wrought by gluttony at dinner parties.

The evils of gluttony were somewhat lessened also by the very leisureliness which characterized the long-drawn programme of the elaborate *cena*. Many banquets lasted eight or ten hours, like Trimalchio's dinner. They were divided into acts, as it were: in the interval after the entrées a concert was accompanied by the gesticulations of a silver skeleton; after one roast there was an acrobatic turn and Fortunata danced the *cordex*; before dessert there were riddles, a lottery, and a surprise when the ceiling opened to let down an immense hoop to which little flasks of perfume were attached for immediate distribution.[157] It was very generally felt that no dinner party was complete without the buffooneries of clowns, antic tricks of wantons around the tables,[158] or lascivious dances to the clatter of castanets, for which Spanish maidens were as renowned in Rome as are the Aulad Nail among the Arabs of Algeria today.[159] Pliny the Younger found nothing amusing in such entertainments: 'I confess I admit nothing of this kind at my own house, however I bear with it in others.'[160] The Pantagruelian feast which such interruptions helped the diners to digest often ended in an orgy whose indecency was aggravated by the incredible lack of embarrassment displayed.

As among the Arabs still, belching was considered a politeness, justified by philosophers who thought the highest wisdom was to follow the dictates of nature.[161] Pushing this doctrine even further, Claudius had considered an edict authorizing other emissions of wind from which even Arabs refrain,[162] and the doctors of Martial's day recommended that people take advantage of the liberties championed by a well-meaning but ridiculous emperor.[163] Music of this kind was not wanting at Trimalchio's table. After explaining his own state of health – 'I have such rumblings inside me you would think there was a bull there' – he adjured his guests not to risk injury to their health by self-restraint: 'As far as I am concerned anyone may relieve himself in the dining-room.'[164] Even Trimalchio had the good taste to quit his couch and leave the *triclinium* when pressed by more urgent need. But not all Roman parvenus were so scrupulous. Martial tells of more than one who simply clicked his fingers for a slave to bring him 'a necessary vase' into which he 'remeasured with accuracy the wine he had drunk from it', while the slave 'guides his boozy master's drunken person'.[165] Finally it was not infrequent during the *cena* to see priceless marble mosaics of the floor defiled with spitting.[166] The best way, in fact, to make sure of being able to eat throughout the incredible carousal was to make use of the small room next door: '*vomunt ut edant, edunt ut vomant*'.[167] It is impossible to repress disgust on reading these descriptions, or to deny that wealthy Rome which drained the resources of her empire was saddled with all too many gluttons and topers, even in the circles in which Pliny the Younger moved.

To appreciate the consummate skill of the Roman chef, past

master in the art of so disguising dishes that none could guess their ingredients (*ut nemo agnoscet quid manduces*),[168] we need only hear Petronius vaunt the exploits of his chef: 'If you want it, he will make you a fish out of a sow's belly, a wood pigeon out of bacon, a turtle-dove out of a ham, and a chicken out of a knuckle of pork. There could not be a more valuable fellow.'[169] To realize the progress of gastronomy in his day and the excellence and variety of the food supplies which were at the gourmet's disposal for varied combinations, we may read the Thirteenth Book of Martial's *Epigrams*.[170] Fish were caught in the gulfs and bays adjacent to the city; shell-fish, large and small, in the Mediterranean. Game abounded in the Laurentine and Ciminian forests. The open country near at hand supplied from its flocks and herds meat and milk in every form, the cheeses of Trebula and Vestini, and also vegetables of every sort: cabbages and lentils, beans and lettuce, radishes and turnips, gourds and pumpkins, melons and asparagus. Picenum and and the Sabine country were renowned for the quality of their oils. The pickles with which eggs were seasoned came from Spain. Pork came from Gaul, spices from the East; wines and fruits from all the sections of Italy and the world; apples, pears, and figs from Chios, lemons and pomegranates from Africa, dates from the oases, plums from Damascus. Every kind of food had its amateurs and connoisseurs. From Juvenal alone a collection could be made of gourmands whose mouths watered to see the abundance of the market: 'the dirty ditch digger who remembers the savour of tripe in the reeking cookshop';[171] 'the youth who has learned from the hoary gluttony of a spendthrift father to peel truffles, to preserve mushrooms, and to souse beccaficos in their own juice';[172] the prodigal who for 6,000 sesterces bought a mullet that he coveted;[173] the gourmet Montanus, who 'could tell at the first bite whether an oyster had been bred at Circeii or on the Lucrine rocks'.[174]

It would be a mistake, however, to believe that every senator was a Montanus; and just as false to imagine that every Roman dinner was like the orgies we have cited. While these grotesque scenes were taking place, many other Romans were partaking of a discreet and charming meal at which the mind had as much play as the appetite, and the disciplined service excluded neither moderation nor simplicity. Thanks to a letter of Pliny the Younger we know the kind of *cena* Trajan presided over in his villa at Centumcellae (Città Vecchia):[175] 'We were every day invited to Caesar's supper, which for a prince was a modest [*modica*] repast; there we were either entertained with interludes [*acroamata*], or passed the night in the most pleasing conversation.' Pliny himself accepts as a rare and welcome gift the 'very fine thrushes' sent him by Calpurnius[176] and the pullet which reached him from Cornutus: 'Weak as my eyes still are, they are strong enough to discern that it is extremely fat.'[177] He accepted an invitation to dinner from Catilius Severus (consul in 115), 'but I must make this condition beforehand, that you dismiss me soon and treat me frugally. Let our table abound only in philosophical conversation, and let us enjoy even that within limits.'[178] A letter of his preserves the menu he had prepared for Septicius Clarus in which he jestingly boasts of

the expense I was at to treat you – which let me tell you was no small sum. I had prepared, you must know, a lettuce and three snails apiece; with two eggs, barley water, some sweet wine and snow ... Besides all these curious dishes, there were olives, beets, gourds, shallots, and a hundred other dainties equally sumptuous. You should likewise have been entertained either with an interlude, the rehearsal of a poem, or a piece of music, as you like best; or (such was my liberality) with all three. But the oysters, chitterlings, sea-urchins, and Spanish dancers of a certain – were, it seems, more to your taste![179]

The same good taste reigned among the humbler middle classes. Let us inspect, for instance, the *cena* which Martial arranged for seven guests:

My bailiff's wife has brought me mallows that will ease the stomach, and the various wealth the garden bears; among which are squat lettuce and clipped leek, and flatulent mint is not wanting nor the salacious herb [*eruca*]; sliced eggs shall garnish lizard-fish served with rue and there shall be a paunch dripping with the tunny's brine. So much for your *hors d'œuvre*. The modest dinner shall be served in a single course – a kid rescued from the jaws of a savage wolf, and meat balls to require no carver's knife, and beans, the food of artisans, and tender young sprouts; to these a chicken, and a ham that has already survived three dinners, shall be added. When you have had your fill I will give you ripe apples, wine without lees from a Nomentan flagon which was three years old in Frontinus' second consulship [A.D. 98]. To crown these there shall be jests without gall, and a freedom not dreaded next morning, and no word you would wish unsaid.[180]

Even simpler and more amusing is the dinner which Juvenal proposes to his friend Persicus:

And now hear my feast, which no meat market shall provide. From my Tiburtine farm there will come a plump kid, tenderest of the flock, innocent of grass, that has never yet dared to nibble the twigs of the dwarf willow, and has more of milk in him than blood; some wild asparagus, gathered by the bailiff's wife when done with her spindle, and some lordly eggs warm in their wisps of hay together with the hens that laid them. There will be grapes too, kept half the year, as fresh as when they hung upon the vine; pears from Signia and Syria, and in the same baskets fresh-smelling apples that rival those of Picenum.[181]

It is pleasing to think it was menus like these that were enjoyed during his holidays at Pompeii by the townsman who had painted on the walls of his *triclinium* the wise mottoes which we still read there, breathing decency and dignity:[182]

Let the slave wash and dry the feet of the guests, and let him be mindful to spread a linen cloth on the cushions of the couches.

> *Abluat unda pedes puer et detergeat udos;*
> *Mappa torum velet lintea nostra cavel*

Spare thy neighbour's wife lascivious glances and ogling flatteries, and let modesty dwell in thy mouth.

> *Lascivos voltus et blandos aufer ocellos*
> *Coniuge ab alterius; sit tibi in ore pudor.*

Be amiable and abstain from odious brawlings if thou canst. If not, let thy steps bear thee back again to thine own home.

> *Utere blandiis odiosaque iurgia differ*
> *Si potes, aut gressus ad tua tecta refer.*

We may be very sure that similar restraint was generally ob-

served by the plebeians in their Guild banquets. Let us call to
witness the regulations of the Funeral College founded at Lanuvium
in A.D. 133.[183] The college organized six feasts a year: two on the
respective anniversaries of the sanctuaries of Antinoüs and Diana, the
hero and the goddess under whose protection this 'College of
Salvation' was placed; four on the anniversaries of the deaths of its
benefactors, the three Caesennii and Cornelia Procula. The rule
was that the president of the banquet (the *magister cenae*) should see
to it that each guest received as his share a loaf costing two asses,
four sardines, and an amphora of heated wine. The *magister* decided the order in which his colleagues should take their seats in
accordance with the list of precedence or *album*. Finally it was his
duty to prescribe penalties for any who misbehaved: 'If anyone
leaves his seat and takes another in order to create a disturbance, he
shall pay a fine of four sesterces; if anyone insults another or makes a
noise he shall pay twelve sesterces; if it is the master of the ceremonies who is insulted the offender shall be fined twenty sesterces.' The
virtues of ancient Rome seem to revive in this association of the
humble folk of a Roman suburb in the time of Hadrian. We seem
to see a new feeling come to birth, which is all to the honour of
the 'Brothers' of Lanuvium: a sense of brotherhood which unites
them in life as it will afterwards reunite them in death, while in
anticipation of their death they meet together to subscribe jointly
for the cost of their respective obsequies and to win salvation in
another world.

This same feeling of brotherhood, even stronger because nourished
by a higher ideal and enlightened by the truths of the Gospel, drew
together the Christians of Rome at the end of their day's work, in
those *cenae* to which their communities had given the Greek name
of 'love' (ἀγάπη). Since the first century they had been wont to
sup together, 'praising God and eating their meat with gladness
and in singleness of heart'.[184] At the end of the second century they
displayed among each other the charity of brothers, for 'the poor
shared in the provisions of the rich, but they suffered nothing vile
and nothing immodest therein.' Thus, as Tertullian writes, they do
not recline to eat till they have offered a prayer to God. They eat
according to the measure only of their hunger. They drink only as is

seemly for chaste people. They satisfy their hunger as people mindful that they must adore God in the night. They converse as knowing that God is listening.[185]

The pictures of Petronius, the *Epigrams* of Martial, the *Satires* of
Juvenal only too clearly impress upon us all the sordid and depraved
side of Roman life. But now, alongside this, we see a certain
nobility in the everyday conduct of the best people in Rome that
commands our admiration: in the daily life of the humble citizen
and the plebeian, in the modesty of Trajan's court, in the frugality
of the meals to which Pliny the Younger and the poets invited their
friends, in the good-humoured *cenae* where the faithful of Antinoüs
and Diana crowded fraternally round their tables; and above all in
those serene '*agapes*', where the Christians lifted up their hearts in
the joy of knowing the divine presence in their midst.

# LIST OF ABBREVIATIONS USED IN
## SOURCES OF INFORMATION AND NOTES

| | |
|---|---|
| AJA | American Journal of Archaeology |
| Ann. épigr. | Année épigraphique |
| Atti-CNSR | Atti del Congresso nazionale di studi Romani |
| BC | Bullettino della Commissione archeologica comunale di Roma |
| CIL | Corpus Inscriptionum Latinarum |
| Class. Phil. | Classical Philology |
| CRAI | Comptes Rendus de l'Académie des Inscriptions et Belles Lettres |
| DS | Daremberg-Saglio, Dictionnaire des antiquités grecques et romaines |
| JÖA | Jahreshefte des österreichischen archäologischen Instituts in Wien |
| JRS | Journal of Roman Studies |
| MA | G. Lugli, I Monumenti Antichi di Roma e Suburbio, Vols. II and III. Rome, 1934–8 |
| MAAR | Memoirs of the American Academy in Rome |
| MAI | Mémoires de l'Académie des Inscriptions et Belles Lettres |
| Mél. | Mélanges d'archéologie et d'histoire de l'École française de Rome |
| ML | Memorie della reale Accademia nazionale dei Lincei |
| NS | Notizie degli Scavi di Antichità |
| PA | S. B. Platner and T. Ashby, A Topographical Dictionary of Ancient Rome. Oxford, 1929 |
| RAP | Rendiconti dell' Accademia Pontifia |
| RE | Pauly-Wissowa-Kroll, Real-Encyclopädie der klassischen Altertumswissenschaft |
| Rh M | Rheinisches Museum für Philologie |
| RL | Rendiconti della reale Accademia dei Lincei |
| SG | L. Friedländer, Darstellungen aus der Sittengeschichte Roms (reference is made to the 10th edition edited by Georg Wissowa, Leipzig, 1922) |
| SHA | Scriptores Historia Augustae. |
| Skrifter | Skrifter utgivna av svenska institutet i Rom |
| TAPA | Transactions of the American Philological Association |
| ZA | G. Lugli, I Monumenti Antichi di Roma e Suburbio, Vol. I, 'La Zona Archeologica'. Rome, 1930 |

# SOURCES OF INFORMATION

A WORD may be appropriate explaining the method which I have adopted in editing this book before the immediate subject of sources is approached. First of all, M. Carcopino granted me generous permission to settle all matters pertaining to the present English edition without further consultation. I take this occasion to express publicly my appreciation of his confidence, and accept, at the same time, full responsibility for the form in which the book now appears.

Comparison with the original French edition will show the changes which have been made. They consist chiefly in additions. The notes have been greatly augmented, and M. Carcopino's short bibliographical introduction has been expanded into the present chapter. In carrying out the work which these additions entailed, I have kept one purpose uppermost in mind: to make the book as a whole more useful to lay reader and classical scholar alike, while respecting the author's views and interpretations of the evidence. Hence, the alterations in the text have been made chiefly to present more complete and precise descriptions of the matters discussed, and the conclusions drawn from the data by M. Carcopino have remained virtually untouched. In some cases, I should have preferred to consult M. Carcopino with regard to a few of the changes before undertaking them, but the circumstances under which the revision was made did not allow lengthy or swift correspondence.

With regard to the notes, they consist of references to the ancient sources and to modern books and articles dealing in a comprehensive way with matters discussed in the text. Wherever in the text direct reference is made to an ancient source, the document is cited. On the other hand, where a problem is involved depending on a large mass of scattered evidence which must be carefully analysed and combined in order to reach valid conclusions of a general nature, it seemed best to cite a book or article in which the complete evidence had been so handled by a competent scholar. Needless to say, I have attempted to cite the most recent studies of the subjects in question, especially those which contain a bibliography of earlier works and an evaluation of the conclusions reached therein. It will seem in some cases that the point of view expressed in the works which I have cited differs from that of M. Carcopino, but this, of course, is the unavoidable result of evidence which is often fragmentary or contradictory and which must be interpreted necessarily with a certain amount of hypothesis.

To begin with the information given us by the ancient authors, classical literature, both Greek and Roman, has long been thoroughly examined for references to all the different aspects of Roman daily life, from such purely material objects as clothes and furniture to the customs and institutions which governed the Roman in his relations with his fellow individuals and with society as a whole. From the time of Trajan we have the *Satires* of Juvenal, the *Epigrams* of Martial, and the *Letters* of Pliny the Younger as our most important sources of information. But earlier and later authors supply us with many details from their own times which we may apply safely to the period with which this book is primarily concerned. Of these, Petronius and Seneca, both of whom wrote in the reign of Nero, deserve particular mention, the former for the realistic picture which he paints of the lower strata of Roman society, the latter for his many allusions to the life led in the circle in which he moved – the circle of the court and the nobility. Furthermore, the distinctly biographical character of the history written by the Roman historians of the empire – especially Suetonius and the later writers known collectively as the *Scriptores Historia Augustae* – makes their works a far richer source with regard to daily life and manners than we might expect from historians inspired by a more profound and philosophical concept of their task. All in all, then, although they often fail us, our literary documents must be the starting point for any serious study of daily life in ancient Rome.

With the authors, moreover, we must also consider the information conveyed by documents incised or engraved on stone or metal. The information afforded by inscriptions is particularly valuable in the field covered by this book. Many of its aspects could not have been discussed in more than a cursory manner had not inscriptions furnished the details. Whether in treating the racial composition of the population of Rome, the constitution of a guild or religious sect, or the regulations governing the use of vehicles within city limits, the most reliable information will be found preserved on stone or bronze and in many cases it will be the only information available.

Furthermore, we cannot even afford to neglect the simple epitaph of a few lines. Whereas the literary text is apt to give us general information about social customs and the behaviour of the individual, the epigraphical document almost always furnishes a fact or facts, even if it is no more than the name given a man who exercises a certain trade, the age at which a girl married, or the street in which a certain product was sold. It can readily be seen that when thousands of these inscriptions have been divided into categories and compared, even the shortest and least informative, when viewed by itself, has contributed to a statistical piece of information which could not have been obtained through any other source.

Finally, our epigraphical material is continually increasing as excavations bring new inscriptions to light, while it is only through new interpretations or combinations of well-known literary passages that the authors can be made to throw new light on the field.

Like the epigraphical material, the archaeological is constantly growing and for the same reason. The monuments uncovered in all parts of the Roman Empire, from the Rhine to the Euphrates and the Sahara to the Black Sea, both illuminate and are illuminated by literary texts and inscriptions. For our immediate subject, the life lived by the Roman in Rome, the remains and excavations of the city proper, together with those of the Italian towns of Pompeii, Ostia, and Herculaneum, are naturally of the greatest importance. Much of ancient imperial Rome has survived in the Rome of the Empire and we can see today with our own eyes many of the buildings which were familiar to the ancient citizen. In other words, the remains of Rome give us an adequate conception of the public background against which the Roman moved.

But Rome, which since the days of the old republic has been of such vital importance, for spiritual or material reasons, to the development of Western civilization, tells us less archaeologically about the private life of her citizens under the empire. When many of the most splendid and impressive public monuments of the ancient city perished utterly, it could hardly be expected that dwelling houses would survive the building and rebuilding of some two thousand years. Thus, although we have remains of dwelling houses, either buried under later construction or unearthed by excavation, these remains are scanty in comparison with those of ancient Ostia.

As the suburb of Rome whose history ended with classical antiquity, Ostia gives us a clear conception of how people were housed in the Rome of the empire. As M. Carcopino has pointed out in the text, a serious mistake prevailed among classical scholars for many years, in that the Pompeian private house or *domus* was assumed to have been as typical of Rome as it was of Pompeii. The unearthing of Ostia has shown up the mistake and the apartment house or *insula* which is barely mentioned in the manuals of twenty years ago is receiving by now the attention it deserves as the most important type of dwelling in the city.

This does not mean, however, that we can dispense with Pompeii and Herculaneum in reconstructing daily life in Rome. The most abundant and illuminating supply of the household objects used in Italy under the early empire has come from the ruins of Pompeii, and now that excavations have been resumed at Herculaneum, we may expect a substantial increase in our knowledge of *instrumenta domestica*. Moreover, we need not assume that the same wide divergence existed between the household objects of Pompeii and those of Rome as existed between housing conditions in the two cities. The problem of sheltering masses of people varying in size within given localities is vitally affected in its solution by a number of factors, economic, geographic, and climatic, which do not apply with the same force to the cultural implements used within different groups of a society which enjoys fundamentally the same cultural patterns throughout. This was as true of antiquity as it is of modern times, and as the same basic forms of household implements prevail among us, whether in the metropolis or the country town, so may we use the furnishings of the Pompeian house to reconstruct the private background of the Roman of Rome.

To summarize, then, no complete or relatively complete picture of Roman life in the city of Rome under the empire can be pieced together without combining the information provided by the three fields of literature, epigraphy, and archaeology. Preference must be given, wherever possible, to material which is directly connected with the city: inscriptions and monuments from Rome and literary references which mention life in the city specifically. Where these fail us, we must have recourse to the smaller Italian towns. But we must here remember to exercise discrimination and to select the kind of material which appears applicable to the larger city not only on the basis of its intrinsic character but also with regard to the local peculiarities of its place of origin.

It is not the purpose of this chapter to give a comprehensive list of modern works dealing with the various aspects of Rome and Roman life treated in this book. Pertinent discussions are cited in the notes at the appropriate place where the nature of their connexion with the subject under discussion is easily understood – something which cannot always be deduced from the mere citation of a book or article in a bibliographical list.

There are certain books, however, of a general nature to which the author and editor are particularly indebted and wish to acknowledge their debt. They are works which deserve to be recommended to all those who may care to undertake further study or reading in the field. Although frequently cited and well known to the classical scholar, a few words about them may be of interest from the point of view from which the present book was written.

The two great classical encyclopedias

PAULY-WISSOWA-KROLL: *Real-Encyclopädie der klassischen Altertum-swissenschaft*

DAREMBERG-SAGLIO: *Dictionnaire des antiquités grecques et romaines*

will be found as indispensable for work in the field of Roman daily life as in any other aspect of Classical Antiquity. M. Carcopino in his bibliographical note to the French edition freely admits his great indebtedness to the *Dictionnaire* and, for that reason, I have seen fit to cite it more often in the notes than the *Real-Encyclopädie*. In all cases I have compared the corresponding articles in both publications, and where they have seemed equally reliable and complete I have not burdened the notes with a double reference. On the other hand, in cases where the German work seemed superior, either in the material collected or its interpretation, I have not hesitated to refer to both works, or in cases where the French work was plainly incorrec or antiquated, to the German work alone. In this connexion, it will be noted that most of the articles cited from the *Real-Encyclopädie* are of fairly recent date.

Among general works on Roman daily life, there are two manuals which are outstanding as compilations of factual information:

J. MARQUANDT: *Das Privatleben der Römer* (2nd ed. by A. Mau, Leipzig, 1886)

H. BLÜMNER: *Die römischen Privat-Altertümer* (Munich, 1911)

Both authors have made a thorough examination of classical literature for information pertaining to their subject, and their documentation, so far as written evidence is concerned, leaves little or nothing to be desired. From our present point of view, archaeology and epigraphy are somewhat slighted, but it must be remembered that material in both these fields has increased vastly within recent years and that with the increase has come both a keener realization of the importance of such material and a greater knowledge of how to use it. Both authors confine themselves strictly to facts and ignore the social and philosophical implications of the customs and institutions which they describe; but as source-books their works remain invaluable.

Of a somewhat different nature is

L. FRIEDLÄNDER, *Darstellungen aus der Sittengeschichte Roms* (10th edition by Georg Wissowa, Leipzig, 1922; English translation from the 7th German edition by J. H. Freese and L. A. Magnus, London, 1908–13).

Friedländer, whose enormous learning in the field is also preserved in a series of brilliant commentaries to Juvenal, Martial, and Petronius, presents a number of comprehensive monographs in book form on different manifestations of Roman life under the empire. The documentation is complete and many subjects are treated which are fascinating in themselves and exceptional enough not to have found a place in the general manuals which deal with customs and institutions common to the average Roman – sight-seeing and tourist travel, for instance, or the ways in which the very wealthy managed to spend their money. What is more, Friedländer does not hesitate to draw instructive comparisons between Roman and later times, which in many cases has a salutary effect on traditional judgements, which were first made, as it would seem, *in vacuo*, and thence kept inviolate from any healthy light which comparison might have cast upon them.

Finally, we must turn to

SAMUEL DILL: *Roman Society from Nero to Marcus Aurelius* (London, 1925)

for a general exposition and estimate of what was thought and felt in Rome during this period. While admitting the unadulterated materialism which strikes us forcibly in our chief literary sources, we must recognize at the same time that religious and philosophic trends were in motion which were not only of overwhelming importance for the future history of Western civilization, but part also of the 'mentality' of anyone who lived among them, whether he was conscious of them or not. For the influence on the Roman mind of religion, both traditional and Oriental, superstition, and philosophy in the period with which this book deals, the book of Dill is to be highly recommended.

These general books, however, fail us in one regard: they tell very little about the city of Rome as the physical milieu of its inhabitants, and we must turn to a different type of work for this information.

The archaeological remains of ancient Rome are bewildering in their magnitude and complexity. Innumerable articles and monographs have been published dealing with individual monuments or the problems which they present, and this material is widely scattered in the many journals devoted to the study of classical antiquity. Fortunately the greater part of this material was gathered together and summarized within recent years by Samuel Ball Platner, whose unfinished manuscript was completed, revised, and published by Thomas Ashby in

*A Topographical Dictionary of Ancient Rome* (Oxford, 1929).

The work is arranged alphabetically. Under each heading the description and history of the monument in question are given, based upon the complete ancient evidence, existing remains, and scholarly reconstruction. With regard to modern works, reference is made not only to specialized articles, but also to the books and manuals in which the monument is discussed. The bibliography is remarkably complete, and as one eminent topographer has stated, the book constitutes a new foundation for all discussion of ancient Rome.

Of a somewhat different character are the three volumes of Giuseppe Lugli,

*I Monumenti antichi di Roma e Suburbio* (Rome, 1930, 1934, and 1938).

The first volume represents a second, revised edition of Professor Lugli's *La zona archeologica di Roma* which appeared in 1925. The work is written for the general reader by an expert, whose more specialized investigations in the field are well known to the student of Roman archaeology. The first volume deals with the section of Rome which contains the most important remains of the ancient city which lie on or about the Capitoline and Palatine hills and extend to the Tiber at the *forum Holitorium* and the *forum Boarium* and to the southern outskirts of the city along the Appian Way. The second volume takes up the monuments which can be treated as types better than topographically. A prefatory chapter gives a history of Roman building activities from the period of the kings to the first barbarian invasions. This is followed by chapters on the city walls, fountains, bridges, aqueducts, etc. The topographical method is adopted again in the third volume which covers the parts of Rome not described in the first. These are chiefly the *campus Martius*, the remaining hills, and the region across the Tiber.

On the whole the documentation is thin and the work must be used with some caution. But the opinions of a scholar of Lugli's experience and eminence deserve careful consideration and his work should be used in connexion with the more factual and conservative dictionary of Platner-Ashby.

In the text of this book, mention is found of two important sources of information which need a separate word of explanation. One is the

## Forma Urbis Romae

At the beginning of the third century A.D., a marble plan of the city of

Rome was affixed to the north wall of the *templum sacrae urbis* which faced the Forum of Vespasian. The temple had burned down in A.D. 191 and been restored by the Emperor Septimius Severus. It is probable, although direct evidence is lacking, that an earlier plan was set up in the same place by Vespasian when he built the original temple. This plan may have served as a model for the one erected by Severus and his son Caracalla, but contemporary allusions in the later plan prove that it was more than a servile copy of its predecessor.

Since the middle of the sixteenth century, many fragments have been found. All those which had come to light by 1874 were collected and published with an exhaustive commentary by

H. JORDAN: *Forma Urbis Romae* (Berlin, 1874).

New fragments, however, have since been discovered and a much needed new edition has been promised. At present all extant fragments are being studied and pieced together in the *Antiquarium Comunale* at Rome. On the *Forma*, besides Jordan's work cited above, see

O. RICHTER: *Topographie von Rom* (2nd ed., Berlin, 1901) 1–8.

G. LUGLI: *RAP* XIII (1937) 86, n. 27.

## The Regionaries

The *Regionaries* are two descriptions of the city of Rome according to the fourteen administrative regions into which it was divided by Augustus. One is called the *Curiosum*, a name found in the oldest manuscripts, the other the *Notitia*, a name given it in the Renaissance. They both derive from a common original, now lost, which appears to have been compiled in the reign of Constantine between the years A.D. 312 and 315. It is likely that the compiler of the original drew upon an earlier description of the city written under Diocletian. The view is generally accepted that the *Notitia*, as it has come down to us, was written after A.D. 334 and before A.D. 357, while the *Curiosum* falls within the period extending from A.D. 357 to the reign of Honorius. The failure of both documents to mention any Christian monument is striking and makes a date later than the fourth century rather improbable.

Both *Regionaries* are divided into three parts. The first contains a list of the most important monuments by regions, beginning with the first and continuing through the fourteenth. At the end of each regionary section, the number of private houses, apartment houses, public fountains, etc., within the pertinent region is given.

The second section contains a list of monuments by categories. It gives the number of libraries and the height and location of the obelisks in Rome. These are followed by the number and names of the bridges, hills, campi, fora, basilicae, public baths, aqueducts, and roads.

The last part is a *breviarium* or summary in which the sum total is given for the monuments already enumerated region by region, in the first part, with the notable addition of certain groups previously omitted.

The *Regionaries* were used as a source by the author of an ecclesiastical history from Constantine to Justinian. The work, written in Syriac, is commonly attributed to Zacharias of Mytiene, and one of the books now lost contained a description of Rome which has survived as an excerpt.

On the *Regionaires*, see

L. PRELLER: *Die Regionen der Stadt Rom* (Jena, 1846).
H. JORDAN: *Topographie der Stadt Rom II* (Berlin, 1871) 1–236; 540–74.
O. RICHTER: *Topographie von Rom*, 6–9; 371–89.
GRAFFUNDER: *RE* IA 477–80.

The text is also printed in

L. URLICHS: *Codex Urbis Romae Topographicus*, 1–27.

On Zacharias, see

JORDAN: op. cit. 149–52; 174–8.

Translations of the Syrian text are given in

H. JORDAN: op. cit. 575–7 (Latin).
F. G. HAMILTON, E. W. BRADY: *The Syriac Chronicle known as that of Zachariah of Mytilene* (London, 1899) 317–19 (English).


### Ostia and Roman Housing

I have mentioned above the importance of Ostia for our knowledge of housing conditions in ancient Rome. For a selected bibliography on Ostia in general, we have

A. W. VAN BUREN: *A Bibliographical Guide to Latium and Southern Etruria* (4th ed., Rome, 1938) 31.

Of the more recent discussions of Roman housing, the following is a selected list of those which have seemed most pertinent.

A. MAIURI: *Atti* I CNSR VII (1929) 161–72
A. BOETHIUS: *Skrifter* II (1932) 84–97
R. C. CARRINGTON: *Antiquity* VII (1933) 133–52
A. BOETHIUS: *AJA* XXVIII (1934) 158–70
P. HARSH: *MAAR* XII (1935) 7–66
A. BOETHIUS: *Skrifter* IV (1935) 164–95
A. BOETHIUS: *Scritti in onore di B. Nogara* 21–31 (1937)
G. LUGLI: *RAP* XIII (1937) 73–98

### Pompeii and Herculaneum

With regard to the antiquities of Pompeii and Herculaneum, we are fortunate in having a recent edition of

A. W. VAN BUREN: *A Companion to the Study of Pompeii and Herculaneum* (2nd ed., Rome, 1938).

In dealing with Pompeii, the author has divided his work into sections covering the various aspects of the city and its life. The ancient evidence, literary or epigraphical, is cited and reference is made to the latest books or articles devoted to the subject under discussion. To the general bibliography on page 13, I would add

HELEN H. TANZER, *The Common People of Pompeii* (Baltimore, 1939).

This book, by presenting a well-documented picture of daily life in Pompeii, invites a comparison between the business and social activities of a relatively small Italian town and those of the city of Rome as described by M. Carcopino. It also contains an excellent bibliography.

To Professor Van Buren's bibliography of Herculaneum on page 36, we may add two articles:

H. MARROU: *Annales de l'École des Hautes Études de Gand* I (1937) 81–107.
R. HORN: *Die Antike* XIV (1938) 355–66.

Both of these works pretend to be no more than general surveys, but they are particularly welcome in view of the dearth of detailed technical reports on the discoveries of recent years.

Finally, the latest archaeological publications on Rome, Ostia, Pompeii, and Herculaneum can be found most conveniently in the

## SOURCES OF INFORMATION

*Bibliographie zum Jahrbuch des Deutschen Archäologischen Instituts.*

This is an annual publication, the second section of which is organized topographically so that the books and articles pertaining to a given locality are gathered together under the appropriate place name.

HENRY T. ROWELL

# NOTES

## PREFACE

1. Juvenal, 11, 78–9.

## *PART ONE*

### CHAPTER I
### THE EXTENT AND POPULATION OF THE CITY

1. On the Forum of Trajan, see *PA* 237–45; *ZA* 58–85; Paribeni, *Optimus Princeps* II 65–100; and Ricci-Colini-Mariani, *Via dell' impero* (No. 24 of the *Itinerari dei musei e monumenti d' Italia*) 122–30.

2. This information is contained in a recently found fragment of the 'Fasti Ostienses', *Ann. épigr.* 1933, no. 30, ll. 54–6. It covers events from A.D. 108 to 113. The more important commentaries are those of Calza, *NS* 1932, 188–202; Carcopino, *CRAI* 1932, 363–81; Huelsen, *Rh M* LXXXII (1933) 362–80; and Groag, *JÖA* XXIX (1935), Beiblatt 177–204. On the gladitaorial games mentioned in this fragment, see Degrassi, *RAP* XII (1936) 183–4.

3. The most recent publication of the column is that of K. Lehmann-Hartleben, *Die Trajansäule* (1926), with 73 photographic plates. The author is primarily interested in the monument as a work of art. For its value as a historical document, see the earlier publications of C. Cichorius, *Die Reliefs der Traiansäule* (volumes II and III of the text refer to volumes I and II of the plates, respectively), and E. Petersen, *Trajan's dakische Kriege nach dem Säulenrelief erzählt*.

4. On Trajan's burial within the *pomerium* reported by Eutropius, VIII 5, 2,

see the views of Labrousse (*Mél.* LIV [1937] 191–2) which reaffirm the validity of the ancient source.

5. *CIL* V 960; cf. 959. The many interpretations of this text in connexion with Dio's notice, LXVIII 16, 3, are summarized by Lehmann-Hartleben, op. cit. 4–7.

6. The final official publication of the market has not yet appeared. A monograph by Ricci, *Il Mercato di Traiano* (Rome, 1929), is summarized in *Capitolium* V (1929) 541–55. See also Ricci-Colini-Mariani, *Via dell' impero* 115–20. For other discussions, mostly of a popular nature, see the Bibliography in *BC* LXI (1933) 253–7.

7. See Boethius, *Roma* IX (1931) 446–54.

8. *Amm.* XVI 10, 15.

9. The wealth furnished the empire by the conquest of Dacia has been discussed in detail by Carcopino, *Dacia* I (1924) 28–34. Some of his views have been attacked by Syme, *JRS* XX (1930) 53–70, and accepted by Degrassi *RAP* XII (1936) 182.

10. Marrou, *Mél.* XLIX (1932) 93–110.

11. This interpretation was first advanced in detail by Theodor Birt, *Die Buchrolle in der Kunst* 269–82; cf. *Rh M* LXIII (1908) 39–57. But see Lehmann-Hartleben, op. cit. 3.

12. Lehmann-Hartleben, op. cit. pl. XXXVII

13. On Trajan's public works apart from the Forum, see Paribeni, op. cit. II 23–64.

14. Lipsius, *De Magnitudine Romana* III 3.

15. Dureau de la Malle, *Économie politique des Romains* I 340–408.

16. Lot, *La Fin du monde antique* 80.

17. On the *pomerium* and its extension, there are two detailed discussions of recent date: J. Oliver, *MAAR* X (1932) 145–82 and M. Labrousse, *Mél.* LIV (1937) 165–99; cf. *PA* 392–6.

18. G. Saeflund's masterly work on the Servian Wall, *Le mura di Roma repubblicana* (Lund, 1932), supersedes all previous discussions.

19. Orosius, V 18, 27. This notice probably has nothing to do with Sulla's extension of the *pomerium* attested by Gellius, XIII 14, 4; Seneca, *Brev. Vit.* 13, 8; and Tacitus, *Ann.* XII 23.

20. *CIL* I 206, ll. 20; 24; 50.

21. See F. Clemuti, *Roma imperiale nelle XIV regioni Augustee; PA* 444–7; and under *Regionaries* in chapter on Sources.

22. *Res Gestae*, 13.

23. The latest comprehensive discussion of the Aurelian Wall is I. Richmond, *The City Wall of Imperial Rome* (Oxford, 1930).

24. A Blanchet, *Les Enceintes de la Gaule romaine*.

25. For the extent of the city beyond the Aurelian Wall, see the figure in *PA* 394 and the discussion of the several regions, ibid. 445–7.

26. Paulus, *Digest* L 16, 2: '"Urbis" appellatio muris, "Romae" autem continentibus aedificiis finitur, quod latius patet'; cf. ibid. 87; 147. Also Macer, ibid, 154: 'Mille passus non a miliario urbis, sed a continentibus aedificiis numerandi sunt.'

27. On the religious significance of this institution, see L. R. Taylor, *The Divinity of the Roman Emperor* 184–90.

28. Pliny, *NH* III 66.

29. For the *Regionaries*, see chapter on Sources. The number 307 for the *vici* is the sum total of the *vici* given region by region, a figure more reliable than the 324 given by the *breviarium* of the *Curiosum* and Zacharias. Even so, our manuscript tradition does not allow exact numbers. Cf. Calza's table, *RL* XVI (1917) 67, where the total is given as 305.

30. The numbers varied from time to time, but it is clear that Caesar, at the end of his reign, reduced the number of those on the corn-dole to 150,000 (Suetonius, *Julius* 41; cf. Dio, XLIII 21, 4. Plutarch, *Caesar* 55, 3 and Livy, *Epit.* 115, confuse this dole list with the complete population). The distributions of Augustus, usually affecting over 250,000 citizens, went as high as 320,000 in 5 B.C. (*Res Gestae* 15), but the one provided by his will sank to 150,000 (Suetonius, *Augustus* 101; Tacitus, *Ann.* I 8; Dio, LVII 14, 2). In general, see Kahrstedt, *SG* IV 10–21, who discusses Beloch's conclusions, *Die Bevöllerung der griechischrömischen Welt* 392–412. On the class of citizens who received Augustus' donations, see Ensslin, *Rh M* LXXXI (1932) 345–50.

31. Dio LXXVI 1, 1, speaks of 200,000 men including the troops in Rome. These last may be estimated at 25,000 and must be subtracted from the whole as not belonging to the civil population.

32. Carcopino, *Roma* XVI (1938) 493–8.

33. Eusebius, *Chron.* II p. 133 ed. Schoene.

34. The scholiast on Lucan (*Pharsalia* I 319=III p. 53 ed. Weber) says that Rome needed 80,000 *modii* of grain per day (29,200,000 *m.* per year). Assuming a consumption of 5 *modii* per month per person or 60 *modii* per year, we arrive at a figure (486,666) slightly higher than the one given in the text.

35. Cicero, *Verr.* II 3, 72. He speaks of 33,000 *medimni* (198,000 *modii*) as a month's supply for the *plebs Romana*. At 5 *modii* per month per individual, we get a little under 40,000 people.

36. See n. 30 above.

37. Suetonius, *Julius* 41.

38. Aurelius Victor, *Epitome* I 5–6; Josephus, *Bellum Iudaicum* II 383–6. On the relation of grain consumption to the population, see Oates,

*Class. Phil.* XXIX (1934) 101–16.

39. *Res Gestae* 15.

40. Cuq, *MAI* XI (1915) 279–335.

41. Lot, *La Fin du monde antique* 80; 85.

42. Suetonius, *Julius* 41.

43. Tacitus, *Ann.* XV, 41.

44. SHA *Pius* 9, 1.

45. Oates, op. cit. (see n. 38 above) reaches the figure 1,250,000 for the Augustan Age.

46. Martial, XII 8, 1–2.

## CHAPTER II
### HOUSES AND STREETS

1. On Roman housing in general, see chapter on Sources.

2. Carcopino, *Mél.* XXX (1910) 397–446.

3. On Ostia in general, see chapter on Sources.

4. See p. 17 above.

5. Munoz, *Campidoglio* (1930) 45–52; *MAAR* XII (1935) 61.

6. *AJA* XXXI (1927) 406–10; *ZA* 402.

7. *NS* 1917, 9–20.

8. *PA* 156–8; *ZA* 269–79.

9. *MAAR* XII (1935) 29–30.

10. On the *Forma Urbis Romae*, see chapter on Sources.

11. Livy, XXI 62.

12. Cicero, *De Leg. Agr.* II 96.

13. Vitruvius, II 8, 17.

14. Strabo, V 3, 7.

15. ibid. XVI 2, 23.

16. Juvenal, 3, 190–96.

17. Gellius, XV 1, 2.

18. Aristides, *Or* XIV p. 324 ed. Dindorf.

19. Aurelius Victor, *Ep.* 13, 13; cf. *Digest* XXXIX 1, 1, 17.

20. Tertullian, *Adv. Val.* 7.

21. Martial lived on the Quirinal *ad pirum* (I 117, 6) near the temple of Flora (V 22, 4; VI 27, 1–2) in a rented apartment (I 108, 3). Later, he acquired a house (IX 97, 8), also on the Quirinal (X 58, 10).

22. Juvenal, 3, 198–202.

23. In *CIL* IV, 138, the following parts of the insula Arriana Polliana at Pompeii are offered for rent: '*tabernae cum pergulis suis et cenacula equestria et domus*'; cf. ibid. 1136.

24. Cicero, *Pro Marco Caelio* 7.

25. For a unit composed of shop and living apartment, see *Digest* XXXIII 7, 7; cf. L 16, 183.

26. *Digest* XII 2, 9; XIII 7, 11, 5. On the renting of houses and apartments, see Herdlitczka, *RE*, Suppl. VI 385–7; Genco and Massano, *Atti* III *CNSR* I (1935) 452–63.

27. Cicero, *Har. Resp.* 49; Velleius, II 77 (cf. Dio, XLVIII 38); Suetonius *Tib.* 15.

28. Suetonius, *Julius* 46.

29. On the *horti Maecenatis*, see *PA* 269.

30. Pollio: Frontinus, *De Aquaeductibus* 21; Sura: Martial, VI 64, 13; cf. Merlin, *L'Aventin dans l'antiquité* 327; 332; 341–2.

31. Flavius Sabinus, *CIL* VI 29788; Martial, see n. 21 above.

32. SHA *Commodus* 16, 3; *Pertinax* 5, 7; cf. Dio, LXXII 22, 2.

33. On the *Nova Urbs* which was built after the fire of A.D. 64, see Boethius, *Skrifter* II (1932) 84–97; Lugli, *RAP* XIII (1937) 83–93.

34. Martial, I 108; IV 64; cf. VII 17.

35. Boethius in *Scritti in onore di B. Nogara* 21–32; cf. Calza, 'Le origini

latine dell' abitazione moderna',
*Architettura e arti decorative* III (1923).

36. Pliny, *NH* XIX 59; cf. Martial,
XI 18.

37. Augustine, *Confessiones* IX 23.

38. Petronius, 60.

39. Pliny, *NH* XXXIII 57.

40. Calza, *RL* XXV (1917) 75, followed
by Lugli, *RAP* XIII (1937) 97, assumes
an average area of 200 square metres
per *insula*.

41. Vitruvius, II 8, 17.

42. Juvenal, 3, 190–96.

43. *Digest* XIX 2, 3; cf. n. 26 above.

44. Plutarch, *Crassus* 2, 5.

45. On the *vigiles*, see P. K. B. Reynolds,
*The Vigiles of Imperial Rome*.

46. Juvenal, 14, 305–8.

47. ibid. 3, 199–207.

48. ibid. 197–8.

49. *Digest* I 15, 2.

50. Juvenal, 3, 198–9; cf. Martial, XII
32.

51. n. 46 above.

52. cf. Caroline L. Ransom, *Couches and
Beds of the Greeks, Etruscans and
Romans*, and Gisela M. A. Richter,
*Ancient Furniture* 130–35.

53. Ritcher, op. cit. 137–42.

54. ibid. 119–24; 127–9.

55. Juvenal, 6, 91.

56. Seneca, *De Clementia* I 9,7.

57. Pliny, *Ep.* II 17, 21; cf. VII 21, 2.

58. Juvenal, 7, 203; Martial, I 76, 14;
Seneca, *Dial.* X 10, 1.

59. Henzen, *Acta Fratrum Arvalium* p. 14.

60. Richter, op. cit. 125–7.

61. Martial, VII 53; cf. II 44.

62. On the silver vessels with gold rims
(*chrysendeta*), see Martial, II 43, 11;
VI 94, 1; XI 29, 7; XIV 97.

63. Mau-Kelsey, *Pompeii* 202; 204. In
general, see Chipiez in *DS* II 1035–40.
Window-panes, which were comparatively rare in Italy, were quite
common in the *villae* of Gaul; Cumont, *Comment la Belgique fut romanisée*
44, n. 3.

64. Pliny, *Ep.* IX 36, 1; cf. VI 21, 2.

65. On heating arrangements, see
Thédenat, *DS* III 345–50.

66. *Via dell' impero* 40.

67. On stoves and braziers, see Gachon,
*DS* II 1194–7.

68. Frontinus, *De Aquaeductibus* 65–73;
cf. the table in Ashby, *Aqueducts of
Ancient Rome* 30. The *Tepula*, then fed
from other aqueducts, and the *Traiana*,
not opened until A.D. 109, are not included in the estimate.

69. The date is given in the 'Fasti
Ostienses', *Ann. épigr.* 1933, no. 30,
ll. 11–12. On the aqueduct, Ashby,
op. cit. 298–307.

70. Frontinus, op. cit. 103; 105.

71. ibid. 108–9.

72. Martial, IX 17, 5–6.

73. Juvenal, 6, 332.

74. Paulus, *Sententiae* III 6, 58; cf. *Digest*
XXXIII 7, 12, 42.

75. *Digest* I 15, 3, 5.

76. Pliny, *NH* XXXVI 104–8.

77. On the *Cloaca Maxima*, *PA* 126–7.

78 *MAAR* XII (1935) 25.

79. *DS* III 988.

80. Suetonius, *Vespasian* 23.

81. On public latrines in general, see
*SG* IV 310–11.

82. See n. 66 above.

83. Martial, XI 77, 1–3.

84. In this connexion, we may recall
the amusing frescoes recently discovered in Ostia (Calza, *Die Antike* XV
[1939] 99–115). On the goddess
Fortuna, see Carcopino, *Journal des
savants* (1911) 456–7.

85. A. Ballu, *Les Ruines de Timgad* I 112–14

86. See the description in *DS* III 988.

87. Suetonius, *Vespasian* 23.

88. Attested for the Insula Sertoriana;
*CIL* VI 29791.

89. Livy, XXXIX 44, 5.

90. Lucretius, IV 1026.

91. Juvenal, 6, 602. On abandoning
babies there, see Carcopino, *Mémoires
de la Société des Antiquaires* LXXVII
(1928) 58–86, esp. 76–85; cf. Cumont,
*Égypte des astrologues* 187, n. 1.

92. Juvenal, 3, 269–72.
93. *Digest* IX 3, 5, 1–2.
94. ibid. 3, 5, 7.
95. Diodorus, XXXI 18, 2.
96. Juvenal, 3, 223–5.
97. Petronius, 95.
98. ibid. 98.
99. Pliny, *NH* III 66.
100. ibid. 67.
101. Tacitus, *Ann* XV 38; 43.
102. See n. 33 above.
103. On the terminology, see Chapot, *DS* V 781–3.
104. On *vici* within the city, see Grenier, *DS* V 861–3. On the balconies, *Codex Just.* VIII 10, 12, 5b.
105. *CIL* I² 593, l. 54.
106. ibid. ll. 32–49.
107. Varro, *De Lingua Latina* V 158.
108. Martial, VII 61; Juvenal, 3, 247.
109. Martial, VII 61.
110. On the perils of the night at Rome, see Juvenal, 3, 268–314.
111. *Digest* I 15.
112. Petronius, 79.
113. On the congestion and noise of Rome, Juvenal, 3, 232–67; Martial, I 41; XII 57; Seneca, *De Clementia* I 6, 1.
114. *CIL* I² 593, ll, 56–67; cf. *SG* IV 22–5.
115. See Cuq, *DS* II 1390.
116. Suetonius, *Claudius* 25, 2.
117. SHA *Marcus* 23, 8.
118. ibid. *Hadrian* 22, 6.
119. Juvenal, 3, 236–59; cf. Martial, XII 57.

## CHAPTER III
### SOCIETY AND SOCIAL CLASSES

1. On the *honestiores* and *humiliores*, see Mommsen, *Römisches Strafrecht* 1031–49.
2. On the composition and the social and economic position of the equestrian order under the empire, see Arthur Stein, *Der röm. Ritterstand* (1927), especially chap. II, III, and VI.
3. On the political career open to knights, see Hirschfeld, *Die kaiserlichen Verwaltungsbeamten²* 411–65.
4. On the order and its qualifications, see O'Brien-Moore, *RE* Suppl. VI 760–66.
5. Offices open to senatorials alone are summarized by O'Brien-Moore, ibid. 777–8.
6. On such titles, see Hirschfeld, *Kleine Schriften* 647–55; cf. *SG* IV 77–81.
7. Suetonius, *Domitian* 13; cf. Aurelius Victor, *Caesares* 11, 2; Pliny, *Panegyricus* 45; 55; Martial, X 72, 3–4.
8. Tacitus, *Hist.* I 4.
9. On the propagation of Roman citizenship, under the empire, see the recent book of A. N. Sherwin-White, *The Roman Citizenship* 167–227.
10. Juvenal, 3, 62–5; cf. Seneca, *Ad Helviam* 6.
11. See the recent discussion of his life by G. Highet, *TAPA* LXVIII (1937) 480–506.
12. Martial, IV 45; I 49; 61; X 103; 104. On Martial's home in Rome, see chap. II, n. 21.
13. On Pliny and Como, see Mommsen, *Étude sur Pline le Jeune* 74–7.
14. On the origin of senators under Trajan, see P. Lambrechts, *L'Antiquité classique* V (1936) 105–14; under later emperors, the same author's *La Composition du sénat romain de l'accession au trône d'Hadrien à la mort de Commode*.
15. SHA *Severus* 19.
16. See the analysis of the evidence by Jotham Johnson, *Excavations at Minturnae*; II Inscriptions: part I 49–113.
17. *CIL* XIV 2112.
18. *Digest* XLVIII 8, 11.
19. Suetonius, *Claudius* 27; *Digest* XL 8, 2.
20. *Digest* I 12, 1. On Seneca's attitude toward slaves, see *Ep.* 47; *Clem.* I 18; *Ira* III 35; *Benef.* III 18.

21. Suetonius, *Domitian* 7; cf. *Digest* XLVIII 8, 4, 6.
22. SHA *Hadrian* 18, 7–8.
23. Gaius, I 53.
24. Juvenal, 14, 126; 1, 92; 6, 475–84.
25. ibid. 1, 92.
26. ibid. 6, 475–84.
27. ibid. 14, 15–22.
28. Martial, VIII 23; I 101.
29. Pliny, *Ep.* I 21, 2.
30. ibid, V 19, 6–8.
31. ibid. VIII 16.
32. ibid. I 4, 4.
33. ibid. I 12, 7.
34. ibid. IX 36, 4.
35. ibid. III 14.
36. Appian, *BC* II 120.
37. On freedmen in general, see the comprehensive study of A. M. Duff, *Freedmen in the Early Roman Empire.*
38. Suetonius, *Augustus*, 40; Dio, LV 13. The laws were the *Fufia Caninia* and the *Aelia Sentia;* cf. Duff, op. cit. 31–5.
39. Gaius, I 29–32b; cf. Duff, op. cit 74–85.
40. Frank, *American Historical Review* XXI (1916) 689–708.
41. The evidence has been compiled by Stech, *Klio* Beiheft X (1912) 127–30.
42. See chap. I n. 9.
43. On imperial slaves and freedmen, *SG* I 35–74.
44. On the 'cabinet', Hirschfeld, *Verwaltungsbeamten* 318–42.
45. Suetonius, *Domitian* 14; Dio, LXXVII 15.

46. On Hadrian's equestrian 'cabinet', Hirschfeld, op. cit. 476–9.
47. Juvenal, 3, 131–2.
48. *CIL* VIII 10570; 14464.
49. Martial, XIII 12, speaks of 300 *modii* of grain, presumably per annum. At 5 *modii* per month per person, we get a family of five people.
50. Galen, *De Affectuum Dignotione* 20, 13 = V 49 Kuhn.
51. Juvenal, 9, 140–41.
52. ibid. 14, 322–8.
53. G. Billeter, *Geschichte des Zinsfusses im griechisch-römischen Altertum* 179–228.
54. Martial, VII 73.
55. ibid. IV 37.
56. ibid. XII 10.
57. Pliny, *Ep.* II 4, 3.
58. Petronius, 71.
59. See chap. I n. 9.
60. Juvenal, 3, 166–7; cf. 14, 126.
61. ibid. 9, 142–4.
62. Martial, VII 53.
63. Juvenal, 7, 141.
64. Petronius, 47; cf. 37.
65. See n. 38 above.
66. Gaius, I 43.
67. Pliny, *NH* XXXIII 135.
68. Athenaeus, VI 272 e.
69. *PA* 161–2.
70. On the pay of these civil and military officials, see V. Domaszewski, *Bonner Jahrbücher* CXVII (1908) 111; 118; 139; 141–69.
71. Martial, V 56.
72. ibid. VI 8.
73. ibid. X 47.

## CHAPTER IV
### MARRIAGE, WOMAN, AND THE FAMILY

1. Gaius, III 17. On the *patria potestas*, see W. W. Buckland, *A Text-Book of Roman Law*² 100–141, and the recent studies of Kaser, *Zeitschrift der Savigny Stiftung* Röm. Abt. LVIII (1938) 62–87; 88–135.
2. Buckland, op. cit. 372–4.
3. Cicero, *De Officiis* I 54.

4. Dionysius, *Ant. Rom.* II 26–7; Gellius V 19; *Digest* XXVIII 2, 11.
5. *Digest* XXV 3, 4.
6. See chap. II, n. 91.
7. Musonius, 15B; cf. Powell, *Archiv für Papyrusforschung* XII (1937) 175–8.
8. *CIL* XI 1147. See F. G. de Pachtere, *La Table hypothécaire de Veleia;* cf.

Carcopino, *Revue des études anciennes* XXIII (1921) 287–303.

9. Sallust, *Catiline* 39; Dio, XXXVII 36; Val. Max. V 8, 5.

10. *Codex Justinianus* 9, 17, 1. But cf. Ulpian, *Digest* XLVIII 8, 2.

11. *Digest* XLVIII 9, 5.

12. ibid. XXXVII 12, 5.

13. ibid. XLVIII 9, 5 (from the middle of the third century).

14. Pliny, *Ep.* IX 12.

15. Martial, III 10.

16. Pliny, *Ep.* IV 2.

17. On the different forms of marriage, see E. P. Corbett, *The Roman Law of Marriage* 68–106.

18. Pliny, *Ep.* I 9.

19. Pliny, *NH* XXXIII 28; Juvenal, 6, 25; *Digest* XXIV 1, 36; cf. Corbett, op. cit. 1–23.

20. Gellius, X 10.

21. For detailed descriptions, see Blümner, *Römische Privat-Altertümer* 349–61; or Lécrivain, *DS* III 1655–8. On marriage and the *gens*, see Rose, *The Roman Questions of Plutarch*, XX 101–8.

22. Duchesne, *Origines du culte chrétien* 445.

23. Lucan, *Pharsalia* II 370–71.

24. Gaius, I 144; cf. Cicero, *Pro Murena* 27.

25. Gaius, I 173; Ulpian, *Reg.* XI 22.

26. Gaius, I 145.

27. *Digest* XXIII 1, 11; cf. L 17, 30.

28. cf. Favez, *Bull. Soc. Ét. des Lettres de Lausanne* (Oct. 1933) 1–9.

29. SHA *Hadrian* 11, 3.

30. Tacitus, *Ann.* VI 29.

31. ibid. XV 62–4; cf. Carcopino, *Points de vue sur l'impérialisme romain* 247–8.

32. Pliny, *Ep.* III 16.

33. ibid. VI 24.

34. Martial, XI 53 (Rufina); IV 75 (Nigrina).

35. ibid. X 35; cf. 38.

36. Pliny, *Ep.* VIII 5.

37. ibid. IV 19.

38. ibid. VI 4; 7.

39. ibid. I 14.

40. ibid. IX 36.

41. ibid. VIII 10; 11.

42. Martial, XI 53.

43. ibid. X 63.

44. Juvenal, 6, 398–412.

45. ibid. 434–56.

46. Pliny, *Ep.* I 16, 6.

47. Juvenal, 6, 448–51.

48. ibid. 1, 22–3; 61–2; 6, 246–64.

49. Petronius, 67; 70–76.

50. Juvenal, 6, 300–305.

51. ibid. 425–33.

52. ibid. 509.

53. ibid. 282–4.

54. Pliny, *Ep.* VI 31.

55. Juvenal, 11, 185–9.

56. On the *Lex Iulia de adulteriis*, see Corbett, *The Roman Law of Marriage* 133–46, esp. 146.

57. Cato in Gellius, X 23.

58. Martial, VI 4.

59. Juvenal, 2, 29–33.

60. Dio, LXXVI 16, 4.

61. On divorce in early Rome, see Corbett, op. cit. 218–28.

62. Cicero, *Philippics* II 69.

63. Val. Max. II 9, 2.

64. ibid. 1, 4; Gellius, X 15.

65. Val. Max. V 3, 10–12. Of the names cited by Valerius, one is completely unknown (Antistius Vetus). The two others could belong to people of the second half of the third century B.C., if Valerius' source was the second decade of Livy, now lost.

66. By the second century A.D., women had acquired the same privilege even in a marriage *cum manu*; Gaius, I 137A.

67. On the fifth marriage of Sulla, see Carcopino, *Sylla ou la monarchie manquée* 217.

68. Plutarch, *Pompey* 4; 10; cf. Carcopino, op. cit. 190–91.

69. cf. Plutarch, *Caesar* 10, 6.

70. ibid., *Cato Minor* 36; 52.

71. ibid., *Cicero* 41; cf. Dio, XLVI 18, 3.

72. Jerome, *Adversus Jovinianum* I 48; Pliny, *NH* VII 158.

73. Dio, LIV 16; Suetonius, *Augustus* 34.
74. The general conclusions are those of E. Cuq, *Les Institutions juridiques des Romains* 172. On the dowry, see Corbett, op. cit. 182–98.
75. Horace, *Odes* III 24, 19.
76. Paulus, *Sent.* II 21B, 2; Justinian, *Inst.* II 8.
77. Martial, V 61.
78. Juvenal, 6, 212–13.
79. ibid. 460.
80. Martial, VIII 12.
81. Juvenal, 6, 142–8.
82. *Digest* XXIV 2, 2, 1.
83. Juvenal, 6, 224–30.
84. Martial, VI 7.
85. *Digest* XXIV 3, 64.
86. ibid. I 61.
87. Seneca, *De Beneficiis* III 16, 2.
88. Juvenal, 6, 224.
89. Martial, VI 7, 5.

## CHAPTER V
### EDUCATION AND RELIGION

1. On concubinage in general, see J. Plassard, *Le Concubinat romain sous le Haut Empire*. For Marcus Aurelius, SHA *Marcus* 29, 10. Vespasian had already set a precedent for such behaviour; Suetonius, *Vespasian* 3.
2. Pliny, *Ep.* III 14, 3.
3. Martial, VI 71.
4. ibid. VII 64.
5. ibid. VI 39.
6. ibid. XII 58.
7. Juvenal, 3, 65–6; Martial, I 34.
8. Plutarch, *Cato Maior* 20. Cf. the example of Aemilius Paulus who was always present at the studies and exercises of his sons unless prevented by public business; Plutarch, *Aemilius* 6.
9. Pliny, *Ep.* VIII 14, 6.
10. The three are mentioned together by Tacitus, *Dialogus* 28. On Cornelia, see also Plutarch, *Gracchi* 1; Cicero, *Brutus* 104; 211; Quintilian, I 1, 6.
11. Such clubs are attested from the first to the fourth century; Suetonius, *Galba* 5, 1; Jerome, *Ep.* 43, 3; cf. *CIL* VI 997; XIV 2120.
12. Pliny, *Ep.* VII 24.
13. Tacitus, *Dialogus* 29.
14. Quintilian, I 1, 4.
15. ibid.
16. ibid. I 1, 8.
17. Pliny, *Ep.* III 3.
18. Plautus, *Bacchides* 162.
19. Boissier, *Fin du paganisme* I 149.
20. On the fees collected by such teachers, see Horace, *Satires* I 6, 75; Ovid, *Fasti* III 829; Macrobius, 12, 7. A *magister ludi* of Capua eked out his fees by writing wills; *CIL* X 3969.
21. Although *plagosus* Orbillius was properly a *grammaticus*, we may cite him here as the best-known example; Horace, *Ep.* II 1, 70; cf. Suetonius, *De Grammaticis* 9. On his successors, Juvenal, 1, 15; Martial, X 62, 10; XIV 80. In general, Plutarch, *Caesar* 61, 1.
22. Quintilian, I 3, 16–17.
23. ibid. I 1, 24–6.
24. Seneca, *Ep.* 94, 51.
25. On education and the State under the empire, see Barbagallo, *Lo Stato e l'educazione pubblica*. On Vipasca, *CIL* II 5181, l. 57: 'ludi magistros a procuratore metallorum immunes es [se placet].' It should be noted that the schoolmaster follows the shoemaker, barber, and fuller in the list of regulations governing their activities.
26. Philostratus, *Vitae* II 1, 10. Quintilian, I 1, 25, suggests alphabets of ivory or of pastry.
27. Vegetius, *De Re Militari* II 19.
28. Apuleius, *Florida* 20.
29. On the first Greek teachers in Rome, see Gwynn, *Roman Education from Cicero to Quintilian* 34–58. For Greek

influence on the intellectual life in general and the reaction to it, see F. Leo's masterly chapter, *Geschichte d. römischen Literatur*, 259–368.

30. Suetonius, *Rhet.* 2.

31. See Marx's ed., 153.

32. Suetonius, *Rhet.* 1; Gellius, XV 11; cf. Cicero, *De Or.* III 93. For the underlying political motives, see Gwynn, op. cit. 65–6.

33. On Caesar, Carcopino, *César* 974. On Quintilian, Eusebius, *Chron.* a. Abr. 2104, II p. 161 ed. Schoene.

34. Dio, LXV 12–13; Suetonius, *Vespasian* 18. On the intellectual policy of Vespasian, see Hertzog's commentary to *Ann. épigr.* 1936 nr. 128 in *Sitzungsberichte d. Preussichen Akademie*, phil.-hist. Klasse XXXII (1935) 968–1019; cf. Levi, *Romana* 1937, 361–7.

35. Suetonius, *Rhet* 1; Plutarch, *Cato maior* 22.

36. Carcopino, *César* 974–5; cf. chap. I, n. 10.

37. On child prodigies under the empire, see Marrou, Μομσικὸς ἀνήρ (Paris, 1937) 196–207.

38. Marrou, *Saint Augustin et la fin de la culture classique* (Paris, 1937). See esp. chap. II.

39. Juvenal, 6, 184–99; Martial, X 68.

40. On Lucian and his lecture tours, see Croiset, *Essai sur la vie et les œuvres de Lucien*.

41. On the substitution of Latin for Greek in the Roman Church, see P. Monceaux, *Histoire de la littérature chrétienne* 42; A. Puech, *Histoire de la littérature grecque chrétienne* II 8. In contradistinction to Rome proper, Roman Africa had been very superficially Hellenized; see W. Thieling, *Der Hellenismus in Kleinafrica*.

42. *IG* XIV 2012.

43. *CIL* VI 33929; cf. XI 6435.

44. Suetonius, *Gram.* 16.

45. *SHA Hadrian* 16.

46. On Juba as writer and scholar, see

S. Gsell, *Histoire ancienne de l'Afrique* VIII 251–76.

47. Sallust, *De Bell. Iug.* 21, 2.

48. Tacitus, *Dialogus* 36, 1.

49. Aristotle, *Rhet.* I 3.

50. On Hermagoras, see *RE* VIII 693–5.

51. Cato, fr. 14.

52. Diomedes, *De Declinatione Exercitationis Chriarum*, I 310 Keil.

53. Quintilian, I 9, 3.

54. Suetonius, *Gram.* 5.

55. For an annotated edition of the *Suasoriae*, see William A. Edward, *The Suasoriae of Seneca the Elder*.

56. Seneca, *Suasoriae* 6; 7.

57. ibid. 1; 4.

58. ibid. 5; 2.

59. ibid. 3.

60. Suetonius, *Rhet.* 1.

61. ibid.

62. See the edition of H. Borneque, *Sénèce le rhéteur – Controverses et Suasoires*.

63. Seneca, *Controversiae* IX 2.

64. ibid. VII 2.

65. On the part played by *mores* in Roman law, see Steinwenter, *RE* XV 290–98.

66. Seneca, *Controversiae* VIII 2.

67. ibid. IX 1.

68. ibid. X 5.

69. ibid. II 7.

70. ibid. I 6.

71. ibid. IV 4.

72. ibid. I 2.

73. Gellius, XVII 12.

74. Marrou, *Saint Augustin* 53–4.

75. Seneca, *Ep.* 106, 12.

76. Petronius, 1–4.

77. Tacitus, *Dialogus* 35.

78. Juvenal, 7, 150–70.

79. On the base materialism attested by dozens of epitaphs, see Brelich, *Aspetti della morte nelle iscrizioni sepolcrali dell'impero romano* (Budapest, 1937) 50.

80. cf. F. Cumont's admirable analysis of the official and traditional religion, *Les Religions orientales dans le paganisme romain*[4] (Paris, 1929) 25–7.

81. Boissier, *La Religion romaine d'Auguste aux Antonins*, II 141–2.
82. See Ovid's lively description; *Fasti* III 523–42.
83. Juvenal, 12, 1–16.
84. ibid. 2, 149–52.
85. Petronius, 44.
86. ibid.
87. Tacitus, *Hist.* V 5.
88. Tacitus, *Germania* 9.
89. Pliny, *Ep.* VIII 8; Boissier, *Religion* II 171.
90. ibid. IX 39.
91. ibid. IV 8.
92. On the beginnings of the imperial cult, see L. R. Taylor, *The Divinity of the Roman Emperor*; on its development under the Flavians, K. Scott, *The Imperial Cult under the Flavians*.
93. Suetonius, *Vespasian* 23. cf. the cynical words of Caracalla about his brother Geta whom he had had assassinated: '*Geta sit divus dum non sit vivus*'; SHA *Geta* 2.
94. Suetonius, *Domitian* 13; cf. Martial, V 8; VII 34; IX 66.
95. Pliny, *Panegyricus* 11, 3; 68, 1; cf. 67, 4.
96. ibid. 14, 1.
97. Tacitus, *Hist.* I 1.
98. See Boyancé, *Le Culte des Muses*, for this 'religious' aspect of the philosophical schools.
99. J. Bidez, *La Cité du monde et du soleil chez les stoiciens*.
100. On Figulus, see Carcopino, *La Basilique pythagoricienne de la Porte Majeure* 196–206.
101. Lydus, *De Mensibus* IV 59 (p. 113 Wünsch).
102. *PA* 283–6.
103. Gauckler, *Le Sanctuaire syrien du Janicule* (Paris, 1912).
104. Suetonius, *Nero* 56.
105. On the cult of Mithra at Capua, *NS* 1924, 353–75; at Rome, *CIL* VI 732.
106. See Cumont's brilliant conclusions in *Les Religions orientales* 181–94; also,

Alda Levi, *La patera d'argento di Parabiago* (Rome, 1936).
107. Juvenal 3, 62.
108. Josephus, *Antiquities* XVIII 3, 4–5; cf. Tacitus, *Ann.* II 85.
109. Juvenal, 6, 532–4; cf. 550; 553; 585.
110. ibid. 540–41; 548–50.
111. ibid. 512–16.
112. ibid. 313–17.
113. ibid. 522–9.
114. ibid. 580–81.
115. Petronius, 39; 62; 74.
116. Tacitus, *Hist.* II 50; Boissier, *Tacite* 146.
117. Pliny, *Ep.* I 18.
118. ibid. II 20.
119. ibid. I 18.
120. ibid. VII 27.
121. Lagrange, *Revue biblique* XXXI (1919) 480.
122. Cumont, op. cit. 23–41.
123. Juvenal, 10, 340–50.
124. Persius, 2, 71–5.
125. Statius, *Silvae* I 4, 128–31. The profoundly inspired prayer of the Stoic Demetrius recorded by Seneca, *De Providentia* 5, 5, has been compared to the *suscipe* which ends the spiritual exercises of Saint Ignatius; cf. Father Delehaye, *Légendes hagiographiques* 170, n. 1.
126. On the religion of salvation of Antinoüs, see Dietrichson, *Antinoos* (Oslo, 1884). I prefer his conclusions to those of Pirro Marconi, *ML* XXIX (1923) 297–300.
127. On the *collegium salutare* of Bovillae, see Carcopino, *RAP* IV (1925–6) 232–46. For the one at Lanuvium, *CIL* XIV 2112.
128. On this imperial policy which continues throughout the second century, see Aymard, *Mél* LI (1934) 178–96.
129. See Graillot, *Le Culte de Cybèle* (Paris, 1913) 151.
130. Pliny, *Ep* X 96.
131. Tacitus, *Ann.* XV 44; Suetonius, *Claudius* 25; *Nero* 16.

132. On the famous passage of Suetonius, *Claudius* 25, 4: *Iudaeos, impulsore Chresto, assidue tumultuantes Roma expulit* (Claudius), see Duchesne, *Hist. anc. de l'Église* I 55, and Janne, *Mélanges Bidez* (Brussels, 1934) I 531–2. Christians did not have their own quarter; Abbé Vieilliard, *Bull. Soc. Antiq.* (1937) 104.

133. Josephus, *Ant.* XIV, 8–10; cf. Suetonius, *Caesar* 84.

134. Tacitus, *Ann.* II 85; cf. Suetonius, *Tiberius* 36. The details are given by Josephus, *Ant.* XVIII 3, 5.

135. Juvenal, 14, 96–106.

136. Dio, LXVII 14, speaks thus of Flavius Clemens.

137. St Paul, *Phil.* 4, 22.

138. Tacitus, *Ann.* XIII 32.

139. Suetonius, *Domitian* 10; Dio, LXVII 12.

140. Suetonius, *Domitian* 15; Dio, LXVII 14.

141. Tacitus, *Hist.* III 65; 75.

142. Mâle, *Revue des deux mondes* XLIII (1938) 347.

143. Eusebius, *Chron.* a. Abr. 2110, II p. 143 ed. Schoene; *Hist. eccl.* III 18; cf. Duchesne, op. cit. 217 n. 2.

144. But on this early dating, see P. Styger, *Die röm. Katakomben* (Berlin, 1933), esp. 9–10.

145. On the initial illegality of Christianity, see Carcopino, *Rev. études latines* (1936) 230–31.

146. cf. Loisy, *Les Mystères païens et le mystère chrétien* (Paris, 1922) 363.

147. Duchesne, op. cit. 198.


# PART TWO

## CHAPTER VI
### THE MORNING

1. On the Julian calendar, see Kubitschek, *Grundriss d. antiken Zeitrechnung* 99–109; Bickermann, in Gercke-Norden, *Einleitung in d. Altertumswissenschaft* III 5, pp. 19–21.

2. The Ides fell on the fifteenth in March, May, July, and October; on the thirteenth in the remaining months; the Nones fell on the fifth in the months when the Ides were the thirteenth, and on the seventh in the other four months.

3. E. Maass, *Die Tagesgötter in Rom. und den Provinzen* 265–83. For dating by market days (*nundinae*) see W. F. Snyder, *JRS* XXVI (1936) 13–18.

4. Dio, XXXVII 18, 2.

5. On the civil day of the Romans, Greeks, and Babylonians, Macrobius, I 3, 2; Gellius, III 2, 2. In general see

Sontheimer, *RE* 8A, 2011–23, esp. 2020–23.

6. On ancient ways of measuring time, see Ardaillon, *DS* III 256–64; Rehm, *RE* VIII 2416–33.

7. On the late introduction of the 'hours' into Rome, Censorinus, XXIII 6. On the primitive division of the day into two, Pliny, *NH* VII 212; Gellius, XVII 2, 10.

8. On the *Graecostasis*, Varro, *L.L.* V 135. Apart from an embassy of Alexander the Great, which is probably a fiction of the annalists, the Greeks sent no deputation to Rome before the victories of Demetrius Poliorcetes (Strabo, V 2, 5).

9. On the division of the day into four, cf. Censorinus, XXIV 3.

10. On the first solar sundial, which dates

not from 293 but from 263 B.C., Pliny, *NH* VII 213–14.

11. cf. ibid. 214: '*nec congruabant ad horas eius lineae . . . paruerunt tamen ei annis undecentum.*'

12. ibid.: '. . . *donec* Q. *Marcius Philippus, qui cum* L. *Paulo fuit censor, diligentius ordinamentum iuxta posuit, idque munus inter censoria opera gratissima acceptum est.*'

13. On the first water-clock introduced into Rome, cf. ibid. 215.

14. On the great *solarium* situated between the *Ara Pacis* and the Aurelian Column, *CIL* VI 702; Pliny, *NH* XXXVI 73; *PA* 366–7.

15. Vitruvius, IX 9, 5.

16. Petronius, 26.

17. ibid. 71.

18. Seneca, *Apocolocyntosis* 2.

19. On the discrepancies between the Roman civil day and the natural day, Censorinus, XXIII 2.

20. Martial, XII 57.

21. Juvenal, 14, 59–63; cf. Horace, *Sat.* II 4, 81–2. On the various kinds of brooms, Pliny, *NH* XVI 108; XXIII 166; Martial, XIV 82. On the ladders, *Digest* XXXIII 7, 16.

22. Pliny, *Ep.* II 17, 9.

23. Pliny, *NH Praef.* 18.

24. On men who turned night into day, Seneca, *Ep.* 122.

25. Persius, 3, 1–7.

26. Horace, *Sat.* I 6, 122.

27. Martial, XII 18, 13.

28. Isidore, *Origines* XX 10, 8.

29. Pliny, *Ep.* III 5, 8; cf. Suetonius, *Vespasian* 21.

30. On the Apoxyomenus of Lysippus and the Bride of Parrhasius which adorned the cubiculum of Tiberius, Carcopino, *Mél.* XL (1923) 267–307.

31. Acro on Horace, *Sat.* I 6, 109; Juvenal, 6, 264.

32. Martial, XIV 119; XI 11, 5; *Digest* XXXIV 2, 27, 5.

33. On the stuffing used for cushions, Martial, XIV 159, 160, 161; cf.

Juvenal, 6, 88. On cushions, Petronius, 32; 78.

34. On the *stragula* and *operimenta* (or *opertoria*), Varro, *L.L.* V 167; Seneca, *Ep.* 87, 2.

35. For the *tapetia*, Martial, XIV 147; *Digest* XXXIII 10, 5. For *lodices* and *polymita*, Martial, XIV 148; 150.

36. Varro, *L.L.* V 167; *Digest* XXXIII 10, 5.

37. Martial, XII 18, 17–18; cf. Arnobius, *Adv. Nat.* II 68.

38. On Roman clothing in general, see the recent book of L. M. Wilson, *The Clothing of the Ancient Romans* (Baltimore, 1938).

39. Like Cato of Utica (Asconius on Cicero, *Pro Scauro* p. 29 ed. Stangl) and the Cethegi (Horace, *A.P.* 50 and Porphyrio *ad loc.*). Varro, in Nonius XIV p. 867–8 Lindsay, states that when Roman dress consisted solely of a *licium* and a toga, it was customary to wear the toga to bed.

40. Martial, VII 67, who, however, is referring to a woman athlete.

41. With the exception, perhaps, of agricultural labourers, whence the name *campestria* commonly given to the *subligaria* of workers; Pliny, *NH* XII 59.

42. Quintilian, XI 3, 138.

43. The *tunica talaris* when worn by a man was considered a sign of effeminacy; Cicero, *Verr.* II 5, 31; 86; *Cat.* II 22.

44. Suetonius, *Augustus* 82.

45. Gellius, VI 12; cf. Nonius, XIV p. 860 ed. Lindsay.

46. Pliny, *Ep.* III 5, 15.

47. On the toga, see L. M. Wilson, *The Roman Toga*, and the observations of V. Chapot, *Mémoires de la Société des Antiquaires de France* LXXX (1937) 37–66.

48. L. Heuzey, *Histoire du costume antique*, 232. On the final triumph of Roman costumes over Greek, and its cultural significance, see M. Bieber,

*Entwickelungsgeschichte der griechischen Tracht* 44.

49. Athenaeus, V 213B.

50. Livy, III 26.

51. Tertullian, *De Pall.* 5; *ita hominem sarcina vestiat.*

52. Juvenal, 3, 147; Martial, I 103, 5; VII 33, 1; X 11, 6; X 96, 11.

53. Augustus always kept a toga in readiness in his bedroom in case of being summoned out hastily on public business; Suetonius, *Augustus* 73.

54. Suetonius, *Claudius* 15, but only in cases where Roman citizens were involved.

55. Martial, XIV 124.

56. SHA *Commodus* 16.

57. Martial, X 51, 6; cf. Juvenal, 3, 171–2.

58. On the appearance of the *synthesis*, see McDaniel, *Class. Phil.* XX (1925) 268–70. As a festive garment, it was also worn instead of the toga during the Saturnalia; Martial, VI 24, XIV 1; XIV 141.

59. Juvenal, 3, 171–2.

60. Suetonius, *Vespasian* 21.

61. Martial, XI 104, 3–4.

62. Mau-Kelsey, *Pompeii* 358.

63. Suetonius, *Vespasian* 21.

64. Suetonius, *Domitian* 16.

65. Ausonius, *Ep.* 2.

66. Suetonius, *Caesar* 45. On the barber in antiquity, see F. W. Nicolson, *Harvard Studies in Classical Philology* II (1891) 41–56.

67. On the disadvantages of open-air barber shops, *Digest* IX 2, 11. On the barbers of the Subura, Martial, II 17; on those of the Carenae, Horace, *Ep.* I 7, 45–51. They also congregated near the temple of Flora: *ad Florae templum ad tonsores.*

68. Seneca, *De Brev. Vit.* XII 3.

69. Horace, *Ep.* I 7, 46–51.

70. This is implied in Horace, *Sat.* I 7, 3.

71. Martial, VII 64, 1–2; Juvenal, 10, 225–6. In the price-fixing edict of Dio-

cletian, a visit to the barber cost two *denarii* (32 cents).

72. Plutarch, *De Audiendis Poetis* 8.

73. Suetonius, *Nero* 51.

74. Suetonius, *Augustus* 79.

75. Quintilian, XII 10, 47; Martial, II 36, 1.

76. Horace, *Ep.* I 1, 94–5.

77. SHA *Hadrian*, 26, 1.

78. Martial, X 83.

79. ibid. III 43.

80. ibid. II 29, 9–10.

81. Cicero, *Pro Sestio* 18.

82. Martial, VI 55.

83. ibid. II 12.

84. ibid. 29.

85. Horace, *Odes* II 15, 10.

86. Gellius, III 4.

87. Suetonius, *Caesar* 45.

88. ibid. 67.

89. Plutarch, *Cato Minor* 53.

90. Plutarch, *Antonius* 18.

91. Suetonius, *Augustus* 23.

92. Dio, XLVIII 34, 3; cf. Carcopino, *Revue historique* CLXI (1929) 228–9.

93. Crinagoras in the *Palatine Anthology* VI 161.

94. Suetonius, *Caligula* 10; *Nero* 12; cf. Dio, LXI 19, 1.

95. *NS* 1900, p. 578.

96. Suetonius, *Nero* 12; Petronius, 29.

97. Juvenal, 3, 186; 8, 166.

98. Ovid, *Ars Amatoria* I 517.

99. Many bearded soldiers are depicted on Trajan's Column. A long beard was part of the unkempt appearance affected by many professional philosophers under the empire; Seneca, *Ep.* 5, 2; Persius 1, 133; Musonius, p. 88 ed. Heuse. It was worn also by charlatans and beggars who posed as philosophers; Gellius, IX 2.

100. Martial, VII 95, 9–13.

101. *Digest* IX 2, 11.

102. On the straight razor of the empire, see M. Della Corte, *Ausonia* IX (1914) 139–54.

103. Pliny, *NH* XXXVI 165.

104. Plutarch, *Antonius* 1. It is significant that the shaving-brush never appears among the equipment of *tonsores* depicted on funeral bas-reliefs.
105. Petronius, 94.
106. Martial, VI 52.
107. *Digest* IX 2, 11.
108. Suetonius, *Augustus* 79.
109. Martial, VII 83.
110. ibid. VIII 52.
111. ibid. XI 84.
112. Pliny, *NH* XXIX 114.
113. Martial, III 74.
114. ibid. X 65, 8.
115. Juvenal, 13, 51 and schol. *ad. loc.*; Pliny, *NH* XXVIII 250; 255; XXX 132; 133; XXXII 136.
116. Suetonius, *Caesar* 45; cf. Pliny *NH* XXXII 136.
117. Martial, VIII 47.
118. SHA *Hadrian* 26; cf. Dio, LXVIII 45.
119. Martial, XI 23, 6.
120. ibid. X 38; cf. 35.
121. Pliny, *Ep.* IX 36.
122. ibid. VII 5.
123. Petronius, 77.
124. ibid. 47.
125. Martial, XI 104, 7–8.
126. *Digest* XXXIV 2, 25.
127. Juvenal, 6, 501–4.
128. *CIL* VI 5539; 7297; 8959; 9370; 33784.
129. Macrobius, II 5, 7.
130. Juvenal, 6, 487–93.
131. Martial, II 66.
132. Pliny, *NH* XXVIII 191; Martial, XIV 27; cf. 26.
133. *Digest* XXXIX 4, 16, 7.
134. Ovid, *Ars Amatoria* III 211; Juvenal, 2, 93; Martial, IX 37, 6.
135. Ovid, *Ars.* III 216; 197; I 515; Martial, XIV 56; Scribonius Largus, 59–60.
136. Ovid, *Ars.* III 229.
137. Martial, IX 37.
138. Petronius, 66.
139. Ovid, *Ars* III 187–92.
140. Apuleius, *Met.* XI 3.
141. Arnobius, *Adv. Nat.* II 23.
142. On sunshades, Juvenal, 9, 50; Martial, XI 73, 6; XIV 28.

## CHAPTER VII
### OCCUPATIONS

1. On clients in general, *SG* I 225–35.
2. Martial, VI 88; cf. I 59; Juvenal, 1, 121.
3. Juvenal, 1, 95–126.
4. Pliny, *Ep.* III 12, 2.
5. Martial, I 49, 35–6.
6. ibid. IX 49; X 11; 73; 96. On Saturnalian gifts, ibid. V 19; 84; VII 53.
7. Juvenal, 1, 101; cf. 3, 126–30.
8. Martial, VI 88.
9. Juvenal, 1, 120–26.
10. Rostovtzeff, *Storia economica* 40; 238–9.
11. See pp. 69, 80 above.
12. See Carcopino, *La Loi de Hiéron* 188–9.
13. Petronius, 119.
14. Calza, *Guida*; Carcopino, *Ostie* 13–
15. For the inscriptions, *CIL* XIV 4549.
15. Carcopino, op. cit. 18. The identification is accepted by Wickert, *CIL* XIV, Suppl. p. 844.
16. *CIL* XIV 51, revised and restored ibid. p. 844. On the altar, Paribeni, *Guida del museo delle Terme²* 264.
17. On imports, see the recent book of Helen J. Loane, *Industry and Commerce of the City of Rome (50 B.C.–A.D. 200)* 11–59.
18. On the *horrea*, *PA* 260–63.
19. See p. 17 above. It is clear that the building of this market dealt a mortal blow to all the special markets, *forum olitorium, cuppedinis, piscatorium,* mentioned almost exclusively in texts relating to the republican period.

20. Waltzing, *Corporations professionnelles* IV 1–49.
21. *PA* 479. The bas-reliefs are reproduced and described in Rostovtzeff, *Storia economica* pl. IV.
22. See p. 61 above.
23. See pp. 38–9 above.
24. *CIL* VI 9525.
25. ibid. 9540–42.
26. ibid. 33892.
27. ibid. 9758; 9759.
28. ibid. 9739–57.
29. ibid. 9614–17. The last three, being freedwomen, were perhaps domestic servants.
30. ibid. 9562–613. In the imperial household, we find two *medicae* (6851, 7581) as against fifteen *medici* (8895–910).
31. ibid. 9875–84; 33907.
32. ibid. 9493; 9941 (as against six *tonsores*, 9937–42).
33. ibid. 9726–36 (eleven in all).
34. ibid. 9720–24 (five in all).
35. ibid. 9901b.
36. ibid. 9801.
37. ibid. 9683.
38. ibid. 9980.
39. ibid. 9961–79 (*vestifici* or *vesticarii*).
40. ibid. 9496–8.
41. ibid. 9891–2.
42. Gide, *Étude sur la condition privée de la femme* 152; cf. Buckland, *A Text-Book of Roman Law*² 167.
43. Suetonius, *Claudius* 18–19; Gaius, I 32.
44. Gaius, I 34.
45. The word *pistrix* is even missing from Dessau's *indices*, *ILS* IV p. 739. Legislation concerning adultery classed saleswomen with prostitutes; Paulus, *Sent.* II 26, 11; 'cum his quae publice mercibus vel tabernis exercendis procurant adulterium fieri non placuit'.
46. See n. 43 above.
47. On the *porticus Minucia* as the place where grain *tesserae* were distributed, see B. Wall, *Skrifter* II (1932) 31–54.

48. Reinach, *Répertoire de reliefs grecs et romains* I p. 375.
49. W. Helbig, *Wandgemälde* no. 1502.
50. Reinach, op. cit. III p. 405.
51. Helbig, op. cit. no. 1496.
52. Reinach, op. cit. III p. 44.
53. Helbig, op. cit. nos. 1496, 1497, 1498.
54. Martial, X 80; IX 59; VIII 6.
55. Helbig, op. cit. no. 1501; Reinach, op. cit. III p. 403.
56. Helbig, *Führer*³ II no. 1837.
57. Helbig, *Wandgemälde* no. 1500.
58. Ibid. nos. 1493, 1495.
59. In Apuleius, *Metamorphoses* I 24–5, Lucius does his own shopping.
60. Petronius, 79.
61. Martial, VIII 67.
62. ibid. IX 59, 21.
63. See above p. 176. This was also the hour for relieving the guard; Martial, X 48, 1–2.
64. Martial, IV 8, 3–4. The same conclusions may be drawn about the miners of Vipasca from *CIL* II 5181, l. 19.
65. Pliny, *Ep.* III 5.
66. Martial, VIII 67, 3.
67. Gellius, XVII 2, 10 = XII Tables I 6.
68. This can be inferred from Martial, VI 35, where seven water-clocks are mentioned as an exception.
69. Pliny, *Ep.* II 11, 14, states that in a case in January he was granted sixteen water-clocks, which allowed him to speak for over five hours.
70. Martial, VI 35.
71. Suetonius, *Augustus* 29.
72. Suetonius, *Vespasian* 10.
73. On the location of this tribunal, see Mommsen, *Ges. Schr.* III 319–26.
74. See Seston, *Mél.* XLIV (1927) 154–83.
75. See Vigneaux, *Essai sur l'histoire de la Praefectura Urbis* (Paris, 1896) 125.
76. SHA *Antoninus* 10.
77. On the Basilica Iulia, *PA* 78–80; C. Huelsen, *The Forum and the Palatine* (trans. by H. H. Tanzer) 15–18.

78. Pliny, *Ep.* VI 33, 3; cf. I 18, 3; IV 24, 1; II 14 and V 9.
79. Quintilian, XII 5, 6.
80. Pliny, *Ep.* II 14, 9.
81. ibid. 14, 5.
82. See p. 275.
83. Pliny, *Ep.* VI 33, 1; 7–8.
84. ibid. II 14, 1.
85. ibid. VI 31, 13.
86. ibid.
87. *P. Oxy.* 33. The document together with a newly discovered fragment is discussed by C. B. Welles, *TAPA* LXVII (1936) 7–23.
88. Suetonius, *Augustus* 35; cf. O'Brien-Moore. *RE* Suppl. VI 766–7.
89. *PA* 143–6, Huelsen, op. cit. 30–31.
90. Seneca, *De Provid.* V 4, contrasts the idleness of the street loafers with the industry of the Senate which *per totum diem saepe consulitur.*
91. Pliny, *Ep.* II 11.
92. ibid. III 4; 9.
93. ibid. 9, 23.
94. Nepos, *Atticus* 13; Fronto p. 20 ed. Naber.
95. On the libraries in Rome, see C. E. Boyd, *Public Libraries and Literary Culture in Ancient Rome*; on provincial libraries, R. Cagnat, *Les Bibliothèques municipales dans l'Empire romain.*
96. Horace, *Ep.* I 20, 1–2.
97. Seneca, *De Beneficiis* VII 6, 1.
98. Martial, IV 72; XIII 3, cf. Quintilian, *Praef.*
99. Martial, I 2; 113; 117.
100. ibid. I 117, 13–17; XIII 3, 3; cf. I 66, 4.
101. This can be inferred from Juvenal, VII 86, where he says that Statius will starve unless he sells his virgin *Agave* to the mime Paris.
102. Gaius, II 73; 77.
103. Martial, XI 3; cf. XI 108; XIV 219.

104. Suetonius, *Tiberius* 61, 3.
105. Suetonius, *Domitian* 10, 1.
106. Suetonius, *Caesar* 56, 7; *Caligula* 34, 2. See also Carcopino, *Journal des savants* CXXI (1936) 115.
107. Isidore, *Origines* VI 52; Seneca, *Controversiae*, IV Preface 2.
108. Suetonius, *Augustus* 89, 3.
109. Suetonius, *Claudius* 41.
110. Pliny, *Ep.* I 13, 3.
111. Suetonius, *Domitian* 2, 2.
112. On the Athenaeum in general, *PA* 56.
113. Aurelius Victor, *Caesares* 14, 3.
114. Pliny, *Ep.* V 17; VIII 12.
115. Persius, 1, 15–21; Pliny, *Ep.* V 17; IX 34.
116. Pliny, *Ep.* IV 19, 3.
117. Juvenal, 7, 39–47; Pliny, *Ep.* III 18, 4; Tacitus, *Dialogus* 9.
118. Pliny, *Ep.* V 17.
119. Juvenal, 7, 40–47.
120. Pliny, *Ep.* VIII 21; cf. III 18, 4.
121. Petronius, 90; Horace, *Sat.* I 4, 74–5.
122. Pliny, *Ep.* VIII 21.
123. ibid. VI 17, 3; Cf. VIII 21, 4; III 18, 4.
124. ibid. I 13.
125. ibid. 18, 2.
126. ibid. VI 15.
127. ibid. 17.
128. ibid. VII 17, 1; III 18; V 5, 2–4.
129. ibid. III 10; IV 7.
130. ibid. IX 27.
131. ibid. VIII 21; V 17; VI 15; Juvenal, 7, 82–7; 1, 52–4.
132. Pliny, *Ep.* VII 17.
133. ibid. V 3; VII 17.
134. Horace, *Sat.* I 4, 76–8.
135. Suetonius, *Caligula* 53, 2. On this point, see E. Albertini, *La Composition dans les ouvrages philosophiques de Sénèque*, esp. 298–325.
136. cf. the opinion of Petronius, 1–5.

## CHAPTER VIII
### SHOWS AND SPECTACLES

1. Juvenal, 10, 77-81.
2. Fronto, *Princip. Hist.* p. 210 ed. Naber.
3. The fundamental work on the Roman calendar is by Mommsen, *CIL* I² pp. 205-339. It is based on the complete evidence known up to 1893. For later evidence, see Leuze's report in Bursian's *Jahresbericht* 227 (1930) 97-139, which covers the new discoveries through 1928. The most convenient survey, indicating day by day when games and holidays were celebrated both in the early and the later empire, is contained in Wissowa's *Religion und Kultus der Römer* 568-93. For the religious festivals, see Warde Fowler, *Roman Festivals*, under the appropriate date, as well as Frazer's commentary to the *Fasti* of Ovid when the festival falls within the months of January-June inclusive. Finally, we must mention the comprehensive study of the *Feriale Duranum* which has just been published by Fink, Hoey, and Snyder in Volume VII of the Yale Classical Studies. It is the latest and most comprehensive work dealing with parts of the imperial calendar and contains much useful general information in the introductory sections.
4. On the kinds of days and their designations, see Mommsen, op. cit. pp. 289-90; Wissowa, op. cit. 434-9; Fowler, op. cit. 8-10.
5. Since the discovery of the pre-Julian calendar of Antium published by Mancini, *NS* 1921, 73-126, the designation NP which appears there can no longer be considered an innovation connected with Caesar's reform of the Roman year. Mancini's suggestion, op. cit. 81, that it served to distinguish the joyous holidays from those commemorating sad events is as reasonable as any.
6. The computations in this section are

chiefly based on the calendar as given in Wissowa, op. cit. 568-93, and are adjusted to later evidence where necessary.
7. They probably began on 17 January instead of 21 January, as held by Mommsen and Wissowa; see Carcopino, *CRAI* 1923, 71.
8. For the holidays commemorating the events of Caesar and Augustus, see the convenient list in J. Gagé's edition of the *Res Gestae Divi Augusti* 163-85.
9. In making this computation, no day was included which was not expressly designated as *feriae* in an official calendar except the forty-five traditional religious holidays and the days devoted to public games.
10. For a list of extant *ferialia*, see Yale Classical Studies VII (1940). The most important is the *feriale Duranum*, there published for the first time, which contains a list of the days celebrated by the Roman army under Severus Alexander with religious rites.
11. Dio, LX 17, 1.
12. Tacitus, *Hist.* IV 40.
13. SHA *Marcus Aurelius* 10, 10.
14. Mommsen, op. cit. p. 300.
15. On these games, see Gagé, *Recherches sur les jeux séculaires.*
16. 4,941 pairs of gladiators fought in the games lasting 117 days which Trajan gave to celebrate his conquest of Dacia (*Ann. épigr.* 1933, no. 30, ll. 13-14; cf. Dio, LXVIII 15, 1 and De Grassi, *RPA* XII [1936] 182-4).
17. These *ludi piscatorii* are not mentioned in the ancient calendars. It was apparently a holiday for the fishermen alone; cf. Ovid, *Fasti* VI 239: '*festa dies illis qui lina madentia ducunt.*'
18. Festus, *s.v.* Piscatori ludi pp. 274; 276 ed. Lindsay. On the meaning of the passage, see Carcopino, *Virgile et les*

*origines d'Ostie* 119–20, and Frazer on Ovid's *Fasti* IV 169–71.

19. On the October Horse, see Fowler, op. cit. 241–50; on its place in the history of horse sacrifice in antiquity, see Hubbell, *Yale Classical Studies* I (1927) 181–92.

20. On gladiatorial games in general, see Schneider, *RE* Suppl. III 760–84; *SG* II 50–76; on their religious origin, Piganiol, *Recherches sur les jeux romains* 126–36; on the role of the state in the *munera*, Carcopino, *César* 515.

21. Festus *s.v. munus* p. 125 ed. Lindsay.

22. Tertullian, *De Spect.* 12.

23. Ausonius, *Ecl.* 23, 35–6.

24. Suetonius, *Augustus* 40.

25. Quintilian, VI 3, 63, relates that Augustus rebuked a Roman knight for drinking during the games, saying: 'If I want refreshment, I go home.' The knight is said to have retorted not without wit: 'But if you go home, Caesar, you are sure to find your place again when you come back.' On the division of spectators according to social categories, see D. Van Berchem, *Distributions de blé et d'argent sous l'empire* 61–2.

26. On the circus *pompa*, see Piganiol, op. cit. 15–31.

27. Ovid, *Amores* III 2, 43–62.

28. On these superstitions, see the extremely curious texts collected by P. Wuilleumier in his article on 'Le cirque et l'astrologie', *Mél.* XLIV (1927) 184–209, and notably Cassiodorus, *Var.* III 51; Isidore of Seville, XVIII 36; *Anthol. Lat.* I 197.

29. Pliny, *Ep.* VI 5: *propitium Caesarem ut in ludicro precebantur;* cf. Dio LXXVIII 2, 3; on the handkerchiefs, SHA *Aurelian* 48, 5.

30. Pliny, *Pan.* 51.

31. Pliny, *NH* XXXIV 62; cf. Suetonius, *Tiberius* 47.

32. Plutarch, *Galba* 17, 5.

33. Titus thus got rid of Vespasian's enemies; Suetonius, *Titus* 6.

34. Dio, LIV 17, 4–5; cf. Suetonius, *Augustus* 45, 5.

35. Suetonius, *Augustus* 43–5.

36. *Res Gestae* 22.

37. Martial, X 41.

38. The figures are given in the *Fasti Antiates, CIL* I² p. 248.

39. Fronto, *Princip. Hist.* p. 210 ed. Naber.

40. On these games in general, see *SG* II 21–50.

41. *PA* 111–13.

42. ibid. 113–14; 370–71.

43. ibid. 114–20.

44. On Consus, God of the Circus, see Piganiol. op. cit. 1–14.

45. Livy, VIII 20, 21; cf. Ennius, fr. 47 Vahlen.

46. Livy, XXXIX 7, 8.

47. Livy, XLI 27, 6.

48. Pliny, *NH* VIII 20–21; Suetonius, *Caesar* 39.

49. Pliny, *NH* XXXVI 102, says 250,000, but this figure undoubtedly refers to the circus of his own time after the enlargements of Nero. Dionysius of Halicarnassus, III 68, who wrote under Augustus, reckons 150,000 places. Modern estimates of the seating capacity vary from 140,000 to 385,000 spectators; cf. *PA* 119.

50. Dio, XLIX 43, 2.

51. Pliny, XXXVI 71; *PA* 367.

52. *Res Gestae* 19. It is mentioned by Augustus in a letter to Livia, Suetonius, *Claudius* 4.

53. Cassiodorus, *Var.* III 51, 4.

54. Suetonius, *Claudius* 21, 3.

55. Pliny, *NH* VIII 21.

56. Pliny, *Pan.* 51; cf. Dio, LXVIII 7, 2; Pausanias V 12, 6; *CIL* VI 955.

57. Jordan, *Topographie* II 558.

58. *CIL* VI 944.

59. Dio, LIX 7, 2–3; LX 27, 2. It was an exceptional occasion, the *ludi saeculares*, on which Domitian gave 100 races in a day. To fit them all in, he had to reduce the laps obligatory for each race

from 7 to 5; Suetonius, *Domitian* 4, 3.

60. Juvenal 10, 36–40.

61. On the factions, see *SG* II 32–40.

62. Jordan, op. cit. 551; 595; cf. Le Blant, *Mél.* VI (1886) 327–8.

63. Plutarch, *Sulla* 35, 3–5.

64. Ovid, *Ars Am.* I 135–64.

65. See the detailed analysis of these inscriptions by Drexel in *SG* IV 179–96.

66. *CIL* XV 6250 on the horse *Corax*; cf. Pliny, *NH* VIII 160.

67. cf. *Recueil de Constantine* 1880 and the figure in *DS* I 1198.

68. *CIL* VI 10048.

69. *CIL* VII 10047.

70. Audollent, *Tabellae Defixionum* nos. 15; 159.

71. Juvenal, 7, 112–14; Martial, IV 67; X 74.

72. *CIL* VI 10048; see the analysis in *SG* IV 179–96.

73. *SG* II 28–9.

74. Suetonius, *Nero* 16.

75. Martial, V 25, 10.

76. ibid., XI 1.

77. ibid., X 50.

78. *CIL* VI 33950; 10050; 10049.

79. Martial, XI 1, 9–16.

80. Juvenal, 11, 193–202.

81. See Statius' description of a day at the circus under Domitian (*Silvae* I 6; cf. Suetonius, *Domitian* 4, 5).

82. Suetonius, *Vitellius* 7, 1; Dio, LXV 5, 1. For Caracalla, see Dio, LXXVII 10; cf. LXXVIII 8, 2.

83. Marcus Aurelius, *Meditations* I 5.

84. On the number of dramatic performances under the Republic, see L. R. Taylor, *TAPA* LXVIII (1937) 284–304.

85. Pliny, *Ep.* IX 6, 3.

86. Juvenal 9, 142–4.

87. *Ann. épigr.* 1933, no. 30, ll. 35–7.

88. *PA* 515–17; Lugli (*ZA* 346; cf. 390–91) assumes with Ashby that each of the *loca* reckoned in the *Regionaries* represents only one square foot, whereas the minimum space necessary

for a seated spectator is a foot and a half (44 cm.).

89. *PA* 513.

90. ibid. 513–15.

91. On Roman theatres in Italy and the provinces during the empire, see M. Bieber, *The History of the Greek and Roman Theater*, 356–90.

92. Tacitus, *Ann.* XI, 13; XII 28, cf. Quintilian, X 1, 98.

93. On masks and costumes, see M. Bieber, *Die Denkmäler zum Theaterwesen im Altertum* 155–74; for masks alone, Bieber, *RE* XIV 2093–105; 2076–83; for costumes, C. Saunders, *Costume in Roman Comedy*.

94. On the Hellenistic, probably Alexandrine, origin of the pantomime, see L. Robert, *Hermes* LXV (1930) 106–22.

95. On Roman tragedy, see the recent article of Ziegler, *RE* 12A 1981–2008, esp. 1994–8; 2001–4. On plays under the empire, Bieber, *History* 391–428.

96. Suetonius, *Caesar* 84, 2–frg. XV Ribbeck.

97. Tacitus, *Ann* XIII 15.

98. Cicero, *Tusc. Disp.* III 44–frg. V Vahlen.

99. Diomedes, p. 491 Keil.

100. See Bieber, *History* 315–25.

101. On the civil status of actors, see Warnecke, *Neue Jahrb. f. d. klassische Altertum* XXXIII (1914) 95–109.

102. Dio, LIV 17, 4–5; Suetonius, *Augustus* 45, 5; Macrobius, *Sat.* II 7, 12–19.

103. Tacitus, *Ann.* I 77; cf. Suetonius, *Tiberius* 37.

104. Tacitus, *Ann.* XIII 25; 28; Suetonius, *Nero* 16, 2.

105. Tacitus, *Ann* XIV 21.

106. Tacitus, *Dialogus* 29.

107. Suetonius, *Domitian* 3; Dio, LXVII 3, 1.

108. Macrobius, *Sat.* II 7, 12–19.

109. Livy VII 2; Val. Max., II 4, 4.

110. Quintilian, XI 3, 86–8.

111. Lucian, *De Saltatione* 67.

112. Juvenal, 7, 86-7.
113. Lucian, op. cit. 37-61.
114. Macrobius, *Sat.* II 7, 16.
115. Josephus, *Ant.* XIX 1, 13.
116. Suetonius, *Nero* 21, 3.
117. Juvenal 6, 64-6.
118. Pliny, *Pan.* 54.
119. Dio, LXVIII 10.
120. Paribeni, *Dioniso* VI (1938) 210.
121. Plutarch, *Quaest. Convivales* VII 8, 3.
122. Cicero, *Ad. Fam.* IX 26; *Ad Attic.* IV 15; *Pro Plancio* 30.
123. Euanthius, IV 1 p. 21 ed. Wessner. On the Roman mime in general, see *SG* II 113-18; Wüst, *RE* XV 1749-61; Boissier, *DS* III 1903-7. A scene from a mime is reproduced in a relief from the theatre at Sabratha (Guidi, *Africa Italiana* III [1930] 38-9; Bieber, *History*, 421).
124. Cicero, *Ad Attic.* XIV 3, 3; cf. Macrobius, *Sat.* II 7, 4.
125. *Poetae Latini Minores* III p. 245.
126. Suetonius, *Caligula* 57; Juvenal 8, 187-8; Tertullian, *Adv. Val.* 14.
127. On the plots, see *SG* II 113-14.
128. Val. Max., II 10, 8; Martial. III 86; cf. *SG* II 115-16.
129. Martial, *Spect.* 7.
130. On the *munus* as a human sacrifice, see Piganiol, *Recherches sur les jeux romains* 126-36.
131. Terence, *Hecyra*, Prologue II 31-4.
132. Cicero, *In Vatinium* 37.
133. Cicero, *Ad Fam.* II 3, 1.
134. Pliny, *NH* XXXIII 53; cf. Plutarch, *Caesar* 5, 4 and Suetonius, *Caesar* 10.
135. *CIL* I² 594 (*Lex col. Genetivae Iulae*) LXX; LXXI.
136. Dio, LIV 2, 4 (22 B.C.).
137. Tacitus, *Ann.* IV 63.
138. Suetonius, *Claudius* 24; cf. Tacitus, *Ann.* XI 22.
139. *Res Gestae* 22.
140. The last of the magistrates' extraordinary *munera* which our sources record are those offered in A.D. 70 for the *natalis* of Vitellius by the consuls of that year; Tacitus, *Hist.* II 95.
141. This method of presentation continued in small towns into the age of the Antonines; cf. *CIL* V 7637.
142. Pliny, *NH* XXXVI 116-20.
143. ibid. 118.
144. *SG* IV 208.
145. Dio, XLIII 22, 3.
146. The world *amphitheatrum* first appears in Vitruvius, I 7, 1; then in *Res Gestae* 22; cf. *SG* IV 209.
147. *PA* 11.
148. On the *Amphitheatrum Flavium* (Colosseum), see *PA* 6-11.
149. ibid. 357.
150. ibid. 5-6; Lugli, *MA* III 490.
151. *PA* 358.
152. On gladiatorial games in general, see *SG* II 54-76; Schneider, *RE* Suppl. III 760-84; Lafaye *DS* II 1563-99. The best illustration of imperial *munera* is the superb mosaic from Zliten published by Aurigemma, *I mosaici di Zliten* 131-201.
153. *CIL* I² 593, l. 123; SHA *Hadrian* 18, 8; Seneca, *Ep.* 87, 15; Juvenal, 6, 216.
154. On the gladiatorial training schools, see *PA* 319-20.
155. ibid. 582.
156. See the detailed discussion in *SG* IV 258-67.
157. On these contests, see *SG* II 77-92; IV 268-75.
158. See Martial, *Liber Spectaculorum*, where the *venationes* given at the dedication of the Colosseum are described.
159. This is indicated by Pompeian inscriptions where the *venatio* is classed with such extra attractions as *athletae, vela*, and *sparsiones*; cf. *CIL* IV p. 71.
160. Suetonius, *Claudius* 21, 3; Dio, LXI 9, 1.
161. Suetonius, *Titus* 7.
162. *CIL* XIV 4546.
163. Plutarch, *Non Posse Suav.* XVII 6; Tertullian, *Apol.* 42.
164. Suetonius, *Claudius* 21, 6.

165. *CIL* V 5933.
166. Juvenal, 3, 36.
167. *CIL* IV 4280.
168. Martial, *Spect.* 20.
169. Carcopino, *CRAI* 1932 pp. 375-7.
170. *CIL* X 7297.
171. *Ann. épigr.* 1933, no. 30, ll. 1-2; 13-14; 54; cf. n. 16 above.
172. Cicero, *Tusc.* II 41.
173. Pliny, *Pan.* 33.
174. The disgust felt by Seneca in describing one of these contests is obvious; *Ep.* 7.
175. Strabo, VI 2, 6.
176. Aurigemma, *Mosaici* 182; 184; 192; cf. *CRAI* 1913 pp. 444-7.
177. Suetonius, *Claudius* 34.
178. On the *Actiaca*, see Gagé, *Mél* LIII (1936) 37-100.
179. Hartke, *RE* XVII 42-8.
180. *SG* IV 276-80.
181. *PA* 495-6; 371.
182. Martial, IV 54; XI 9; cf. IX 35, 9-10.

183. *Digest* III 2, 4, 1.
184. Pliny, *Ep.* IV 22.
185. For a list of amphitheatres in Italy and the Provinces, see *SG* IV 205-40.
186. cf. L. Robert, *Revue de philologie* LVI (1930) 36-8.
187. SHA *Hadrian* 18; cf. *Digest* XLVIII 8, 11.
188. *Ann. épigr.* 1933, no. 30, ll. 1-2.
189. *CIL* II 6278 and Mommsen's commentary, *Ges. Schr.* VIII 499 ff.; SHA *Marcus* 11, 4.
190. Seneca, *De Tranquillitate Animi* II 13.
191. Dio, LXXII 22, 2; SHA *Commodus* 12.
192. Martial, *Spect.* 7; cf. n. 126 above.
193. Martial, VIII 30.
194. Tertullian, *Apol.* 15.
195. SHA *Sev. Alex.* 44; cf. Lugli, *ZA* 346.
196. *Cod. Theodos.* XV 12, 1.
197. Theodoret, *Hist. Eccl.* V 26.

## CHAPTER IX
### AFTERNOON AND EVENING

1. Martial, VII 61.
2. ibid. X 5.
3. Juvenal, 16, 7-34.
4. Martial, *Spect.* 3, 1-10; Juvenal, 3, 60-72.
5. Martial, I 41, 7.
6. ibid. VIII 61; XI 79; IX 22, 14 (the last a reference to horseback).
7. The elder Pliny was carried about Rome in a *sella* so that his literary studies might not be interrupted. He rebukes his nephew for wasting time in walking; Pliny, *Ep.* III 5, 16. On the *lectica* and *sella* (*gestatoria*) in general, see Girard, *DS* III 1004-6; the history of the *lectica* in Rome is given in detail by Lamer, *RE* XII 1076-83. Particularly pertinent to this period are Juvenal, 3, 240-42; 6, 349-51; Martial, IX 11.
8. Petronius, 28.

9. Martial, VI 80.
10. Seneca, *De Provid.* V 4.
11. *PA* 427; *ZA* I 334.
12. Martial, II 14, 1-10; cf. III 19.
13. Pliny, *NH* XXXIV 31; XXXV 114, 139; XXXVI 15, 22, 24, 28, 34, 35.
14. Martial, III 19.
15. ibid. IX 35.
16. Juvenal, 1, 87-93.
17. The laws are given in the *Digest* XI 5, 2 and 3; cf. Cicero, *Phil.* II 56, Horace, *Odes* III 24, 58; Ovid, *Tristia* II 472. For the exception made during the Saturnalia, see Martial, XI 9. On gaming in general, see Humbert, *DS* I 180.
18. *Tali* had only four marked faces, *tesserae* six as in our modern dice. For methods of playing, see the two articles of Lafaye, *DS* V 28-31; 125-8.

19. On *capita aut navia*, see Saglio, *DS* I 897; on *par impar*, Lafaye, *DS* IV 322. For Augustus, Suetonius, *Augustus* 71.

20. Described by Lafaye, *DS* III 1889–90.

21. Cicero, *De Off.* III 77, cf. *De Fin.* II 52; Petronius, 44; Fronto, *Ep.* I 5 p. 13 ed. Naber; St Augustine, *De Trin.* VIII 5, 8.

22. *CIL* VI 1770.

23. There is an excellent description of these games in Owen's commentary to Ovid's second book of the *Tristia*, pp. 250–59. For the *latrunculi* see also Lafaye, *DS* III 992–5; for *duodecim scripta*, Saglio, *DS* II 414–15.

24. On Canus, see Seneca, *De Tranq. An.* 14, 7; on Piso, *Laus Pisonis*, 190–208; cf. schol. to Juvenal (Valla) V 109.

25. Martial, VII 71, 7; *CIL* XIII 444.

26. Over one hundred of these impromptu playing boards have been found in the city of Rome; cf. Lamer, *RE* XIII 2003.

27. See Lafaye, *DS* IV 115–16. The most complete source is Ovid, *Nux* 73–86.

28. *Digest* XI 5, 1.

29. ibid. XXIII 2, 43, 1.

30. *CIL* IX 2689.

31. *NS* 1911, 431; 457. If we recall that the ass was famous in antiquity for its sexual appetite, the *cognomen* of these young women (*asellae*) is not unintelligible; cf. Mallardo, *Rivista di Studi Pomp.* (1934) 121–5; (1935) 224–8.

32. The emperor Nero had similar inns set up along the Tiber when he sailed down to Ostia; Suetonius, *Nero* 27.

33. Schol. to Persius, I 133.

34. Seneca, *De Provid.* V 4. The *illo tempore* as shown by the context is the equivalent of the entire day, *totum diem*.

35. On baths, public and private, see the articles of Saglio, *DS* I 648–64 and Benoi, *DS* V 214–19, and Blümner, *Privat-Altertümer*, 420–35.

36. Plutarch, *Cato Maior* 20. 5. This attitude was still prevalent in the time of Cicero, *De Off.* I 129.

37. Varro, *L.L.* IX 68; cf. Blümner, op. cit. 421.

38. Pliny, *NH* XXXVI 121.

39. loc. cit.

40. The *Regionaries* give 856; Jordan, *Topographie* II 573.

41. Seneca, *Ep.* 86, 9; Martial, III 30, 4; VIII 42; Horace, *Sat.* I 3, 137. Juvenal, 2, 152 with schol., informs us that children were admitted free, but that women had to pay more than men (6, 447). This is confirmed by the fees charged at Vipasca in Lusitania, where women paid an as as against half an as for men, while children were free of charge; cf. *CIL* II 5181, l. 19.

42. Pliny, *NH* XXXVI 121; cf. Dio, XLIX 43 and Blümner, op. cit. 42, n. 8.

43. On the *thermae* in general, see *PA* 518–20. On free access, Dio, LIV 29. With reference to Martial, III 36, 6, Mau doubts that free access was granted in perpetuity, *RE* II 2749; but Fronto states expressly that the public *thermae* were free to all, *Epistulae Graecae* V p. 247 ed. Naber.

44. *PA* 531–2.

45. ibid. 533–4.

46. ibid. 534–6. The date of dedication is given by the 'Fasti Ostienses', *Ann. épigr.* 1933, no. 30. l. 10.

47. *PA* 520–4.

48. ibid. 527–30.

49. ibid. 525–6.

50. *ZA* I 419.

51. Of the *triplices thermae* (the baths of Agrippa, Nero, and Titus) frequented by Martial, X 51, 21, he had the greatest admiration for those of Nero, VII 34, 5; cf. II 48, 8.

52. It was the gymnasium and the palaestra as places of moral corruption that the Romans censured particularly; Cicero, *Tusc.* IV 70, *De Rep.* IV 4; cf. Plutarch, *Quaest. Rom.* 40. Roman

youths had always exercised on the Campus Martius to prepare themselves for the hardships of military service.

53. For condemnation of Greek methods of exercise under the empire, cf. Pliny, *NH* XXIX 26, XXXV 168; Seneca, *Ep.* 88, 18; Tacitus, *Ann.* XIV 20.

54. SHA *Sev. Alex.* 24; *Tacitus* 10. But at Vipasca in Lusitania the bath was kept open until the second hour of the night; *CIL* II 5181, l. 19.

55. Juvenal, 11, 205.

56. Martial, X 48, 3.

57. SHA *Hadrian* 22.

58. SHA *Sev. Alex.* 24.

59. Martial, III 36, 6.

60. ibid. XIV 163.

61. Pliny, *NH* XXXIII 153; Quintilian, V 9, 14; Martial, III 51 and 72; VII 35; XI 47; Juvenal, 6, 419 (but here we may be dealing with a private bath; cf. Friedländer's commentary *ad loc.*).

62. SHA *Hadrian* 18; cf. Dio, LXIX 8. Another part of Hadrian's general regulations for bathing is contained in 22 of the *Life*. *CIL* VI 579, which warns women against entering the men's pools, does not seem to have come from a public bath.

63. *CIL* II 5181, l. 19 ff.: '*omnibus diebus calefacere et praestare debeto* (scil. *conductor*) *a prima luce in horam septimam diei mulieribus et ab hora octava in horam secundam noctis viris*'.

64. This assumes that Hadrian's decree prohibiting public bathing before the eighth hour applied to men alone.

65. Petronius, 27.

66. On ball games in general, see Lafaye, *DS* IV 475–8. Section 9 of the article, p. 477, deals with the *trigon*.

67. op. cit. section 7.

68. op. cit. section 3.

69. op. cit. section 4.

70. op. cit. 476. According to Martial, XIV 47, the *follis* is the ball for young boys and old men, not for young men.

71. On the punching bag (*Corycus*), see Saglio, *DS* I 1541.

72. Fencing against a dummy or stake (*ad palum*) was an important part of the training of new recruits and gladiators; *Vegetius*, I 11 and 12. But it was also practised by those who fenced for sport alone; Juvenal, 6, 274 (in this case, a woman); Martial, VII 32.

73. Martial, VII 32.

74. On the *trochus*, see Lafaye, *DS* V 492–3.

75. Juvenal, 6, 421; Martial, VII 67; XIV 49.

76. Martial, VII 67, 4–5.

77. ibid. IV 19; cf. XIV 126 and Pottier, *DS* II 616.

78. *ZA* I 425.

79. Juvenal, VI 422–3.

80. Pliny, *NH* XXVIII 55.

81. Petronius, 28.

82. Martial, V 42.

83. ibid.

84. SHA *Hadrian* 17.

85. Petronius, 28.

86. On these libraries, see *ZA* I 420. For libraries in the baths of Diocletian, cf. SHA *Probus* 2.

87. *ZA* I 417–18.

88. ibid. 207.

89. Seneca, *Ep.* 56, 2; Martial, XII 19; *Digest* III 2, 4.

90. Martial, XII 70; Quintilian, I 6, 44; Seneca, *Ep.* 122, 6.

91. Columella, I 16; Juvenal, 6, 419–29; Seneca, *Ep.* 15, 3; Pliny, *NH* XIV 139.

92. Juvenal, 1, 143–4.

93. SHA *Commodus* 11, 5.

94. *CIL* VI 15258; cf. *Palatine Anthology* X 112.

95. Octave Homberg, *L'Eau romaine* (Paris, 1935).

96. Juvenal, 10, 356.

97. The emperor Vitellius, for example; cf. Suetonius, *Vitellius* 13; Dio, LXV 4, 3.

98. Festus, *s.v. cena* p. 49 ed. Lindsay.

99. Pliny, *Ep.* III 5, 10–11.

100. Galen, *De Sanitate Tuenda* V 332, p. 143 ed. Koch in the *Corpus Medicorum Graecorum;* cf. Paulus Aegineta, I 23.

101. Martial, XI 104, 4.

102. Galen, op. cit. VI 412, p. 181 ed. Koch. It consisted of bread alone.

103. Suetonius, *Claudius* 34.

104. Martial, XIII 31. For Martial's breakfast hour, cf. VIII 67.

105. Seneca, *Ep.* 83, 6.

106. Fronto, *Ep.* IV 6 p. 69 ed. Naber; Galen, op. cit. V 332-4; Martial, I 49, 14; XIII 13.

107. Pliny, *Ep.* III 5, 10.

108. Seneca, *Ep.* 83, 6.

109. See *Revue de Paris* (1 June 1938), 885 ff.

110. Suetonius, *Nero* 27; for Vitellius, see n. 97 above.

111. Pliny, *Ep.* III 1, 8–9.

112. Martial, XI 52; cf. X 48.

113. Pliny, *Ep.* III 5, 13.

114. Suetonius, *Nero* 27.

115. Petronius, 79, where some of the guests leave at midnight.

116. Juvenal, 8, 9–12.

117. Vitruvius, VI 3, 8.

118. Val. Max., II 1, 2.

119. Suetonius, *Claudius* 32; cf. Tacitus, *Ann* XIII 16. This custom was preserved in a conservative ceremony such as the banquet of the Arval Brotherhood as late as the third century, *CIL* VI 2104, l. 12; but Plutarch already knew of children reclining at table, *Quaest. Convivales* VII 8, 4.

120. Columella, XI 19.

121. In Gaul there does not seem to have been any fixed custom, since we find both men and women seated and reclining at the banquets depicted on the funeral reliefs; see Espérandieu, *Recueil des bas-reliefs de la Gaule romaine* VI, nos. 5154; 5155; VIII 6449; 6489.

122. Martial, V 70. See the painting from Pompeii depicting a tavern scene reproduced in *D S* I 973.

123. Martial, V 79.

124. Plutarch, *Cato Minor* 56.

125. On the *triclinium* in general, see the recent article of Hug, *RE* XIIIA 92–101.

126. Petronius, 31.

127. Martial mentions *stibadia* seating seven and eight persons, X 48, 5–6, XIV 87; cf. SHA *Elagabalus* 29. A couch for twelve was an exception; Suetonius, *Augustus* 70, SHA *Verus* 5.

128. Vitruvius, VI 7, 3; Athanaeus, II 47 f.

129. Martial, XII 29, 12; XIV 138.

130. Horace, *Satires* II 8, 10.

131. Juvenal, 11, 133, mentions knives with ivory and bone handles. According to Martial, XIV 22, cf. III 82, 9, the best toothpicks (*dentiscalpia*) were made of mastic wood, but a feather might be used. Trimalchio had one of silver; Petronius, 33.

132. Both these types are mentioned by Martial, XIV 120 and 121; cf. VIII 71, 9–10; 33, 23–4.

133. Petronius, 31.

134. ibid. 60; Martial, II 37, 7; VII 20, 13.

135. Juvenal, 1, 94–5.

136. Macrobius, *Sat.* III 13, 10 ff. He describes a banquet of the *pontifices* on the occasion of the inauguration of Lentulus as *flamen Martialis*. It is analysed in *D S* I 1282.

137. Petronius, 31.

138. ibid. 33.

139. ibid. 35.

140. ibid. 36.

141. ibid. 40.

142. ibid. 59.

143. ibid. 60; there seem to have been two desserts, cf. 68.

144. ibid. 68.

145. ibid. 72–3.

146. On ancient wines in general, see the excellent article of Jardé *D S* V 912–24. Martial had a particularly low opinion of wine from Marseilles; X 36, XIII 123, XIV 118. He classes Vatican wine with vinegar, X 45.

*Falernum*, however, he twice characterizes as *immortale*; IX 93; XI 36, 5.

147. The label of one of Trimalchio's wines read: '*Falernum Opimianum annorum centum*'; Petronius, 34.
148. Martial, I 11; VI 89.
149. See Jardé, op. cit. 921.
150. On the *commissatio*, see *DS* I 1373.
151. Martial, I 71; VIII 51, 21; XI 36, 7; XIV 170.
152. Pliny, *NH* XIV 91.
153. Pliny, *Ep.* II 6.
154. Martial, IX 2.
155. Juvenal, 5, 24–155.
156. Pliny, *Ep.* II 6.
157. Petronius, 34–5; 52–3; 58; 60.
158. Pliny, *Ep.* IX 17.
159. On these dancing girls from Cadiz, see Juvenal, 11, 162–4; Martial, V 78, 26–8.
160. Pliny, *Ep.* IX 17, 2.
161. Cicero, *Ad Fam.* X 22, 5; Juvenal, 3, 107; Martial, X 48, 10; Pliny, *Panegyricus* 49.
162. Suetonius, *Claudius* 32.
163. Martial, VII 18, 9–10.
164. Petronius, 47.
165. Martial, III 82, 15–18; cf. VI 89, 1–2; XVI 119; Petronius, 27.
166. Juvenal, 11, 175; cf. Pliny, *NH* XIV 146; Vitruvius, VII 4, 5.
167. Seneca, *Cons. ad Helviam* X 3; cf. Juvenal 6, 425–33; Martial, VII 67, 9–10.
168. Apicius, IV 2 (132).
169. Petronius, 70.
170. On Roman food in general, see Fournier, *DS* I 1141–69; Orth, *RE* XI, 944–82. See also Bilabel's discussion of Roman cook-books, ibid. 941–3.
171. Juvenal, 11, 79–81.
172. ibid. 14, 6–10.
173. ibid. 4, 15–16.
174. ibid. 140–42.
175. Pliny, *Ep.* VI 31, 13.
176. ibid. V 2.
177. ibid. V 21, 4.
178. ibid. III 12, 1.
179. ibid. I 15.
180. Martial, X 48.
181. Juvenal, 11, 66–74.
182. *NS* 1927, 93–4; cf. Della Corte, *Case e abitanti a Pompei*, pp. 120–21.
183. *CIL* XIV 2112; cf. G. Boissier, *La Réligion romaine* II 283.
184. *Acts of the Apostles* II 46.
185. Tertullian, *Apologeticus* 39, 17–18.

# INDEX

Accius, 245

Achilles, 250

Acilii Glabriones, 154, 155

Acquataccio (River Almo), 26

Actiaca, games founded by Augustus, 227–67

*Actio rei uxoriae*, 111–12

Actium, 143, 268

Adultery, 107–9, 210; *Lex Iulia de adulteriis*, 108; re-enactment by Domitian, 108; recast by Septimius Severus, 109

Aedis Martis, 25–6

Aegisthus, 250

*Aelia Sentia*, 320, n. 38

Aelius Aristides, 36

Aemilia, wife of Pompey, 110

Aemilius Paulus, 322, n. 8

Aemilius Scaurus, 99

Aeneas, 250

Aërope, the wife of Atreus, 250

Aesop, 126

Aetolians, Roman campaign against the, 164

Afer, 81

Africa, province of, grain, 28, 196; Saint Augustine, 125; governed by Sallust, 129; elephants, 261

Africanus, fortune-hunter, 81

Agamemnon, 133, 249

*Agape* (ἀγάπη), 156, 229, 300

Agave, 250

*Ager Romanus*, 22

*Agnatio*, 89

*Agon Capitolinus*, 227, 268, 280

Agrippa, improvements in Roman sewers, 51; innovations at chariot races, 235, 242; founding of the baths of Agrippa, 277–8

Albulae, quarries of, 257

*Album*, census list, 28; list of precedence, 299

Alcestis, 101

Alexander the Great, 130, 132, 146;

command regarding beards, 178; statue and group by Lysippus, 272

Alexander Severus, 270, 278; Life of, 281

Alexandria, 163, 195; water-clock, 164; Museum of, 124, 215; Library of, 215

Alexandrine thought, and neo-Pythagoreanism, 145

Alphabet, method of teaching, 119, 120, 121

Alps, province of the, 66

Ammianus Marcellinus, record of Constantine's admiration of the Forum of Trajan, 18

Amphitheatre, punishment of criminals, 65, imperial shows and spectacles, 224, 253–68, 269; Pompeii, 256; of Taurus, 256; Amphitheatrum Castrense, 257; Flavian Amphitheatre, *see* the Colosseum

Anatolia, cults of, 146

Andromache, 186

Animals, sacrifice as part of marriage ceremony, 95; sacrifice of the 'October horse', 228; wild beasts used in the arena, 258; emperor's menagerie, 260; tame animals used in circus acts, 260; numbers slaughtered in the arena, 261; punishment of criminals, *ad bestias*, 266

Anna Perenna, festival of, 138

Annona, mythical personification of the year's food supplies, 27; numbers fed, 27, 28, 79, 194; amount of grain needed each year, 28; temple of Annona Augusta, 195; worship by the guilds, 196; *tessera* entitling one to her bounty, 202

Antiates, ships captured from the, 163

Antinoüs, Bithynian slave in whose honour Hadrian founded a religion, 151–2; obelisk of, 25; college of salvation, 70, 151, 152, 299

Antiochus of Syria, 164

Antiquaries, 204

*Antiquarium Comunale*, 310

Antistia, divorced wife of Pompey, 110

Antoninus Pius, 30, 72, 75, 144, 152; originated in Nemausus (Nîmes), 69; decree condemning slaying of slave as homicide, 71; example of monogamy, 114; tribute to wife, 152

Antonius Creticus, 181

Antony, Marc, 132, 179, 180, 267

Anubis, 147

Apollo, 267

Apollodorus of Damascus, architect of the Trajan group, 17, 19

Apoxyomenus, the, of Lysippus, 231

Appian of Alexandria, on the position of the Roman slave, 72

Appianus, defiance of Commodus, 211

Apuleius, owner of House of Gamala, 34

Apuleius, 123; to whom Isis appeared, 189

*Aqua Traiana*, 50, 278

Aqueducts, connected with market fishponds, 17; built by Trajan, 19, 50; as part of the fortification, 25; overflow used to flush sewers, 51; listed in *Regionaries*, 311

Aquileia, discovery of pocket sundials at, 165

Aquinum, birthplace of Juvenal, 68

Arabia, conquest of, 9; porphyry and incense, 197

Ara Coeli, discovery of ruins under the, 34

Aragon, home of Martial, 68

Arbuscula, mimic-actress, 252

Ardeatine Gate, 25

Argiletum, district devoted to handicraftsmen and booksellers, 215

Aristonicus, 123

Aristotle, the three types of eloquence, 130

Arithmetic, method of teaching, 119, 121

Arles, 126, 136, 195

Armenia, 263

Armilustrium, festival of the consecration of arms, 225

Arria the Elder, wife of Caecina Paetus, 99

Arriana Polliana, *insula* rentals, 317 n. 23

Artisans, condition of, 198, 204, 205

Arx, the Citadel, 23

Asia, senators from, 69

Asinarian Gate, 25

Asinius Pollio, 39; completion of Roman library, 215, 216

Astrology, Roman faith in, 146, 148–9, 230; introduction of seven-day week, 161–2

Astronomy, 129

Atargatis (Dea Syra), temple of, 145, 146

Athena, temple of, 135

Athenaeum, built by Hadrian in Rome, 217

Athenaeus, estimate of slaves in household, 84

Athens, educational model for Rome, 123, 125; sundials, 162, 163

Atia, mother of Augustus, 118

Atina, Cicero's defence of a citizen of, 252

Atrectus, bookseller, 215

Atreus, 250

*Atrium*, entrance hall, 35, 48; household place of sacrifice, 95

Attic art, renaissance under Hadrian, 127

Atticus, copying studio, 214–15

Attis, liturgy of, 145, 146, 150, 151

Auctus, 203

*Auditoria*, 217, 219

Augurs, participation in dedication of City of Rome, 22; Pliny's election to College of Augurs, 141

Augusta, feminine imperial title granted Livia, 98, 152

'Augustus', imperial title of divinity, 67

Augustus (Octavius), 19, 43, 46, 66, 67, 95, 114, 143, 176, 188, 212, 248, 251; Forum of, 13; organizes fourteen divisions of Urbs, 24–5, 26, 309, 310; old fortifications dismantled, 24; special administration of the *vicus*, 26–7; advance in population, 28–9; *Res Gestae*, 29, 232, 235; generosity, 28–9; restrictions on height of houses, 16; incorporation of outside districts,

39; fire-fighting night watchmen, 44; on manumission of slaves, 74; marriage by 'usus', 93; marital laws and guardianship, 96–7; laws against adultery, 108–9; on divorce, 111–12, 113; concubinage, 116; education, 118; jurisprudence, 124, 181, 208; extinction of his family line, 142; divinity of emperor, 152; establishing the twelve months, 161; obelisk of Montecitorio a sundial, 165; clothing, 172; hairdressing and shaving, 176, 178–9; legislation on corporations, 203–4; enthusiasm for public readings, 216; *Ludi Fortunae Reducis*, 225; holidays, 227; on wearing the toga, 229; buttressing power by use of games and spectacles, 231–2, 254; obelisk of Rameses II, 235; races, 237; Theatre of Marcellus, 244; *naumachia*, 257; criminals *ad bestias*, 266; Greek games, 268, 280–81; Portico of Octavia, 272; gambling games, 274

Aulus Fulvius, 90

Aulus Gellius, 36, 94

Aulus Plautius, 154

Aurelia, mother of Caesar, 118

Aurelian Wall, 21, 22, 25; fortification, 25–6

Aurelius Victor, Egyptian grain supplied to Rome, 28

Ausonius, *Ephemeris*, occupations of a day, 175; appeasement by gladiatorial slaughter, 229

*Auspex*, 66, 95, 96

Authors, condition under Roman system of publishing, 215–16

Aventine Hill, 23; residence of Asinius Pollio, and meeting place of Roman plebs, 38; within the Roman sewerage system, 52, 54; system of warehouses, 196–7; Circus Maximus, 234–5; *thermae* dedicated by Trajan, 278

Babylon, 132, 162

Baetica, birthplace of Trajan and Hadrian, 69; meats to Rome, 197;

extortions of Classicus, and his trial, 213, 214

Bakeries, at Pompeii, 49; inducements to set up Roman shops, 202

Baltic, amber from the, 197

Balzac, *Physiologie du mariage*, 183

Banishment, punishment of *honestiores*, 66; of early Christians, 154, 155

Banking, 198; banking operations forbidden to women, 202

*Banquet of Thyestes*, 101, 250

Barbers and barbershops, 61, 176–80; apprenticeship, 181

Bartoli, Professor, excavations beneath the Church of Sant' Adriano, 213

Basilica Iulia, description, 208; assembly of the *centumviri*, 208; draught-boards scratched on the steps, 210, 275

Basilica Ulpia (Trajan), 14, 15, 18, 20

Basilicae, 272; enumerated in *Regionaries*, 311

Baths, public, 10, 277–86; baths of Caracalla (*thermae* of Antoninus), 18, 278, 280, 284, 285; largest public baths built by Trajan, 9, 18–20, 278, 279, 285; Herculaneum and Pompeii, 47; *thermae*, 174, 271; women's attendance, 191, 281, 282; built by the Caesars, endowed by philanthropists, 277–8; census of baths, 277; baths built by Agrippa, 278; *thermae* erected by Nero, 278; baths of Titus, 278; *thermae* built by Trajan in memory of Licinus Sura, 278; *thermae* of Constantine, 278; baths of Diocletian, 278; description and types of baths, 278–81; hours for bathing, 281, 282; mixed bathing, 281; restrictions, 281; games at the bath, 280, 282–4; evils of the bath, 286; 'Palace of Roman Water', 286; baths of Stephanus, 288; enumerated in the *Regionaries*, 311

Bathrooms, 49

Bathyllus, mime, 251

Beds and furnishings, 171, 184–5

Bel, 146

Bellona, 61, 147

Belvedere Torso, 285

Betrothal, 93–4; decree by Augustus against breach of, 111

*Bibliopolae*, 215

Bibliothecae Ulpiae, libraries of Trajan, 15, 20

Bidez, Joseph, demonstration of the debt of Stoicism to the Semites, 145

Bilbilis, Aragon home of Martial, 68, 170, 192

Billeter, researches of, 79

Birth rate, falling, in upper classes, 111

Bithynia, 152

Bizerta (Hippo-Diarrhytus), 196

Blanchet, Adrien, study of walled towns in Gaul, 25

Blandina, torture of, 267

Boethius, A., 40

Boileau, *Embarras de Paris*, 61

Boissier, Gaston, story of the tutor-slave, 119; piety of the pagan Romans, 138–9, 140–41

Bona Dea, 147

Bossuet, 152

Bovillae, 22, 151

Bridges, enumerated in *Regionaries*, 311

Brindisi, 133

Britannicus, 85, 247

Britons, 154

Brothels, 276

*Bruma*, 274

Brutus, 96

Building, regulation of, under Trajan, 19–20; incentive to building, under Nero, 73

Buildings, frequent collapse of, 36, 43, 44, 62; restrictions on height, 36

Burial forbidden within *pomerium*, 16, 23

Businessmen, 193; hours of business, 204

Cabinet, Imperial, slaves and freedmen, 75; Hadrian's reservation for members of the Equestrian Order, 77

Caecina Paetus, 99–100

Caelian Hill, 39; (Mons Caelius), 236; (Caelius), 256

Caelius Rufus, annual rent, 37

Caere, 23

Caesar, Julius, 54, 95, 124; congestion of Forum, 18; enlargement of Urbs, 24; population, 27; triumph 45 B.C., 28; *Censor Morum*, 28; residence in Rome, 39; gold stool, 46; decree on care of streets, 58; decree regarding night traffic, 61, 62; loyalty of Legions, 67; patrician families, 74; marriages, 110; mother's interest in his education, 118; interest in grammar and rhetoric, 124–5, 130; appoints Sallust governor of province of Africa, 129; the god Caesar, 143; Jewish colony in Rome, 153; twelve months of the year, calendar reform, 161; the toga, 172; fastidiousness, 176; clean shaven, 179, 183; Curia, 213; first State Library in Rome, 215; *Ludi Victoriae Caesaris*, 225; holidays to commemorate significant events in his life, 225–6; inattention at spectacles, 232; improvements in Circus Maximus, 235, 254; Theatre of Marcellus, 244; *canticum* from Pacuvius' *Armorum Iudicium* sung at his funeral, 246; assassination, 252; Greek games, 268; gardens bequeathed to the people, 272. *See also Leges Iuliae*

Caesennii, benefactors of 'College of Salvation', 299

Calchas, 133

Calendar, days and hours, 161–9; Julian reform, 161; solar calendar, 204; stone calendars, 224; calendars of festivals, *ferialia*, 224–8 *See also Fasti*

Calendar of Philocalus, record of games and public holidays, 227

Calends, the 161, 212, 226

Calenus, 184

Caligula, 252; claims to dynastic divinity, 67; Egyptian cults welcomed back, 146; shaving as a religious rite, 179; pronouncement on Seneca, 221; building of the Circus Gai, 234; races under, 237; assassination of, 251

Calpurnia, wife of Pliny the Younger, 102, 103, 105, 184

Calpurnia Hispulla, 103

Calpurnius Fabatus, 103

Calpurnius Piso, 217; mythology of the constellations, 221

Calvina, 81

Calza, Guido, research on houses, 34; reconstruction of Casa dei Dipinti, 41-2

Campagna, the, suburban villas, 39; frescoes, 203

Campi, enumerated in *Regionaries*, 203

Campus Martius, 256, 309; plain dedicated to military exercises, 23-4; a portion released for dwelling-houses, 23-4; temples, tombs, etc., 33; obelisk of Montecitorio, a sundial, 165; Saepta Iulia, 272; *thermae* of Nero, 278

Cantabrians, campaign against, 179

*Cantica*, recitatives or lyrics, 246, 247, 248, 249, 250; *canticum* from Pacuvius' *Armorum Iudicium* sung at Caesar's funeral, 246

*Capilli Indici*, 187

Capitol, the, 24; Temple of Jupiter, 80, 139; (Capitoline Jove), 179, 272
*See also* Capitoline Hill; Citadel

Capitoline games, 126

Capitoline Hill, 16, 23, 309

Capua, 23, 134, 146, 234, 256

Caracalla, 242; baths (*thermae* of Antoninus), 278, 279, 284, 286; plan of Rome, 309-10

Carinae, the, 39

Carneades, academician, 124

Carthage, 125, 195; Christian martyrs, 267

Casa dei Dipinti (House of Paintings), Ostia, reconstruction, 41-3

Cassiterides (Scilly Isles), tin from the, 197

Castle of S. Angelo, 257

Castra Praetoria, 208,

Catachresis, in grammar, 128

Catiline, insurrectionist, 90; destroyed by Cicero, 60

Catilius Severus, 297

Cato the Elder (the Censor): sanitation, 54; treatment of his plough oxen, 69; rigorous family discipline, 91, 118; penalty for adultery, 108; admired

by Hadrian, 127; influence on oratory, 130; represented as bearded, 178; attitude to the public baths, 277

Cato the Younger (of Utica), marriage to Marcia, 97; divorce and remarriage to Marcia, 110-11; shaven daily, 179; vow on defeat of the senatorial army, 289

Catullus, *Laureolus*, 252, 253, 269

*Cavea*, spectators' seats, 234; description, 236, 239, 249, 258; Circus Maximus, 244

*Cena*, 287, 288

*Cenae*, religious, 299

*Cenacula*, dwelling apartments, used as a basis for computing Roman population, 30; description, 35, 40; confined to upper storeys of buildings, 37; danger in case of fire, 37, 45; lack of heating arrangements, 48; lack of water, 50; sanitation, 51-2; sub-letting, 55-6, 184

Census, Rome, January 1939, 21; census of *vici*, 26; census of 86 B.C. abandoned, 28; catalogue of different categories of population substituted and made standard, 28, 29, 30
*See also Regionaries*

'Centenaries' of the Eternal City, 227

Centumcellae (Cività Vecchia), Trajan's country house, 210, 297

*Centumviri*, 208, 212

Centurion, annual salary, 86

Ceres, temple of, rebuilt by Pliny, 141

Cerialia, public holidays, 225

Cess trenches, 52, 54

Chaldean cult, 147, 148

Chariot races, 234-43, 270, 274

Charon, 263

Children, parental authority over, 90-91, 92; emancipation, 91

China, silk from, 188, 200

Chios, fruit from, 296

Christian Church, martyrs, 101, 153, 154, 155, 267; Latin adopted by the, 126; converts in the directing classes, 154; requickening of virtue, 157; Christian emperors stop arena butcheries, 270; *cenae*, 299; failure to

Christian Churches - *contd*
mention Christian monuments in *Regionaries*, 310
Christianity, advent of, 152, 153-7; analogies between Christianity and the pagan mysteries, 156
Chrysippus, Stoic philosopher, 119
Church of the Holy Cross at Jerusalem, 257; of Saint Mary of the Angels, 278; of Saint Peter, 259; of Sant' Adriano, excavations beneath, 213
Cicero, 36, 54, 87, 131, 132, 214, 252, 275; *In Verrem*, free grain, 28; and Catiline, 60; *De Officiis*, the Roman family, 89; divorce, 110-11; treatises, 124; study of his works in classes, 127; murdered by Popilius Laenas, 134; College of Augurs, 141; lucubration, 170; mania for litigation, 207; published works, 215; *Tusculan Disputations*, 247; defence of a citizen of Atina, 252; popular reaction to the murder of Caesar, 252; opinion on gladiatorial combat, 265
Cimber, Martial's miser, 82
Ciminian forests, 296
Cimon, son of Miltiades, 135
Cincinnatus, 173
Cinna, 22, 110
*Cinyras and Myrrha*, 250
Circuses, 234-43; Agonalis, 268-9; Flaminius, 24, 40, 234, 244; Gai, 234; Maximus, 234-6, 244, 263
Cirta (Constantine), capital of Numidia, 129
Citadel, the, 23
See also the Capitol
Citizens, classifications of, 65, 68; manumission of slaves and rights of citizenship, 73
Civil cases, 206, 207-9, 224
Città Vecchia (Centumcellae), 210, 297
Claqueurs, 209
Classicus, Caecilius, trial and punishment for extortion, 213-14
Claudia Rufina, 101, 104
Claudius, 9, 200, 245, 295; Caesar's decree regarding night traffic, 62; emperor by his dynasty's divinity,

67; decree regarding sick or infirm slaves, 70; outfitting merchant ships, 70, 202; cabinet recruited from freedmen, 75; murder, 85; treatment of wife of Senator Caecina Paetus, 100; reformation of religious cults, 146; Christianity, 153; decree regarding toga, 174; women's hairdressing, 186; writer of history, 216; holidays, 224, 226; cost and equipment of games, 233, 235; gladiatorial shows, 254, 260, 267
Claudius Ariston, 210
Claudius Marcellinus, 213-14
Cleopatra, 267
*Clepsydra*, 164, 165, 206-7
'Client', 191-3
Clitumnus, river of, and adjacent pastures, 139, 140, 151
Clivus Argentarius, 58; Capitolinus, 58; Publicius, 59; Victoriae, 197
*Cloaca Maxima*, 51
*Cloacae*, 52, 54
Clodius Albinus, of Hadrumetum, 69
Clothing, 289, 304; men's, 172-4; women's, 171-2, 185-6
*Coemptio. See* Marriage
*Cognatio*, 89
Colleges devoted to the gods, 70, 146, 151; *collegium salutare*, 152, 299
Colonnade of Quirinus, 242
Colosseum (Amphitheatrum Flavium), 18, 233, 236, 256-61, 268; cross, in memory of the Christian martyrs, 267
Column of Marcus Aurelius, 19, 36
Column of Trajan, 14, 15, 17, 19; Trajan's ashes deposited in the base, 16
Columns of Theodosius and Arcadius, Constantinople, 19
*Comitia*, 22, 123, 203, 231
Commagenian priests, 147
Commentary, as taught in grammar class, 128
*Commissatio*, drinking match, 293
Commodus, attends gladiatorial school, 39, 271; flogging of colonist volunteers, 78; congregation of Mithra, 152; decree on use of toga, 173-4; abused by a condemned man, 211-12;

slaughter of arena animals, 261;
over-use of the bath, 286
Como, 69; Lake Como, 101
Concubinage, 116–18
Condemnation *ad bestias*, 270; *ad metalla*,
65, 270
*Confarreatio. See* Marriage
Confiscation, as a punishment, 66;
imperial enrichment by, 81
*Congiaria*, 17, 27, 29, 79, 90
*See also* Annona
*Coniunctio sanguinis*, 89
Conscript Fathers. *See Patres conscripti*
Constantine, city of (Cirta), 129
Constantine, Emperor, admiration of
Trajan's Forum, 18; decree on the
murder of a son by his father, 90;
supply of victims for arena stopped,
270; compilation of the *Regionaries*, 310
Consualia, 225
Consus, altar to, 234
Cooking arrangements, 49, 61
Copyists, vagaries of, 29, 128; copying
studio of Atticus, 214–15
Corellius Rufus, 71
Corinth, bronzes of, 194
Corneille, 46; *Cid*, 246
Cornelia Procula, 299
Cornelius Minicianus, 214
Cornutus, 297
Corporations, 195–222
Cotton stuffs from India, 188
Country villas, 218
Courts, congestion of, 207; description
of a hearing, 209–10
Crassus, 44
Cretan labyrinth, 251
Creticus, M. Antonius, 181
Criminal prosecutions, 208
Crito, physician to Trajan, 75
Critolaus, 124
Crucifixion of *humiliores*, 65
Ctesibius, inventor of water-clock, 164
Cumont, Franz, analysis of Roman cults,
145, 150
Cuq, Édouard, research into the popula-
tion of Rome, 30, 31
*Cura corporis*, men, 175; women, 185
Curia of Julius Caesar, 76, 193, 212, 222

Curio the Younger, 255
*Curiosum. See Regionaries*
Curius Dentatus, 9
Curtius, *Puteal* of, 208
Curule chair, 46, 208–9, 213
Curule magistrate, 237
Cybele (Great Idaean Mother of the
Gods; Lady of Salvation; *Mater deum
salutaris*), cult of, 145, 146, 147, 150,
152, 182, 225, 229
Cyniphs, 180
Cytheris, 252

Dacia, 211; conquest of, 9; plunder used
to build Trajan's Basilica, 14–15;
episodes pictured on Column of
Trajan, 15; second campaign, 75;
captives, 75, 116; gold, 197
*See also* Decebalus
Dalmatia, gold from, 197
Damascus, fruit from, 296
Dancing, 249
Day, division of the, 162–3
*See also* Calendar
Dea Syra. *See* Atargatis
*Death of Hercules*, 270
Decalogue, the, 153
Decebalus, 15, 82
Decimus Laberius, 253
Delmatius, 126
Demetrius Poliorcetes, 163
Depilatories, 183
*Depositio barbae*, 179
De Rossi, G.-B., on conversions to
Christianity, 155
Diadochi, the, 130
Diana, double invocation with Anti-
noüs, 70–71, 151, 299, 300
Diana, Hill of, 80
Dice games, 274
Dido, 105, 250
*Dies Dominica*, 162; *fasti*, 206, 224;
*legitimi*, 212; *nefasti*, 224; *solis*, 162
*Digest*, on refund of rent in case of
tearing down an *insula*, 43–4; on
damages in case of slops thrown
from windows, 55; prosecution of
criminals, 60

Dinner, 287–300

Dio Cassius, *congiarium*, 27; Christian martyrs, 154; seven-day week, 161; shows and spectacles a barrier against revolution, 232

Diocles, 241

Diocletian, reconstruction of the Curia, 212; of Theatre of Pompey, 245; decoration of Campus Martius, 256; baths, 279; early description of Rome, 310

Diogenes, 124

Diomedes, 131, 174

Dionysius, 272

*Divi*, 67, 142, 229

Divination, 148–9

Divorce, 109–15

Doles, 10, 78

   See also Annona; *Conglaria*; *Sportulae*

*Dominus et deus*, 67, 142

Domitia, Empress, 248

Domitian, 56, 70, 113, 140, 151, 249, 260, 281, 290; edict against street display of merchandise, 59; assassination, 76, 142, 175; law against adultery, 109, 115; Temple of Isis, 146; persecution of Christians, 154, 155; decree regarding use of toga, 174; action against literary production, 216; as a poet, 217; munificence at the races, 242; Theatre of Pompey, 245; *Laureolus*, 253; Colosseum, 257; gladiatorial combat, 263, 265; Greek games, 268, 280

Domitilla, sister of Domitian, 76

Domitius Afer, 209

*Domus*, enumeration in *Regionaries*, 29, 30, 31; etymology, 30; description of house, 34, 35, 42, 305; ground-floor apartment, 37, 40, 51, 56; sanitation, 52–3

*Domus Aurea*, 256, 278

*Domus divina* of the Caesars, 64

Dorus, publisher of Cicero and Livy, 215

Dowry, action of a divorced wife to reclaim it, 111–12; *propter liberos, impensas, res amotas, mores*, 112; legal safeguard, 112; hold on the husband, 113

Drama, death of the Roman, 245, 246

Duchesne, Monseigneur, 96; comparison of Christian ritual with Roman nuptial rite, 95–6; Christian and pagan brotherhoods, 156

Duilius, 163

Dureau de la Malle, distribution of population of ancient times, 20

*E manubiis*, legend on Trajan's Basilica, 14

Eburones, the, massacre of Caesar's lieutenants, 179

Economic liberalism of the first Antonines, 86

Economic system and condition of the masses, 87–8

Education, 116–38; primary, 118–22; popular education a failure, 122, 129; Greek influence, 123, 124, 125, 126, 127, 128, 268–9; schools of Hellenistic type in Rome, 123; political power of superior education, 123

Egypt, 71, 271; grain supplied Rome, 28, 196; imperial revenues, 81; religious cults, 145, 146; Far East caravan ports, 189

Elephants, 129, 235

Elis, a fable of the people of, 134

Eloquence, 268; a threat to government, 124; emptied of all real content, 125; three types, 130–31; condemnation of eloquence, 130; prizes at the *Agon Capitolinus*, 268

Encolpius, 282

Ennius, 127; *Andromache*, 247

Epicureanism, 145

Epirota, Q. Caecilius, 127

Epitaphs and obituary inscriptions, 70, 84, 85, 104, 117, 125, 304

Equestrian Order (*Equites*), amount of fortune necessary, 66, 79, 81, 86, 254; symbol, a gold ring, 73; place in imperial cabinet, 77; etiquette of a 'client', 192; seats at the Circus Maximus, 236

Esquiline, fifth region of Rome, 24; gardens of Maecenas, 39

Esquiline Hill, 23, 80, 256; warehouses, 197

Etruscans, experience in drainage of marshes, 52; clothing, 173; bronze razors, 180; human sacrifice, 229

Euphrates, 189; captives from, 116; amphitheatres, 269

Eurysaches, tomb of, 199

Eurythmius, 211

Eusebius, 155

Evadne, 101

Exegesis, 128

*Factiones*, 237, 242

*Familia gladiatoria*, 259

*Familiae serviles*, 83

Family instability through divorce, 109–15

Far East, riches to Rome, 9; pepper and spices, 17; routes to the, 86; silks, 197

Farnese Bull, 285

Farnese Palace. *See* Palazzo Farnese

*Fasti* of Ovid, 127

*Fasti Ostienses*, 244, 265, 266

Faustina the Elder, wife of Antoninus Pius, 114, 152

Favorinus of Arles, 126, 136

Felicitas, Christian martyr, 267

Feminism, 98, 103–9; confined to upper classes, 201

*Feriae*, 224, 225; *publicae*, 206; *privatae*, 226

*Ferialia*, 226

Festus, 228, 228–9

Fez, 53

Fezzan, ivory, 197

Ficulea, 22

Fidenae, 22

Fire, danger from, 38, 44, 45; Juvenal, 37; precautions against, 51; fire of A.D. 64, 30, 57, 153, 235, 256; A.D. 80, 146; A.D. 104, 278; A.D. 191, 310; in the reign of Antoninus Pius, 30

Fishing contest, 228

Fishponds, market, 17; Nero's, 256

Flamen Dialis, 93

Flamines, the, 62

Flamininus, L. Quinctius, 134

Flaminius Nepos, 234

Flamma, the gladiator, 265

Flavia Domitilla, aunt, 154, 155

Flavia Domitilla, niece, 155

Flavian Amphitheatre. *See* the Colosseum

Flavian period, 19, 63, 75, 83, 98, 124, 146, 154, 186, 236

Flavius Clemens, 154, 155

Flavius Sabinus, 154

Flora, games in honour of (Floralia), 225, 229, 253; statue, 285

Food supply, organization of, 199, 223 *See also* Annona

Foot races, 225, 268

Footwear, 171, 174

Foreigners in Rome, 66, 271 *See also* Peregrini

*Forma Urbis Romae*, 309

Fortifications dismantled by Augustus, 24

Fortunata, wife of Petronius' Trimalchio, 106, 185

Fortunes, 79, 81

Forum, Roman, 49, 51, 53, 58, 125, 170, 215, 223; *fora* enumerated in *Regionaries*, 311

Forum of Augustus, 13

*Forum Boarium*, 309

Forum of Caesar (*Forum Iulium*), 49, 53, 125

*Forum Holitorium*, 309

Forum of Ostia, 194–5

Forum of Peace (Vespasian), 215, 310; survey register of the Urbs, 34

Forum of Trajan, 13, 14, 18, 19, 125

Frank, Tenney, on the emancipated population of Rome, 74

Fregenae, 22

Frejus, in the Provençal plain, 71

Friedländer, L., 241; documentation on Roman life, 307–8

Frontinus, 50, 275

Fronto, 223, 233

Frusino, estates at, 56

*Fufia Caninia*, 83, 320, n. 38

Funeral college, Lanuvium, 70, 151, 299
  See also Colleges
Funeral processions, 62
Furniture, 44–7, 171, 217, 304
Fuscus, charioteer, 242

Gabii, 22
Gaetulians, 235
Gaius, jurist, 97; on manumission of slaves, 83; on divorce, 114
Galba, 231
Galen, 287
Galerius Tracalus, 209
Gallia Narbonensis, 69, 268
Gallinaria, forest of, 60
Gallitta, tried on charge of adultery, 210
Gambling, 242–3, 273–4
Games, 62, 223–43; attempt to acclimatize Greek games in Rome, 267–8, 274–5; in baths, 283–4
  See also Ludi
Garrison, Rome, 29, 79, 316, n. 31
Gauckler, Paul, 146
Gaul, defence against Germanic-hordes, 24, 25; senators from, 69; wool, 196; Caesar, the conqueror, 225; theatres, 245, 270; pork from, 296
Gismondi, I., reconstruction of Casa dei Dipinti, 42
Gladiatorial combats (hoplomachia), 208, 229, 253–5, 258, 262, 269, 270, 274; restrictions on, 254; gladiatorial troupes, 259, 269; training schools, 259
  See also Munera
Gladiators, 260–7
Glass, trinkets, 61; from Phoenicia, 197; none for windows, 47
Gnomon, 164, 166, 167
Golden House. See Domus Aurea
Gracchi, the, 118
Grain, distribution of free, 27, 28, 29, 79
  See also Annona
Grammar of Palaemon, 105
Grammarian, routine teaching, 122–30, 132; bilingual, 124
Granicus, battle of, 272
Greece, influence on Roman education, 123, 124, 125, 126, 127, 128, 267–8;
  on Roman culture, 125; Greek revolution, 130; influence on religion, 145–6; divisions of day and year, 162–3; clothing, 173; marble, 196; influence of the Hellenic theatre, 245–6
Greek, use of, in the Christian liturgy and writings, 126
Guilds, 191; banquets, 299–300

Hadad and Atargatis, temple of, 146
Hadrian, 9, 75, 97, 104, 144, 152, 177, 197, 243; erection of commercial city of Ostia, 9; command of army against the Parthians, 16; burial of Trajan's ashes in the Column, 16; remission of taxes, 18; insulae of Ostia, 42; Roman traffic decree, 62; titles of nobility, 66; born in Spanish Italica, 69; restrictions on abuse of slaves, 70, 269; cabinet, 77; Far East, 85–6; inheritance of a son's estate by his mother, 89; murder of a son by his father, 90, 91; affection for his wife, Sabina, 98, 116; schools, 121; jurisprudence, 124; Greek epigrams, 126; renaissance of Attic art, 127; cult of Antinoüs, 151; Christianity, 155; bearded, 183; generosity, 202; public readings, 217; Life of Hadrian, 281; conduct of the baths, 281–2, 285
Hadrumetum (Tunis), 69
Haghrab, 54
Hairdressing, 176–7; women, 186–7
Hammamet, Gulf of, 196
Hannibal, invasion of, 23, 35, 136
Heating, 48–9
Heliopolis, 235
Heraclea. See Table of Heraclea
Herculaneum, ruins of, archaeological evidence, 9, 306, 312; country houses, 34; baths, 47; cooking arrangements, 49; sanitation, 51–2; bedrooms, 184; absence of women in paintings, 202
Hercules, 221, 262; Death of Hercules, 270; statue of, 285
Hermagoras, the rhetorician, 130
Hermes, 236

Hermes Psychopompos, 263
Hermogenes, of Tarsus, 216
Herodes Atticus, 121
Heuzey, Léon, on the Roman style of
    dress, 173
Hills of Rome, 23, 311
    See also each by name
Hippo, 125
Hippo-Diarrhytus, 196
Hippodrome of Constantinople, 235
Historia Augusta, 29, 98, 281, 284, 304
Holidays, 224, 225, 226, 227
Homer, 105, 126, 148, 149
Honestiores, a class of the citizen body,
    65–6; senators and knights, 66
    See also Senatorial, Equestrian Order
Honorius, 245, 270, 310
Hoplomachia. See Gladiatorial combats
Horace, 112, 170, 215, 221; Epistles, 127,
    177
Horologium, 'counter of hours', sundial
    or water-clock, 162, 163, 164; horolo-
    gium ex aqua, water-clock (clepsydra),
    164, 165, 166
Horoscopes, 149, 197
Horrea, 197
Hortensius, the orator, 110, 111, 239
Hour, variations in the Roman, 162–3,
    166–7, 168, 204–5
House of Livia, 34; of Gamala, Ostia, 34
Household objects, 169–70, 290–91, 292,
    305–6
Houses, 33–63; release of land for
    dwelling purposes, 24; modern aspects,
    34–42; archaic aspects, 42–64
Human sacrifice, 229–30, 254
Humiliores, 65
Hylas, pantomime-actor, 249
Hypocausis, 48, 53, 279, 280

Iberian Peninsula, 197
Ibn Khaldun, Berber sociologist, 20
Icarus, 221
Ides, the, 161, 212, 227
Incitatus, charioteer, 242
Income, 79–80, 81, 86, 87
India, riches to Rome, 197
Indus River, 189

Infant prodigies, 125
Infants, abandonment of, 54, 90
Ingenui, 65, 69, 72
Inheritance laws, 89
Insula of Felicula, 30, 31, 36, 40
Insulae, apartment houses, 57, 59, 305;
    enumerated in Regionaries, 29, 30, 34,
    35, 40, 311; confusion in interpreta-
    tion of the Latin words, 30; com-
    parison with the domus, 34–5; height,
    35; description, 40–41; Ostia, 42;
    heating, 49; Roman ground plans,
    42; sub-letting, 43–4, 56, 184; sanita-
    tion, 52–3
    See also Building regulations; Build-
    ings
Io, 148
Iphicrates, 135
Iphigenia, 133
Iphigenia in Tauris, Euripides, 251
Iran, 145
Isidorus, C. Caelius, 83
Isis, cult of, 145, 147; Temple of, 146,
    148
Itys, 251
Iulius Cerialis, 288
Iulius Tiro, 210
Ius civile, 68
Ius gentium, 68
Ius Latii, 73
Ius naturale, 68
Ius trium liberorum, 89, 202

Janiculum, 39, 146
Janus, Temple of, 24
Jason, 250
Javolenus Priscus, 219
Jerusalem, Temple of, destroyed, 153
Jews, 140; colony in Rome, 153; Tibe-
    rius' shipment of 4,000 Jews to
    Sardinia, 153; victory of Titus, 236
Josephus, record of grain, 28–9; first
    production of Cinyras and Myrrha, 250
Juba II, Mauretania, 129
Julia, wife of Pompey, 110
Julian family extinct on death of Nero,
    67
Julius Canus, the Stoic, 275

Julius Frontinus, 141

Junius Mauricus, 268

Juno, 139; Temple of Juno, 272

Jupiter, 134, 148, 233; Temple of Jupiter, 80, 140, 179, 272; games, 229

Jurisprudence, 124

Justice and politics, 205–214

Justinian, 311

Juvenal, *Satires*, 138, 304; fire in Rome, 37, 44–5; collapse of houses, 43–4; indolence of great ladies, 46; water-carriers, the scum of the slaves, 50; injury from missiles from windows, 55; muddy streets of Rome, 59; night-time perils, 60; traffic jams, 61; night traffic, 62; on provincial immigrants, 68, 147; born at Aquinum, 68; treatment of slaves, 68, 274; degradation of paying court to slaves, 77; an adequate income, 79; a lawyer's standing judged by his slave retinue, 82; himself an ex-officer of limited means, 86; on learned women, 105, 106; women as gluttons, 107; adultery, 107–8; to the husband of a wealthy wife, 112; divorce, 113–14; enthusiasm for Greek, 125; on would-be orators, 136; religion, 139, 140, 151; scepticism, 139; aversion for the Jews, 140, 153; on exotic cults, 147, 148, 149; Christianity in Rome, 152; hair-dressers and barbers, 176, 179; ladies' hairdressing, 186, 187; etiquette of the 'client', 193; on the renting of private *auditoria*, 218; bread and circuses, 223; at the circus, 241–2; gambling, 243, 273; baths, 280–81, 282; women athletes, 284; *mens sana in corpore sano*, 286; self-indulgence, 294; gourmands, 296; idea of a pleasing dinner, 298; sordid side of Roman life, 300; commentary by Friedländer, 308

Kashgar (Issidon Scythica), 189

Knights, 66

*See also* Equestrian Order

Labourers, 195, 198, 199–200; hours of labour and recreation, 204–5

Labour, forced, at the mines, 65, 270

Lady of Salvation, 152

*See also* Cybele

Laenas, M. Popilius, 164

Lanuvium, funeral college, 70, 151, 299

Laocoön group, 286

Larcius Licinus, retinue of claqueurs, 209

Larcius Macedo, assassinated by household slaves, 72, 117

Latin language and literature, 69; superseded by Greek under grammarians and rhetoricians, 123, 124, 125, 126–7; adopted by Christian Church toward middle of third century, 126; training of orators, 130; trained in an artificial literature, 132; decay of Latin letters, 137; prizes for Latin poetry, 268; literature as a source of information, 306, 312

*Latini Iuniani*, 73

Latinus, pantomimist, 253

Latrines, 49, 52–4

Laurentine forest, 296

Laurentine villa of Pliny the Younger, 68, 169

Laureolus. *See* Catullus

Lavinium, 22

*Lectus*, 45, 289; beds made of gleaming exotic woods, 45; single beds, 45; a double bed, 45, 184

*Leges Iuliae*, on adultery, 108; on divorce, 111; on dowry, 111, 113

Legionaries, power to proclaim emperors, 67

Leisure, employment of, 227–34

Leonidas, 132

Leptis Magna (Tripoli), 69

Leuconian flocks, 171

*Lex Cornelia*, against gambling, 274

*Lex Petronia*, forbidding a master to deliver his slaves to the beasts without a judgement, 70

*Lex Publicia*, against gambling, 274

*Lex Titia*, against gambling, 274

Liberal arts, 128, 217

*Libertas Restituta*, 76

*Liberti*, 73, 77, 80

Libraries, public and municipal, 215; librarians as propagandists, 216; gathering places, 285; enumerated in the *Regionaries*, 311

Libraries built by Trajan. *See* Bibliothecae Ulpiae

Library of the Museum of Alexandria, 215

Library of Rome, State, 81

Licinius Sura, 39, 149

Lighting arrangements, 47, 170, 282

Ligurian marble, 63

Lipsius, Justus, 20, 247

Litigation, 207–8, 212

Livia, wife of Augustus, 186; granted title of 'Augusta', 98; house of on the Palatine, 203; *Ludi Palatini* in memory of Augustus, 225

Livius Andronicus, 126, 249

Livy, 216; incident of the ox which climbed to the third storey, 35–6; works published, 215

Loans, 80–81

Lot, Ferdinand, estimate of Roman population, 21, 30, 31

Lucan, 28; *Pharsalia*, 127

Lucian, 126, 137, 250

Lucifer, 288

Lucina, crypt of, 155

Lucius Caesar, 177

Lucius Verus, 177

Lucretius, *De Rerum Natura*, 54

Lucus Furrinae, 146

*Ludi*, 224–5, 227, 231, 232–3, 237–8, 244, 245, 255, 263; *Apollinares*, 224, 229, 233; *Ceriales*, 224, 229; *Florales*, 224; *Fortunae Reducis*, 225; *Martiales*, 225; *Megalenses*, 224 (Megalesian festival), 232, 245; *Palatini*, 225; *Plebei*, 224, 245; *Romani*, 224; *Victoriae Caesaris*, 225; *Victoriae Sullanae*, 225

*Ludus gladiatorius*, 259

*Ludus ingenuarum artium*, 217

*Ludus litterarius*, 119, 121, 126

Lupus, character by Martial, 87, 293

Lusitania, 121

*Lustrum*, 72

Lycia, 245

Lycomedes, daughters of, 250

Lydus, slave-tutor, 119

Lyons, amphitheatre, 267

Lysippus, the Apoxyomenus of, 231; group, Alexander and his generals, 272–3

*Macaris and Canace*, 251

Macedonia, 269

Macrinus, 102

Macrobius, 187, 291

Maecenas, 39, 218

Maenads of Priapus, 147

Madaura, 122, 125

*Magister*, head of each of fourteen regions of Rome, 26; serving at the sanctuary of a god, 70; teacher in a school, 120, 126; trainer in a gladiatorial *ludus*, 238; *magister cenae*, president of a banquet, 299

Mainz, dyes from, 187

Mâle, Émile, 154

*Manes*, 70, 139, 255

Manumission, various methods, 73; restrictions regarding testamentary manumission, 73, 83; manumission of a slave concubine and her children, 116–17; *toga praetexta*, a symbol of manumission, 133

Marcellus, 178, 179; theatre of Marcellus, 244, 257, 270

Marcia, wife of Cato of Utica, 96, 110

Marciana, sister of Trajan, 186

Marcus Aurelius, wealth given into public treasury, 18; decrees on night traffic extended, 62; semi-victories, 75; inheritance by children from their mother, 89; concubinage, 116; *Meditations*, 126; stoicism, 144, 269; lucubration, 170; wisdom and goodness as an emperor, 212; deduction in number of holidays, 226; personal indifference to gambling, 243; effort to humanize gladiatorial combat, 269–70

Marianus, 113

Marius, 123

Marius Priscus, 213, 214

Market of Trajan, 14, 17, 40, 47, 198; excavations, 34

Marriage, 89–115; three types: *confarreatio, coemptio, usus*, 94; the ceremony, 94–5; *cum manu*, 97–109; *sine manu*, 97, 98, 110, 112
*See also* Betrothal

Mars, 109, 152; sacrifice of the race-horse, 228

Mars Ultor, temple of, 225

Marsyas, enclosure of, 208

Martial, *Epigrams*, 9; home in an *insula* on the Quirinal, 37, 39, 317, n. 21; Saturnalian gifts, 47, 82; lack of household water, 49–50; muddy streets, 59; Bilbilis, home in Aragon, 68, 170; flogging of slaves, 71; estimate of size of a family, 78; epigram on one man's many houses, 80; fortune-hunting mortgagers, 80, 81; lost confidence in the value of work, 87; wastrel sons, 92; gallery of accomplished women, 101, 104–5; adultery, 107, 108, 117; comment on marriage to a wealthy woman, 113, 184; on divorce and re-marriage, 114; ridicule of Greek enthusiasm, 125; Christianity, 152–3; insomnia and night traffic, 169; a visit to Pliny, 171; hour of rising, 170; the ex-barber who became a wealthy landowner, 176; opinion regarding hairdressing, 176–8; on the perfumes used by a man, 178; on shaving, 180, 183; epitaph to a barber, 181; woman's hairdressing, 187; hours of labour, 205; the judicial world, 206, 207; publication of the *Epigrams*, 215; expenditures by consuls and praetors, 233; gambling, 242; use of condemned criminals in plays ending in their deaths, 253; tame animal acts, 260; on the liberation of best of the duellists, 265; Greek games, 268; porticos and their works of art, 273; gambling allowed during the Saturnalia, 274; chess, 275; monuments and buildings, 279; hour for bathing, 281; mixed bathing, 281;

games at the bath, 283; gift of a cloak, 283; three phases of the hygienic bath, 284; hour of dinner, 288; on practice of grading quality of food to standing of guest, 293; unpleasant manners, 295; on the excellence of food, 296; a dinner he served, 297; *Epigrams* show a sordid and depraved side of Roman life, 300; source of information, 304–5

Marulla, 116

Mathematics, 124, 129

Matidia, niece of Trajan, 186

Matron, Roman, 98–104

Matronalia, the, 225

Mauretania, 66, 129, 197

Maximus, Martial's epigram against a certain, 80

Maximus, Q. Sulpicius, infant prodigy, 126

Meals, 287–300

Medea, 250

*Medici*, doctors, 201; veterinary surgeons, 238

Menander, 126

Menus, 290–95

Merchant ships, outfitting of, 73, 202

Meroe, 148

Messalina, 186, 187

Messalla, M. Valerius, 164

Metaphysics, taboo in the curriculum, 125

Meton, sundial of, 162

Metrovian Gate, 25

Mevia, 106

Middle class, condition of, 78, 79, 86, 87

Miltiades, 135

Mimes, 252–3, 269

Minerva, 139; festival of Quinquatrus, 120, 225; Temple of Minerva, 146

Minturnae, 70

Minucius, Portico of, 202, 223

Misenum, fleet of, 257

Mithra, cult of, 145, 146, 152

Mithridates, 173

Modena, 179

Molière, 105; *Bourgeois Gentilhomme*, 131

Mollicius, M. Aurelius, 242

Montanus, 296

Montecitorio, obelisk of, 165
Monte dei Cenci, 244
Monte Giordano, 268
Months, naming of the, 161
Mucia, wife of Pompey, 110
*Mucius Scaevola*, 269
*Municipia*, 174, 252, 259, 266
*Munera*, gladiatorial combats decreed for an emperor, 227, 229; a method of directing mass emotion, 231; human sacrifice, 253; restrictions on number, 254; contractors of gladiator troupes, 259; dawn to dusk, 260; *venationes*, 260, 261; numbers of animals slaughtered, 261; description, 262–5; a means of revenge and murder, 266; *munera sine missione*, combats from which none escaped alive, 266; the morning massacre, 266; opposition, 267; efforts to humanize, 269
Museo Nazionale delle Terme, 195, 278
Museum of Alexandria, 124, 215
Music, 128, 268
Musonius Rufus, 90, 98, 126
Mustius, Pliny's architect, 141
Mysticism, Oriental. *See* Religion
Mythology, taught by the grammarian, 128

Naples, 269
Narbonne, 195
Narcissus, slave of Caesar, 76
Nasica, P. Cornelius Scipio, 164
*Natalium restitutio*, in the manumission of slaves, 73
*Naumachia*, 19, 223, 256, 259, 260, 265
Naumachia Vaticana, 257, 259
Neo-Pythagoreanism, 145
Nero, 9, 304; attempt at re-planning city, 57; Julian family extinct at his death, 67, 142; imperial claim by virtue of dynasty's divinity, 67; on treatment of slaves, 70; inducement to capital for building purposes, 73; treatment of Seneca's wife, 99, 101; goddess Atargatis, 146; Christianity and Christian martyrs, 153, 154; hairdressing, 177; shaving, 179; consecration of first beard, 179; silk caravans, 188; rebuilding of the circus, 235–6; generosity at the charioteers' banquet, 242; public readings, 245; trap for Britannicus, 247; banishment of actors, 248; himself an actor, 251; gladiatorial combat of opposing categories, 263; Neronia, 268, 280; public baths, 278; length of dinners, 288
Neronia, Nero's revival of Greek games 268, 280
Nerva, 140; congestion of Forum, 20; adoption and succession of Trajan, 68, 104; survivors of senatorial families, 74; successor of Domitian 76; proclaimed divine by his son Trajan, 142
Niceros, perfumes of, 178, 184
Nigidius Figulus, 145
Nigrina, 101
Nile, statue of, 146; papyri from, 197
Nîmes (Nemausus), 69
*Niobe*, 250
Non-citizen. *See Peregrini*
Nonianus, 217
*Notaria*, 201; *Notarius*, 103
*Notitia*. *See Regionaries*
Nubia, hippopotami of, 261
Numa, palace of, 228
Numidia, 129; exploitation by Romans, 194; marble, 196–7

Obelisks, Temple of Minerva, and the Pantheon, 146; enumerated in *Regionaries*, 311; of Antinoüs, 25; of Montecitorio, 165; of Rameses II, 235
*Obsequium*, 72, 116, 191
Occupations, 191–222
Octavia, sister of Augustus, 129, 186, 272; Portico of Octavia, 272
Octavius, 235
  *See also* Augustus
'October Horse', sacrifice of the, 228
Odeum, the, 268
Oedipus, 249; *Oedipus Coloneus*, 251
*Officiales*, 206
Oil, storehouses, 17; from Picenum, 296

Olympians, the Roman pantheon's likeness to the Greek, 138

Olympic games, 280

Oratory in popular education, 122, 127–8, 129, 130–31, 132

Oratory of Saint Bernard, 278

*Ordines*, 66

Ormisda, Persian ambassador, 18

*Ornamenta*, 185–90

*Ornatores, ornatrices*, 84, 187–8, 201

Ostia, 133; recent excavations, 10, 34, 305, 311; sea water to the Roman market fishponds, 17; municipal individuality, 22; docks, 34; House of Gamala, 34; *tabernae*, 38; likeness of buildings to modern ones, 40; an inn surrounded by green trees, 41; *insulae*, 42; Casa dei Dipinti, 47; heating arrangement of houses, 49; lack of running household water, 51; sanitation, 51, 52; public latrines, 53; Hellenistic influence on religion, 146; Forum of Ostia, 194; port of Rome, 194, 195, 196; warehouses, 197; *Fasti Ostienses*, 33, 265

Ovid, *Fasti*, 128; suggestions on women's make-up, 188, 189; the circus, 239

Oxyrhynchus papyri, 211


Pacuvius, 245; *Armorum Iudicium*, 246

Paestan fields, 272

'Palace of Roman Water', 286

Palaemon, *Grammar*, 105

Palaestra, 10, 106, 277, 280, 282, 284

Palatine Hill, reserved for emperor, 23; excavations, 34, 309; House of Livia, 34, 203; decorated *forica*, 53; imperial slaves, 83; hearings in the emperor's basilica, 208; sanctuary of Cybele, 225; adjoined by the Circus Maximus, 234, 236

Palazzo Barberini, 256; Caetani, 234; Capitolino, 256; Colonna, 23; Farnese, 18, 38, 238, 285; Sermoneta, 244; Taverna, 268; Venezia, 256

Pallas, imperial slave, 76

Palmyra, 146

Pamphylia, 245

Pandataria, island of, a place of banishment for condemned Christians, 154

Panniculus, pantomime-actor, 253

Pantagathus, Martial's epitaph to his barber, 181

Pantheon, the building, 36, 146; Roman pantheon, the cult, 137

Pantomime-actors, *See* Mimes

Pantomime plays, 248, 249, 250

Paribeni, Robert, Column of Trajan, 19; Roman tragedy, 251

Parilia, the, 225

Paris, markets, 19; population density, 21; area, 23; transport, 33; *maisons*, 35; Opera, 246

Paris, pantomime-actor, 248, 250

Parrhasius, 135

Parthenius, Greek chamberlain to Domitian, 76, 175

Parthians, Roman campaign against, 9, 16, 98, 188

Pasiphae, 251

Pasiteles, 272

Passennus Paulus, elegies of, 221

*Pastillarii*, 199

*Pater familias*, authority of the, 89–90

Paternus, cousin of Pliny, 71

*Patres conscripti*, 76, 123, 143

*Patria potestas*, 89–90, 91, 93

*Patronus*, 72, 116–17, 191

Paulina, wife of Seneca, 99

Paulus, praetorian prefect, 50

Paxaea, wife of Pomponius Labeo, 99

*Pax Romana*, 27

*Peregrini*, 29, 65, 68, 76, 79, 258

Pergamum, 79, 123

Peristyle, 35

Perpetua, Christian martyr, 267

Perseus, 164

Persia, silk caravans, 188–9

Persicus, 298

Persius, 151, 170

Petosiris, 148

Petronius, 275; satirical romance, 9; the *insula*, 56; *Satyricon*, 56; ridicule of the schoolroom's pompous phrases, 136; Roman exploitation of conquered territory, 194; skill of Roman chef,

295–6; pictures sordid side of Roman life, 300, 304; Friedländer's commentary, 308
*See also* Trimalchio

Pharsalus, eve of, 289

Phidias, 134; statue of Venus, 273

Philaenis, 283

Philhellenes, 267

Philippus, Q. Marcius, 164

Philomela, 251

Philomusus, Martial's wastrel, 92, 273

Philosophy, banished from Rome, 124, 145; publication in Greek of the philosophers, 126; treatment during the Middle Ages, 128
*See also* Stoicism

Phoenicia, glass from, 197

Phrygian cult, 147

Phrygian marbles, 45

Physics, taboo in the curriculum, 125

Piazza Colonna, 34; del Cinquecento, 22; del Popolo, 235; di Grotta Pinta, 244; Navona, 268; San Pietro, 234

Picenum, oil from, 296

Pincian Hill, 25, 33, 39

Piso, consul, 275

Pistoclerus, 119

Plantin, 87

Plautus, 105, 245; *Menaechmi*, 251

Plebs, the, Sulla's release of dwelling space for, 24; public assistance, 27; Augustus' gift of 60 *denarii* each, 29; *plebeii* (the *humiliores*), 65; need for the dole and spectacles, 78, 223, 231; prosperity after the campaigns of Trajan, 85; rise of great magnates from the ranks, 87; funeral colleges, 151; the *munus*, 255; *lusiones*, 269; noon *prandium*, 287; guild banquets, 299

Pliny the Elder (the Naturalist), *vici* in the lustrum of A.D. 73, 26; flowered balconies, 41; admiration of Roman houses and streets, 57; quoted on *familiae serviles*, 83; the sundial of Catana, and the first *horologium* in Rome, 164; *profecto enim vita vigilia est*, 170; lucubration, 170, 205; on shaving, 182; hours spent in writing,

205; Circus Maximus, 236; exasperation at Caesar's trick theatre, 255; amusement at trained animals, 260; sculpture in the Portico of Octavia, 272; number of public baths, 277; three phases of hygienic bath, 284; daily meals, 287, 288; on gluttony and selfishness in a host, 294

Pliny the Younger, 47, 117; *Letters*, 10; room furnishings, 46; Cisalpine birthplace, 68; Laurentine villa, 68, 169; estates in Tuscany, 68; treatment of slaves, 72; friendship with his slaves, 71; amount of his estate, 81, 83; manumission of slaves, 83; liberalism with regard to friend's children, 91–2; encumbrance of betrothals, 93; letter regarding the elder Arria, 99; love of wife and husband, 101; his wife, Calpurnia, 103, 105, 184; division of his wealth, 104; education and good taste in women, 105; letter regarding a centurion in Trajan's army, 107–8; every parent his child's teacher, 118; 'piety' and scepticism, 139–40; the divinity of a Caesar, 143; superstition, 148; Christianity, 153; lucubration, 170; independence of each of the married pair in their home, 184; *clepsydrae*, 207; feeling against the 'low rout of claqueurs', 209; speeches before the *centumviri*, 209; on the Senate transformed into a High Court, 213, 214; public readings, 217, 221; *Panegyric*, 231, 236; appearance of the emperor at the games, 231; Circus Maximus, 236; deplores craze for circus, 243; opinion on human sacrifice at the combats, 266; feeling against Greek games, 269–70; time for dinner, 288; gluttony and selfishness in a host, 293–4; disgust at dinner entertainments, 295; charming and frugal meals, 296–7, 300; *Letters* a source of information on Roman life, 304

Plotina, wife of Trajan, 98, 114

Plotius Gallus, 123

Plutarch, 180

Plutocracy, and living standards, 78–88
Policing arrangements, 60
Politics, political power of good education, 123; taboo as a course of public instruction, 125; justice and politics, 205–14; discussion proscribed, 207; excitement of races a substitute for politics, 243; permitted in a pantomime, 252–4
Pollentia, goddess of might, 235
Polydoxus, race-horse, 240
Polytheism, 144, 148
*Pomerium*, Trajan's burial within the boundaries, 16; burial of ordinary mortals forbidden, 16; not the definite limits of Imperial Rome, 21, 22, 23; the sacred orbit, 22; religious character, 23; overflow of population, 24; Aurelian Wall, 25
*Pompa Circensis*, 236
Pompeia, wife of Caesar, 110
Pompeii, archaeological evidence, 9, 34, 305, 306, 312; country houses, 34; frescoes, 42; area of *domus*, 42; baths, 47; heating arrangements, 49; bakeries, 49; sanitation, 52, 53; street paving, 59; washroom, 174; absence of women in the paintings, 201–2; wall mottoes, 298
Pompeius Musclosus, 241
Pompeius Saturninus, wife of, 105
Pompey, feeding of 486,000 people in 57 B.C., 28; residence in the Carinae, 39; several wives, 110; Circus Maximus, 235; plethora of combats, 254; Greek games, 268
Pomponia Graecina, suspected of being a Christian, 154
Pomponius Graecinus, 155
Pomponius Labeo, 99
*Pone muros*. See *Pomerium*
Ponte Rotto, 51
Pontia, island of, internment of Christians, 155
Pontifex Maximus, 93, 228
Pontine marshes, 60
Pontius Epaphroditus, charioteer, 241
Popilius Laenas, 134
Population of Rome, 19–32, 78–9;

growth, 26–32; racial composition, 304
*See also* Census
Porta Capena, first region of Rome, 25
Portico of the Argonauts, 272; of Europa, 272; of a Hundred Pillars, 272–3; of Minucius, 223; of Octavia, 272; of Pompey, 272
Portrayal of character, in rhetoric, 131
Portus, port of Rome, 196–7
*Praefectus praetorio*, 208; *urbi*, 66, 70, 208, 258, 275; *vigilum*, 60, 71
*Praeficae*, 62
Praeneste, 23, 43
Praenestine Gate, 25, 260
*Praetor hastarius*, 208; *peregrinus*, 208; *urbanus*, 208
Praetorian Guard, 142, 261
Praxiteles, statues of Cupid and Venus, 273
Precincts of Rome, 20–26
*See also* Regions
Priapus, 147
Priesthood, highest posts held by Senatorial Order, 66
Princeps, the, First of the Senate and the People, incarnation of gods, guardian of the auspices, 66; descent to earth, 143
Priscilla, catacomb of, 155
Prisoners of war, 75
Probate case, 211
*Procne and Tereus*, 251
Proculeia, Martial's anecdote about, 232
*Procuratores*, 77, 260; salary, 86
Professions, liberal, 205–6
Prometheus, 135, 253
Proscriptions of 43 B.C., 134
Provincials, effect of immigration on the social plane, 68–9, 146
Ptolemy Physkon, 123
Public assistance. *See Congiaria;* Doles; *Sportulae;* Annona
Public funds, subsidy for festivals of the gods, 138
Publilia, wife of Cicero, 111
Publilius Syrus, 253
Publishers, the rise of, 214–15
*Pulvinar*, 230, 232, 235, 236, 258, 262

Punic War, First, 163
Punishment, graded to type of citizen, 65–6; in the schoolroom, 120, 122
Puteal of Curtius, 208
Puteal Libonis, 207–8
Pydna, battle of, 164
Pylades I, pantomime-actor, 232, 249–50
Pylades II, 251
Pyrrhus, Roman wars against, 163

Quadratus, Apologia, 155
Quartan Fever, an oration by Favorinus of Arles in honour of, 136
Quinquatrus, festival in honour of Minerva, 120, 225
Quintilian on the qualifications of a child's nurse, 114; the tutor, 114; on schoolroom punishment, 120; teaching the alphabet, 121; improvement in teachers, 121; most famous of professors, subsidized by the imperial regime, 124; weakening of Hellenic influence, 125; Institutio Oratoria, 131, 215; feeling towards elaborate hairdressing, 177; crowding of law courts, 209; on the pantomime-actor, 249
Quirinal Hill, 17, 18, 19; Martial's quarters, 37, 39, 68; Vespasian, 39; thermae of Constantine, 278

Races. See Chariot races; Foot races
Racilia, wife of Cincinnatus, 173
Racine, Athalie, 246
Rameses II, obelisk of, 235
Reading, the teaching of, 119, 127–8
See also Recitationes
Recitationes, 216–22; the curse of literature, 216, 221–2; building of the Athenaeum in Rome, 217
Red Sea, the route from the Far East, 189
Refugees from Asia and Egypt, first professors of grammar and rhetoric, 123
Regia, the, residence of Julius Caesar, 39; sacrifice of the 'October Horse', 228

Regio Transtiberina. See Transtiberina
Regionaries, 310; record of vici, 27; population, 27, 28, 31–2; forica, 53–4; loca at the Circus Maximus, 236; at the amphitheatre, 258; source material, 310; used by Zacharias of Mytilene, 29, 311–12
    Notitia, begun A.D. 334, 27, 310–11; dwelling-houses, domus and insulae, 29, 30, 31, 32, 40; vagaries of the copyist, 29
    Curiosum, A.D. 357, 29–30, 310
Regions (administrative) of the Urbs, 310; position and extent, 24–5, 26; census of the vici, 26–7; other streets, 58; described in Regionaries, 311
Regulus, advocate, 92, 149
Relationship, agnatio and cognatio, 89
Religion, of slaves, 70; decay of traditional religion, 137–44; Oriental mysticism, 137, 144–53; festivals, 138, 227–30; respect for religious forms, but personal scepticism, 139–41; imperial divinity, 142, 143, 230; Greek influence, 144–6
Rentals of houses and apartments, 56
Republican Wall, 23, 39, 58
Research, Roman attitude towards disinterested, 129
Rex sacrorum, chariot of the, 62
Rhetores Latini, compelled to stop teaching, 124
Rhetoric, study of, 119, 122–5; use of Latin interdicted, 124; impractical rhetoric, 129–37; Greek rhetoric, 130; forced into a strait-jacket of six parts, 130; falsification of history, 132–3
Rhetorica ad Herennium, 123
Rhodes, 123
Ricci, Corrado, excavations, 13, 16
Roads, enumerated in Regionaries, 311
Robigalia, festival of the, 225
Romanus, Pliny's letter to his friend, 140
Roscius of Ameria, 60
Rostovtzeff, M., 10, 193
Royal Laws. See Twelve Tables
Ruga, Sp. Carvilius, 110
Rutilus, 71

Sabina, wife of Hadrian, 98, 114

Sabine country, 296

Sabratha, Tripoli, 196, 245

Saepta Iulia, 203, 204; in the Campus Martius, 272

Saint Augustine, 41, 125, 275

Saint Jerome, *Chronicle*, census of Rome, 28

Saint Monica, 41

Saint Paul, *Epistles*, greetings *in domo Caesaris*, 154

Saint Peter, statue on the Column of Trajan, 15, 17; 'Chair of St Peter', 46

Salarian Gate, 25

Salii, dance of the, 225

Sallust, married to Terentia, Cicero's divorced wife, 111; governor of the province of Africa, 129; *De Bello Iugurthino*, 129

*Saltus Burunitanus*, 78

Salvation, idea of, spread to religious foundations, 151, 156
See also *Collegium Salutare*

Salvius Iulianus, 97

Samnites, 260, 263

San Pietro, excavation of a cess trench, 52

Sardinia, shipment of 4,000 Jews by Tiberius to, 153; ship outfitters, 195

Saturn, conjunctions of, 148

Saturnalia, 225, 247, 274, gifts, 47, 82; 192; gambling allowed, 276

Scepticism of Juvenal and his contemporaries, 139

*Schola*, use of chairs, 46; meeting place of a guild or college, 46

Scholars and teachers supported by the State, 120

Scipio Aemilianus, 178

Scorpus, a charioteer, 241; on his death, 241

Scribonianus, revolt of, 100

Sculpture, Roman, use of brilliant colours, 16; renaissance of Attic art under Hadrian, 127

Scyros, 250

Secundus, book publisher, 215

Secundus, P. Pomponius, 245

Selius, 272

*Sella curulis*, 46
See also Curule

Selurus, the bandit, 266

Semitism, Stoic debt to, 145

Senatorial Order, armies mobilized against the democratic government of Rome, 28; one of the orders of the *honestiores*, 66; *vir clarissimus*, 66; headed by the emperor, 66; compels Nerva to adopt Trajan, 68; made up of Romans and provincials, 69, 80; senatorial families, 74; subserviency to 'slave' cabinet, 75; assassination of Domitian, 76; decree of imperial divinity, 152; heavy duties of a senator, 206, 212–13; seats at the circus, 235; arch consecrated by the Senate to Titus' victory, 236; votes won by spectacular scenes at the amphitheatre, and law passed disqualifying any magistrate so elected, 254; Senate participation in the Neronia, 268

*Senatus-consulta*, on the treatment of slaves, 71; confirming laws against gambling, 274

*Senatus consultum Orphitianum*, right of children to inherit from the mother, 89

*Senatus consultum Tertullianum*, admits a mother's right under certain conditions to inherit from her son, 89

Seneca, champion of human rights of slaves, 71; Nero's fatal command, 99; on divorce, 116; treatises included in the curriculum, 127; Roman 'time', 166–7; condemnation of his writings by Caligula, 221; *munera sine missione*, 266, 270; Campus Martius, 272; on the temptation of dives, 276; source of information on the court and nobility, 304

Seneca the Elder, teacher of rhetoric, 132; *suasoriae*, 132, 133, 136

Septicius Clarus, 297

Septimius Severus, recipients of the *congiarium*, 27; survey register of the Urbs, 34; Insula of Felicula, 36; cadastral survey, 42; born in Tripoli,

69; recasts law against adultery, 109; *thermae* of Antoninus, 278; restoration of *templum sacrae urbis*, 310

Serapis, 145

Seres, 188, 194

*Servi*, 69; conspirators against Domitian, 76; *servi atrienses*, indoor servants, 83
See also Slaves

Servian Walls, 35

Servius, commentator, 128

Servius Tullius, 22, 23

Seven Hills of Rome, 58

Sewers and sewage, 51–2
See also Cloacae

Sextia, wife of Aemilius Scaurus, 99

Shaving, a religious rite, 179

Ship outfitting, 73, 202

Shows and spectacles, 10, 223–70

Silk caravans from China, 188–9

Silverware, usual Saturnalian gift, 47, 192

Slaves, considered in estimating population of Rome, 29, 79; water-carriers, 50–51; night attendants, 59; *res mancipi*, 65; humanity displayed towards slaves, 69; slavery and manumission, 69–74; epitaphs, 70, 84, 85; replenishment through the wars, 75, 116; Roman reverses and invasions, and drying up of slave sources, 75; ineligible for grain distribution, 79; suffix-*por* added to owner's name, designation of a slave, 83; growth in number per household, 82–3; testamentary manumission, 83; categories of slaves by name of speciality, 84; concubinage, 116–17; tutors, guardians, and servants of children, 119; tale of a slave boy and the *toga praetexta*, 133; *collegium salutare*, 152; *cura corporis*, 180, 204; duties to the *patronus*, 192; place at the circus, 258; impressment into gladiatorial troupes forbidden, 269

Slums, 55

Social classes, 65–88

Social discipline, 63

Social values, confusion of, 74–8

Social War, 91 B.C., 27

*Solaria*, 165

Solstice, 168

Sosii, the, book publishers, 215

Spain, senators from, 69; oil exports to Rome, 196; pickles, 296

Spanish Italica, birthplace of Trajan and Hadrian, 69

Spes, goddess of hope, 70

Spice market, 16

*Spina*, 230, 234

*Sponsiones*, 242, 263; repressive legislation, 274

*Sportulae*, 191, 192, 243
See also Doles; *Congiaria*

Stadium, the, 223

*Stationes arcariorum Caesarianorum*, 17

Statius, *Silvae*, 9, 186; *Thebais*, 127, 221; a confession of faith in the value of personal religion, 151; Christianity, 152

Stephanus, participant in murder of Domitian, 76; baths of, 288

Stock exchange, 86, 198

Stoicism, influence on Roman law, 97; debt to Semitism, 145; divination, 150; Marcus Aurelius' effort to reduce importance of the *munus*, 269

*Stolata*, 140

Strabo, on the height of the houses of Tyre, 36

Streets and traffic, 57–64; fire hazard, 57; categories of, 58; Caesar's order regarding clean streets, 58; paving, 58–62; hucksters, and Domitian's edict, 59, 60; lighting, 60; dangers of night travel, 59, 60; Caesar's decree regarding night traffic, 61

Strigil, 284

*Suasoriae*, 133; Seneca the Elder, 132; artificiality, 133

Sub-letting, practice of, 55, 56, 184

Subura, the, 16, 39, 228

Suetonius, Caesar's order regarding census forms, 30; forfeits 'Ministry of the Pen' for his disrespect for Hadrian's wife, 99; *suasoriae*, 133; belief in dreams, 149; Christianity, 152–4; details of Augustus' caprices, 172; the morning rising of Vespasian,

Suetonius – *contd*
174; last hours of Domitian, 175;
fastidiousness of Julius Caesar, 176;
biographical character of histories as
source material, 304

Sulla, 256; release of portion of Campus Martius for dwelling purposes,
24; dark streets, 60; marries Valeria,
sister of Hortensius, 110, 239; clean
shaven, 179; pretensions to divinity,
225; Greek games, 268

Sulpicia, poems of, 101; wife of Calenus,
184

Sundial of Catana, captured in Sicily,
163; set up in Rome, 163

Sundial of Meton, 162

Sundials, 162–8; used in setting up the
water-clock, 164–5; obelisk of Montecitorio, *gnomon* of a giant dial, 165;
Trimalchio's fantastic idea of a tomb,
166; pocket dials (*solaria*), 165
*See also* Horologium; Clepsydra

*Synthesis*, 174, 289

Syria, legionaries, 9; haste of Syrians
to assume citizenship, 68; religious
influence, 145; Roman campaign
against, 164; glass from, 197; Syrtes,
the, 180; ivory from, 197


*Tabernae*, market booths, Trajan's market, 16; ground floor of humbler
*insulae*, 37, 56; description, 37;
entrance to upper floors, 38, 39;
single room used to house tenant's
family as well as his wares, 38;
crowds, 61; allotted by Caesar to
studies, 125; *horrea Galbae*, 197; type
of merchant, 197; barbershops, 176

Taboos for protection of *pomerium*, 23

Tacitus, fire of A.D. 64, 30, 57; on the
choice of emperors, 67; the tragedy
of Seneca's wife, 99; loss of practical
value of rhetoric, 129, 136; scepticism,
with respect for religious rites, 140;
praetor, consul, and proconsul, 140;
Jews, 140; *Germania*, 140; under
Trajan, liberty and harmonious rule,
144; superstitions, 149; Christianity,

152, 153; *Histories*, Christian martyrs,
154; *histrionalis favor*, 248

Tagaste, birthplace of Saint Augustine,
125

*Tali*, 274

Tarentum, 163

Tarpeian Rock, 139

Tarquin the Proud, 148

Taurus, C. Statilius, 256

Taxes, replenishment of imperial purse
from the maintenance of, 81–2;
immunity for primary school, 121

Teachers, State subsidy of, 120, 124;
refugee-teachers, 123; women, 201

Telesilla, 114

Telesphorus, Bishop, 155

Temple of Annona Augusta, 195;
Atargatis (Dea Syra) and Hadad,
145, 146; Athena, 135; Castor, 215;
Isis, 145, 146; Janus, 24; Jerusalem,
destroyed A.D. 70, 153; Jupiter (Jove),
80, 139, 179, 272; Juno, 272; Mars
Ultor, 225; Minerva, 146; Vesta, 80

*Templum sacrae urbis*, 22–3, 310

Terence, 105; works used in the schoolroom, 127; the theatre, 245, 251;
*Andria*, 251; *Hecyra*, 254

Terentia, wife of Cicero, 111

Tertullian, 252; absurdity of the Valentinians, 36; on human sacrifice in
gladiatorial combat, 229; the Christians, 299

Terpsichore, 250

Terra Mare, 180

*Testamento*, manumission by, 63

*Tesserae*, 202, 258, 274

Textual criticism, 128

Thalamus, Nero's barber, 182

Theatre of Balbus, 244; Marcellus,
244, 257, 270; Pompey, 244, 245

Theatres, 223, 243–54; expenses paid
by the State, 224, 244; description
of Roman theatres, 244–5; too big
for the play, 245, 246; degradation
of the Roman theatre, 251; Caesar's
double theatre changeable into an
arena, 255–6

Thédenat, Abbé, on *cloacae* and *insulae*, 52

Theodoric, the Ostrogoth, 245

*Thermae. See* Baths

Thermopylae, 132

Thersites, 136

Thespiae, 273

Thracian gladiators, 260, 263

Thrasea, son-in-law of Caecina Paetus, 100

Thyestes' feast, 101, 250

Tiber, the 33, 68, 146; canalized by Trajan, 19; Campus Martius, 24; *regio Transtiberina*, 24, 26; depository of city sewage, 51; dancing on the banks, festival of Anna Peranna, 138; temple to Atargatis excavated, 146

Tiberius, decrees regarding second-class citizenship, 73; accompanied to wars by his wife, 99; ebbing belief in imperial divinity, 143; banishes Egyptian cults, 147; measures against Jews, 153; decoration of his bedchamber, 170; clean shaven, 179; decree concerning literary works, 216; manipulation of petitions by mass emotion, 231; misanthropy, 233; riots over rival actors, 248; restrictions on giving a *munus*, 254

Tibur (Tivoli), 22, 257

Tiburtine farm, Juvenal's, 298

Tigellinus, death of, 231

Tigris, the, 116, 189

Timgad, 53

Tiridates, King of Armenia, 263

Titinius Capito, 218

Titles of nobility, 66

Titus, censor, 26, 57; imperial victory over the Jews, 236; completion of amphitheatre, 256; Colosseum inaugurated, 261; combats at Circus Maximus, 263; public baths, 277

Tivoli (Tibur), 22, 256

Toga, the, 172; description and variations, 173–4; essential in a client's attendance on his patron, 192; Augustus' decree for the wearing of the toga, 229; *toga praetexta*, 72, 133; *toga virilis*, 179

*Tonsores*, barbers, 84; hairdressers, 175–9, 201; perils of attending the wayside barber, 181; hours of labour, 204–5

Torlonia, Prince Giovanni, 197

Trade, extent and variety, 198–9
*See also* Corporations

Traffic congestion, 12, 61; decree concerning night traffic, 61–2

Tragedy, transformed to opera and to the ballet forms, 246, 251; born of Greek tragedy, 247; decline, 247

Trajan, 9, 32, 39, 50, 54, 56, 77, 79, 80, 91, 104, 140, 165, 186, 191, 243, 249, 269, 304; group of buildings, 14; equestrian statue in Forum, 14, 17; death, 15, 16; Trajan's inscription on the Column, 16; description of the group, 17; renovation of the Urbs, 19; restriction on height of buildings, 36; policy of the Urbs, 44; night traffic, 63; feeling with regard to imperial divinity, 67; loyalty of the Legion, 67; adopted by Nerva, 68; born in Spanish Italica, 68; inducement to set up bakeries, 73, 202; campaigns, 75, 85; cabinet recruited from freedmen, and slaves, 76; confiscates treasure of Decebalus, 82; simple tastes, 85; punishment of a father for treatment of his son, 91; Trajan's wife's loyalty, 98, 114; decree punishing adultery, 107–8; victories, 116, 188; generosity to education, 124; recommends Pliny to the College of Augurs, 141; proclaims divinity of his adopted father Nerva, 142; no special claims to personal divinity, 143–4; *Panegyric*, 144; hairdressing, 177; clean shaven, 179; Portus of Trajan, 197; tribunal at Centumcellae, 210; presides at Senate High Court in trial of Classicus, 213; interest in the Colosseum, 233; Circus Maximus, 236; caters to circus tastes of his subjects, 244; restrictions on actors, 251; Amphitheatre Castrense, 257; *Naumachia Vaticana*, 259; slaughter of animals, 261; release of surviving gladiators, 265; mimic combats, 269; *thermae* as memorial to Licinius Sura, 278; modesty of his court, 300

Trajan – *contd*
See also *Aqua Traiana;* Basilica Ulpia; Bibliothecae Ulpiae; Column of Trajan; Forum of Trajan; Market of Trajan
Transtiberina (Trastevere), fourteenth region of Rome, 24; street hawkers, 61
Transylvanian mines, 9
Trastevere (Transtiberina), 24
Trebula, cheeses of, 296
*Tribunicia potestas,* 29
Trimalchio, wealthy freedman, hero of Petronius' satirical romance, elaborate dining-room, 42; bed of solid silver, 45; guests who lost their way home, 60, 204; estimate of his estate, 81; vast number of slaves, 83-4; gluttony of his wife Fortunata, 106; superstitions, 149; dining-room clock, 166; instructions as to tomb and sundial, 166; golden pyx, 179; sleeping arrangements, 185; present of a *chiromaxium* to his favourite, 272; at the bath, 282, 283, 285; dinners, 288, 291, 295; table manners, 295
Tripoli (Leptis Magna), 69, 245; mosaic, 266
Tropes, 128
Tryphon, 216
*Tunica,* clothing, 94, 172
Tuscany, Pliny's estates in, 68; marbles of, 196
Tuscus, race-horse, 240
Twelve Tables, width of streets, 58; a mother's inability to inherit from her intestate son, 89; father's right of life and death over his children, 90; right to divorce a wife without appeal, 109-10; part of school curriculum, 126; on the conduct of civil suits, 206
Tyre, height of houses, 36

Ucalegon, Juvenal's, 45
Ulpian, on fires in Rome, 45; missiles dropped from chamber windows, 55
Ulysses, 128
Ummidia Quadratilla, 119

Urine, industrial use of, 54
*Usus. See* Marriage

Valentinians, 36, 37
Valeria, wife of Sulla, 110, 239
Valerianus, Q. Pollius, book publisher, 215
Vallis Murcia, site of Circus Maximus, 234
Varus, defeat of, 179
Vatican Hill, Circus Gai, 234
Vegetius, on literacy among new recruits, 122
Vehicles, regulations governing use of, within Urbs, 61-4, 304
Veii, 12
Velabrum, the, 23, 236
Velia, the, 256
*Venationes,* 261-2, 266, 269
Venus, 109, 152, 250
Vertumnus, statue of the god, 215
Vespasian, 39; censor, 26; licensed rights to sewage, 54; aggregate length of streets, 57; loyalty of the Legion, 67; exile of philosophers, 125; jest about his divinity as emperor, 143; Christianity, 154; early waking hours, 170, 174; congestion of the courts, 207; reduces number of holidays, 226; Flavian amphitheatre, 233, 256; an original *forma urbis Romae,* 310
Vestalia, festival of, 225
Vestals, the, 62, 94, 228
Vestini, cheese of, 296
*Vestis. See* Clothing
Vesuvius, eruption of A.D. 79, 9, 34
Via Appia, 58, 59, 309; Biberatica, 16, 34, 37, 47; dei Cappellari, 40; dei Cerchi, 34; dei Tribunali, 40; dell' Abbondanza, 276; delle Finanze, 23; del Mare, 244; Labicana, 58, 260; Lata, seventh region of Rome, 24; Latina, 58, 197; Nova, 58; Ostiensis, 58; Sacra, 58, 208, 228
Victor, race-horse, 240
*Vicus,* separate administration, 26; census, 26; enumerated in *Regionaries,* 27;

*insulae per vicus*, 39; congestion, and decree of Caesar, 61
Vicus Tuscus, 197, 215
Vienne in Gallia Narbonensis, 269
Villa Ludovisi, 38
Vinalia, festival of the, 225
Vipasca, imperial mines, 121, 281
Virgil, the *Aeneid*, 45, 129; poems of, 87, 105; in the schoolroom, 127; reminiscences of, 221
Virro, Juvenal's, 294
Vitalis, pantomime-actor, 252
Vitellius, interest in *factiones* of chariot races, 242; hour of dinner, 288
Vitruvius, on height of Roman houses, 36; law on thickness of walls, 42–3; description of water-clock, 165
*Vivarium*, 260
Volcanalia, festival of Vulcan, 225
Volsinii, 43
*Volumen*, 19; at the booksellers, 215; harmed by public readings, 221–2; chests for the protection of, 285.
Vulcanus, fish sacrifice to, 228

Waltzing, catalogue of corporations, 198, 199–200
Water-clock 164, 165, 166
    *See* Clepsydra; Horologium ex aqua

Water system, aqueducts, municipal channels and private conduits, 50; lack of household system, 44, 50
Weapons, of gladiators, 260, 262–3
Wells, 50
Wills, under Hadrian, women permitted to draft, 97
Windows, lack of glass, 47
Wine, storehouses, 17; wine from Italy, 196; used at *commissatio*, 293
Women, right to make wills under Hadrian, 98; guardianship, 97; standing during empire, 98–9; loyalty as confidantes of their husbands, 98–102; gallery of accomplished women, 101–3; feminism and demoralization, 103–9; and marriage, 183–5; clothing, 185; toilet of, 185–90; daytime hours, 191, 204; in professions and occupations, 200–203
    *See also* Betrothal; Marriage; Matron
Workmen's living quarters, 201
Writing, in the school curriculum, 119, 120, 121

Xerxes, 132

Zacharias of Mytilene, *Regionaries* used by, 29, 311

# FOR THE BEST IN PAPERBACKS, LOOK FOR THE 🐧

In every corner of the world, on every subject under the sun, Penguin represents quality and variety – the very best in publishing today.

For complete information about books available from Penguin – including Puffins, Penguin Classics and Arkana – and how to order them, write to us at the appropriate address below. Please note that for copyright reasons the selection of books varies from country to country.

**In the United Kingdom:** Please write to *Dept E.P., Penguin Books Ltd, Harmondsworth, Middlesex, UB7 0DA.*

If you have any difficulty in obtaining a title, please send your order with the correct money, plus ten per cent for postage and packaging, to *PO Box No 11, West Drayton, Middlesex*

**In the United States:** Please write to *Dept BA, Penguin, 299 Murray Hill Parkway, East Rutherford, New Jersey 07073*

**In Canada:** Please write to *Penguin Books Canada Ltd, 2801 John Street, Markham, Ontario L3R 1B4*

**In Australia:** Please write to the *Marketing Department, Penguin Books Australia Ltd, P.O. Box 257, Ringwood, Victoria 3134*

**In New Zealand:** Please write to the *Marketing Department, Penguin Books (NZ) Ltd, Private Bag, Takapuna, Auckland 9*

**In India:** Please write to *Penguin Overseas Ltd, 706 Eros Apartments, 56 Nehru Place, New Delhi, 110019*

**In the Netherlands:** Please write to *Penguin Books Netherlands B.V., Postbus 195, NL–1380AD Weesp*

**In West Germany:** Please write to *Penguin Books Ltd, Friedrichstrasse 10–12, D–6000 Frankfurt/Main 1*

**In Spain:** Please write to *Longman Penguin España, Calle San Nicolas 15, E–28013 Madrid*

**In Italy:** Please write to *Penguin Italia s.r.l., Via Como 4, I-20096 Pioltello (Milano)*

**In France:** Please write to *Penguin Books Ltd, 39 Rue de Montmorency, F-75003 Paris*

**In Japan:** Please write to *Longman Penguin Japan Co Ltd, Yamaguchi Building, 2–12–9 Kanda Jimbocho, Chiyoda-Ku, Tokyo 101*